T0301122

Searching for Juliet

SEARCHING FOR JULIET

The Lives and Deaths of
Shakespeare's First Tragic Heroine

SOPHIE DUNCAN

sceptre

First published in Great Britain in 2023 by Sceptre
An imprint of Hodder & Stoughton
An Hachette UK company

1

Copyright © Sophie Duncan 2023

The right of Sophie Duncan to be identified as the Author of the Work has been
asserted by her in accordance with the Copyright, Designs and Patents Act 1988.

All rights reserved. No part of this publication may be reproduced, stored
in a retrieval system, or transmitted, in any form or by any means without
the prior written permission of the publisher, nor be otherwise circulated
in any form of binding or cover other than that in which it is published and
without a similar condition being imposed on the subsequent purchaser.

A CIP catalogue record for this title is available from the British Library

Hardback ISBN 9781529365177
Trade Paperback ISBN 9781529365153
eBook ISBN 9781529365139

Typeset in Dante by Hewer Text UK Ltd, Edinburgh
Printed and bound in Great Britain by Clays Ltd, Elcograf S.p.A.

Hodder & Stoughton policy is to use papers that are natural, renewable
and recyclable products and made from wood grown in sustainable
forests. The logging and manufacturing processes are expected to conform
to the environmental regulations of the country of origin.

Hodder & Stoughton Ltd
Carmelite House
50 Victoria Embankment
London EC4Y 0DZ

www.sceptrebooks.co.uk

For my parents, who gave me my love of Shakespeare,
and for my wife, whom I first met at Shakespeare's house.

Contents

List of Illustrations

8 Charlotte Cushman as Romeo by Charles D. Fredricks & Co (New York: 1858), 102 x 64 mm. University of Washington Libraries, Special Collections, PH Coll 75.175. © BG/OLOU/Alamy Stock Photo.

9 Bronze statue of Juliet by Nereo Costantini (originally 1969) and 'Juliet's Balcony' at 'La Casa di Giulietta', via Cappello, Verona. © Stefanos Kyriazis/Alamy Stock Photo.

10 Franco Zeffirelli directs John Stride and Judi Dench in rehearsals for *Romeo and Juliet* (Old Vic, London, 1960). © Keystone Features/Hulton Archive/Getty Images.

11 Richard Beymer and Natalie Wood in *West Side Story* (13 December 1961). © ScreenProd/Photononstop/Alamy Stock Photo.

12 Paramount Pictures promotional poster for the American release of Zeffirelli's *Romeo and Juliet* (1968), featuring Lord Snowdon's portrait of Leonard Whiting and Olivia Hussey in the title roles. © Album/Alamy Stock Photo.

13 Promotional still of Claire Danes as Juliet in Baz Luhrmann's *Romeo + Juliet* (1996). © Pictorial Press Ltd/Alamy Stock Photo.

14 Admira Ismić and Boško Brkić, in an image photographed by Chris Helgren (Reuters, 26 May 1993). © REUTERS/Alamy Stock Photo.

15 Michael Byrne (Romeo) and Siân Phillips (Juliet) in Sean O'Connor and Tom Morris's *Juliet and Her Romeo* (Bristol Old Vic, 2010). © Donald Cooper/Alamy Stock Photo.

16 Gwen Ffrangcon-Davies (Juliet) and John Gielgud (Romeo) in the May 1924 Regent Theatre production, London. © Sasha/Hulton Archive/Getty Images.

17 Platinum print of Gwen Ffrangcon-Davies by Nicholas Sinclair (1991), 377 x 376 mm, NPG x38420, National Portrait Gallery. © Nicholas Sinclair. All rights reserved, DACS 2023.

Introduction

A thirteen-year-old girl is at a party. A man wants to marry her. Her father thinks she's too young, that married life will damage her – but after all, the man has a title.

Gatecrashers arrive. They're young men from the city's other powerful clan, her family's opponents in a deadly feud. She doesn't recognise them. Perhaps she's too young to go out much in public. Perhaps she's never been to a party before. But one of the gatecrashers likes what he sees. This boy, slightly older than she is, has been dragged to the party by friends. On the way, he'd felt a premonition that something terrible would happen. He'd only come in the hope of seeing a different young woman.

Instead he sees her. Juliet.

Within a week, the boy and girl are dead. Suicides. Their bodies discovered together inside a family grave. In the interim come marriage, murder, sex and drugs, creating the violent, unstoppable plot of Shakespeare's first great tragedy, and the definitive romance of Western literature.

The star of the play is Juliet. This sheltered, Veronese child-bride becomes her play's living heartbeat. William Shakespeare wrote *Romeo and Juliet* in 1595, two centuries after Dante mentioned the feuding Montagues and Capulets in his poetry, and a century after the earliest Italian versions of her love story. This makes Juliet a child of the Italian Renaissance: the era of da Vinci, Raphael and Michelangelo; of Petrarch's sonnets for the unattainable Laura; of international expansion and the birth of capitalism in the city-states of Florence and Venice. Juliet is locked away from all these revolutions in art and culture. So cloistered is her life that she can only leave her parents' home to visit her priest. And yet, such is Juliet's courage and resourcefulness that she orchestrates her clandestine marriage to Romeo, forgives him for murdering her cousin, defies her parents, fakes her own death and ultimately takes her own life rather than be coerced into bigamy or deprived of her love. She never sees her fourteenth birthday, but has endured as a romantic and sexual icon for over 400 years. This book is about that girl.

Why not Juliet *and* her Romeo? It seems perverse to focus only on one half of literature's most famous lovers. I separate them because, despite being indivisible in death and in the popular imagination, they spend most of their lives divided. Shakespeare's most famous couple appear onstage together in just five scenes: her father's party; the iconic balcony scene, in which they cannot touch; the moments before their marriage; their parting before banishment; and their death scene, in which one or both are always insensible.

The lovers have also been remembered in radically different ways. In the final moments of Shakespeare's play, Juliet's father-in-law Lord Montague vows that she will be commemorated as 'true and faithful Juliet' (5.3.201).[1] Romeo has not been so lucky, with his name entering the English language as an insult, the dictionary definition not just of 'a lover or sweetheart' but, more ominously, of a 'seducer or habitual pursuer of women [. . .] c.f. lothario'.[2] Romeo and Juliet may be history's greatest lovers, but their respective afterlives are very different. If *Romeo and Juliet* is the story we tell ourselves about what it means to be young, passionate, and doomed, Juliet's is the story we tell about what it means to be a young woman in love.

It is Juliet who the world has most loved to remember: as a talisman, a tourist trap, a sexual icon, a paragon of innocence, and a romantic ideal. You can buy a keyring of her right breast in Verona, and attach a 'Juliet balcony' to your newly built home. On her wedding day in 1930, my great-grandmother Muriel, an English teacher, wore a 'Juliet cap', a closely-worked, embellished cloche attached to a long veil. Inspired by Edwardian performances of the play, the Juliet cap was popular throughout the twentieth century, including with Jacqueline Bouvier and Grace Kelly – although Muriel Kirlew got there first.

Even a full generation before Shakespeare's play, one of the earliest Italian-language versions of the Romeo and Juliet story circulated exclusively under the name of its heroine – *La Giulietta*. It is

Juliet around whom the Veronese tourist industry has, for centuries, revolved.[3] For actors, there is no comparison: Juliet is an epoch-making part, the definitive young Shakespearean heroine, a role that actresses love to recall fifty, even eighty years later. Romeo, frankly, doesn't come close in the canon of male Shakespeare roles. Even watching John Gielgud – the most successful Romeo of the early twentieth century – the great Shakespearean critic Ivor Brown confessed that although '[i]t may be heresy to say' it, 'Romeo is a great name, but not a great part'.[4]

We tell ourselves that Romeo and Juliet were the greatest lovers who ever lived. Crucial to this is the idea that the 'star-crossed lovers' (1.0.6) are the paragons of romance precisely because of their tragedy. To be 'star-crossed' for the Elizabethans meant being ill-fated twice over: both by the circumstances of your natal astrology – the negative alignment of planets and constellations at the moment of your birth – and 'crossed' in the sense of being defrauded or cheated. The lovers' death is thus as inevitable as it is unfair. The Chorus that begins the play reiterates that Romeo and Juliet are not only 'star-crossed' but also share a 'death-marked love' (1.0.9). Their love is not merely defined by the violence and death all round them but marked *for* death. Doomed.

What is the appeal of a 'death-marked love', surrounded by life-threatening parental disapproval? Who would want to be 'star-crossed'? I spend much of my academic life trying to answer these – and other – questions about Shakespeare at the University of Oxford. In 2019, during our summer 'long vacation', I headed to Verona as part of a research fellowship. Having been born and brought up in Stratford-upon-Avon – the playwright's real-life birthplace – I was curious to see this other hive of Shakespearean tourism: the fictional birthplace of his most famous heroine. In Verona, thronging tourists sighed over sites marketed as the originals of Juliet's house and balcony. How many of these travellers, I wondered, would really approve if their children or friends chose partners from families they despised? How many of the study-abroad students who haunt Verona, earnestly journalling and soulfully captioning Instagram posts, could defend their current love affair against decades of familial sniping or insurmountable opposition? What proportion of the relationships between the jet-setting retirees in tour groups actually began in the face of parental ire but thrived nonetheless? One evening in Verona, I attended an interactive, promenade performance of *Romeo and Juliet*, in which the actors invited the audience's longest-married couple (fifty-three years) to stand in for the teenage lovers during the ball scene. They were American; the bilingual narrator asked them where they met. The man explained that he saw his wife at a drive-in cinema, eating pizza with girlfriends. He didn't add, 'And our parents had a blood feud'.

Today, most couples who marry still meet each other through mutual friends or in the workplace, sharing overlapping interests and concerns. Newspaper advice columns coax widows and divorcees to join hobby clubs to discover 'like-minded people'. Dating apps match people beyond their immediate circles, but few users would deliberately seek out a partner with a wildly different background; a MAGA-hat-wearing rifle enthusiast is unlikely to swipe right on an eco-warrior advocating for open borders. Yet Western culture's template for romance is two dead teenagers whose lives and families are linked only by street brawls, opprobrium, and blood.

For decades, psychologists talked about the 'Romeo and Juliet effect': a one-off, hugely influential study from 1972 that misleadingly claimed familial opposition to a relationship actually strengthened lovers' bonds.[5] I say 'misleadingly' because no study has ever managed to replicate that single set of results. On the contrary, a much larger 2014 study proved that parental (and wider social network) disapproval made partners trust each other less and criticise each other more, leading to overall reductions in love and commitment, and a greater likelihood of break-ups.[6] Beyond the laboratory, the impact of intrafamilial conflict is corroborated by everything from self-help titles like *Toxic In-Laws: Loving Strategies for Protecting Your Marriage* (2002) and the anguished *What Do You Want From Me?: Learning to Get Along with In-Laws* (2009), to Reddit's r/JUSTNOMIL (where 'MIL' stands for 'Mother-in-Law') subforum, a seething cauldron of meddling, madness and Munchausen's, with 1.3 million subscribers.[7]

To understand Juliet's literary longevity is as much to unravel our fascination with 'star-crossed' lovers as it is to recognise her as the character who drives the play. Despite facing the predicaments of a fairy-tale heroine – trapped high up in the parental home, swallowing a magic potion, supposedly to be awoken by true love's presence, if not kiss – she tries to be the architect of her own destiny. She exchanges two kisses with a nameless stranger, and within hours is initiating their marriage – despite discovering that he's the son of her family's enemies. She offers to elope with him. She breaks every taboo, and knows she's doing it: in being 'too fond', too desperately in love with Romeo, she confesses to him that she risks being thought 'light' (2.1.140–41). It's an innocent-sounding word, but one that, in the sixteenth century, implied promiscuity, licentiousness, and immorality. Shakespeare's contemporary John Lyly used the word 'light' to describe the beautiful Helen of Troy, whose adultery with Paris provoked the Trojan War.[8]

A single day after meeting Romeo, Juliet's clandestine marriage is not only a stunning rebellion against a society that deems her the property of her parents, but – blasphemously – it's disguised as a trip to the confessional. We follow Juliet to the threshold of her wedding night, where she confides to us how she feels about her imminent loss of virginity, in strikingly egalitarian terms. For a girl who has come to define heterosexual romance – the epitome of girl-meets-boy – her imagery is strikingly gender-fluid. She is the 'impatient child' and Romeo her newest dress: the beautiful 'new robes' she longs to wear to the ball (3.2.29–31). Together, she and Romeo are the interchangeable 'pair of stainless maidenhoods' to be lost to each other (3.2.13).

Shakespeare created Juliet in an age where the women of love poetry were frequently as glittering and distant as celestial bodies, following the traditions of the Italian poet Francesco Petrarca. When Elizabeth I's celebrated courtier and diplomat, Sir Philip Sidney, wrote a long love-sonnet-sequence, he called his unattainable heroine 'Stella' – Latin for 'star'.[9] And yet, when Juliet is rhapsodising over her new husband and lover, he is the one she imagines being turned into constellations:

Take him and cut him out in little stars
And he will make the face of heaven so fine
That all the world will be in love with night (3.2.22–4).

When confronted with forced marriage, Juliet exhorts aid from Friar Laurence by threatening her suicide, and is prepared to descend into a vault of putrefying corpses to escape with her husband, a convicted murderer. Ultimately, she kills herself rather than either rejoin her parents or resign herself to widowhood in a convent. All the while, we bear witness.

This book tracks Juliet's lives and deaths through 400 years of reinterpretation, from Elizabethan boy-players to twenty-first-century warzones. Some of the Juliets you'll find here are well-known, like *West Side Story*'s Maria. Others, including Regency child actress Jenny Cibber or nineteenth-century star Mary Anderson, are today barely remembered outside academic circles. The Juliets range from high-glamour calendar models to enslaved women, and from theatrical pioneers to the victims of war.

Each incarnation in this book embodies a moment where the Juliet myth and society's ideas about young women were brought most vividly into relief. Juliet's re-imaginings show us how our social and cultural perspectives on romance, on tragedy, and on the nature of teenage girls have shifted – and how they have stayed the same. In writing *Searching for Juliet*, I wanted to explore how the glowing aura of a literary and theatrical classic can sometimes dazzle us into ignoring the dark things which Shakespeare's cultural prestige has been used to legitimise.

In the twenty-first century, studios, theatres, and critics all value directors and performers who promise novelty in a Shakespeare revival, vaunting the 'new', the 'innovative', that can 'show us the play for the first time'. But the overwhelming majority of people who come to *Romeo and Juliet* bring to that encounter some aware-ness of the four-hundred-year myth surrounding it. Perhaps they've heard Taylor Swift's *Love Story* (2008), her multi-platinum country pop single in which Juliet is a smalltown princess with an overbearing dad, or Martin Solveig's disco house classic *Juliet & Romeo* (2019), which relocates the couple to Ibiza, forever on the dancefloor. My generation grew up on Baz Luhrmann's kitsch-heavy 1996 film, starring pretty Leonardo DiCaprio and perfect Claire Danes. That film's 90s aesthetic proved so iconic that it merited a 2021 retrospective in *Vogue*; today, stills from Luhrmann's cinematography are emblazoned on ASOS t-shirts, bought by children who don't remember the film's release. A case in point: celebrity offspring Brooklyn and Nicola Peltz Beckham (b. 1999 and 1995, respectively) attended a 2022 Halloween party dressed as DiCaprio and Danes, reinvigorating tabloid speculation about an alleged feud with Brooklyn's parents. *Romeo and Juliet* remains a phenomenally popular set text wherever English is spoken or taught, introduced to thousands of teenagers just as they're experiencing the play's own themes – love, desire, and adolescent anger – for the first time. It's an extraordinarily powerful text, shaping the minds of generations of young people. Juliet's myth is crucial to this.

In 2010, I worked as a tour guide in Shakespeare's Birthplace, the wooden-framed, sixteenth-century house in which the playwright was almost certainly born. Our 3,000 daily visitors came from all over the world, whether on individual pilgrimages or gruelling group coach trips. They spoke dozens, if not hundreds, of different languages, and plenty had never seen or read a Shakespeare play. At the end of the tour, our visitors made it to the gardens, where a troupe of local actors performed Shakespeare scenes on-demand. Regardless of age, language, group size, or country of origin, the play people most frequently requested was *Romeo and Juliet*. And the character they wanted to see was Juliet on her balcony. Juliet has shaped ideas both of romance and of Shakespeare himself, and she needs to be part of the conversation whenever we talk about either.

Through four hundred years of Juliet's lives and deaths, valorising the star-crossed suicide of a thirteen-year-old has come at a price: a price often paid by young girls, whether in Georgian London or on a sun-soaked film set in Rome. The story of Shakespeare's Juliet unfolds not only between the pages of play-texts but during some of the most painful eras in human history: the transatlantic slave trade, the rise of fascism in Europe, and the suffering of twenty-first-century Afghanistan. Juliet's character and story have also inspired some of our most beloved music and film, from ballet and opera to *West Side Story* and the cinematography of Baz Luhrmann.

Even as Juliet's story travels in very different directions, the power of Shakespeare's play reasserts itself. As Shakespeare's audience and

readers, we have intimate access to Juliet's inner life that even
Romeo doesn't share. Romeo is equipped with Friar Laurence,
Benvolio, and Mercutio as devoted friends, as well as a set of
concerned parents and a faithful servant, Balthasar. He shares his
motives and feelings with them throughout the play, then leaves a
tell-all letter for his father, which is later read onstage. Juliet, meanwhile, is frequently alone – with us. Only we see her impatience as
she waits for the Nurse. Only we witness her glorious rhapsody of
sexual excitement as she anticipates her wedding night, her 'love-
performing night' with Romeo. She confides in us that, 'O, I have
bought the mansion of a love/ But not possessed it, and, though I
am sold,/ Not yet enjoyed' (3.2.26–8).

The Nurse never discovers Juliet's secret fury when she urges
her charge to betray Romeo – 'ancient damnation!' (3.5.235).
Romeo and Friar Laurence never know of the trauma Juliet
experiences when left entirely alone with the potion, feeling the
'faint cold fear' that 'almost freezes up the heat of life' (4.3.15–
16) as she contemplates the 'loathsome smells' of the tomb,
which she fears will drive her mad if she isn't 'strangled' by the
lack of air (4.3.34–45). Nor do they know of the visceral night-
mares of 'mangled' Tybalt's ghost, 'fest'ring in his shroud'
(4.3.41–51), which she has to confront in order to trust them and
take the drug. Only we hear her heart-wrenching lament over
Romeo's corpse. At so many of the pivotal moments in Juliet's
life, we are alone with her – including, after the Friar's retreat, at
that life's very end. Unlike Romeo, Juliet leaves no letter for her
parents; her bitter resolution, taken against the Nurse, that
'Thou and my bosom shall henceforth be twain' (3.5.240) opens
a rift with her entire family that persists beyond the grave. We,
the audience, keep her secrets.

The intimacy and iridescence of Shakespeare's portrayal mean
that we each see our own Juliet. For the desperate and lovelorn who
write to her even today at the Juliet Club in Verona, Juliet is both
advisor and goddess. For those drawn to the heat of her passion, she
is an object of desire. At times in history – particularly when a society's debates over the status of women have been especially fraught
– Juliet has been a problem, an exotic Mediterranean whose rebellion needed to be quashed. Whatever her reception, and whatever

the incarnation, she has always been there, embodying the world's ideas of love and desire.

In writing Juliet, Shakespeare invited us into a new kind of intimacy with a new kind of heroine. She is Shakespeare's first tragic heroine, and the most famous lover who never lived.

I

Shakespeare's First Tragic Heroine

The year 1598 was momentous for English literature. The poet and playwright George Chapman's translation of Homer's *Iliad* appeared in print, revolutionising the study of classical texts. John Florio, Elizabethan England's greatest linguist and lexicographer, published *A World of Words*, an Italian–English dictionary that used quotations to illustrate words' meanings – the first English dictionary to do so. Ben Jonson's great comedy *Every Man in His Humour* appeared on both stage and page. The late Christopher Marlowe – a murdered rock star of a playwright – made his final, posthumous foray into print with the tragic love poem *Hero and Leander*, a romance of forbidden love helpfully completed by none other than George Chapman (who, what with the *Iliad*, spent 1598 overachieving). Not yet Elizabeth's heir, James VI of Scotland published *The Trew Law of Free Monarchies*, which unsurprisingly argued that kings should be given their own way. Meanwhile, in Oxford, Thomas Bodley re-founded the University's Bodleian Library, abandoned since the Reformation, to house what would become Britain's greatest and most beautiful collection of books.[1] Beyond print, sonnets were circulating in manuscript for those in the know – the young John Donne, described at this time as 'a great visitor of Ladies, a great frequenter of Plays, a great writer of conceited Verses', had begun producing his religiously erotic and erotically religious poems.[2]

Meanwhile, an obscure commonplace book called *Palladis Tamia* was published. It appeared without fanfare in the autumn of 1598, its author an aspirant scribbler named Francis Meres.

At thirty-three, Meres was a failed poet, a little-known translator and an absolutely disregarded writer of sermons. His benevolent kinsman, the high sheriff of Lincolnshire, had been unable to help Francis into politics. Francis was also a failed academic, despite – as he liked to remind people – being a 'Master of Arts of Both Universities'.

Palladis Tamia isn't much good. Most of the material is unoriginal, cribbed from classic Latin texts in circulation at the time, and works on Elizabethan education. Even the one chapter that did make its mark on literary history – 'A comparative discourse of our English poets, with the Greeke, Latine, and Italian poets' – shamelessly stole from the lit-crit luminaries of the time, like Sir Philip Sidney and his *An Apology for Poesy*. But there are moments, amidst the recycling, where Meres finds a new voice. He fulsomely praises contemporary writers and, with equal enthusiasm, shares scandalous gossip about their lives. In doing so, he gives us our first vivid glimpse of William Shakespeare as a successful young writer.

Meres was a big fan. He called Shakespeare 'hony-tongued', praising the sweetness of the poet's 'sugred Sonnets among his private friends' (Meres either was a 'private friend' or hoped we'd think so). He said that if the Muses – the nine Greek goddesses of the arts and astronomy – were alive and speaking English, they'd all speak in Shakespearean verse. He compared Shakespeare's work to the Greek poet Horace, declaring that both would outlast 'kings and kingdoms'. And, of course, he celebrated the best of Shakespeare's plays so far. Among them, Meres's review of *Romeo and Juliet* stands out; he doesn't just praise the play, but showcases a moment from live performance, vividly recalling how 'true-harted *Julietta* did die upon the corps of her dearest *Romeo*'.[3] Since Meres, cultural authorities from William Wordsworth to *Playboy* magazine have agreed that *Romeo and Juliet* is the greatest love story ever told. 'Star-crossed lovers' recur everywhere from Verdi's 1871 opera *Aida* to *The Hunger Games*, appearing as a ubiquitous trope in soap operas, pop songs and gossip columns. And yet, in the mid-1590s, when Shakespeare sat down and wrote the romance that would define literary love for the next four centuries, he might justifiably have seemed the last playwright to pen anything of the kind.

The most startling difference between *Romeo and Juliet* and Shakespeare's earlier plays is Juliet herself. As befits Shakespeare's first eponymous heroine, she has more speeches, appears in more scenes, and speaks a greater percentage of her play than any of his previous female characters. Juliet is the second-largest role in the play, after Romeo. Revisiting Shakespeare's back catalogue, it's initially impossible to work out where she came from. Shakespeare had first made his name with the occasional comedy and huge chronicle histories staged by a variety of London theatre companies, including four lengthy adaptations of Raphael Holinshed's *Chronicles* (1587), which dramatised England's fifteenth-century civil wars to exciting and bloody effect (*Henry VI Parts 1, 2, and 3* and *Richard III*). At best, the women in these plays are brilliant cameos, enjoying a few great moments, such as the witch-conjuring Duchess of Gloucester in *Henry IV Part 2*, or Anne Neville, seduced over her father-in-law's corpse into marrying his murderer, the future Richard III. Margaret of Anjou appears in all four plays, evolving from captive princess in *Henry VI Part 1* to vengeful queen mother and angry relict in *Richard III*, but it takes the entire quartet to stitch together the equivalent of one leading role. Shakespeare may also have contributed to a range of other historical and contemporary tragedies, only one of which – *Arden of Faversham* (1592) – stars a strong female character. Alice Arden is an adulterous murderess who can't scrub her husband's blood out of the floorboards – Lady Macbeth in beta, rather than a first-draft Juliet. Overwhelmingly, Shakespeare's early historical women are mothers and consorts, appended to plays named for – and fascinated by – men.

Shakespeare's earliest tragedy, *Titus Andronicus* (1592), offers two female roles. Lavinia speaks only fifty-nine lines before being raped and mutilated into silence, while Tamora – the transgressive Queen of the Goths – is confined to just five of the play's fifteen scenes. Although commercially successful, *Titus* did not immediately encourage Shakespeare to write more theatrical tragedies. When bubonic plague closed London's playhouses for nearly two years after June 1592, Shakespeare concentrated on two long poems. *Venus and Adonis*, published in June 1593, was the first Shakespearean text in print, followed by *The Rape of Lucrece*, a year later. Both centre on women, and despite some comic sequences in *Venus and Adonis*, they meditate on desire, coercion, death and despair. It's possible – if we squint – to trace a link from Lucrece's suicide, undertaken to avoid the imputation that her rape had been consensual adultery, to

Juliet's fatal desperation to remain a faithful wife. But the link is faint: the defiant, sexually frank teenage strategist is nowhere in the crushed Roman matron.

Even when the playhouses reopened, Shakespeare didn't immediately return to writing tragedies. The London theatre scene was changing. Several of Shakespeare's previous plays had been collaborations undertaken with Oxbridge-educated 'university wits', including George Peele (*Titus Andronicus*), Christopher Marlowe, and Thomas Nashe (*Henry VI Part 1*). But Marlowe had been murdered in a 1593 tavern brawl while under government surveillance for 'monstrous opinions', including, according to fellow tragedian Thomas Kyd, that Jesus and St John had been lovers.[4] The hard-living Peele would shortly die 'by the pox', and Nashe, the sole survivor, had temporarily abandoned playwriting for religious feuding, prose-writing and satire. Shakespeare was now writing solo, and doing so for a new theatre company.

Before the plague, Shakespeare had been associated – as a writer and actor – with several companies. The most recent was the Lord Strange's Men, who were under the patronage of the cultured and charming Ferdinando Stanley, 5th Earl of Derby. But in April 1594, a week before Shakespeare's thirtieth birthday, Ferdinando died so excruciatingly of 'yellow jaundice', wasting, 'vehement hickocke' (hiccups) and vomiting bloody bile that 'many learned men [. . .] suppose[d] him to be bewitched'.[5] Shakespeare's theatrical patron was gone, and with him his troupe. To his great good fortune, Shakespeare joined a new company: the Lord Chamberlain's Men. Their patron, Henry Carey, was the queen's cousin (and perhaps half-brother).[6] Shakespeare was one of eight founding members, or 'sharers', who bought a share in the company, entitling them to a literal share of each performance's revenue.

Shakespeare, now thirty, would soon be rich. Within a decade of co-founding the Lord Chamberlain's Men, he had land, property, a gentlemanly coat of arms and a mansion in his hometown, Stratford-upon-Avon.[7] The company also brought Shakespeare artistic rewards: for the first time, he could write and act exclusively for and with a coherent group of principal actors. No longer a precarious quill-for-hire, he had the stability to produce better, more consistent artistic work – and to co-own the products of his labour.[8]

Among his fellow sharers was Richard Burbage, son of James Burbage, an actor and joiner who built London's first permanent playhouse. Richard became Shakespeare's leading man: his first Hamlet, Lear, Othello and – almost certainly – Romeo. Another sharer was John Heminges, who seems to have leaned towards theatre management, and who edited the First Folio. Heminges's co-editor, actor Henry Condell, also had shares, as did Will Kemp, a well-established celebrity clown famous for his jigs, athleticism and self-contained comic 'merriments'. There were also hired men: minor actors hired for a fixed fee. And then there were boys.

Boy actors were (we think) aged between twelve and twenty-one, and (we know) played all the female roles on the early modern stage, from Shakespeare's early chronicle heroines to more mature roles like Lady Macbeth and Cleopatra. Adolescence – euphemistically termed the 'flower of youth' – was the subject of early modern parenting manuals and scientific works that clarify that puberty (including the vocal changes that could scupper a male Juliet's career) happened later for the Elizabethans than it does today. The Office of Christian Parents (1616) agreed with The Problems of Aristotle (1595) that male puberty began at fourteen, with voices breaking at fifteen. Today, male puberty begins, on average, at twelve – but can start as early as nine.[9] Henry Cuffe's The Differences of the Ages of Man's Life (1607) estimated that the advent of 'mossie excrement of haire' on a boy's 'cheeks and other hidden parts' could be 'prorogued until the eighteenth year', giving boy actors longer careers in female roles than we might initially assume.[10] In Shakespeare's time, boys in female roles were apprenticed to older players and – if they were lucky – later transitioned to adult careers on stage. It was this collection of children, sharers and actors-for-hire that would combine to perform Shakespeare's greatest love story – and among them, the boy who would so delight Francis Meres as 'true-harted Julietta'. But not just yet.

★

Shakespeare had always loved comedy. Critics speculate now that he might have finished his earliest solo play, The Two Gentlemen of Verona, before leaving Stratford for London. He kept his hand in comedy throughout the late 1580s with The Taming of the Shrew and the inclusion of much gruesome humour in history plays like *Richard III*. After joining the Lord Chamberlain's Men, in an extraordinary burst of comic energy, Shakespeare produced *The Comedy of Errors* (1594), *Love's Labour's Lost* (1595), the now-lost *Love's Labour's Won* (1595) and *A Midsummer Night's Dream* (1595–6). Each of the extant plays contains a role designed as a vehicle for star clown Will Kemp. The bumbling Costard in *Love's Labour's Lost* and Bottom in *A Midsummer Night's Dream* epitomise the malapropisms, confusion, hilarity and low cunning of his performances. But in these comedies, Shakespeare was also steadily building opportunities for the boy-players. His new plays required more boys than the histories had: where *Henry VI Part 1* needed just two (and even the unwieldy *Richard III* and *Henry VI Part 2* only five or six boys opposite more than twenty adult men), now *Love's Labour's Lost* cast a minimum of six, and *A Midsummer Night's Dream* up to eight. These female roles were also more prominent. *The Comedy of Errors*, *Love's Labour's Lost*, and *A Midsummer Night's Dream* each has a woman among the three largest roles – in *The Comedy of Errors*, the voluble Adriana only narrowly misses top billing, and still has significantly more lines than her husband.[11]

Looking back on Shakespeare's early history plays, we can recognise in his queens and duchesses the first sketches of the older tragic women he'd create in the 1600s. Alice Arden, Joan of Arc and Duchess Eleanor's witchy ambitions anticipate Lady Macbeth, while Margaret's disastrous momager would evolve into the controlling Roman matriarch Volumnia, the *grande dame* of *Coriolanus* (c. 1605–8). But by 1595, Shakespeare was also an expert in the comedic tropes that would sustain the rest of his career: identical twins, mistaken identity, amusingly reluctant or rebarbative lovers, and a variety of improbably effective disguises. It was a winning formula for comic fun. And then he created Juliet.

Juliet Capulet is amazing. She confronts Romeo with the prospect of marriage within six hours of their first kiss, insists that he schedule their wedding within twenty-four hours, and then suborns a much older servant to confirm arrangements. This helicopter-parented heiress – one of only four Shakespearean heroines to appear alongside both parents, and the only protagonist – seems confined to Casa Capuletti except to attend confession. On the two occasions she manages to escape, she conducts a secret marriage with the son of her parents' great enemy, and plans to fake her own death with the help of the family priest, respectively. Having previously (and correctly) noted that being discovered in her father's orchard would be enough to get Romeo killed, she loses her virginity to Romeo in her childhood bedroom, under her parents' roof and very nearly their noses: a move that would be bold even for twenty-first-century teenagers. After Romeo is banished for murdering her beloved cousin, and Paris – the titled kinsman of Verona's prince – is forced on her as a spouse, Juliet reaches a point at which many girls might take the Nurse's advice and marry the prince. Instead, she not only sticks with Romeo, but endures a huge argument with her terrifying parents, furiously discards the Nurse (her only confidante), drinks what she fears may be poison despite her own intense necrophobia, and finally kills herself rather than rely any longer on the weeping, dithering friar whose judgement she once revered. She is both a consummate actress and blazingly sincere. And her roots lie not in the medieval dowagers of Shakespeare's early histories, but in the rebellious girls of his new comedies.

Instead of asking why Shakespeare wrote *Romeo and Juliet*, we need to ask: for whom did he write it? It's true that he dutifully included another Kemp vehicle, in the relatively minor role of the Nurse's servant Peter; Shakespeare gives himself away by writing 'Enter Will Kemp' instead of 'Enter Peter' in the manuscripts that became the basis of *Romeo and Juliet*'s second quarto version (1599). But this is the desperate shoehorning of a company star into a play that doesn't really fit him. The evidence shows that Shakespeare was writing for another actor. The film *Shakespeare in Love* (1998) speculated on this possibility, imagining England's first actress in the form of Gwyneth Paltrow's rebellious Lady Viola de Lesseps, who, cross-dressed as actor 'Thomas Kent', inspires Joseph Fiennes's Shakespeare to write the greatest love story of all time. The only plot point more improbable than this unconvincing passing is when Viola marries Colin Firth's Earl of Wessex and the film expects us to feel sorry for her. The first Juliet's genesis had nothing to do with disguised female aristocrats. Instead, it was a case of a very gifted and unusual boy-player: one whose talent recurs throughout Shakespeare's early comic plays.

The Comedy of Errors has two major female roles to showcase the boy-players: the witty and defiant Adriana, who complains of gender inequality, and her sweetly compliant sister Luciana, who preaches patience and resignation. This counterpoint is typically Shakespearean: later characterisations juxtapose an ale-loving, dilettante Prince Hal with his warlike namesake Harry Hotspur (*Henry IV Part 1*, 1597), while half-brothers Edgar (virtuous, boring) and Edmund (mad, bad, seduces two sisters) duel to the death in *King Lear* (c. 1605). But this counterpoint is especially obvious in Shakespeare's comic women. In *Love's Labour's Lost*, Rosaline is the wittier, livelier gentlewoman to the Princess of France's amusing but serene, well, princess. She's even a contrast in her looks: for the first time, Shakespeare specifies a heroine's appearance beyond mere beauty. Rosaline is unfashionably dark, we are told, even though her admirer Berowne swears she is 'born to make black fair' (4.3.257).

It's an unusual choice. But in his next extant play, Shakespeare does it again. *A Midsummer Night's Dream* presents us with Helena and Hermia, beautiful young women who have been best friends from childhood, and whose existing romantic complications – Demetrius has forsaken Helena for Hermia, who loves Lysander – quadruple when fairies interrupt Hermia and Lysander's elopement, and both young men profess their love to Helena. Unaware that Demetrius and Lysander have been dosed with a love-potion-laced flower, Helena and Hermia trade blame and insults, and the scene devolves into a catfight more gloriously funny than anything else Shakespeare had yet written. Their argument confirms what we already suspect: that the defiant, quick-witted Hermia 'was a vixen when she went to school' (3.2.324), and that passive-aggressive Helena prides herself on being 'a right maid for [her] cowardice' (3.2.302) and having 'no gift at all in shrewishness' (3.2.301). But we also learn two more things. First, Hermia is dark, unfashionably and even undesirably so; the racist insults of her (temporarily) revolted paramour Lysander see her described as an 'Ethiope' (3.2.257) and 'tawny Tartar' (3.2.343). Hermia is dark like Rosaline (accordingly, Helena has traditionally been cast as blonde), and quick-tongued, like both Rosaline and Adriana.

Second, Hermia is short – and sensitive about it enough to be violently insulted when Helena calls her a 'puppet' (3.2.288), and to

respond by calling her a 'painted maypole' (3.2.296). Hermia para-
noidly assumes that Lysander has deserted her because Helena has
'urged her height', seducing him with her 'tall personage' (3.2.291–
2). Like Rosaline, Hermia is feistier, wittier and quicker-tempered
than her nearest female counterpart. She is also darker and smaller.
Post-*Romeo and Juliet*, Shakespeare would go on to write another
diminutive brunette in the long shadow of a taller woman in *Much
Ado About Nothing* (1598–9); when comparing her to Beatrice,
Benedick dismisses Hero as 'too low for a high praise, too brown for
a fair praise, and too little for a great praise' (1.1.163–5).

This sequence implies that there were (at least) two talented boy-
players on the Lord Chamberlain's Men's books in the mid-1590s,
one of whom was significantly smaller and darker than the other,
and whose performances leading up to Hermia in *A Midsummer
Night's Dream* impressed Shakespeare enough to create Juliet for
him. Admittedly, Juliet's hair colour and complexion are never specified. But there is one clue as to her build. Juliet also appears in key
scenes alongside the Nurse and Lady Capulet. As the youngest
woman onstage, it makes sense for a small, slight boy to play Juliet.
Given the play's emphasis on her youth and physical frailty, the
effect would be ludicrous if she outstripped her mother and the
Nurse in height, or looked more mature than either.

The plot of *A Midsummer Night's Dream* tells us even more about
Shakespeare's thinking, and how Shakespeare's first tragic heroine
is descended from a play ostensibly built around Will Kemp's turn
as Bottom the Weaver. In this play, the young Hermia faces death if
she refuses her father's choice of suitor. Unlike Lord Capulet, Egeus
knows his daughter loves Lysander, and Shakespeare allows
Lysander to contest the capriciousness of Egeus's dislike. Lysander
is 'as well derived [. . .] as well possessed [. . .] as fairly ranked' as the
favoured Demetrius – if not more so (1.1.99–110). Egeus's loathing
of Lysander seems as arbitrary and irrational as the Capulet–
Montague feud. His sole accusation is that Lysander has 'bewitched
the bosom' of Hermia with the standard range of love poems and
presents (1.1.27–45), but it's openly acknowledged that Demetrius
has already 'made love' to Hermia's best friend Helena and 'won
her soul' (1.1.106–8). Hermia, unlike Juliet, immediately elopes
with her lover, and after much magical intervention returns to

Athens as a triumphant bride; Juliet dies. In *A Midsummer Night's Dream*, the couples' eventual wedding reception includes an hilariously botched production of *Pyramus and Thisbe*: the classical story of secret lovers from neighbouring, feuding families who end up killing themselves.

Written close together, the romances of Hermia and Lysander and Romeo and Juliet feel like a diptych. That Shakespeare also parodied the plot in his mockery of *Pyramus and Thisbe* shows how profoundly preoccupied he was with the theme, and its potential to fail as well as succeed onstage. The 'star-crossed lovers' of *Romeo and Juliet* embody Lysander's axiom that 'the course of true love never did run smooth' (1.1.134), and the twenty-first-century graffiti of this line at Casa Giulietta, Juliet's 'birthplace' in Verona, show how frequently the line is misattributed. Hermia avoids the state-sanctioned death her father desires for her because she runs away. Juliet dies because she doesn't. In that sense, *Romeo and Juliet* is a play about what happens when Hermia stays.

★

Lovers triumphantly defying an unreasonable parent had been a standard comic plot since ancient Greece, where the angry father figure – later known to the Romans as *'senex iratus'* – imperilled young love but was ultimately thwarted. Shakespeare would have been intimately aware of this as a classically educated master of the form. With this narrative ancestry, *Romeo and Juliet* should set up the young lovers to win. Their parents are as preposterously averse to each other as Egeus is to Lysander – more so, even, since nobody can *define* the 'ancient grudge'. Even Lord Capulet admits hostilities could easily be suspended (1.2.3). Shakespeare makes the feud such an inexplicable, arbitrary void that modern adaptations routinely feel compelled to fill it. Accordingly, they recast the Capulets and Montagues along racial or sectarian lines that attribute their enmity, in the words of the great Katherine Duncan-Jones, to 'antagonisms between races that are all too recognisable, and recognisably intransigent'.[12] This choice misinterprets Shakespeare. There is nothing substantial about the feud: no power imbalance, not even a meaningful difference between the houses. The Montagues and Capulets are not only 'alike' but overlapping. Montague-ally Mercutio and his otherwise unmentioned 'brother Valentine' make the guest list for the Capulets' ball (1.2.67), and the two households share a confessor in Friar Laurence – that most intimate counsellor. Rather than a forbidden tryst, Juliet and her Romeo ought to be a highly eligible match.

In the Elizabethan comedy playbook, the lovers' marriage, rather than their deaths, should resolve the 'ancient grudge'. Friar Laurence's notion that the clandestine wedding 'may so happy prove / To turn your households' rancour to pure love' (2.4.86–8) isn't necessarily foolish – or without precedent. Other Shakespearean marriages ratify peace deals: Richmond and Elizabeth (*Richard III*), Henry V and Princess Katherine (*Henry V*) and Miranda and Prince Ferdinand (*The Tempest*). Moreover, Shakespeare handily equips each lover with a comic sidekick – Juliet's Nurse and Romeo's Mercutio – whose bravura displays of wit and bawdy keep the audience laughing for the play's first three acts. Another point in Romeo and Juliet's favour as potentially comic – and thus surviving – characters is that, although rich, the lovers aren't royal. Theatrical tragedies before *Romeo and Juliet* typically depicted the downfall of nations, with the protagonists' misadventures not only leading to their own deaths but also to regime change. *Titus Andronicus* ends with Lucius (the eponymous protagonist's son) becoming Roman emperor; Marlowe's *Edward II* (c. 1587–92) ends with Edward's gruesome assassination by red-hot poker and his son's accession. Romeo and Juliet's deaths may devastate their families, but Prince Escalus remains on the throne. Verona endures.

Most strikingly for the play's comedic credentials, Juliet offers to elope. Hermia has to wait for Lysander to propose their runaway scheme, but Juliet is as active and ingenious about hers as she is about anything else. In Act 2, Scene 2 – now immortalised as the 'balcony scene' – Juliet volunteers to abscond with Romeo, promising that 'all my fortunes at thy foot I'll lay / And follow thee my lord throughout the world' (2.2.147–8). It's a resounding echo of Hermia and Lysander's gambit to escape the 'sharp Athenian law' (1.1.162). Juliet's offer never recurs, but the moment clarifies the kind of heroine Juliet believes herself to be: a resourceful survivor about to elope. In other words, the heroine of a comedy.

Unfortunately, she is mistaken. For all its structural misdirection, *Romeo and Juliet* is upfront about its ending. The play was first printed as a quarto – a squarish, smallish book made from printing eight pages on a single sheet of paper (four on each side), then folding and cutting the paper to create four leaves. A folio, by contrast, was the larger, more expensive format, using twice as much paper: sheets folded in half. Eighteen of Shakespeare's plays were first printed in quarto form. The first quarto of *Romeo and Juliet* appeared in 1597, followed by a second quarto in 1599. The title of the first quarto advertises 'An EXCELLENT Conceited Tragedie', and the second 'The MOST EX-cellent and lamentable Tragedie', while the Chorus promises 'misadventured piteous overthrows', 'death-marked love' and the 'children's end' (1.0.4–11). Cosmopolitan early modern theatregoers might also have recognised the plot as derived from a succession of sad poems and novellas about tragic Italian teenagers. In writing his first tragic heroine, Shakespeare put the kind of woman he'd perfected in his comedies – rebellious, rebarbative, and romantic – into a very different sort of play. Juliet's tragedy is that she isn't, as she imagines herself to be, in *A Midsummer Night's Dream*.

Crucial to what makes Shakespeare's Juliet distinctive is this tension between the surrounding tragedy and Juliet's drive to live. Portents of death and disaster centre on Romeo: he is the one who intuits 'some consequence, hanging in the stars' of his ball attendance that will result in 'untimely death' (1.4.106–11), who dreams of himself as dead (5.1.6) and whom Juliet pictures in a grave (3.5.55–7). Both threaten suicide, but Romeo makes his threat an entire act before Juliet does – and for Juliet, it's primarily an ultimatum to force the Friar's help. When she does take the coma-inducing drug, she dreads death by poison, being 'stifled in the vault' or taking her own life while 'distraught' and 'dash[ing] out [her] desperate brains' (4.3.24–54).

Shakespeare's determined Juliet is a marked departure from the play's most immediate source material: Arthur Brooke's 1562 *Tragicall Historye of Romeus and Iulliet,* a verse translation that popularised a fourteenth-century myth from Italian and French literature for English readers, and William Painter's 1567 *Palace of Pleasure,* which transfigures Brooke's story into prose with few alterations. Brooke's heroine is not only constantly rehearsing for death, but in fact almost dies early after Romeus's banishment, when 'dedly panges' see her 'draw no more her breath'. Only strenuous efforts save Juliet: Brooke vividly describes how the Nurse 'wringes/ her fingers and her toes' to revive her. Brooke's Juliet invariably cries 'bitter teeres' at the moments when Shakespeare's Juliet is at her most rhapsodic; in Brooke's balcony scene, her eyes as 'fountaynes ronne' (14v), while on her wedding night, crying again, she seems 'like betwixt [Romeus's] arms to faint' (24r). Once Romeus is banished, 'joylesse Juliet' becomes suicidal, graphically threatening 'Hedlong to throw her selfe/ downe from the windows height,/ And so to breake her slender necke' (45v). Soon, she is offering to 'perce my brest,/ with sharpe and bloody knife', calling her mother 'the murdresse of my life' when the Capulets try to cure her depression with a wedding (52r; 54r). Unsurprisingly, the Juliet of Shakespeare's sources is glad to sacrifice herself in death, telling the deceased Romeus in Brooke's poem that she 'willing/ offers to thee her gost' (78r). This sustained despondency and death drive is all the more striking given that, unlike Shakespeare's Juliet, both Brooke's and Painter's Juliets have intensely loving parents and three months' happiness with Romeus. Brooke's Juliet is also three years older than Shakespeare's Juliet, and Painter's four. When Shakespeare transplanted his comic heroine into a tragedy, to exploit the talents of the boy-player who'd conquered Rosaline and Hermia, he made her an age – thirteen – that Elizabethan audiences would have found scandalously, recklessly young.

Despite modern misapprehensions, the average first-time bride was twenty-two in Shakespeare's day, with lower-class girls frequently marrying between twenty-four and twenty-seven. In fact, there were two (albeit failed) Parliamentary attempts to raise the age of consent for girls from twelve to fifteen during Shakespeare's lifetime.[13] Although Shakespeare's Lady Capulet calculates that she had Juliet at thirteen (1.3.73–4), Lord Capulet is uneasy about even marrying Juliet to the Prince's kinsman, warning him 'too soon marr'd are those so early made' (1.2.13). 'Marr'd' carried connotations of mutilation around the turn of the seventeenth century; the King James Bible (1611) used it to describe Christ's face, assaulted and weeping, during the Passion. England's own royal family was acutely aware of the danger of early marriage.

Aged thirteen, Margaret Beaufort had barely survived delivering the future Henry VII. Forty-two years later, when Henry's nine-year-old daughter, also called Margaret, was sought as a bride for James IV of Scotland, both Beaufort and her daughter-in-law vehemently objected. As Henry told the Spanish ambassador, 'they fear the King of Scotland would not *wait* [original emphasis], but injure her and endanger her health'.[14] Margaret eventually went to James at thirteen, the same age as Juliet; her first three children all died, and the first two deliveries nearly killed her, too.

Shakespeare's Juliet embarks on an incredibly dangerous course of action at an uncommonly vulnerable age. Perhaps Shakespeare wanted to heighten the tragedy by making its most innocent victim especially young. Perhaps, too, Juliet's age heightened the personal stakes for him: Susanna, Shakespeare's eldest child, turned thirteen the year *Romeo and Juliet* was first performed.[15] Susanna would ultimately marry in her mid-twenties – and marry well, to local physician John Hall – but if Shakespeare shared one attribute with his character Lord Capulet, it was careful concern for the family wealth. Most unusually, in his last will and testament, Shakespeare left lands and money directly to his female relatives – sister and daughters – rather than their husbands.[16]

In any case, the whirlwind of Juliet's experience in Shakespeare's play feels even more pronounced because Shakespeare aggressively truncates the timeframe he inherited from Brooke and Painter. While Brooke and Painter's lovers enjoy three months of unperturbed secret marriage, Shakespeare's Juliet goes from first kiss to second death in less than a week. Crucially, Shakespeare also scraps Brooke's relentless moral condemnation of the lovers. Brooke's preface vilifies them for 'thrilling themselves to unhonest desire, neglecting the authoritie and advise of parents' and 'abusing the honorable name of lawefull marriage'; he intends his readers 'to rayse [. . .] an hatefull lothyng of so filthy beastlynes'. Instead, Shakespeare's Chorus and Prince consistently blame the parents: the Prince vehemently so, declaring that 'a scourge is laid upon [their] hate' and that 'heaven' has 'found means to kill [their] joys with love' (5.3.2915). Shakespeare instead makes Juliet the play's source of moral authority. It is Juliet who pronounces her relationship with Romeo 'too rash, too unadvised, too sudden' (2.2.118), who notes that oaths may 'prove false' and who wishes she had 'dwel[t] on form' (2.2.88) rather than risk seeming 'light' (2.2.99). Brooke's narrator is the poem's moraliser; Shakespeare's Juliet is the perceptive centre of the play.

The role of Juliet offered an astonishing opportunity for Shakespeare's boy actor, turning that boy's trajectory of diminutive, brunette, quick-witted women to devastatingly tragic advantage. Crucially, we now know who he was. Shakespeare's first Juliet was a boy-player named Robert Gough, who lived to be honoured by the royal household and see his own son achieve even greater fame playing women's roles. Critics have long disagreed over whether Robert or another boy, Alexander Cooke, would have originated Juliet. Both performed key roles in a now-lost play called *The Second Part of The Seven Deadly Sins* (originally written c. 1585, but restaged in the 1590s).[17] We know this because of the play's surviving 'back-stage plot', a document summarising entrances and exits, and other details such as props. For a long time, this 'backstage plot' was thought to date from the early 1590s, before the time Shakespeare was writing *Romeo and Juliet*, when the key personnel who would have formed the cast might well have been different. However, research by David Kathman proves the 'plot' dates from 1598. Cooke was not bound as an apprentice until 26 January 1598, after *Romeo and Juliet* was on stage, and so could not have been Shakespeare's first Juliet.[18]

We can only speculate about Robert Gough's earliest years. His father may well have been the actor Thomas Goffe (a variant spelling that Robert would use at his own children's baptisms). Thomas was a London barber-surgeon and travelling performer who acted at court with Sir Robert Lane's Men at Christmas in 1571 and shared the major responsibility of receiving their payments.[19] Goffe migrated to the Earl of Lincoln's Company in 1572–3, probably as a result of 1572 legislation that demanded travelling players have aristocratic patrons. Poor old Sir Robert Lane didn't qualify, but it's possible that Robert Gough's Christian name is a nod to his father's former patron.[20] Born in the early 1580s, evidence suggests young Robert was apprenticed to Thomas Pope. Pope was a comic actor – and strong contender for the first Falstaff – who toured Denmark and Germany with an English company before joining Strange's

Men in 1593. He acted there alongside Burbage, Shakespeare, and Augustine Phillips, before all four joined the Lord Chamberlain's Men as sharers.[21] Pope bequeathed 'all his wearing apparel' to Gough and fellow actor John Edmans, a common gesture from masters to (current or former) apprentices.[22]

After Gough and Cooke became co-stars in the company, Gough seems to have played younger characters; even if he was technically older, he evidently continued to have a younger playing age, implying a particularly diminutive, youthful appearance.[23] Although Cooke couldn't have been the first Helena to Gough's Hermia, or the first Princess of France to Gough's Rosaline, it's likely he took over these roles. By the time Cooke was apprenticed, the most plausible originals – Henry Condell and Christopher Beeston – were respectively twenty-one and nineteen, ageing out of female characters. Cooke is a good candidate for Beatrice to Gough's Hero in *Much Ado About Nothing* (c. 1598–9), and Rosalind to his Celia in *As You Like It* (c. 1599). In *Twelfth Night*, the diminutive Gough may also have played Maria (perhaps with Cooke as Olivia), another Shakespearean woman noted for her petite stature – other characters ironically call her a 'giant' or 'Penthesilea', the name of an Amazon queen (1.5.199; 2.3.172). If he did play Hero and Maria, Gough would have seen the Lord Chamberlain's Men transfer from the Theatre in Shoreditch – unimaginatively named because it was England's first permanent playhouse – to the Globe. The Theatre's landlord, Giles Allen, claimed the building was his when the Burbages' land-lease expired in 1598. That Christmas, while Allen celebrated at his country retreat, the actors – Gough perhaps among them – and carpenter Peter Street demolished the Theatre and carried its timber, piece by piece, to Street's warehouse. In spring 1599, they ferried the wood across the Thames to Southwark, where Street built the Globe.

By the time *Twelfth Night* opened at the Globe, Gough was reaching the end of his boy-player career. He had played Juliet for the last time. Although he would ultimately join the royal court as an officer, a 'Messenger of the Chamber', his family connections with the theatre lasted for the rest of his life. In February 1603, Robert married: like Shakespeare, he was a precociously young husband. His bride was Elizabeth Phillips, sister of the actor and Globe sharer

Augustine Phillips, and the step-sister of Thomas Pope, Gough's probable former master.[24]

Robert and Elizabeth had five children in eleven years. The couple named their youngest son Alexander, perhaps in memory of Alexander Cooke, who had died a few months before the baby's birth.[25] The two former boy-players had remained close neighbours, living in St Saviour's Parish for the rest of their lives. The young Alexander Gough, like both his father and namesake, became a boy-player, starring aged twelve as the concubine Caenis in Massinger's *The Roman Actor* (1626). After the Restoration, seventeenth-century historian James Wright described him as the 'Woman Actor at Blackfriars', who, after the Puritans closed the theatres, organised secret performances in aristocrats' homes. Like his father, he had evidently 'made himself known to persons of Quality'.[26]

Robert Gough died in 1625. He was one of very few Chamberlain's Men who survived to see himself listed among the 'Principall Actors in all these Plays' in Shakespeare's First Folio, outliving Shakespeare himself, Burbage, Augustine Phillips, Will Kemp, Thomas Pope, Alexander Cooke, and Nicholas Tooley, many of whom had most likely appeared in the first *Romeo and Juliet* in 1596.[27] We don't have a precise date for the production, but it most likely happened at the Shoreditch Theatre, before plague closed London's theatres on 22 July. Gough thus brought Shakespeare's first tragic heroine to life in the oldest and greatest of the London playhouses, on the unusually large stage where he had already created witty, triumphant comic women. What would his performance have been like? And what of his acting? In *Hamlet*, Shakespeare offers a definition of good acting: 'to hold, as 'twere, the mirror up to nature, to show virtue her own feature, scorn her own image' (3.2.17–19). Hamlet exhorts actors to speak 'trippingly on the tongue'; lightly and fluently, maintaining a 'temperance' and 'smoothness' even in the 'whirlwind' of 'passion' (3.2.1–6). He demands a reciprocity between voice and body: 'suit the action to the word, the word to the action', never overstepping 'the modesty of nature' (3.2.14–15). One of Hamlet's demands suggests that what Shakespeare valued was a resemblance to contemporary manners, showing 'the very age and body of the time his form and pressure' (3.2.18–19). Given Gough's long career in Shakespearean roles, we must assume that his acting met at least some of these demands for fluid delivery, smoothness, and realism. And given the anti-theatricalists' complaints about players' lavish costumes and potential for boy-players to seduce men into sodomy, we may also assume he looked gorgeous. Francis Meres's description of Juliet as 'true-harted' suggests an emphasis on Juliet's unshakeable fidelity to Romeo in those early performances. Gough was playing close to his own age, with more lines than Shakespeare had ever given him: the summer plague must have been not only a medical terror, but a bitter personal blow.

*

Romeo and Juliet was first printed in 1597: this first quarto has been dubbed a pirate version, a memorial reconstruction, or heavily edited text for touring – as the company did to Faversham, Dover, and Bristol in the summer of 1596.[28] But its frontispiece makes one unusually helpful claim: that *Romeo and Juliet* had been 'often (with great applause) plaid publiquely'. The assertion of applause is striking, and it is the only early quarto to make any such claim for a Shakespeare play. Evidently, Shakespeare's new tragedy and new heroine were as popular as they were innovative – no wonder somebody wanted to cash in by rushing an unauthorised text into print.

In an age before mass literacy, *Romeo and Juliet* was so popular with readers that it sold out five quarto editions by 1637 – the same number as *Hamlet*, and a figure exceeded by only four of Shakespeare's other plays. Early readers assiduously annotated and even corrected their quarto and Folio editions: a teenage John Milton added the Prologue when he found it missing from the First Folio, along with enthusiastic marginalia to mark his favourite lines.[29] Choice quotations from the play appeared in the newly fashionable anthologies of extracts from contemporary literature. *Romeo and Juliet* was the most-cited Shakespeare play in Robert Allott's *England's Parnassus* and also makes a strong showing in John Bodenham's *Bel-vedére*, published in 1600.[30]

The play's popularity obviously irritated Shakespeare's contemporaries. By 1598, John Marston was mocking fans' habit of quotation, sneering that they spoke 'naught but pure Iuliat and Romeo'.[31] Marston also parodied the balcony scene in his play *Jack Drum's Entertainment* (1601), where three enthusiastic wooers congregate beneath the heroine's window.[32] Henry Porter's splendidly titled *The Two Angry Women of Abington* (1599) saw young lovers with feuding mothers interrupted at the same moment by a variety of relatives.[33] Quotations from Juliet appear six times in the commonplace book of dedicated theatre fan Edmund Pudsey, compiled between 1596–1602 and a rare survival of its kind. Juliet even delighted the Archbishop of Canterbury, William Sancroft, who mentions her twice in his commonplace book.[34] Juliet had other clerical fans: her desire to keep Romeo like a 'wanton's bird' was compared to God's love for 'his Saints' in Nicholas Robertson's university sermons in 1620–1: the first step towards her popular canonisation as the patron saint of love.[35]

Where quotation led, fanfiction followed. Shakespeare's Juliet became the subject of a range of extraordinary and – to say the least – varied creative responses, beginning soon after her stage debut. In 1599, well within the period when Gough was still playing Juliet, London publisher and literary opportunist William Jaggard (whose later Shakespeare credits included a 1619 'False' Folio before its legitimate 1623 successor) released *The Passionate Pilgrim*. This twenty-one-poem anthology was solely attributed to Shakespeare, but was in fact a ragbag also containing work by Christopher Marlowe, Sir Walter Raleigh, and assorted other poets, including some still unidentified today. Shakespeare's degree of cooperation on the volume is unknown, but when *The Passionate Pilgrim* was reprinted in 1612 with extracts from Thomas Heywood's poem *Troia Britannica*, Heywood claimed that he and Shakespeare were 'much offended' that Jaggard 'presumed to make bold with his name'.[36] The title of the anthology is itself an allusion to *Romeo and Juliet*, reflecting how closely Shakespeare was associated with the play; at their first meeting, when Romeo addresses Juliet as a 'saint', she responds by calling him a 'pilgrim'. Within the anthology, one anonymous poet riffs on Juliet's 'Parting is such sweet sorrow / That I shall say goodnight till it be morrow' (2.2.184–5), writing an alternative Romeo whose Juliet 'at my parting sweetly', throws 'gazes to the East', then concludes, 'Good night of day now borrow / Short night tonight, and length of thyself tomorrow', echoing the play's obsession with the night / dawn boundary.[37] Cambridge undergraduate Thomas Prujean's dreadful poetry collection *Aurorata* (1644) includes the sub-Ovidian poem 'Juliet to Romeo', purportedly correspondence during Romeo's Mantuan exile. Juliet's declaration (worth reading aloud) that "Thy breath is alwayes so delicious/ As if thou hadst command o'er Zephyrus' is crashingly representative of Prujean's oeuvre.[38]

Prujean's rhapsody and Marston's sneer about 'Iuliat and Romeo' have one thing in common: Juliet comes first. Rather than the play's published title, *Romeo and Juliet*, its inverted final phrase, 'Juliet and her Romeo', defined the play in the popular imagination. In 1623, it became the only play directly referenced in the commendatory poems to the First Folio, that supreme monument to Shakespeare's work, when Leonard Digges declared it 'impossible' to out-do the 'Passions of Juliet, and her Romeo'.[39] When Milton wrote the Prologue into his copy of the First Folio, he did so under the hand-written title 'The Prologue to *Juliet and Romeo*'.

One anecdote reinforces the play's gathering mythos. In the nineteenth century, the Bodleian Library's Falconer Madan undertook 'a detailed description of the wear and tear' to the Bodleian's First Folio, sacrilegiously sold in 1660 but recovered in 1838, to discover 'which plays were most popular with early seventeenth-century readers'.[40] The most popular of all, Madan found, was *Romeo and Juliet*: the pages were stained and thinned with tears. As Emma Smith notes, the book might well have become tearstained after 1660 – but the idea is tantalising.[41] The play also seems to have been popular abroad: Martin Wiggins speculates that it was in the repertory of an English troupe who performed at Bavaria's Nördlingen in January 1604, twice at the Court of Saxony in 1626, and again in Dresden in 1646.[42]

What is certain is that through the first fifty years of the play's theatrical life, invoking 'Juliet and her Romeo' signalled especially tragic content for readers and audiences. It was even used to describe same-sex love. In Gilbert Swinhoe's *Tragedy of the Unhappy Fair Irene* (published 1658 but possibly written far earlier), Paeologus learns that his fiancée Irene is dead, and promptly stabs himself: ordinary tragic content. But then his male servant Demosthenes immediately vows, 'I was inseparable in life/ And will not be disjoyn'd in death' and, according to the stage directions, 'stretches himself close down by the Corps [of Paeologus], and with the same Dagger kills himself'. The onlookers readily identify the two men's bodies as 'a Spectacle of like Woe/ To that of *Juliet*, and her *Romeo*', and the play ends.[43] The stage picture, it seems, had become as powerful and familiar as the play's language: one cued the other. In 1640, Oxford academic Richard Goodridge commended Jacques Ferrand's controversial manual on 'erotique melancholy' as helpful even in love affairs 'of as much direfull woe/ As that of Juliet and Hieronymo'.[44] Hieronymo (or Hieronimo) was the protagonist of Thomas Kyd's *The Spanish Tragedy* (c. 1582–7), the most influential revenge tragedy in six decades.[45] This political bloodbath created the tragic blueprint that plays like *Hamlet* follow – and which the lyrical, romantic *Romeo and Juliet* largely subverts. By linking 'Juliet and Hieronymo', Goodridge discards Romeo to equate Juliet with the ultimate tragic hero of early modern theatre: she had become its ultimate heroine.

Despite all these tributes, none quite exceeds the immediacy of Francis Meres's 1598 description of how 'true-harted *Julietta* did die upon the corps of her dearest *Romeo*'. What makes Meres's description so remarkable is that this is not an action specified by the text: Juliet simply 'stabes herselfe and falls' (Folio text). Today, we expect Juliet to die on Romeo's 'corps', but excitingly, Meres tells us that this familiar tableau is actually a performance tradition dating back to the earliest years of Juliet's life – and death – on stage. What Francis Meres remembered was not Shakespeare's text, however highly Meres rated him as 'the most passionate among us to bewaile and bemoane the perplexities of love'. Instead, Meres was moved by the passion and motion of Shakespeare's boy-player, Robert Gough, whose talent allowed the playwright to create both a new kind of tragedy, and a tragic heroine who would live forever.

2

Everybody Loves a Dead Girl

When Romeo sees his wife's corpse in the tomb, his first thought is how sexy she is. He's just murdered a man, and is surrounded by other corpses, including his wife's cousin, whom he also killed. Nonetheless, nothing detracts from the luminous sexiness of Juliet, his dead thirteen-year-old bride. He describes this allure in the language of erotic jealousy: a piece of paranoid Renaissance rhetoric, in which he professes to 'believe/ That unsubstantial death is amorous', and the 'lean abhorred monster' has imprisoned Juliet 'here in dark to be his paramour' (5.3.102–5). Her asphyxiation becomes Death's kiss, as he has 'sucked the honey of [her] breath' (5.3.92).

Romeo is hardly the first character to link sex, death and Juliet in the play. On discovering Juliet apparently dead in her bed, her own father swiftly imagines that Death has been in the night and had sex with his child: 'Flower as she was, deflowered by him'. The two most important men in Juliet's life both look at her corpse and see an intensely sexual object. She is a 'fair corpse', to be shown off publicly 'in all her best array' (4.4.108–9); she is, to Romeo, a spectacular beauty who makes her tomb 'full of light' (5.3.86). There are four corpses and at least twelve other people onstage by the time the play ends, but Juliet's dead body remains the spectacular centrepiece of the now very crowded tomb.

The dead girl has always been attractive entertainment. In the earliest surviving description of a performance of *Othello*, from 1610, Oxonian clergyman Henry Jackson describes 'famous Desdemona killed before us by her husband', noting that 'although she always acted her whole part supremely well, [. . .] when she was killed she was even more moving, for when she fell back upon the bed she implored the pity of the spectators by her very face'.[1] The heart-rending expression of a boy-player's female corpse begins a tradition still prevalent in Shakespearean performance: a Shakespeare heroine smothered in her bed does not look like a bruised, violated victim disfigured by petechiae, bleeding lips and burst blood vessels, but like an attractive young woman lying with her eyes shut.

Shakespeare was not alone in his celebration of the female corpse. In Thomas Heywood's domestic tragedy *A Woman Killed With Kindness* (1603–7), the adulterous wife Anne Frankford demonstrates her remorse by starving herself to death. In doing so, she not only conveniently writes herself out of the narrative – clearing the way for her husband's remarriage – but, through her self-starvation, erases and desexualises her rebellious body. Middleton took his obsession further in *The Second Maiden's Tragedy* (1611), where the heroine's onstage corpse becomes the villain's necrophiliac love-object, painted to look more alive. In the eighteenth century, the new novel form saw heroines die their way out of sexual subjection, or be gorily murdered in early Gothic novels.

A threnody of dead girls in nineteenth- and twentieth-century fiction swiftly writes itself: Little Nell to Beth March, Juliet to JonBenét. Highbrow Scandi noir and the most derided slasher flicks rely equally on serial killers with a penchant for nubile blondes – from those murdered before the opening credits to the manacled survivor who screams in her underwear while the hero races against time. Inside Catholic churches, martyred virgins offer us their ecstasy, while troubled celebrities become angels once they overdose. Writers before and after Edgar Allan Poe have agreed that 'the death, then, of a beautiful woman is, unquestionably, the most poetical topic in the world'.[2]

We garb ourselves in dead girls – or at least, in their garments. High-fashion brands routinely pose models as corpses to sell designer clothes and accessories – a 2006 Jimmy Choo ad staged Molly Simms dead in a car boot, with Quincy Jones-as-murderer brandishing a spade. In 2014, Marc Jacobs posed singer Miley Cyrus beside an apparently drowned model on a moonlit beach.[3] Photographer Izima Kaoru's 1995–2008 series *Landscape with a Corpse* varies the theme by basing the images on each model's 'fantasy of a perfect death', including 'which designer clothing they imagine wearing when people discover their dead body'.[4] This may unsettle you, as it unsettled me – why should fashion models have ready-made fantasies of a 'perfect death'? But patriarchal society forces women to prepare for, imagine, and simultaneously obsessively avoid our own deaths. This begins in adolescence, when girls are necessarily taught that some men (and it is overwhelmingly men) are murderous predators from whom they are always at risk.

Society instructs girls that it is their responsibility to cheat death by not walking or dressing or existing in certain times, manners and locales. Rebecca Solnit takes it furthest: 'To be a young woman is to face your own annihilation in innumerable ways or to flee it or the knowledge of it, or all these things at once'.[5] Adolescent dead girls are frequently depicted as culpable, hapless, reckless. In fiction, as Alice Bolin notes, they are 'wild, vulnerable creatures' whose bodies are both 'a wellspring of, and a target for sexual wickedness'.[6] Girls are taught by society to fear the danger in the darkness, while society secretly believes that the danger was in girlhood all along. Hollywood has, for Bolin, a 'necrophiliac quality', and the young Rebecca Solnit gave away her television after a night in San Francisco when 'a young blonde woman was being murdered on each channel'.[7] Nonetheless, the lust for the beautiful bodies of dead young white women is much older than America. When a girl is dead, she can be loved as never before.

Western culture loves a saint, but never more so than when it can fashion her from the corpse of a sinner. Death vindicates the fallen woman. Like the suspected witch drowned on a village ducking-stool, her demise proves that she was a nice girl all along. In asking, 'When lovely woman stoops to folly, [. . .] What art can wash her guilt away?', and answering that the only choice 'is to die', eighteenth-century writer Oliver Goldsmith acknowledged a truth recognised by Shakespeare – whether or not the 'folly' were real.[8] In *Much Ado About Nothing*, a priest advises Hero, wrongly accused of being unchaste, to fake her own death to 'change slander to remorse' and mortify her fiancé (4.1.211). Queen Hermione does the same thing for sixteen years in *The Winter's Tale*.

By the nineteenth century, death was the standard and implicitly desirable fate for the sexually rebellious woman. In Alexandre Dumas's *La Dame Aux Camélias* (1848), courtesan Marguerite Gautier's emotional self-sacrifice and horrific death from

tuberculosis redeem her, impressing even a priest. In Thomas
Hardy's *Tess of the D'Urbervilles* (1893), when Tess is arrested for her
rapist's murder, carrying an inevitable sentence of death, she
declares herself 'almost glad – yes, glad!' The deaths of Marguerite
and Tess curtail careers that would have blotted their menfolk's
lives. As Tess tells her husband Angel at the moment of her arrest,
'now I shall not live for you to despise me'.[9] Tactfully, Tess bequeaths
Angel her box-fresh younger sister, the untainted 'Liza-Lu', whose
description by Hardy as 'half girl, half woman – a spiritualised
image of Tess, slighter than she, but with the same beautiful eyes'
hammers home that pious Liza is Tess caught early, by Angel and
not by the rapist Alec. Primed, as Tess notes, for Angel to 'train her,
and teach her, and bring her up for [his] own self', Liza-Lu is groom-
able by the 'right' man instead of the wrong one. Marguerite and
Tess retain their youth, if not their virtue: the narrator of *La Dame
Aux Camélias* feels that by killing beautiful Marguerite, 'God has
been merciful' in destroying her 'before the coming of old age, the
courtesan's first death'. That avoiding the ageing process is one of
the compensations of premature death has become such a tenet of
Western culture that 'Forever Young' is a typical comment on
condolence cards, funerary wreaths and monuments, and – inevitably – social media. The implication is that, for the young and beautiful, life runs inevitably downhill.

   If the dead girl was also an artist, that art is indivisible from her
death. Too often, considerations of Sylvia Plath's poetry and novel
count down to the freezing morning in February 1963 when she
barricaded herself in the kitchen and lay down with her head in the
oven. The final play by Sarah Kane, *4.48 Psychosis* (1999), was
reviewed as a '75-minute suicide note', and the line 'I shall not speak
again' taken as prophecy, because Kane had died aged twenty-eight
by suicide before the play's first night.[10] In fact, the play ends hope-
fully, with a request for light. Male artists who die before their time
are also subject to schlocky retrospectives, especially if they were
queer. Joe Orton's biographer John Lahr writes as if Orton's murder
by his mentally ill partner Kenneth Halliwell was the predestined
climax of Orton's promiscuous, uproarious and thus (to Lahr)
necessarily doomed life.[11] For some, Oscar Wilde's extraordinarily
prolific and often beautiful literary works are precursors to his

downfall – the 1895 imprisonment for gross indecency, the 1900 death in a Parisian hotel. In truth, many of Wilde's friends were shocked by revelations of his sexuality, and Wilde died not of disgrace but of otogenic bacterial meningitis caused by a pustulant ear tumour, curable today with antibiotics and surgery.[12]

Homophobia fuels these perceptions of Orton and Wilde as death-driven and doomed, but worshipping elegant dead women is so culturally intrinsic that dead female artists themselves become art. In 2013, *Vice* published a photoshoot by Annabel Mehran and Annette Lamothe-Ramos, in which they styled each model as a famous woman writer who died by suicide, posed at the moment of that writer's death.[13] Virginia Woolf hugs a rock, calf-deep in a river. Beat poet Elise Cowen lies face-down on a sidewalk, bare legs exposed almost to her buttocks. Sylvia Plath gazes into the oven, hair in tangled ringlets. The dead female writer, no matter her talent, becomes the dead girl Muse, the subject of art and not its creator.

Ideally, the dead girl's death must further the development or hasten the tragic crisis of a man, whether he's Lord Capulet or King Lear, whether she's Evangeline St Clare or Dora Copperfield – but then everyone moves on. Apart from occasioning a personal revenge quest or religious conversion, the consequences of the fictional dead girl's death are rarely systemic. Whether we sob over Little Nell or lament the abused, drug-addicted demise of *Twin Peaks*'s Laura Palmer, the ideal dead girl's death highlights the injustice of society without compelling anyone actively to seek an alternative. *Romeo and Juliet* does end the feud between the patriarchs Capulet and Montague, but this is unsurprising – for once, there is a dead boy as well as a dead girl.

However she does it, the perfect dead girl dies beautifully. She is herself beautiful, which in Western culture means white, and – as Rebecca Solnit notes – she is preferably blonde. Once she is dead, decomposition and putrefaction rarely apply. Nor, usually, should the manner of her death leave any visible impression on her body. The drowned fallen woman becalmed on the canvas of George Frederic Watts's *Found Drowned* (1850) is no more the bloated corpse with haemorrhaged muscles and abraded, livid features than four centuries' worth of stage Ophelias.[14] Even when Laertes's grave-leaping shenanigans uncover the actress's face in *Hamlet*, this drowned corpse is never more than interestingly pale with (at most) an off-kilter lipstick. There are slight exceptions. If you must be bloody, wear it well: the imprint of a thumb on a white throat is acceptable, although miraculous preservation is preferred. In 1599, three years after *Romeo and Juliet* entered the repertory, the body of Saint Cecilia, virgin martyr, was exhumed from a Roman basilica. Fourteen centuries after her death, the saint's body was 'incorrupt' – unrotted, intact, and with the axe's indentation visible in her neck. Within a year, Baroque sculptor Stefano Maderno had immortalised her in marble: veiled and vulnerable, she lies curled on her side in a red-and-black tomb, the cuts to her neck as white and unblemished as any wound could wish to be.[15]

Although Juliet is a bloodless corpse (at least until her real death), Shakespeare knew blood could also be sexy. Even avoiding vampire territory, blood is permissible if it can be likened to jewellery: blood 'braceleting' or 'glittering' on the wrists or throat. The novice nun Isabella announces in *Measure for Measure* (c. 1602–4):

> The impression of keen whips I'd wear as rubies,
> And strip myself to death as to a bed,
> That longing have been sick for, ere I'd yield
> My body up to shame (2.4.100–3).

Nevertheless, despite this promising start, Isabella dares to survive. The sexuality of death – that which Philippe Ariès calls the 'éroticomacabre' – is key to the 'death-marked love' of *Romeo and Juliet*.[16] Juliet links sex and death at her first meeting with Romeo, declaring that: 'If he be married/ My grave is like to be my wedding-bed' (1.5.133–4). Later, in her erotic rapture before learning of Tybalt's murder, she rhapsodises, 'Give me my Romeo, and when I shall die/ Take him and cut him out in little stars' (3.2.21–2), with a characteristic Renaissance punning on death and orgasm. The Renaissance was fascinated by sex and death: in the 'Death and the Maiden' art motif, where a skeleton fingers nubile flesh, the male viewer not only recalls the inevitability of death but wishes he were Death himself, guaranteed access to so much swooning femininity.[17]

In the tomb, Romeo marvels that death 'Hath had no power upon thy beauty [. . .] Beauty's ensign yet/ Is crimson in thy lips and in thy cheeks, and death's pale flag is not advanced there' (5.3.91–6). To a knowing audience, this is dramatic irony of the most harrowing kind: *hang on, we will Romeo, for God's sake; Friar Laurence is on his way, she's about to come round.* Three scenes earlier, we've heard Lord Capulet pronounce that Juliet's 'blood is settled and her joints are stiff' (4.4.54): the onset of both liver and rigor mortis. Shakespeare is oddly specific about the time the potion will last – forty-two hours – and we know from Friar Laurence that we're at the forty-hour mark. Juliet has spent most of her 'death' in the chill of a subterranean tomb; rigor resolves more slowly in small, less muscular corpses kept at a low temperature. Liver mortis continues, and the relaxed muscles sag as they decompose. But so enraptured is Romeo with his very sexy corpse that he assumes Juliet is a still-beautiful incorruptible rather than consider-ing the possibility that a lack of rigor and liver mortis and grotesquely sagging muscles indicates that something other than death is at work. My assessment of Romeo's grief-stricken oblivi-ousness might seem mean, but William Painter, the author of one of Shakespeare's prose sources for *Romeo and Juliet*, shows both the Capulets and Romeo performing extensive checks that Juliet is *actually* dead – her parents summon 'the most expert Phisitians of the towne', and Romeo in the tomb puts his hands 'uppon the colde stomacke of Iulietta' and touches her 'in many places' to check there are no 'Iudgemente of Lyfe'. There is due diligence. Shakespeare cuts this, and if, like the early modern audience, you're familiar with Painter, Shakespeare's characters seem negligent. Perhaps this gave them hope that Juliet, so readily misidentified as dead, might be going to sit up and give Romeo the embrace for which he is so desperate.

Instead, she gives him her beautiful, theatrical corpse. The stage has always been a valuable source of beautiful dead girls never more gratifying than in their deaths. Unlike Isabella, determined to evade sex altogether by retreating to the convent, Juliet chooses her violent death as an alternative to religious life in 'a sisterhood of holy nuns' (5.3.157). She would rather stab herself, re-consummating her marriage to Romeo, and transforming the bed-turned-bier back into a wedding bed, as the two young lovers are found unmistakeably and eternally joined. Juliet is the perfect dead girl: nubile, beautiful, indistinguishable from a virgin, European, wealthy, and white.

*

This is how Juliet dies, a week before her fourteenth birthday: but she does not stay dead. Beautiful dead girls don't rest in peace. Long after Shakespeare went to his own tomb in the riverside church at Stratford, Juliet's stage death began to fascinate theatregoers – and makers – far more than the ten scenes in which she lives her brief, explosive theatrical life. One hundred years after her first death on stage, the century that gave us Leviathan-shaped pulpits and Spode pottery, Blenheim Palace and Cadbury's chocolate, pornographic snuffboxes, steam engineers and *opera seria* also created a lavish funeral sequence for Juliet – one still visible in modern screen adaptations. Juliet's death ushers in a new century of Juliets. It's the template for how we've understood dead girls ever since.

Apart from performances by clandestine lawbreakers like Alexander Gough, most theatre in Britain stopped in 1642, ended by the Civil Wars and subsequent Republic. The year 1660 saw the Restoration of the monarchy in the form of King Charles II, proclaimed by Parliament on 8 May as having been Britain's lawful king ever since his father's execution in 1649. The new king was exiled in France and preparing to return. William Davenant, the syphilitic poet laureate and self-proclaimed illegitimate son of Shakespeare, went to join Charles, badgering him for theatrical preferment.[18] Thomas Killigrew, a pre-war playwright and fanatical Royalist, was already with the king, and desperate for the same.[19] The king sailed to England later in May, entertaining diarist Samuel Pepys (among others) with hair-raising stories of his disguised escape from England, twelve years earlier. To hear the king tell it, he had been 'travelling four days and three nights on foot, every step up to his knees in dirt'; he was recognised by a Brighton innkeeper, and mistaken for a thief in Rouen.[20] Within six weeks of reaching London, this theatrical king granted his 'trusty and well beloved' Killigrew and Davenant sole warrant for producing plays (Davenant wrote the warrant himself).[21] Having enjoyed both the architecture and the actresses of the French stage, Charles subsequently stipulated that the new generation of British playhouses should be indoor spaces with women playing women's roles. Killigrew hastily converted a tennis court in Vere Street, and British theatre resumed there on 8 November 1660. The King's Company inherited the older actors of the pre-war theatre scene, and many of the plays, while Davenant's Duke's Company – opened in its own tennis court in June 1661 – was primed to adapt stock plays and produce new writing. Within a year, Killigrew was producing plays in a bigger building on Drury Lane.[22]

The first woman to appear on a British stage probably did so on 8 December 1660, as Desdemona in Killigrew's production of *Othello*. The prologue to the performance titillatingly boasted that its speaker 'saw the lady drest; / The Woman playes today, mistake me not', but nobody bothered to record the actress's name.[23] The likeliest candidate is the then twenty-year-old Anne Marshall, who would become one of the most versatile performers of the early Restoration, taking on everything from tragedies and cross-dressed breeches roles to comic heroines such as the witty and vengeful courtesan Angellica in Aphra Behn's *The Rover* (1677). Although England's first actress appeared in a Shakespeare play, Shakespeare at the time of the Restoration was the object of entrepreneurial enthusiasm rather than reverence. The plays were little-read, circulating primarily in the expensive Folio editions of 1623, 1632 (owned by the new king), and 1664. His collaborators were dead – of the Principall Actors listed in 1623, none saw the Restoration – and the last of Shakespeare's surviving children was buried in 1662. Few images of Shakespeare were in circulation, and they were typically of poor quality.[24] When the plays were staged, they were heavily and freely adapted to suit the musical and scenographic enthusiasms of the time. Davenant spliced *Much Ado* and *Measure for Measure* to create *The Law Against Lovers* (1662), and inserted singing and dancing witches into his *Macbeth* (1663–4). In collaboration with John Dryden, Davenant wrote *The Enchanted Island* (1667), an adaptation of *The Tempest* that gives Miranda and Caliban sisters, and Ariel a girlfriend. Thomas Shadwell's operatic version in 1674 also featured an aerial ballet and pyrotechnics.

Romeo and Juliet returned in 1662, at Davenant's Lincoln Inn's Fields theatre, otherwise known as 'the Opera'.[25] The Opera boasted moveable scenery and Britain's first proscenium arch, both of which impressed theatregoer Samuel Pepys more than the play, which he dubbed 'a play of itself the worst that ever I heard in my life'. London's first female Juliet was thirty-five-year-old Mary Saunderson, soon to become the wife of the production's Mercutio, Thomas Betterton, and the most respected actress and acting teacher of the era. The impact of her Juliet, however, seems to have been slight. The Nurse, meanwhile, continued to be played by men until 1735, as a scene-stealing comic turn, which minimises the impact of her betrayal of Juliet.

Davenant's management also produced the first Restoration adaptation of *Romeo and Juliet*, written by James Howard. Only one anecdote survives of the production, noting that Howard's version 'preserv[ed] both Romeo and Juliet alive'.[26] What followed was more significant.

In 1679, the country seemed to be once again on the brink of civil war. Despite Charles's many lovechildren, he had no legitimate child to succeed him. Instead, the Heir Presumptive was James, Duke of York, the king's Catholic brother. The powerful Earl of Shaftesbury proposed a Parliamentary bill to exclude James from the succession on the grounds that a Catholic king might rule via absolute monarchy, as Louis XIV of France was doing across the Channel. Anti-Catholic hysteria had also been fuelled by a hoax called the 'Popish Plot', a fictitious conspiracy that posited an extensive Catholic network plotting to kill the king. During the two-year Exclusion Crisis that followed, three bills were presented to Parliament – and each time, Charles dissolved Parliament to prevent them passing.

Responding to the national mood, dramatist Thomas Otway gave *Romeo and Juliet* a Roman revamp for Killigrew's company. Otway belonged to a new political faction: the Tories, who opposed James's right to succeed his brother. Otway's play transformed the essentially domestic tragedy into a political conflict at a moment of political crisis: *The History and Fall of Caius Marius*. Its premise is all too familiar – the Caius Marius of the title is Lord Montague's equivalent, leader of the plebeians. Young Marius (Romeo) secretly marries Lavinia (Juliet), daughter of Metellus, Roman patrician and Old Marius's enemy. Otway's tragedy is even bleaker in its exploration of unjust parental behaviour than Shakespeare's: Old Marius murders Lavinia's father in front of her, and she stabs herself. Lavinia's imprecation is far in excess of Mercutio's 'a plague a'both your houses' in *Romeo and Juliet* (3.1.108). She curses: 'now let Rage, Distraction and Despair/ Seize all Mankind, till they grow mad as I am.'[27] The Roman feud remains unresolved.

Although Otway's play is forgotten today, *Caius Marius* introduced an innovation with a long theatrical legacy. In Otway's equivalent of the tomb scene, now in a 'Church-yard', Lavinia revives before Marius has died of the poison, heightening the pathos as she briefly regains the 'soveraign Charm' of Marius's 'Embraces', only for Marius to find the 'World's gross air [. . .] burdenous' and die in her arms.[28] The lovers' joy is as intense as it is brief.

In opera, the benefits of Romeo's early revival include an extra duet for lovers who, in Shakespeare's play, only share four scenes of dialogue. Romeo dying so shortly before Juliet awakes is already horribly unlucky, but having him poison himself literally a heartbeat or two before she stirs is appalling. Shakespeare's Romeo never realises his mistake – poison ends his tragedy. Allowing him to see Juliet wake gives him the unbearable knowledge that his death is not merely futile, but catastrophic for his wife. Juliet, meanwhile, has an even worse fate in the revised sequence. Shakespeare sees the wakeful Juliet shift from relief to concern – 'O comfortable friar! where is my lord?' (5.3.148) – before Friar Laurence breaks the news and shows her Romeo's body. If Juliet revives while Romeo is still alive, she swings devastatingly from euphoric reunion to the unparalleled horror and anguish of watching Romeo die. It's the only way to make Shakespeare's tragedy more tragic.

But the Restoration's romantic project comes at a cost. Most adaptations that wake Juliet sooner cut some or all of the scene's many interruptions from Friar Laurence, Balthasar, the Watch, and Paris's Page, enhancing its intimacy. Perhaps this gives Juliet more tragic grandeur in her decision to die, by making it a single-minded response to Romeo's death. But it also greatly reduces the scene's complexity. As Shakespeare writes it, Juliet kills herself under pressure from two kinds of desperation: first, grief, and second, the imminent threat of discovery. Friar Laurence abandons Juliet because he 'dare no longer stay' given the danger of the approaching watch (5.3.159). Juliet is clearly suicidal, trying to find residual poison on Romeo's lips. But the moment of her death arrives because she, too, is under time pressure: she hurries her final, fatal act because she hears something: 'Yea, noise? Then I'll be brief' (5.3.169). The 'noise' is a Veronese Watchman, addressing his boy. Juliet has just refused Friar Laurence's offer of 'a sisterhood of holy nuns' (5.3.157). Neither women nor men offer her a way out now.

In killing herself, Shakespeare's Juliet is not only the bereaved Mrs Romeo Montague: she is a desperate teenager rejecting every form of authority – patriarchal, civic, religious. The doomed interventions of both priestly and state forces remind us of the girl who offered to run away with Romeo, to 'follow thee my lord throughout the world' (2.2.148) as a direct response to the society surrounding them. The seventeenth- and eighteenth-century rewrites escalate the tragic romance of the tomb scene, but they also strip out the mess, the urgency, and the horribly public nature of a sequence that is less grand opera than terrible farce. Out of a cowardly priest, snivelling manservants, the gratuitous death of Paris, and a panicked stabbing triggered by approaching uproar, the writers and composers of the Stuart and Georgian eras created the ultimate romantic tableau. There were textual precedents for this: Luigi da Porto, author of one of the Italian versions of the legend (published posthumously in 1530), briefly reconciled the lovers, just as Otway's far more recent Roman adaptation had done.[29]

But the seventeenth- and eighteenth-century writers and composers were less fans of Da Porto or Otway than they were influenced by the two wildly different actor-managers who ensured that the extended death scene dominated the eighteenth-century stage. The first actor-manager was Theophilus Cibber (1703–58), a dissolute, abusive impresario who helped destroy his daughter's career. The second was David Garrick (1717–79), Georgian England's most celebrated performer, who single-handedly created the Shakespeare industry as we know it today. Both men were involved in the intertheatrical Cibber family feud: a feud so toxic it rivalled that of the play.

When in 1744 Theophilus Cibber staged his own version of *Romeo and Juliet* in an unlicensed season at London's Haymarket, he had closely read his Otway: Juliet revives to enjoy the 'sovereign Charm' of Romeo's embraces before he dies.[30] Cibber couldn't afford to take any chances. The very public divorce of his second wife for adultery had backfired on him horribly – even in sensibility-struck Georgian England, the British public had sided with her – and he desperately needed *Romeo and Juliet* as his comeback.

Theophilus was a mess. Described by actress George Anne Bellamy in her memoir as 'a compound of meanness and extravagance [. . .] ever involved in duplicity and falsehood', topped off with 'the most frightful face [she] ever beheld,' he was the son of visionary actor and Poet Laureate Colley Cibber.[31] Shortly before his retirement in 1733, Colley demonstrated his opinion that Theophilus wasn't worth the powder on his periwig by selling his share of the Drury Lane Theatre patent outside the family.[32] Theophilus had constantly cheated on his late first wife, the docile actress 'amiable Jane' Johnson, with 'sullied dear purchas'd Pleasures' in the form of prostitutes.[33] Jane died, aged twenty-six, in 1732: her successor as Mrs Cibber was the 'very young and very pretty' Susannah Arne, an actress and singer so talented that Handel composed for her.[34] The astute Arne demanded a prenuptial contract guaranteeing her sole use of her theatrical earnings. But the profligate and under-employed Theophilus broke the contract, stole her money, and pimped her out to a younger lover, William Sloper.[35] Luckily for Susannah, Sloper loved her – but when she left her husband to be with Sloper, Theophilus abducted her, then menaced her for years. He published handbills citing 'the Authority I have an undoubted right to' over Susannah and accusing her of seeking to 'Stab my reputation'.[36] He also sued Sloper twice, for 'criminal conversation' and 'detaining' his wife.

By the standards of the day, Susannah should have been an outcast. She was a runaway actress, pregnant by her lover, and the subject of a celebrity trial complete with voyeuristic tavern landlord, who testified to having 'bored Holes through the Wainscoat' to watch Sloper and Susannah having sex.[37] The 1730s was a decade that enjoyed being shocked, thanks to a burgeoning daily newspaper industry, an evangelical revival, and – in Hogarth's *A Harlot's Progress* (1732) – a shared frame of reference for the precise trajectory that sexually rebellious women ought to follow: six etchings of corruption, prostitution, degradation, and death. At the dawn of the following decade, Samuel Richardson's four-volume novel *Pamela, or Virtue Rewarded* (1740) would entrance thousands of readers with its single plotline of a housemaid who avoids getting raped by her lecherous lord, then marries him. It was the perfect climate in which to condemn Susannah Cibber. But Theophilus's cruelty, avarice, and colossal lack of talent were so obvious that the public sided with Susannah, hurling 'Volleys of Apples and Potatoes, and such vile Trash' at Theophilus when he next appeared on stage.[38] A 1738 broadsheet called him a 'crafty Pimp'.[39] Although Susannah left England for Dublin after the second trial, it was a splendid exile – Handel followed her, writing the contralto solo for her in *Messiah*, which premiered there. The chancellor of Dublin's two great cathedrals was reportedly so moved by her performance that he cried out: 'Woman! Thy sins be forgiven thee!'[40]

By 1742, Susannah had returned to the London stage as Desdemona, the ultimate in unjustly accused Shakespearean wives.[41] Theophilus's career was in the doldrums so he decided to rebrand as a romantic lead, playing Romeo in his own adaptation of Shakespeare's play. His wife, his obvious leading lady, was gone. But his *first* wife, Jane Johnson, had left him two children. When Theophilus's ill-fated production opened in September 1744, his onstage lover was his own daughter. Playing Juliet was fifteen-year-old Jane (Jenny) Cibber, in what must have been one of the most unsavoury moments in British stage history.

Theophilus's self-authored prologue to the production makes it all the more revolting. He described his daughter as still in 'the Husk of Infancy', inviting the audience's 'Indulgence' as the catalyst for her dramatic – and sexual – maturity: 'She the fair Bud – and you the rip'ning Sun'. As theatre historian Elaine McGirr notes, Theophilus 'encouraged audiences to leer at his daughter and anticipate her "ripening beauty"'. Jenny still looked young enough to play a little boy in *King John* twelve months after partnering her father, implying that she was still pre-pubescent when presented for audiences to ogle as Juliet.[42] Poor Jenny's Juliet was the puppet of her father, onstage and offstage. In Cibber's text, Juliet and Romeo are betrothed to each other by their fathers before the feud begins.

Rather than a bold act of defiance, Jenny's Juliet thus followed her father's original instructions in loving Romeo; her feelings are learned rather than the spontaneous attraction experienced by Shakespeare's heroine. This turns Juliet into a docile daughter victimised by her father's caprice, rather than a rebel who violates family values in pursuing her own desires.

Meanwhile, Jenny the actress was key to her disgraced father's doomed career reboot. He had exploited her since childhood, and the public knew it. Theophilus had staged a fundraising 'benefit' performance, ostensibly for nine-year-old Jenny and her sister Elizabeth, trading on sympathy for the children in order to fund his lifestyle; a contemporary pseudo-autobiography, attacking Theophilus, described him cynically 'touch[ing] the Public in a tender Point'.[43] When Susannah left him for Sloper, Theophilus had publicly invoked his daughters to emotionally blackmail their stepmother, telling the persecuted Susannah in print that 'my Children starve while you riot'. Susannah, rather than rioting, was pregnant and in hiding.[44]

Jenny had become not only his mascot, but a surrogate: an empty vessel into which Theophilus could pour all the malice he felt for Susannah, and all his desire to control the women in his life. As the full prologue to Cibber's *Romeo and Juliet* made clear, Jenny mattered most as a stand-in for her dead mother. Having failed to destroy his second wife, Theophilus Cibber wanted to use the body of his daughter to resurrect the first. Rather than 'Jenny', Theophilus's prologue calls her 'Jane', the baptismal name she shared with her dead mother. 'Young Jane, the blooming promise of her spring' is overwhelmed by this dead mother's presence:

Her Mother's Mem'ry fresh and fair survives,
And added Lustre to the Daughter gives;
By Nature's Self inspir'd she gain'd Applause,
Let her Remembrance plead the Daughter's Cause.

The closer you look, the worse it gets. Cunningly, Theophilus was not only tying daughter to mother, but both of them to the role of Juliet herself, the girl who comes back from the dead. The deceased Jane 'fresh and fair survives', as attractive to the theatrical public in death as the beautiful, dead Juliet is to Romeo, and (so he believes) the 'amorous' Death himself. 'Young Jane' emerges as a kind of corpse revived, reanimating the woman Theophilus elsewhere called 'the Spouse of my Soul'. The scholar Joseph Roach has written brilliantly of a cultural process called 'surrogation', when one individual is nominated as the effigy of the lost subject, significant only in their ability to body forth what is lost.[45] 'Young Jane' became her mother's effigy, her own individuality deadened by the responsibility of embodying her dead mother. Humiliatingly, the prologue made no mention of Jenny's own talent, and did not stop at comparing her to just one dead relative, urging the audience to remember from what 'Root she came,/ And her just, hereditary Claim' to theatrical attention. Given the toxic destruction wreaked by 'heredity' in Shakespeare's play, the words are jarring. Juliet's 'heredity' leads only to despair and destruction.

Those audience members so strenuously encouraged to remember Jane Johnson through her daughter might also have recalled Johnson's final performance. Just as Theophilus paraded his daughter Jenny as a 'real' teenage Juliet, so had he forced his wife Jane onstage as a 'real' pregnant woman in the lead role of Charles Johnson's *Caelia*, a play about an innocent, exploited fallen woman. After Jane collapsed onstage while playing the victimised Caelia, she died of puerperal fever.[46] Subsequent commentary blamed Theophilus: during the Sloper–Cibber trial, the *Weekly Miscellany* published a long pseudonymous letter denouncing Theophilus as 'the Means of depriving the Theatre of one, or more of its brightest Ornaments'.[47] The only possible other 'ornament' was Jane Johnson. The *Miscellany*'s 'Philodramatus' blamed Theophilus for Jane's death: five years later, Jenny was walking in her mother's footsteps at her father's behest.

The incestuous and exploitative performance horrified David Garrick, who wrote: '[I have] never heard so vile and scandalous a performance in my life . . . the girl, I believe, may have genius; but unless she changes her preceptor, she must be entirely ruined.'[48] Theophilus's aggressive marketing campaign saw him insert 'anonymous' puff pieces in the press, advertising Jenny's 'Innocence and rip'ning Beauty', while insisting via paid-for reviews that his 'most polite Audience' included 'persons of Distinction' and repeat performances by the 'Particular Desire of "Ladies of Quality"'.[49] Although the illegal season was ended when the Licensing Act was enforced,

Jenny played Juliet opposite her father once more, for a benefit where Cibber wrote 'little Jane' an excruciating epilogue. 'Genius, my Dad says, is by nature shown,' she insisted, then invoked 'my dear Mother gone', calling herself only 'her unskill'd infant'. All she could hope for, in the words her father insisted she speak, was to be 'a second Jenny Cibber': the dead young woman brought back to life.

Theophilus's detractors had accused him of secretly using his children's benefit performances to line his own pockets. Now, it was explicit, with Jenny made to propose that she and her father should 'both [the audience's] happy Bounty share', beseeching them to 'pardon the Fondness of my Filial Love'.[50] In this forced submission, Jenny most closely resembled the Juliet of Act 4, Scene 2, when she vows to be 'henceforth [. . .] ever ruled by' Lord Capulet (4.2.22), even as she plans to fake her own death and elope. But Jenny was triply trapped: Theophilus was her father, onstage husband, and playwright. Her only words were his.

Six years later, John Hill recalled with sympathetic distaste that 'little Juliet' would have been 'much more pleasing [. . .] if there had been some gay young fellow for her lover, instead of a person whom we could not but remember, at every sentence she deliver'd concerning him, to be too old for her choice, too little handsome to be in love with, and, into the bargain, her father'.[51] By the time Hill wrote, Jenny's career was over. Too soon 'made' an actress and her father's onstage consort, she had been irrevocably 'marr'd' (1.2.12).[52] In 1761, she married William Ellis, headmaster of Aldenham School, then little more than a struggling Hertfordshire village school, where boys were taught the absolute educational basics.[53] Within a year, she was dead.[54]

Jenny Cibber had been destroyed by her family as thoroughly as Juliet Capulet. For Theophilus, far more a Lord Capulet than a Romeo, wives and daughters were interchangeable commodities, 'baggage' to be exploited (3.5.160). According to the prologue he wrote for her, his real-life daughter Jenny 'beg[ged] a father's fate to share'. She got her wish.

*

David Garrick, meanwhile, was plotting. He became the new licensee at Drury Lane in 1747, and having seen *Romeo and Juliet* succeed

in Dublin the previous year, he edited his own text of the play, casting Susannah Cibber opposite the handsome Irish actor Spranger
Barry.[55] A jealous Theophilus rushed his own version of *Romeo and
Juliet* and a self-aggrandising autobiography into print, compiled in
a single volume along with the libellous handbills he'd published
about Susannah. It was clearly intended to discredit both Garrick
and Susannah – and it didn't work. Susannah's performance was
acclaimed.

Susannah Cibber played a very different kind of Juliet. Where
Jenny Cibber had been the persecuted child, Susannah Cibber was
seen as the doomed, passionate lover. Jenny's Juliet was the creature
of her father, the professional and personal passivity of her performance ensured by having him – and not 'some gay young fellow' –
embrace her onstage and dictate her interpretative choices.
Susannah was the sexual rebel who had risked all for love. As Elaine
McGirr argued, 'in Susannah's hands, Juliet is always already
doomed; there is no hope in her love'.[56] In Garrick's rendering, she
became a tragic, death-marked heroine fit for the sentimental,
sensibility-obsessed Georgian era.

Garrick's adaptation did two vital things to Shakespeare's heroine. Most influentially of all, he gave her a balcony. Shakespeare's
play never mentions one; there is no stage direction in either of the
quartos. In fact, Shakespeare wouldn't have known what a balcony
was. The word 'balcone' only entered English in 1618, two years
after Shakespeare died. When in 1611 Thomas Coryat had published
his enormous European travelogue as *Coryat's Crudities*, he could
only describe this exotic example of Italianate architecture, bemused
but impressed, as 'a very pleasant little tarrasse, that jutteth or
butteth out from the maine building: the edge whereof is decked
with many prety litle turned pillers, either of marble or free stone to
leane over'.[57] Coryat didn't know the word either; there were no
balconies on English buildings. Accordingly, Shakespeare's Romeo
– the product of an Elizabethan pen – only refers to 'yonder window'
(2.1.44). In Shakespeare's theatre, that was most likely a window in
the 'tiring-house', the backstage area where the players attired
themselves. In the earliest printed version of *Romeo and Juliet*, the
stage directions for the lovers' morning-after scene explicitly
discover the lovers 'at the window', through which Romeo escapes

before the arrival of Lady Capulet. Garrick put the balcony in balcony scene, a decision that made Susannah Cibber's Juliet a spectacle as never before, and one that has had theatrical and architectural consequences ever since.

Second, as befitted a promoter of theatrical respectability, Garrick sanitised the play, and along with it the frank desire and rebelliousness of Shakespeare's heroine. Working from Alexander Pope's 1725 edition – which cut puns and 'vile ribaldry' – and silently leaning on Otway and Cibber's adaptations, Garrick created a thoroughly sentimental, demure Juliet in a play also stripped of the most explicit excesses of the supporting cast (notably Mercutio, Gregory and Sampson).

Garrick's Juliet was a decorous seventeen. She did not kiss Romeo in the sonnet-less ball scene. During the balcony scene, Garrick cut Juliet's rejection of 'Montague' as 'not hand, nor foot / Nor arm nor face [. . .] nor any other part / Belonging to a man' (2.2.40–2), due to the possibility of what 'part' might be implied. The possessive sadomasochism of Juliet's urge to keep Romeo as her 'poor prisoner in his twisted gyves' was gone (2.2.179). When the Nurse (also censored for being 'highly disgraceful to the [. . .] dignity of tragic compositions') complained of breathlessness instead of giving Juliet news of Romeo, Garrick expunged Juliet's pert rejoinders, including, 'How art thou out of breadth when thou hadst breath / To say to me that thou art out of breath?' (2.5.31–2), perhaps her funniest lines. Unsurprisingly, Garrick also muffled the eloquent sexuality of Juliet's pre-wedding-night soliloquy. Amidst heavy cuts, she could no longer describe herself as 'sold / Not yet enjoy'd'. Talk of 'amorous rites' and the lovers' 'pair of stainless maidenhoods' disappeared, and the sexual pun in 'Give me my Romeo, and when I shall die / Take him and cut him out in little stars' was eliminated, becoming: 'Give me my Romeo, and when *he* shall die' (3.2.1–31).[58] Garrick also decimated Juliet's other great soliloquy, before taking the potion. Many of Garrick's cuts swiftly became traditional: Juliet's evasive bantering with Paris in Act 4, Scene 1 would not be seen again for over a century. Garrick adopted Otway and Cibber's method of reviving Juliet early, but strictly as a foil for Romeo – of fifty-nine additional lines of dialogue between the couple, she speaks just eighteen.

That Garrick had to cut so much to make Juliet acceptable to respectable eighteenth-century audiences tells us how exceptional, unruly, and vital Shakespeare's youngest and greatest tragic heroine truly is. Not only do Garrick's cuts curtail Juliet's sexual self-confidence and longing, they also make her a far less imaginative heroine: her metaphoric vocabulary can no longer transform Romeo into a bird, a newly-purchased mansion, or a set of constellations to beautify the night. She can no longer break the connection between the Montague name and the Montague body, revealing the artificiality of all familial identities and the pointlessness of the feud. Unable to banter with Paris, we are denied the opportunity to see, even for a moment, what that relationship could have become.

> Paris: Do not deny to him [Friar Laurence] that you love
>   me.
> Juliet: I will confess to you that I love him.
> Paris: So will ye, I am sure, that you love me.
> Juliet: If I do so, it will be of more price,
>   Being spoke behind your back, than to your face.
>   (4.2.24–8)

The quick stichomythia – their alternate lines, each picking up on the other's language – reveals two strong personalities. As in her first exchanges with Romeo, Juliet holds her own, maintaining the formal 'you' even when Paris slips to the intimate 'thou'. He is possessive, calling her 'my lady and my wife', and telling her, 'Thy face is mine' (4.1.18; 35). But it's notable that Juliet, despite her despair and her recent conflict with her family, does not reject him openly, despite having the perfect opportunity so to do. Paris has a superior social position, but Juliet has already decided death is preferable to marriage. Nevertheless, something she hears in Paris's rhythm – the strong iambs and the semantic register of 'deny' – is worth catching and giving back. She inverts 'deny' to become 'confess', and tantalisingly delays the confession that she loves not Paris, but her priest. Paris might be forgiven for reading the delay as deliberately teasing, just as Juliet's own mother and the Nurse have misread her attitudes to Romeo.

Shakespeare had already used stichomythia for lovers (Hermia and Lysander, Romeo and Juliet) and enemies-to-lovers: Richard III seduces Anne Neville over the corpse of her father-in-law, whom he murdered, in shortened stichomythic lines. Later, Shakespeare gives the same rhythm to the sparring Beatrice and Benedick, and uses it to begin the psycho-sexual quagmire that is the closet scene between Hamlet and his mother Gertrude. It's a rhetorical indicator of emotional, and often erotic, intensity. This is also the only conversation we ever witness between Juliet and someone who is neither her husband, parents, nor the Nurse. We learn in it that she can spar with a powerful man even in a moment of despair. We learn, too, that there is verbal chemistry between Juliet and Paris, and are left to speculate on what might have been, had the two of them met on different terms. Paris tells us that Juliet still looks visibly distressed ('Poor soul, thy face is much abused with tears', 4.2.29) and she will shortly threaten suicide to Friar Laurence – but even now, she is as much of an actor and wit as any Shakespearean protagonist. In 1817, the critic William Hazlitt argued that Romeo was 'Hamlet in love', because both 'live in a world of imagination'.[59] But surely the greatest capacity for imagination, planning, and dissembling in the play is Juliet's.

Shakespeare's Juliet was disappearing with every cut, but Garrick's sanitised, partly silenced Juliet pleased the Georgians. The production was successful enough that Susannah Cibber and Spranger Barry, having fallen out with Garrick, decamped from Drury Lane to a 1750 revival at Covent Garden, using Garrick's text.[60] Another competition ensued: Garrick mounted his own production at Drury Lane, starring himself as Romeo opposite nineteen-year-old George Anne Bellamy. For twelve days, the 'Battle of the Romeos' raged. The men – much better served by Garrick's text than their heavily edited leading ladies – received far more coverage than the women. A female audience member remarked, 'Had I been Juliet to Garrick's Romeo – so ardent and impassioned was he, I should have expected he would have come up to me in the balcony; but had I been Juliet to Barry's Romeo – so tender, so eloquent, and so seductive was he, I should certainly have gone down to him!'[61]

Even Bellamy, Garrick's Juliet, spoke fondly of 'the incomparable Cibber' and 'Mr Barry's excellence in performing [. . .] lovers' but Barry's original 1748 performance had been heavily coached by Garrick, who attended Barry and Cibber's rehearsals, and 'communicated all his ideas to the performers' more than a century before the emergence of the modern theatre director.[62] Although in 1750 Garrick's Romeo had to compete with Barry's, the Drury Lane *Romeo and Juliet* was responsible for twelve per cent of the theatre's annual takings that year: the same percentage as in 1748, when the production had faced no rival.[63]

The pressure of competition from Garrick was clear enough that John Rich, the Covent Garden licensee, knew his theatre needed an innovation. Rich was a showman: a huge force in the history of English pantomime, and an impresario who had used the dazzling success of *The Beggar's Opera* (1728) to fund his new theatre.[64] His remedy appealed to the age's spectacular appetites. Rich created a lavish funeral scene for Juliet, inserted between 4.5 (when she is found 'dead') and 5.1 (when Romeo hears the news in Mantua). Thomas Arne – Susannah's composer brother, who had already set songs for *As You Like It* and a revival of Dryden and Shadwell's *The Tempest* – obliged with an orchestral 'solemn Dirge' set for trumpets, flutes, violins, bell, viola, bass, and three-part male choir.[65]

Opinion was divided as to the sequence's success. Although another leading actor-manager, Tate Wilkinson, called it 'very grand', a German writer found it 'stupid and ridiculous [. . .] The costumes are mediocre and the decorations positively bad'.[66] The lyrics emphasise paternal grief, adapting Garrick's lines for Capulet. Capulet's 'But one, poor one, one poor and loving child/ But one thing to enjoy and solace in,/ And cruel death hath catcht it from my sight' becomes 'She was her Parent's Sole Delight/ They had but one and only Child. / [. . .] Death has torn her from their Arms'.[67] The dirge ends by exhorting the audience to 'Witness our Sighs and Groans and falling Tears'.

Garrick panicked. Within three days, Covent Garden playbills were suddenly advertising their own funeral scene, now with not merely (as at Drury Lane) 'the Funeral Procession of Juliet' but 'The Funeral PROCESSION to the MONUMENT of the CAPULETS'. Garrick hired the composer William Boyce, who, with Arne, Handel, and others, had in 1738 co-founded what is today the Royal Society of Musicians.[68] Instead of a mere procession, Garrick's onstage retort to Rich encompassed an 'entire funeral [. . .] with bells tolling, and a choir singing. Juliet, feigning death, lies on a state bed with a splendid canopy over her', with bridesmaids and torch-bearers, while 'choristers and clergy in their vestments walk in front, and the father and the mother and their friends follow'.[69] Garrick's song was longer than Rich's, with three verses and four choruses. Admittedly, his lyrics were no better, addressing Juliet as 'the sweetest flow'r of May', whose eyes 'shone like breaking day' (echoing Romeo's description of her in the balcony scene: 'What light through yonder window breaks?/ It is the east, and Juliet is the sun' 2.2.2–3).[70] Rather than addressing the audience, the dirge ends by addressing Juliet herself, as the 'spotless soul' who must 'look down' and 'give us strength to bear our woe' as an interceding saint. In search of inspiration, Garrick had reached right across Shakespeare's canon. His claim that Juliet did not 'leav[e] behind/ So fair a form, so pure a mind' recalls *Twelfth Night*, where Sebastian eulogises the twin sister he mistakenly believes to be dead: 'she bore a mind that envy could not but call fair' (2.1.18–21).[71] The Juliet dirge's recurring lament, 'She's gone, she's gone', is uttered twice by Lear after the death of Cordelia (5.3.255, 266).

Garrick's lyrics, like his playtext, would hold the stage for the next hundred years.[72] The funeral sequence had its detractors during Garrick's lifetime – the *Monthly Mirror* asked: 'What end is all this pomp, shew, and farce to answer? [. . .] it is absurd and ridiculous'.[73] Count Frederick Kielmansegge, visiting from Germany, could not help find the staged religion 'rather profane', but acknowledged that 'nothing of the kind could be represented more beautifully or naturally'.[74] Francis Gentleman, Irish playwright, critic, and sensibility-savvy editor of Shakespeare, approved on the grounds that 'three-fourths of every audience are more capable of enjoying sound and shew than solid sense and poetical imagination'.[75] Juliet's funeral proved so popular, in fact, that this 1740s innovation has survived in every major film adaptation – and many stage versions – ever since.

Why should a funeral so thrill spectators? Snobbish Francis Gentleman in the *Dramatic Censor* might remind us of Hamlet in his scorn for the masses who understand nothing but 'inexplicable dumbshows and noise' (3.2.11–12), but it's misleading. Certainly, the eighteenth-century stage increasingly mingled music and drama, leading to the rise of melodrama as well as *opera seria*; *Romeo and Juliet* would be adapted into seven different operas before 1800. John Rich and David Garrick, the duelling theatre managers of 1750, could have made a musical spectacle out of the lovers' masquerade meeting (as Franco Zeffirelli would in 1968), the lovers' marriage (first brought onstage in 1849), or the parents' reconciliation.[76] So why didn't they? Crucially, in the mid-eighteenth century, the English funeral was rapidly changing as never before.

Previous upheavals to death rituals had been largely religious. Successive Tudor monarchs had denounced liturgies in the name of the True Faith (whatever that happened to be), followed a century later by revolutionary Puritans (who, unsurprisingly, wanted plain rites) and their Restoration conquerors. By the mid-eighteenth century, England was ruled by Hanoverian Protestants, and fashion, not faith, was the funerary watchword. Aristocratic funerals involved not only 'municipal' delegations but representatives of the entire county. Sir William Blackett's 1728 funeral procession included 'the corporation of Newcastle in all their pomp, preceded by the municipal regalia, then gentry of Northumberland and Durham, and some 1,500 members of Newcastle's incorporated companies. Family, household, parish, municipality, trade, industry, and the higher ranks of society both urban and rural were all represented'.[77] In 1735, when Edmund, Duke of Sheffield, died young, his 'mad with pride' mother staged an enormous funeral reflecting his unmarried juvenility: 'the virginal white of numerous plumes and of the scarves, silk hatbands, favours, and gloves of several participants figured prominently amid the funereal black'.[78] To keep the corpse publicly perfect, an 'effigy of the deceased was placed over the body'.[79]

Even middle-class funerals could distribute invitation cards to mourners. One 1738 card depicted the interior of St Marylebone Church, the London venue for the obsequies of Mrs Mary Thomas.[80] Others were rich in *memento mori*. An invitation to the recipient to 'accompany the Corpse of Mr John Boyfield' in 1747 depicted Death grasping the robe of a young man beside a pile of discarded sceptres, and allegorical figures cutting the 'thread of life'.[81] Cards became decidedly more theatrical – by 1776, the engraving summoning friends to the funeral of Mrs Rebecca Hale depicted the mourners surrounding the body within a curtained tomb identical to the

'discovery space' in which Garrick and his fellow Romeos discovered their Juliets, set into the proscenium arch.[82]

But the biggest driver of interest in funeral pomp was the emergence of the new profession of undertaker. The profession spread
through the early eighteenth century, especially in urban areas. By
the 1730s, they had largely taken over funeral organisation.[83]
Whereas previously the bereaved had had to purchase the torches,
canopies, and mourning gear visible in Juliet's funeral and those of
her real-life counterparts, this new 'set of Men who live by Death'
(according to one 1747 manual) could 'furnish out the Funeral
Solemnity' on a budget.[84] Many were moonlighting joiners, carpen-
ters, or upholsterers: tradesmen and artisans who produced desirable goods for the theatres and homes of the living as well as the
dead.[85] Middle-class consumers could now hope for at least some of
the funereal spectacle they saw onstage. No wonder Juliet's lavish
funeral intrigued them.

England was a country obsessed with death: deathbeds, funerals,
tombs – the *ars moriendi*. Thomas Gray's 'Elegy Written in a Country
Churchyard' (1750), with its reflection that 'the paths of glory lead
but to the grave', is only the best-remembered work of the Graveyard
School – the term now given to a literary movement that ruminated
on death, death rituals, corpses and tombs. *Romeo and Juliet* in its
new funerary form dug deeper into the public mood. James Hervey's
Meditation Among the Tombs (1745) – published in the years between
the Cibber and Garrick revivals – recalls the Capulet–Montague
reconciliation in its emphasis on the graveyard as a place where
'persons of contrary interests, and contradicting sentiments' make
peace: Death has 'brought all their differences to an amicable
conclusion', vowing 'not to perpetuate the memory of injuries'.[86]

Most of this literature, regardless of the author, ventriloquises
the male response to death – a hallmark of both versions of Juliet's
funeral. Where Arne's lyrics expanded on Lord Capulet, Garrick's
playtext downplays the grief of Lady Capulet and the Nurse to priv-
ilege that of Capulet and Paris. Eventually, late-eighteenth- and
early-nineteenth-century Europe would become increasingly interested in the tragic death of the young male artist, whether fictional
or real. Germany had Young Werther, the miserable protagonist of
Goethe's novel *The Sorrows of Young Werther* (1774), and later the

real-life suicide pact of poet, dramatist and novelist Henrich von Kleist. England specialised in poets: in 1770, seventeen-year-old Thomas Chatterton killed himself with opium; John Keats died of tuberculosis in 1821, and Shelley drowned in 1822. But in the mid-1700s, long before dead poets, it was the dead girl who was in literary and theatrical vogue.

Clarissa Harlowe, eponymous heroine of Samuel Richardson's 1748 novel, declines from mental trauma and anorexia after being raped by the libertine Lovelace. She plans her own funeral, but also purchases, lives beside, and writes upon her coffin – itself inscribed with *memento mori*, a broken lily, and depressing biblical quotations.[87] Juliet-like, Clarissa's 'lovely corpse' is wept over by her nurse and family, who 'never saw death so lovely before [. . .] nor had death, which changed all things, a power to alter her lovely features!'[88] Like Garrick's Juliet, Clarissa's corpse is accompanied by 'six maidens'.[89] So obsessed with preserving her beauty is her rapist that he intends to embalm her, adding: 'Every thing that can be done to preserve the charmer from decay shall also be done'.[90] Romeo asks Juliet's supposed corpse, 'Why art thou yet so fair?' In eighteenth-century England, the answer was embalming: practised for centuries, but particularly fashionable among the Georgians.

When the young wife of dentist Martin Van Butchell died in 1775, she was embalmed so successfully that a newspaper epitaph proclaimed: 'Taintless and pure her body still remains,/ And all its former elegance retains.' The 1775 correspondent becomes cheerfully necrophiliac, envying the 'lucky Husband [. . .] a much loved wife at home to keep/ Caress, touch, talk to, even sleep/ Close by her side, when e'er you will', and reflecting that a dead wife could be 'Firm, plump, and juicy as before/ And full as tractable, or more'.[91] Van Butchell himself participated in the embalming, opening his wife's abdomen to 'put in the remainder of Powders', and cleaning 'the face and legs with Spirits of Wine and Oil of Lavender'.[92] Dead bride plus Georgian science seemingly offered the perfect recipe for domestic bliss. The detailed descriptions of Van Butchell's contributions and ingredients *almost* invite the reader to Try This At Home, a full generation before Mary Shelley dreamed up *Frankenstein*.

Meanwhile, medical students learned anatomy from sculptures like Clemente Susini's Wax Venuses, a series of slender nude women with removable organs. The 1780–82 Anatomical Venus has a beautiful face, real human hair, and a pearl necklace. Reclining with her neck extended, she is simultaneously an erotic nude and an incorruptible saint – a preserved body and a violated one. Like Clarissa, Juliet, and young Maria van Butchell, the Anatomical Venus was preserved and displayed for the erotic gaze of men. Death is for the best, and beautiful. The early Gothic novel would be full of slaughtered girls: the most lurid, Matthew Lewis's *The Monk* (1796), features the eponymous monk's rape and murder of the beautiful Antonia, his own sister. The Gothic novel, the full-length prose successor to the Graveyard school of poetry, was condemned by critics and devoured by readers; the poet Samuel Taylor Coleridge called *The Monk* 'a poison for youth' and speculated that the author must habitually read 'lewd and voluptuous tales' akin to, and including, pornography.[93] Shakespeare plays, meanwhile, offered eighteenth-century audiences that enticing dead-girl aesthetic without the cultural disapprobation.

Outside the Gothic graveyard, *Clarissa* – the longest published novel in English at 970,000 words – interrupts its own eroticism with hundreds (if not thousands) of pious reflections on everything from sex to housewifery. Juliet's theatrical funeral in Garrick's text needs no such moralising. The spectator is free to wallow in the thanatophilic spectacle, and even the patriarchs' final reckoning loses the Prince's ominous 'All are punish'd' and promise of deferred retribution. Simultaneously, the strong anti-Catholicism of the early Gothic novel has no equivalent in Georgian stagings of *Romeo and Juliet* – despite its Italianate setting, and the fact that excessive funerary ritual had once been condemned precisely for being too Catholic. Thanks both to sanitising new editions and the birth of the Shakespearean tourist industry following Garrick's 1769 Shakespeare Jubilee, Shakespeare's increasing prestige gave audiences a luridly baroque spectacle of female death, guilt-free and at the heart of British culture.

Garrick died in 1779 and was buried in Westminster Abbey's Poets' Corner. His funeral exceeded any onstage spectacle, centring on 'a coffin covered in crimson velvet, studded with gold nails, with a plate of gold', whose dozen pallbearers included six Dukes and Lords.[94] The funeral procession included celebrities from both the major London theatres, a deputation headed by Doctor Samuel Johnson, and around 140 coaches containing mourners and supporters from across the country.[95] Garrick's colleagues and rivals in the 'Battle of the Romeos' were already nearby: Spranger Barry and Susannah Cibber had both been buried in the Abbey's north cloister, although without visible memorial.[96] Garrick's playtext, made popular by their performances, became the basis for the next wave of translations of *Romeo and Juliet*, by Simon Grynaeus (1758), Christoph Martin Wieland (1762–6) and Johann Joachim Eschenberg (1775–82). Juliet was now a decorous, demure maiden with a lavish funeral scene in the theatre of the continent.[97]

★

Even when the newly fashionable *opera seria* demanded a *liete fine* – or happy ending – that permanently reunited the lovers, these new operas kept lavish funeral sequences and Gothic elements. Epitomising this is the extended tomb scene in Giulio Roberto Sanseverino's two-act Italian libretto for Johann Gottfried Schwanberger's *Romeo e Giulia* (1773). Sanseverino had Romeo passionately kiss Juliet's corpse in what Richard Erkens calls 'a shudder-scene of the Romantic style': the érotico-macabre at its best.[98] But Garrick's eighteenth-century format of briefly reunited lovers, itself a legacy of Otway, still persists in *Romeo and Juliet*'s afterlives. Operas by Zingarelli, Bellini, Vaccai and Gounod all exploit the possibilities of reviving Romeo sooner for a final duet.[99] Bernstein and Sondheim's 1957 musical *West Side Story* sees Tony (Romeo) shot just as he makes it to the arms of Maria (Juliet – who, unusually, survives).[100] Even the Royal Shakespeare Company borrowed from Garrick and popular music. When in 1976 Trevor Nunn and Barry Kyle directed Francesca Annis and Ian McKellen as the lovers, Annis began to revive during McKellen's dying kiss.[101] If anything, modern adaptation is moving closer to Garrick's version than to Shakespeare's. Baz Luhrmann's 1996 adaptation graphically depicts Clare Danes's horror upon waking to Leonardo DiCaprio's death throes, while in Carlo Carlei's 2013 film, Hailee Steinfeld's revived Juliet enjoys a protracted kiss with Douglas Booth's poisoned

Romeo, before he addresses his dying words, 'Thus with a kiss/I die', to a conscious rather than unconscious wife.[102]

Shakespeare removed a lot of the despondent, death-driven misery found in his English-language sources when he wrote the character of Juliet, creating instead a pugnacious heroine who fights for life. But eighteenth-century England – obsessed with the cultures of sensibility, of suffering, and a burgeoning Gothic tradition – put all the death back in. Reviving the lovers intensifies the cruelty of Romeo's mistake in not waiting just a few moments longer. Juliet is thus forced not just to find her husband's corpse but actually to watch him die. The century most committed to tantalising its audience with the possibility of reunion was also the one that savoured every detail of her death. Our ideal of romance isn't just the story of a terrible week in the lives and deaths of a teenage girl and her fugitive husband. It's a commodity, in both senses: a commercial confection of female desirability and theatrical spectacle, sold to audiences in theatre and cinema ever since.

This story, of Juliet the beautiful dead girl, found its most recent chapter in the 2020 Pirelli Calendar, a high-glamour publication produced annually by the Italian tyre company. Entitled *Looking for Juliet*, the calendar and accompanying film saw Paolo Roversi photograph nine performers in character as Juliet. Some of these castings are distinctly non-traditional: queer Chinese singer Li Yuchun (Chris Lee) is a gender-neutral Juliet, while Indya Moore is a trans, non-binary Juliet of Haitian, Puerto Rican, and Dominican descent. But the result is still very familiar: conventionally attractive, female-passing and strikingly underweight bodies posed in frequently thanatophilic ways. Mia Goth, who at twenty-six looks genuinely half her age, is posed half-undressed, pale legs visible through the skeleton of a translucent skirt, and a nearly transparent, highly-structured bodice. Her skin is washed-out, her face discoloured to the point of cyanosis. Her lips are cold and dark; above her black hair, a coronet sparkles like the halo of an angel. At her side, one braceleted hand is the colour of a corpse. Goth glances sideways while walking across frame. Her eyes are hooded, unfocused, exhausted.

Jenny Cibber's Juliet was the product of patriarchal oppression – the frustration of a man determined to rule his daughter when he could no longer rule his wife. David Garrick's Juliet, with her spectacular funeral and her censored speech, was the Juliet for an era that had decided a woman was most powerfully beautiful and emotionally moving when she was silent and dead. Pirelli's calendar and accompanying film, with its mute, skinny heroines, shows how far we haven't come. Without any of Shakespeare's text, this is the essence of Dead Girl Juliet: a Gothic waif who's only moments away from an aestheticised death. This is the kind of death we like to look at – the kind of dead girl our history has handed down to us. But even as Garrick's version of the text prepared for us a blue-lipped blueprint in place of Shakespeare's audacious, transgressive, impatient heroine, British theatres and British theatregoers were trading in (and on) a different kind of death. In the eighteenth and nineteenth centuries, Shakespeare's heroine reached new shores and was used to tell new stories – in the very worst possible way.

3

Country Marks

Juliet was the first Shakespearean heroine on the American stage. In 1730, a doctor called Joachimus Bertrand led an amateur troupe who performed *Romeo and Juliet* in New York: nothing else is known about the production. Garrick's adaptation arrived in 1752, performed by a troupe of touring English actors, Lewis Hallam's London Company of Comedians. *Romeo and Juliet* swiftly became Revolutionary America's favourite Shakespeare play, with East Coast performances as far afield as Charleston and Philadelphia, Williamsburg and Annapolis. After the War of 1812, Regency and Victorian star actors began to make American tours, giving Stateside audiences a chance to see successful London productions. The first homegrown American star to achieve real fame in the play would be Charlotte Cushman in the mid-nineteenth century.

Shakespeare's star-crossed lovers conquered America in Garrick's sanitised, euphemised playtext, staged in the young country's new cities, and earning fortunes for those English stars acclaimed and adventurous enough to make the journey. There is, however, another story to tell. To understand the extent of Juliet's cultural capital, and the kinds of power her image and story had on foreign shores, we need to get beyond the theatres and drawing rooms of a new nation to the colonies of an old one: the British Caribbean. Juliet's story encompasses thousands of other dead girls: dead girls whose deaths were meaningless to a white world that never saw them as truly alive. While the British theatre made Juliet's the most famous female death on the Georgian and Regency stages, the British Empire was killing Juliets of a very different kind. From the Haymarket to Hanover, and from Drury Lane to St David Parish, Jamaica, imperial Britain created Juliets who had never set foot onstage.

England had been colonising the world since the late sixteenth century, occupying Newfoundland, parts of North America, and its first Caribbean colonies during the Elizabethan and Stuart eras. During the eighteenth century, Britain's East India Company (est. 1600) changed its focus from trade to the subjugation of India as a proto-industrialised state under British rule. Today, the EIC would be the worst and most powerful corporation on earth: multi-national, with a private army, and thousands of workers and enslaved people. The company had relied on slave labour since 1621, and would continue to do so until 1843.[1] Britain made its first permanent settlement in Africa in 1661: a river island in present-day Gambia. In 1787, Britain colonised Sierra Leone, and within fifteen years they also owned parts of modern-day Namibia. In South America, meanwhile, the British took Berbice and Demerara in 1781, today parts of Guyana.[2]

Prominent Anglo-Caribbean plantation families and the new 'nabobs' – British colonialists in India – regularly intermarried, moving their children and their capital between Asia, London, and the Caribbean.[3] By 1800, Britain's Indian Ocean territories included Andaman, the Seychelles and a protectorate in the Maldives. But it was in the Caribbean that Britain's slave empire grew fastest in the eighteenth century. Between 1700 and 1750, Britain more than doubled its enslaved population from 114,300 to 285,000, thus also doubling its sugar exports from the Caribbean. Poet and abolition-ist Samuel Taylor Coleridge would later describe tea with sugar as 'sweetened with human blood'.[4] In 1763, the Treaty of Paris confirmed Britain's possession of Dominica, Grenada, St Vincent and Tobago. Overall, the British National Archives estimate that Britain enslaved and transported over 3.1 million Africans across the Atlantic between 1640 and 1807; 2.7 million survived the journey.[5]

British theatre benefitted from, and was intertwined with, the trafficking of enslaved Africans. Bristol's Theatre Royal (today the Old Vic), which opened on 30 May 1766, was funded by several of Bristol's foremost beneficiaries of the trade.[6] Original shareholder James Laroche Jr was the son of Bristol's leading slave-ship agent, who managed over 100 slave ships. Paul Farr, another subscriber, co-owned at least one slave ship. Henry Bright (whose family owned plantations) managed twenty-one slave-trading voyages, while John Coghlan, a later subscriber, ran a further ten.[7] David Garrick himself opened the new theatre, which had been designed by his own Drury Lane carpenter, James Saunders.

The prologue Garrick wrote for the opening night didn't just stress theatre's commercial status – 'That all the world's a stage, you can't deny;/ And what's our stage – a Shop – I'll tell you why: –/ You are the customer, the tradesmen, we' – but relied on maritime imagery reflecting Bristol's trading status: 'Unless your favour in full tides will flow;/ Ship, crew, and cargo, to the bottom go!' Garrick's speaker hoped to become 'rich as a nabob', and invoked 'Shakespeare's golden mines'. Of more immediate concern to the Bristol establishment was Africa's Gold Coast (now Ghana), where Britain's recently established African Company of Merchants controlled British interests in both gold and enslaved people. The new Theatre Royal, it was hoped, would 'From East to West extend this city's fame/ Still to her sons increasing wealth with fame'.[8] Written in iambic pentameter, the prologue mingled – even equated – Shakespeare, theatre, and Bristol's international interests, which were above all in slavery. The records of the colonies Britain supplied with enslaved Africans, and which in turn supplied England's slave ports with wealth, show that Britain was now also exporting Shakespeare – and in particular, Juliet.

We know this from records compiled in the early nineteenth century. In 1807, the British government abolished the slave trade: specifically, the enslaving and transportation of currently free Africans from Africa. If you were already enslaving Africans in British colonies in the Caribbean, you could continue to do so. If one of the women you enslaved gave birth to a child after 1807, you still legally owned that child. But depending on the British colony in which you lived, the colonial administration might require you to register your slaves. This was to 'combat illicit transportation': to check that any fluctuation in your enslaved population count was not due to transportation from Africa (bad) but to sale, purchase, birth, or death (still totally fine).[9] The age, colour and birthplace (whether 'African' or 'Creole', i.e. Caribbean-born) of enslaved people were all recorded, however haphazardly. Still more revealing and misleading were their names.

Although a few enslaved people kept their own names, enslavers of all nationalities frequently renamed enslaved people at the point of purchase, baptism (if it occurred) or – for those born into slavery – at birth, often 'against the wishes of (and sometimes competing with names awarded by) their enslaved parents'.[10] Many enslaved people resisted this renaming, as evinced by first-person accounts by formerly enslaved people such as Olaudah Equiano (c. 1745–97), whose autobiography recalls receiving 'many a cuff' for trying to resist one of his several slave-names.[11] A relatively small proportion of enslaved people were given classical names, although fictional representations of slaves make this seem more common.[12] Others were given geographical, botanical, or animal names.[13]

Increasingly, generic European, often biblical, names were imposed upon enslaved Africans. In the registers for British colonies between 1813 and 1834, the most common names for enslaved women were overwhelmingly Mary, Ann/Hannah, Sarah, Elizabeth, Jane and diminutive versions such as Eliza, Betty, or Nan.[14] But records also reveal a disturbing trend among British colonial slaveowners for giving their slaves Shakespearean names. Fictional beings whose names were recognisable around the globe were invoked to deny real enslaved people their authentic identities. The trend went further: enslaved people received not only the names of Shakespearean characters, but even of white Shakespearean actors. Even half a century after he died, more than 400 enslaved people in British colonies were named Garrick.[15] Besides Shakespeare, the most popular theatrical character names came from *The Orphan*, a play by *Romeo and Juliet*'s Restoration adaptor Thomas Otway, in which both David Garrick and Susannah Cibber had enjoyed huge successes. There was also 'Oronoco'. Oroonoko, originally the eponymous hero of Aphra Behn's 1688 novella, had become better known via Thomas Southerne's 1695 play in which – drawing heavily on *Othello* – the enslaved African prince Oroonoko falls in love with a white woman whom he ultimately murders (with her selfless encouragement).

For men, overwhelmingly the most popular name was Hamlet. Just under 2,900 enslaved people are recorded with this name, rising to approximately 3,500 with variant spellings. A wide variety of character names is represented, extending even to Yorick (of 'alas, poor' fame), who appears only as a skull in *Hamlet* (fifty-seven mentions in the records, rising to 110 with variants). There were also eighty-nine enslaved people called Shakespeare. But by the far the most popular Shakespearean slave name was Juliet. Around 3,355 enslaved women were given this name by their British owners, rising to over 10,000 with variations in spelling – especially common in an era when operatic adaptations presented her as 'Julie' and 'Giulietta'.[16] Romeo was the second-most popular Shakespearean slave name for men (2,203 mentions). Juliet was such a popular name among British slaveowners that there were often multiple Juliets on a single plantation. Sir John Gordon, 5th Baronet of Earlston, owned three Juliets on his Carlton Estate in St James, Jamaica, in 1817: an octogenarian, a sixty-year-old, and a thirty-year-old, all African-born.[17] Four Juliets were enslaved by John Graham Campbell across estates in nearby Westmoreland: they were aged fifty-nine, forty-nine, thirty-four, and thirty.[18] Campbell was a Cambridge-educated lawyer and University of Pennsylvania donor; his schooling and Middle Temple practice placed him in London during the height of Garrick's fame.[19] Whereas Sir John Gordon's Juliets would all have been renamed at some point after they were captured and trafficked across the Atlantic, three of Campbell's Juliets were Caribbean-born, and possibly named by him.

Theatrical names often cluster as a generational marker. Sir John Gordon's eighty-year-old 'Old Juliet' is listed alongside Othello (also eighty) and Polidore (eighty-three), both African-born.[20] It's easy to imagine the trio being purchased and renamed at the same time. The Chief Justice of Tobago, Elphinstone Piggott, enslaved (among many others) two Juliets, a Yorick, and an Oronoco, all within thirteen years of each other in age. On the same plantation, a younger generation of enslaved people were called Romeo, Hamlet, and Horatio.[21] Like Campbell, Piggott was a Middle Temple man who would have known London well – the Masonic Lodge to which he belonged was on Chancery Lane.[22]

Unsurprisingly, you often find a Romeo alongside a Juliet, the former usually older. Such was the case on the Jamaican plantation of Thomas Pepper Thompson, where two enslaved Africans renamed after the lovers died within a year of each other in the early 1820s.[23] This was around the time of Thompson's own death, when his vast estate passed to his mixed-race grandson, Thomas

James Thompson, the wealthy friend of Charles Dickens, and father of suffragist poet Alice Meynell.[24] In 1819, plantation-owner John Alexander's slave Matilda gave birth to a baby girl in St Ann, Jamaica, subsequently named Juliet. The previous year, another enslaved woman, Charity, gave birth to a boy named Romeo.[25] These plantation-owning men 'themed' their slave-names in a given era in the same way dog-owners might a litter of puppies.

Scholars working on slave-naming practices in American plantations note that classical and biblical names were frequently bestowed on the basis of 'the traits most commonly identified' with these 'ancient figures'.[26] Looking at the Shakespearean names chosen by British enslavers, the ones they avoided are revealing. No regicidal Macbeths, and very few Prosperos or Lears; unsurprisingly, businessmen who derived their wealth from enslaving humans didn't give their men the names of defrauded rulers whose rights are ultimately recognised or restored. Nor were there many Banquos, whose descendants (so the witches in *Macbeth* prophesy) will ultimately enjoy the power that temporarily exalts Banquo's commander. Ambitious subordinates are generally overlooked – no Iagos or Malvolios. Goneril, the murderous plotting daughter from *King Lear*, doesn't appear (although there are a handful of Regans). More chillingly, neither do Perdita or Thaisa, believed dead but ultimately restored to their families (in *A Winter's Tale* and *Pericles*).

Instead, just as biblical names for enslaved people evoked figures 'noted for their uncommon suffering, sacrifice, or sin', among the next most popular Shakespearean slave-names for women were Ophelia, Gertrude, Cordelia, and Cleopatra: victimised and frequently sexualised women, blamed and persecuted by men, who end up dead.[27] Some of these resonances help us to understand what it meant to call an enslaved woman Juliet. All five women are considered desirable within their play-worlds. Like Ophelia and Cordelia, Juliet is young and blameless – but far more than either, she is sexualised, without the implied promiscuity of Gertrude and Cleopatra. To name an enslaved child or woman Juliet strongly implies the sexual desirability often ascribed to young, enslaved women, romanticising the sexual exploitation they would very likely face.

Olaudah Equiano wrote in 1789 that it was the 'constant practice' of white men to 'commit violent depredations on the chastity of the female slaves', including raping 'females not ten years old'.[28] John Ferdinand Dalziel Smyth, visiting America in the 1770s, reported that the rape of enslaved women by their masters had created 'beautiful girls, [. . .] who are absolutely slaves in every sense'.[29] Naming these girls and women Juliet was not the only way that plantation-owners romanticised their sex slaves. bell hooks describes masters giving their exploited slaves presents, trying to reframe rape as concubinage or courtship.[30] Harriet Jacobs, writing of her adolescence in late-1820s North Carolina, described enslaved girls as 'reared in an atmosphere of licentiousness and fear', doomed to 'become prematurely knowing in evil things', because 'when she is fourteen or fifteen, her owner, or his sons, or the overseer, or perhaps all of them, begin to bribe her with presents. If these fail to accomplish their purpose, she is whipped or starved into submission to their will'.[31]

Jacobs was enslaved in America, where slavery persisted until 1865; a collection of interviews with (by then octogenarian) survivors of slavery echo her words. Virginia-born former slaves Sam and Louisa Everett described group rapes of 'the prettiest of the young [enslaved] women' by white men in mid-nineteenth-century Virginia.[32] Hilliard Yellerday, interviewed about the experiences of his enslaved parents, recalled the 'general custom' that girls 'were expected to begin bearing children from the master' at 'twelve or thirteen years old'.[33] As Jacobs noted: 'Slavery is terrible for men; but it is far more terrible for women'.[34] Young, fertile, enslaved women were valued at prices sixteen to twenty-five per cent higher than women not expected to bear children.[35] Records suggest that when there were two enslaved women with Shakespearean names on the plantation, they tended to be Juliet and Ophelia: young women exploited and betrayed by their fathers, pushed to the brink or actuality of madness, and dying by suicide. Branding these enslaved women such names ascribes their destiny to some kind of literary precedent – they are 'star-crossed' by Shakespearean plots, rather than by a system created and perpetuated by white men. Named in these ways, their lives become tragic tropes rather than avoidable suffering. Those who encounter them are positioned as readers or audience members, engaged in a literary or theatrical encounter rather than having any responsibility to intervene.

Forcing Shakespearean names on your slaves marked you out as cultured, literate, refined, and even witty, adding some literary cachet to your plantation. Slaveowners' choices reflected a portfolio of cultural interests. On St Vincent, Robert Sutherland enslaved not only a Romeo, three Juliets, and a Polydore, but also a 'Grandison', the hero of Samuel Richardson's 1753 novel *The History of Sir Charles Grandison*.[36] Elizabeth Barrett Browning's poetry-loving uncle, the Yorkshire MP Samuel Barrett, mingled Shakespearean names including Juliet, Ophelia, Orlando, and Hamlet with classical allusions like Pompey and Cato.[37] Barrett was credited by one Parliamentary historian with having struggled with the 'dilemma of being a slave-owning Whig', and accordingly having 'built decent houses, schools and churches for his 1,100 slaves'. The Wesleyan missionary Peter Duncan called him 'a true friend to the religious instruction of the slaves'.[38] There is no record of what those 1,100 enslaved people, Juliets among them, thought of this 'true friend'. George Cunningham, who owned five Jamaican estates over his lifetime, registered in Trelawney in 1817 not only a twelve-year-old Jamaican-born girl called Juliet, but sisters Ophelia (six) and Cordelia (nineteen), along with Hamlet (twenty-six) and an older generation of enslaved people named for eighteenth-century writers like Pope and Swift.[39]

There's a cruel irony to enslaved people denied freedom, literacy, citizenship and a voice being (re)named after Shakespeare's most beloved – and often voluble – characters. This was, after all, an era in which free Black people attempting to make a career on British professional stages were, regardless of the success they achieved, also subject to excruciating racist mockery. Ira Aldridge (1807–67), the first African American actor to achieve major success in Europe, became Poland's highest-paid actor and received honours from the Russian Tsar, but was still victimised by the British press. *The Times* claimed that the 'shape of his lips' made it 'utterly impossible' for Aldridge to speak English properly when he appeared in *The Revolt of Surinam* in 1825. When he appeared as *Othello* at Covent Garden in 1833, *Figaro in London* called him a 'miserable n*****' who 'dishonoured' the stage.[40]

Aldridge was not the first Black Shakespearean in Britain, however. In the 1770s, a Black Irish singer named Rachael Baptiste was almost certainly Britain's first Black Juliet, appearing on stage in Lancashire. Baptiste (born c. 1750) was a hugely successful Irish singer, a 'celebrated Black Syren' who enjoyed a long operatic career in Ireland. She is also rumoured to have played both Juliet and Polly Peachum in English theatres. Written evidence for this first performance by a Black actress is scant, and primarily supplied by two racist anecdotes by John Jackson, a Scottish theatrical scholar of the period. In the first, Jackson hoots at a theatre manager's proposal that Baptiste should appear in a mask, and at the idea of her recent Romeo describing how Juliet's beauty 'hangs upon the cheek of night/ Like a rich jewel in an Ethiop's ear'. Jackson follows it up with a reflection on arrogant actors who are 'so blind to [their] natural defects, that the most glaring infirmities are deemed by [them] as trifling obstacles'.[41]

The irony of trying to trace the acting career of a Black Juliet through records of the racist things people said about her only intensifies when it comes to rediscovering the lives of enslaved Africans through a name – Juliet – that was used to obliterate their identities. Without underestimating the gulf between the imaginary sufferings of one rich fictional teenage girl and the real suffering of centuries of Black women, there's something horribly apt about the naming of these enslaved Juliets. Shakespeare's Juliet is raised in a culture where girls 'younger than she are' ostensibly 'happy mothers made', but as Hilliard Yellerday knew, 'too soon marr'd/ are those so early made' (1.2.12–13). Juliet is a commodity for her own master, her father, who dictates every aspect of her existence, who physically abuses her and vows that if 'you be mine, I'll give you to my friend/ [If] you be not, hang, beg, starve, die in the streets' (3.5.193). Juliet's own marriage, like that of her enslaved namesakes, cannot be recognised, and her attempt to run away from the household that abuses her ends in her death. We know far more about the life of one Juliet who never lived than we do about the Black women who – as Shakespeare became the British Empire's greatest cultural export – received her name.

Hundreds of artists imagined Juliet over the eighteenth and early nineteenth centuries: usually as a well-nourished pink-and-white miss with ringlets. By contrast, records reveal only brief, sometimes distressing details about her enslaved namesakes' appearances. Intermittent references to height reveal a pattern of short stature, probably as a result of poor diet and negligible healthcare. The results for children and adolescents are particularly appalling: one eight-year-old Juliette in Port Lewis, Mauritius, would, at less than forty-one inches tall, be below the first percentile in modern paediatric charts.[42] Another enslaved Juliette in Port Lewis was, at thirteen – the same age as her Shakespearean namesake, and the age at which enslaved girls were expected to start childbearing – just four feet, eight inches tall, more than five inches below the average height for her age today.[43]

The African-born woman registered in 1817 as Juliet, a fieldhand enslaved by Henry Smithson in Berbice (now Guyana), had 'country marks' on her body: ritual scarification from the African community in which she had been born. She also had one other distinguishing mark: Smithson's initials, HS, branded on her right shoulder.[44] Branding is 'one of the most charged symbols of the evils of slavery', designed partly to identify runaways.[45] Historian Karina Keefer, an expert on slavery and branding, notes that: 'Before the trans-Atlantic slave trade, most societies that used slavery did not brand slaves if there was any chance they might be set free'.[46] In branding Juliet, Henry Smithson – and British slaveowners like him – ensured that even if she were granted her freedom, Juliet would never be able to escape the bodily reminder of her enslavement and violation.

Occasionally, Juliets were noted for their beauty. Another African-born fieldhand in Bernice named Juliet was described as 'well made' in the records of slaveowner Henry Welch.[47] In advertisements for fugitive slaves, 'well made' denoted not only physical strength, but also physical attractiveness. Runaway slave Joe was described as 'handsome, well made, and pleasant countenanced' in 1796, while Baltimore slaveowner John Gadsby searched for the 'well made, handsome' Mary in 1809.[48] Welch's Juliet was listed as 'yellow', implying light skin – another marker of attractiveness as far as white enslavers were concerned. The autobiographies of Jacobs and others make it clear how being regarded as 'well made' and attractive by white overseers and enslavers heightened the risk of sexual abuse.

The eighteenth and nineteenth centuries made Shakespeare's Juliet's onstage death a far more spectacular part of her story than ever before. The spectacle of a fictional beautiful dead white girl entertained a British society that was profiting from the exploitation and deaths of real girls on the other side of the world. The fact that enslavers bestowed these names shows us how far the Shakespearean character's sphere of influence reached, and draws our attention to the extreme contrast between the two categories of experience. Coleridge in 1796 described how readers enjoyed weeping over tragic fictional deaths while remaining unmoved by real-life evils: they were 'not nauseated by the stench and filth of the slave-vessel – the fine lady's nerves are not shattered by the shrieks' as long as they didn't have to face them directly. They could enjoy one kind of death and ignore the other.

Many of the enslaved Juliets only make it into the written records if they died between registrations. Some outlived their Shakespearean predecessor, reaching adulthood, but with grim life expectancies – in Westmoreland, Jamaica, John Wedderburn's enslaved Juliet died 'of old age' at just fifty.[49] Similarly, the 1820 death of the African-born Juliet in Hanover, Jamaica, was attributed to 'old age and debility' by the slaveowner Robert Hibbert; she was fifty-two.[50] Hibbert was a merchant and philanthropist who forced enslaved Africans to work 'six days and three nights in the week', providing only 'a weekly allowance of seven or eight herrings to each adult'. Abolitionist Zachary Macaulay reported on Hibbert in his book *Negro Slavery* (1832), following his discussion of Hibbert with a 'general' description of plantation morals, which noted that slaveowners lived in 'open and avowed concubinage with Black or Coloured women', with enslaved girls 'at any early age made the mere instruments of licentious gratification'.[51] Of course, plenty of enslaved children in British colonies failed to live even as long as Shakespeare's heroine. One Juliette, enslaved by Victorina Ferrier in Port Lewis, Mauritius, died aged eight, partially blind 'of a growth,' perhaps childhood cancer.[52] Juliette died in 1832, one year before the abolition of slavery in most of the British Empire.[53] Enslaved children over the age of six became indentured apprentices – had she survived, Juliette would have been fourteen when the majority of British apprenticeships finished in 1838.

The enslaved women and girls called Juliet are dead twice over: forgotten by history, and never legally alive. Under British colonial law, the death of a slave mattered primarily as a devaluation of the enslaver's personal property, rather than as the loss of a life. The original slave codes of Barbados (1661) and Jamaica (1664) specified that a slaveowner could kill their own slave during a punishment without penalty. In 1781, the crew of the overcrowded, under-provisioned Liverpool slave ship the *Zong* threw 132 enslaved Africans overboard during a sickness-stricken slave-trading voyage to Jamaica. The crew massacred the Africans in order to curb infection and claim insurance money through 'general averaging', wherein a captain can claim for cargo loss incurred to save the rest. Despite efforts to prosecute the crew for murder, thus recognising the Africans as humans, the Chief Justice William Murray, 1st Earl of Mansfield, ruled otherwise: the suit was conducted on the basis of lost possessions rather than killed people.[54] The enslaved people had never been living human beings in law.

The Georgian imperialists created and killed their Juliets on plantations across the British Empire. The name Juliet branded enslaved Africans not only as property – their West African heritage obliterated by a European name – but as the property of a person more interested in flaunting their literary knowledge for clout than acknowledging their slaves' humanity. Their new names showed that they belonged to an empire that traded in Shakespeare along with sugar, cotton, and human lives. The name 'Juliet', with all its connotations of just-pubescent desirability, hints at the sexual objectification of young enslaved women and the rape that was inevitable for many. When a Juliet's name is listed alongside a Romeo, or a group of Shakespearean names, there's a suggestion of a sick joke as well as literary pretention. The 'theming' of a generation of plantation workers diminishes them further. Imposing on an enslaved girl the name of a fictional dead girl helped aestheticise the fact that she was part of a system that did not see her as either real or alive. Renaming her as 'Juliet' irrevocably removed the girl's authentic identity, imposing on her a foreign narrative that bound her to her enslavers' culture and system.

This would not be the last time that Juliet would be co-opted by a political agenda. The eighteenth-century obsession with Juliet as a passive, beautiful, dead white heroine, part of a larger Gothic stage picture, still reverberates in our culture today. By 1800, Juliet had become a vessel for a society's fears and fantasies about adolescent girls. The story of the Caribbean Juliets illuminates a moment in history when we see two vital shifts in her story, both of which would recur over the next two centuries. Neither has anything to do with love.

The first is the use of 'Juliet' as cultural shorthand to turn a real person, in whose sufferings we are culpable, into a fictionalised trope, with a predestined 'star-crossed' story in whose outcome we cannot and need not intervene. In the eighteenth and early nineteenth centuries, this was the practice of a group of powerful white enslavers, to aestheticise their brutality with a veneer of culture; in the twentieth century, the popular press would take this practice to new heights to romanticise victims of war, as explored in Chapter 7. The second shift is even more stark: by naming enslaved Africans 'Juliet', British enslavers were telling a story less about their slaves than about themselves, as Juliet became the centre of a story about how a nation – an empire – used its political and economic power to flex its cultural credentials.

This was happening in the Caribbean, far from the stages Shakespeare had written for, or anywhere he had ever seen. Later in the century, the battle for Juliet would return to the city Shakespeare knew best: London. Victorian Britain was confident of its imperialistic rights to rule the globe, but its domestic hierarchies were increasingly unstable. As nineteenth-century England debated a woman's place in society, a new group of star actresses would bring worldwide celebrity and cultural power to their interpretations of Juliet. At the height of nineteenth-century Bardolatry – the worship of Shakespeare as 'the Bard' – star actresses' on- and offstage fame forced them to walk a tightrope between sexual allure and Victorian respectability. For their audiences, there was a new question: was Juliet an angel to be imitated, or a terrible warning?

Her Southern Temperament

In the Upper Library at Christ Church, on a chilly Oxonian after-noon, I have taken my search for Juliet into half a dozen unremark-able grey boxes. Looking through a Venetian window across a wintry Peckwater Quad, I am sifting the worldly leavings of Francis Bridgford Brady, a Middlesex solicitor who died, unknown, in Leigh-on-Sea, Essex, in 1981.[1]

In 1977, Brady wrote in his diligent and looping hand to the Christ Church librarian, asking whether, since Brady had been a Member of 'the House' (he took a Classics degree shortly before the First World War), Christ Church might accept, on his death, the bequest of a 'large miscellaneous collection' of theatrical ephemera. Brady had collected it 'from the 'twenties to the 'sixties, until the material disappeared beneath the counter or soared above my means', a delightful phrase implying that theatrical playbills became salacious contraband at or around the sexual revolution. Brady amassed a collection of Georgian and Victorian playtexts, engravings, 'portraits of actors, scenes from plays', toy theatre images and theatrical memoirs unparalleled in all but a handful of world-famous muse-ums.[2] One of my first jobs as a lowly DPhil student was to sit in a (freezing) cellar and catalogue Brady's toy theatres. A decade on, I've been upgraded from the freezing cellar (now officially uninhabitable, thanks to damp) to share space with Cardinal Wolsey's hat, a 1695 head of Mercury, 40,000 books, and – today – a small fraction of the Brady Collection. They are hand-coloured images from eighteenth- and nineteenth-century toy theatres, and larger individual studies of actors in character, and I am searching for Juliet among them.

In the nineteenth century, toy theatre publishers dispatched several artists to each popular new theatre production in London, with different artists sketching the scenery and actors. I like to imagine these artists as either Hogarthian scamps, mirthful faces flushed as they dashed off sketches with the same verve and vigour they saw onstage, or (alternatively) as jaded, enervated talents cramped by the necessity of reproducing another *Harlequin and Little King Pippin* in Penny Plain/Tuppence Coloured when they could have been off founding Impressionism. The toy theatre publishers all had pleasing Dickensian names, like Skelt and Pollock, and, appropriately enough, Dickens's own illustrator, George Cruikshank, and his brother Isaac, both drew for what became known as the 'juvenile theatre'. One fan, the author Robert Louis Stevenson, recalled 'gesticulating villains, epileptic combats, bosky forests, palaces and war-ships, frowning fortresses and prison vaults – it was a giddy joy'.[3] Surviving Shakespeare productions for toy theatres are rare, but Brady collected some, as well as large portraits of performers in Shakespearean roles.

Set before me is one such box of portraits, including 'Fairburn's Portraits No, 21: Fanny Kemble as Juliet'. The Fairburns were a prolific, accomplished, and occasionally bankrupt family of publishers across the East End who produced stylish prints and scurrilous satires speculating on the Royal Family's sex lives. No such lasciviousness informs their take on Fanny Kemble. Alone in her boudoir, she has a pink-and-white complexion, classically posed limbs, a Roman nose, and opera gloves. Here is a Juliet of the 1830s: statuesque attitudes, puffed sleeves, centre-parted hair in a style favoured by the young Victoria – and by 1990s costume dramas. A veil pinned to her shiny hair is the only concession to the Italian setting, and even that looks like chintz tablecloth. She has a rosebud mouth and no cleavage. Compared to other women the Fairburns drew from the stage – in the same series, the ample 'Mrs Honey as Celestia' features naked legs, golden sandals, a short spangled dress and a prominent bosom – Kemble's Juliet is prim enough for any Jane Austen assembly or royal presentation.

It was just as well. Queen Victoria loved Juliet before she was queen – and even before she'd seen the play. Lithographer Robert John Lane entertained the seventeen-year-old Princess with 'beautiful coloured drawings by Chalon'. According to Victoria's diary, she was especially delighted by 'a very beautiful head and hands of

Juliet after she has taken the draught'.[4] As a young queen, she enjoyed her father figure Lord Melbourne's accounts of Susannah Cibber, 'the best Juliet there ever was', noting that 'Lord M. said the Balcony Scene was the celebrated one'.[5] A year later, when Victoria finally saw Romeo and Juliet for the first time, she found it a 'beautiful Play', writing that 'Miss Emmeline Montague took the part of Juliet, & was charming in the Balcony Scene, but not so good afterwards', as if recalling Melbourne's words.[6]

Not only did Victoria see the play several more times, but the characters became part of Royal Family life; Prince Alfred rode 'dear little "Juliet", who is such a pretty dark chestnut' in the Royal Mews's Riding School, while Victoria's eldest daughter and namesake sketched scenes from Romeo and Juliet at Osborne House.[7] Princess Maud played Juliet in Balmoral tableaux in 1888 ('Maud looked so pretty lying there'), while singers – including Princess Beatrice – regularly entertained the family with extracts from Gounod's 1867 Roméo et Juliette.[8] Victoria idealised the characters, writing: 'What a lovely Play it is! Such youth & freshness in the simple love of Romeo & Juliet for one another'.[9] Charles Dickens, a noted Shakespeare fiend, drew on Romeo and Juliet in his 1838 novel Nicholas Nickleby, when his eponymous hero accidentally stars in a travelling production which embodies all that was bombastic, chaotic, and irresistible about melodramatic 1830s theatre.

Dickens was the dedicatee of his friend Mary Cowden Clarke's The Girlhood of Shakespeare's Heroines (1850), a simultaneously sentimental and dictatorial collection of biographies of Shakespeare heroines' childhoods. Cowden Clarke calls Juliet 'the White Dove of Verona'. Anna Jameson's Characteristics of Women: Moral, Poetical and Historical, better known by its later title Shakespeare's Heroines (1837), breathlessly described 'the inmost sanctuary of Shakespeare's genius, in Juliet's moon-light bower', rejoicing over 'the simplicity, the truth, and the loveliness of Juliet'.[10]

But when, half a century later, in 1888, the Girl's Own Paper ran an essay competition on 'My Favourite Shakespearean Heroine', the results illustrated with two engravings of Juliet in tomb and funeral bier, the editors were shocked to find that their readers, instead of flocking to the white dove of Verona, had 'been particularly hard on poor Juliet [. . .] Juliet is the favourite of some half dozen girls only'. More shockingly still, 'A few of the girls wandered from the subject in a curious manner, and made their essays a vehicle for expressing their ideas on some social problem,' including 'the vexed question of "women's rights"'.[11] The readers' favourite heroine was Portia, the cross-dressing, consummate lawyer (and committed anti-Semite) and heiress of *The Merchant of Venice*. 'Who could imagine Portia being so cowardly as to commit suicide?' wrote one *Girl's Own* reader. 'How different is Portia's love from the mad passion of Juliet!' said another. What had gone wrong?

For the Victorians, Juliet had become both an impossible ideal and a cautionary tale of Mediterranean sexiness: a blonde angel in a white muslin dress, and a precocious 'Southern' rebel with a tenuous grip on her sanity. The iconic actresses who embodied her knew more about the duality, intensity and conflict of Victorian womanhood than most, fighting as they were for respectability in a profession that necessarily traded on their glamour and sexual appeal. Across the nineteenth century, as actresses moved away from the beautiful dying girl of Garrick's text, the gulf between that 'traditional' Juliet and their new interpretations of a fully psychologised, rebellious heroine became as perilous as the gap between the actresses' public images and the colourful chaos of their real lives.

Theatre was Victorian Britain's defining medium: its international, cross-class, endlessly innovative mass entertainment. By 1882, London had fifty-seven theatres and 415 music halls; tens of thousands attended West End theatres nightly.[12] Shows ranged from music halls' sensational bawdy, exemplified by Marie Lloyd's scandalous songs (lyrics including 'She'd Never Had Her Ticket Punched Before') to prestigious and lavishly pictorial Shakespeare revivals at the Princess's Theatre, and, later, Sir Henry Irving's Lyceum. Victorian theatre oscillated between respectability and opprobrium. The Royal Family hosted private command performances at Windsor before Prince Albert's death and (after a long pause) at other palaces, including Balmoral.

Clichés that actresses were automatically regarded as – or actually worked as – prostitutes have been overturned by scholarship. Even the ultra-conservative Victorian actress Mrs Kendal noted that many actresses 'earn their £300 or £400 a year, and that is a very nice competence for a woman [. . .] very much more than she would earn in almost any other career. Besides, she has the blessedness of independence, and that is a great thing to a woman, and especially to a single woman'.[13] Nevertheless, actresses' families routinely had hysterics upon the announcement that their daughter or niece intended to take to the stage. An aunt of the famous Mrs Patrick Campbell wailed that 'the die for evil is cast' upon hearing the news, warning her of 'the shame, the humiliation of seeing yourself despised by decent people'.[14] And as late as Arthur Wing Pinero's hit *The Second Mrs Tanqueray* (1893), when a man must convey to his friends that a woman is sexually 'fallen', he need only say that she 'would have been, perhaps had been, described in the reports of the Police or the Divorce Court as an actress'.[15]

But as poet Matthew Arnold reflected (with something of a sigh), 'the theatre is irresistible'.[16] Never a guiltless pleasure, theatre's slippery status meant that upstanding Victorians desperately craved the performance of virtue from their female theatrical stars: women they could idealise and sexualise simultaneously. The actresses who made the most successful Juliets fulfilled this need, hiding colourful sexual lives, ruthless ambition, and emotional chaos – sometimes all three – and often in plain sight.

Helena Faucit (1817–98) was the 1840s superstar who married Prince Albert's biographer and ended her days as Lady Martin, hosting Queen Victoria at her Denbighshire mansion. Faucit was so lauded for her lifelong ladylike respectability that colleague Madge Kendal sent a wreath inscribed 'Our Example' to her funeral.[17] In fact, after a complicated childhood, the teenage Faucit – whose favourite literary hero had been Milton's Satan – took to the stage at sixteen, trained by actor Percy Farren, the brother of Faucit's mother's lover. Percy and the young Faucit had an emotionally intense relationship; when he disparaged her debut as Juliet, she had a nervous breakdown. In her early twenties, Faucit fell (unrequitedly) for her much older leading man, William Macready, enduring scandalous accusations that she was his mistress – and pregnant. Faucit later toured Ireland, Scotland, and Paris alone, conquering new stages as a European superstar.[18] The first actress to write in detail about the Shakespearean characters she played, Faucit presented Juliet as a psychologically complex, single-minded rebel.

Helena Modjeska (1840–1909), who self-fashioned herself as a dreamy, ladylike beauty, unofficial Polish countess and ambassadress, concealed her own illegitimacy and that of her son behind her husband's exaggerated title, at the same time as becoming Poland's most famous actress, America's highest-paid foreign performer, and a London sensation. She was a workaholic who nearly gave birth on stage. 'Modjeska' was the stage name of her first seducer, the married actor (and probable felon) Gustav Zimajer; fortunately, neither a scurrilous novel based on their relationship nor unfounded rumours that Zimajer was her pimp ever gained traction outside Poland.[19] Her Juliet veered towards madness to graphic onstage effect; one critic marvelled that when Modjeska 'conjured up the horrors of the charnel house, she became almost green with terror'.[20]

By the time Ellen Terry (1847–1928) played Juliet, she was thirty-five, the mother of two illegitimate children from a six-year affair, and trying to extricate herself and her finances from her abusive, alcoholic second husband. She was, nonetheless, the nation's sweetheart, whose interpretations of Shakespearean heroines including Juliet would inspire the suffragettes. She herself derived inspiration from Eleonora Duse (1858–1928), Italy's greatest interpreter of both Shakespeare and Henrik Ibsen. Duse was the daughter of 'a wandering band of Thespians, who knew the bitterest pangs of poverty', who had played Juliet in Juliet's hometown, Verona, in her early teens.[21]

All four actresses became icons, immortalised in china figurines, endless engravings and photographs – and, for Ellen Terry, whom Oscar Wilde dubbed 'Our Lady of the Lyceum', a life-sized waxwork at Madame Tussaud's.[22] The actresses were also, in defiance of convention, attracted to the darker sides of Juliet's character: her thanatophilic drive towards poison and suicide, and – in an era obsessed with ghost stories, horror, and the occult – the Gothic potential of her descent into the tomb. When they spoke about Juliet, these actresses emphasised her emotional strength, often at Romeo's expense. They understood and embodied her sexual passion, often in ways that alarmed and excited Victorian audiences. They walked the agonising tightrope between sainthood and sexuality for their publics.

We know so much about how Victorian actresses felt and worked because this is the first century in which these women could speak to us directly, telling us about Juliet in their own voices in autobiographies, interviews, and public speeches. It's also a century that took theatre criticism seriously, with performances in London or Manchester discussed in the newspapers of Cardiff or Exeter, satirical papers such as *Fun* and *Punch* responding to new productions, and two periodicals devoted exclusively to the theatre industry: the *Era* and the cheaper, more popular (and persistent) *Stage*. The Victorian era was also the zenith of 'Bardolatry', a Shakespeare-adoring sentiment that swirled together nationalist and aesthetic fervour. Not only were there substantial purchases and innovations for the national good – the 1847 purchase of Shakespeare's birthplace and the 1879 inauguration of the Shakespeare Memorial Theatre – but also a huge proliferation of Shakespearean commentaries, curios, and tat.

A Victorian Shakespeare fan could mount a Shakespeare-shaped door-knocker on his threshold, inscribe Shakespearean quotations on his wall (as at Wightwick Manor, Wolverhampton), and fill his what-nots and sideboards with Staffordshire pottery figurines of the playwright and his celebrity characters.[23] Theatregoers collected *cartes-de-visites* (photographs on cardboard) of performers in Shakespearean roles, and flocked to his birthplace. As with visits to Juliet's grave, this became a quasi-religious experience; the nineteenth-century visitor came 'as a pilgrim would to the shrine of some loved saint' on 'holy ground'. Shakespeare's birth-room became another Bethlehem stable, housing 'that illustrious cradle [. . .] where lay that infant who was destined to glorify and exalt our greatest kings'.[24]

Across Britain, home libraries filled up with new Shakespeare biographies and collected editions, all romanticising the writer's speculative family life. Shakespeare fans' mantelpieces bore his image affixed to everything from ceramics to clocks.[25] Upstairs in the nursery, children staged Shakespeare plays in toy theatres, and heard stories from editions that recast the plots in edifying, decorous prose.

Conformity and moral clarity were key; even as eighteenth-century rewrites of the plays began to be replaced by Shakespearean playtexts, these were still heavily edited. One popular editorial tactic was to claim that overly coarse or explicit passages must have been the work of another writer. A play like *Pericles*, a late and genuinely collaborative romance featuring father–daughter incest and a heroine stranded in a brothel, surviving only as a garbled quarto version, caused predictable problems. Victorian editor F. G. Fleay solved this by reshaping everything he thought was *authentic* Shakespeare into a different play, *Marina* – which, coincidentally, cut everything about incest or brothels. Nonetheless, Fleay was praised by fellow Shakespearean Edward Dowden for the 'lovely little romance' that he had 'separated from the coarse work' of' other writers.[26]

Even Oscar Wilde, at other times conspicuously Irish and radical, bought in to the Shakespearean conservative, nationalist agenda. Speaking at the October 1888 unveiling of the Gower Memorial, a group of statues of Shakespeare and his characters, Wilde praised England as 'our land', the British Empire as 'the greatest empire the world has certainly yet seen', and Shakespeare's 'healthy English enjoyment of delightful things' as tradition amounting to fact. Because, despite the newness of these Shakespearean phenomena – the ornaments, the tableware, the libraries, the monuments and public recreations – the essence of Bardolatry was not novelty, but tradition. Even as new editions of Shakespeare's plays filled the shelves, for use by schoolchildren, scholars or the proliferating Shakespeare amateur dramatic clubs, they printed as gospel the inherited stage business of the last hundred years. The vast majority of Shakespeare quartos and folios carry few stage directions, and the three texts of *Romeo and Juliet* are no exception. Yet, crack open a Victorian copy of the play and you'll find detailed annotations telling performers when and where to move, sit and stand. The Victorian actress playing Juliet had her path laid out for her as strictly as any housewife, ensuring she upheld old traditions and never became too passionate – or inventive.

Bardolatry wasn't only the cult of Shakespeare, it was the cult of home. Shakespeare was the Victorians' household god, and elevating him to his rightful place meant keeping everyone else in theirs. John Ruskin, Shakespeare prophet and Oxford's first Slade Professor of Art, invoked Shakespeare in his own manifesto for gender roles. Ruskin argued that in Shakespeare 'the catastrophe of every play is caused always by the folly or fault of a man; the redemption, if there be any, is by the wisdom and virtue of a woman'. This was not, however, a sign that women should be given more authority, let alone equality. For Ruskin, they belonged at home, as real-life Shakespearean heroines, 'infallibly faithful and wise counsellors – incorruptibly just and pure examples – strong always to sanctify, even when they cannot save'.[27]

Other writers aimed their strictures directly at young girls, including Cowden Clarke, in her 1887 article for the *Girl's Own Paper* entitled 'Shakespeare as the Girl's Friend'. Cowden Clarke presented Shakespeare as a paternal source of 'kindliest admonition and wisest counsel', who helped pure girls avoid being 'warped and weakened by circumstance'. Cowden Clarke advised girls to imitate not only Shakespeare's heroines' 'artlessness, guilelessness, modesty, sweetness, ingenuousness and most winning candour' but even their 'mode of utterance' (a tall order). Above all, she celebrated Shakespeare's portrayal of 'the superior fidelity and steadfastness of women' in love; this message for 'the young girl' was in fact a late-Victorian guide to becoming the perfect wife. Nestled between two examples of high-Victorian religiosity – an illustrated Bible verse and a song about Jesus's crown of thorns – she used Shakespeare as scripture, prescribing submission of the most abject kind.

Cowden Clarke praises Hermione in *The Winter's Tale* for showing 'wifely concern' for husband Leontes after he has falsely imprisoned her for adultery, rejected their child and put her on trial for her life.[28] When, in *Cymbeline,* Posthumus pays a servant to murder the similarly innocent Imogen, Cowden Clarke exalts that she 'offer[s] her bosom to the sword'. She concludes that 'Imogen is a perfect exemplar of a devotedly loving wife and a high-minded, large-souled woman'; the good wife not only endures physical and emotional abuse, but is willing to collaborate in her own killing.

Cowden Clarke had fictionalised Juliet's childhood a generation earlier in *The Girlhood of Shakespeare's Heroines,* but faltered when it came to describing what actually happens in the play. In the article, Juliet doesn't make it into Cowden Clarke's pantheon of Shakespearean married women, even though few of Shakespeare's heroines think of themselves so totally as wives. None could be more loyal – Juliet forces herself not to criticise her husband even when he has just killed her cousin. She risks suicide to avoid bigamy, to ensure she can 'live an unstained wife to [her] sweet love' (4.1.88). And finally, when she lies 'bleeding, warm, and newly dead' in front of her parents and the city authorities (5.3.174), she is eulogised primarily as 'faithful Juliet'; 'his lady', Mrs Romeo Montague (5.3.301–2). Cowden Clarke deals with other tragic wives in her article: Desdemona, Brutus's Portia and the women of *Coriolanus* all incur praise and occasionally blame. But on Juliet, she is silent – and no wonder. In her deceit of her family, transgression of their feuding rules, sexual assertiveness and utterly frank desire, Juliet is far from the 'artlessness' and 'guilelessness' Cowden Clarke craves for her readers.

Juliet had become an increasing source of concern for conservative commentators through the nineteenth century. In 1837, even amidst her rhapsody over Juliet's 'moon-light bower', Anna Jameson had concluded by calling Juliet's life and death 'warnings for the youth of this enlightened age'.[29] Ruskin preferred Juliet to Romeo, whom he criticised for 'ruinous impatience', but she did not make his list of twelve 'faultless' Shakespearean women (Virgilia, the wife called 'gracious silence' by Coriolanus, did). An adolescent sexuality such as Juliet's alarmed the Victorians. Until 1875, the age of consent for English girls was twelve – a year younger than Juliet. Later, after journalist W. T. Stead's 1885 exposé on child prostitution and trafficking, entitled 'The Maiden Tribute of Modern Babylon', the so-called Stead Act raised the age of consent from thirteen to sixteen. Juliet, self-assertive and sexually passionate at thirteen, alarmed critics. She also kills herself; suicide was illegal throughout the nineteenth century and remained so in English law until 1961. English commentators on Shakespeare, including Jameson, were quick to blame both Juliet's sexual rebellion and her suicide on her Italian blood.

White imperialism routinely sexualises young girls and women from the global South. Throughout the British Empire, coercive sexual relationships between white men and women of colour were normalised by imperial power structures, creating a racist contrast between the white Northern European lady – sexless, innocent, and virtuous – and the primitive, hypersexual woman of the global South. Although the overwhelming manifestation of this was and is in the cultural mistreatment of Black women, Victorian commentaries on Juliet also sexualised her on the grounds of her Mediterranean 'race'.

As early as 1832, Anna Jameson had blamed Juliet's consent to sex with Romeo on her exotic 'southern temperament' ultimately 'overpowering her reason'. She quoted, too, an old claim that Italian women were 'weak in resisting the first impulses of passion', noting that Juliet shows 'the truly Italian spirit'.[30] Two decades later, Cowden Clarke described Juliet as hitting puberty young in the throes of 'Southern early womanhood'.[31] Actresses whose performances as Juliet were panned traded on Jameson's reflection that 'the love that is wild and passionate in the south' would be 'deep and contemplative' in the more innocent girl of 'the north'. Playing Juliet badly when young became a marker of English purity, reflecting the 'tardier development of an English girl'. Excusing her uninspiring debut as Juliet, Helena Faucit noted that 'an English girl of the age which Shakespeare assigns to Juliet was in every respect a different creature. Development must come later; I certainly was never a precocious child'.[32] Even Ellen Terry, in every way less conservative, felt that Juliet, as 'a passionate young Italian', had 'arrived at maturity sooner' than an English Victorian 'girl of fourteen' who 'seems a mere child'.[33]

The *Christian Lady's Magazine*, a bonkers periodical built fifty per cent on anti-Catholic libel and fifty per cent on angry poems, vilified Juliet and her Romeo for their suicides 'where crime hath raised a tomb/ And Satan claims his right' in a charming ditty entitled 'Verona'.[34] In 1898, the *Wesleyan Methodist Magazine* described adolescents 'especially in the Southern races' as particularly liable to impulsive suicides 'in a pet'.[35] Child suicide terrified the Victorians, not only as a tragedy but as a blasphemous rebellion that destroyed the family line. Above all, child suicide threatened the Victorian fetish of the child as pure, passive, and oblivious to the world's evils.

In Henry Morselli's 1879 treatise on suicide, he declared a 'terrible increase in suicide' across the generations; in 1907, American statistician Arthur MacDonald concluded that levels of reported child suicide, remained 'less than reality'. Increases in girls' suicides were blamed on 'female employment', which engendered 'special difficulties and hardship which overwhelm [girls'] nervous systems and produce [. . .] despair': hysterical madness and despair.[36] Young people intending to kill themselves sent suicide notes to newspaper columns, while lovers' suicide pacts, often as the result of the girl's parents' opposition, became press staples.[37]

Of all the iconic Juliets, Helena Modjeska most brought out this suicidal drive and fragile sanity in a performance remembered for its 'frenzied despair'. Her Juliet 'constantly and uneasily unsheathed' her dagger 'with a glittering and deadly determination to die'. Her soliloquy before taking the poison reduced her to a 'distraught and quivering wreck of girlhood' who fell into 'hysterical frenzy' and 'real madness' after 'the terrible blow which shakes the mental poise of the frail and romantic girl'. Unsurprisingly, Modjeska's Juliet reminded spectators of another suicidal Shakespearean heroine; as her biographer noted, although 'Juliet's mind is not completely shattered like Ophelia's, it is at least unhinged'. Modjeska took poison in the expectation and even the experience of death: 'with her limbs drawn up convulsively, her whole frame quivering, her very teeth chattering, and a cold sweat upon her livid features'.[38] Another critic recalled her 'clutching at and tearing down the hangings of [her] bed'.[39]

Ellen Terry's 1882 Juliet looked, at moments, madder than her 1878 Ophelia. A publicity image shows her with hair dishevelled, the poison-bottle held like the handle of a dagger; another in the same set sees her clutch the side of her neck. Her face looks haggard, and her aesthetic white robe creased until it looks more like a bedsheet than clothing. In an era of stylised poses and heavenward gazes, her frantic, anxious stare reaches straight through and past the viewer, her mouth an asymmetric shadow that nearly splits the face.

The actresses in this chapter were enthralled by Juliet's descent into agony and death. As a child, Helena Faucit loved Juliet for 'what she had to suffer, in which the horror of her tomb, "the being *stifled* in the vault", always my first terror, played a prominent part'. She and a fellow schoolgirl had become obsessed with a vault in their local Lee churchyard: 'A flight of green, slimy-looking steps led down to a massive door with open iron-work at the upper part, and we girls used to snatch a fearful pleasure by peering through it into the gloom within'. The schoolgirls shared 'the attraction [Faucit] felt towards' the tomb: 'We both agreed that in just such a tomb must Juliet have been placed'. Crucially, it was 'the terrible and the tragic' that was 'most alluring', not 'the passion of love': 'It did not interest me. But Juliet's devotion to Romeo, and her resolve to die rather than prove untrue, this I could understand, because all the heroes and heroines worthy of the name, of whom I had read, were always true and devoted'.[40]

When it came to performing the potion soliloquy as an adult, in which Juliet imagines the tomb's 'terrible smells' and hallucinates the ghost of her newly murdered cousin, Faucit would annotate her playtext with lines from Psalm 55: 'My heart is disquieted [. . .] the fear of death is fallen upon me,' and 'Fearfulness and trembling are come upon me, and a horrible dread hath overwhelmed me'.[41] She used her Christian faith to heighten rather than allay the horror of the scene. In Poland, the Catholic Helena Modjeska did likewise, drawing on 'childhood impressions of the Franciscan church, the mysterious vault' of her hometown, where she had sat 'shiver[ing] with fright [. . .] in the warmth of a summer moonlight, fascinated, hypnotised' to prepare her performance. She would also rehearse in a cemetery.[42]

Even Mary Anderson, America's most famous Juliet, and another staunch Catholic, admitted in her retirement that as a Kentucky teenager, she had trekked to Louisville's Cave Hill cemetery to intone Juliet's lines 'through the grilled door of a vault' and 'better realise my heroine's feelings on awakening in her "nest of death, contagion, and unnatural sleep"'. Although Anderson later repudiated the theatre, claiming to have longed 'for the peace and privacy of a domestic life', she still recognised that this Gothic attraction to Juliet was a natural part of childhood: 'What actors we all are, little girls in particular!'[43]

The actresses' frank love of the darker elements of Juliet's experience was a far cry from Cowden Clarke's fictional biography of Juliet's childhood as 'The White Dove of Verona'. Her Juliet is the opposite of the actresses' Gothic girls; her Juliet has no 'curiosity, or excitement, about distasteful things', 'shrinking' from the 'disagreeable' and preferring 'snug safety'. Nor was her Juliet at all active in her own desires, requiring, 'like the clay Pandora', a man 'to make her, from a dreaming child into a sentient, passionate woman'.

Cowden Clarke's child Juliet is a ladylike innocent; she loves flowers, 'natural objects' and pictures, and confesses 'fancied rather than
actual' offences to Friar Laurence. She definitely doesn't hang
around in graveyards communing with ghosts. She's a far more
edifying figure for children's fiction – and a much more boring evening at the theatre. But the gulf between Cowden Clarke's 'gentle,
affectionate little creature' and the spectacular madness of the
actresses sums up the tightrope walked by Victorian culture.
Audiences wanted Juliet to be simultaneously picturesque and
passionate, angelic and spectacular, saintly and sexy – but not *too*
sexy. Nineteenth-century texts, like their eighteenth-century predecessors, continued to cut the frank passion of Juliet's Act 3 mono-
logue, where Juliet characterises her forthcoming night with Romeo
as 'a winning match/ Played for a pair of stainless maidenhoods'
and complains of being 'sold,/ Not yet enjoyed' (3.2.12–13; 27–8).

Conservative Mary Anderson sometimes cut the entire scene, but
even Mrs Patrick Campbell, a consummate *fin-de-siècle* actress who
had achieved national fame playing *femmes fatales* and fallen women,
did not give the speech in full. Several productions, from Helena
Faucit to Henry Irving, also cut all reference to the 'cords' (the ladder
by which Romeo visits Juliet on their wedding night) on grounds of
decency. Like Garrick before them, they also cut moments that
demonstrated Juliet's wit and ability to deceive. Shakespeare's words
challenged the Victorian model of an ideal woman, so instead it was
easier to cauterise her character, making her less complex and less
contrary. Acting opposite Henry Irving at the Lyceum, Ellen Terry
was not allowed to play the sequence where Juliet, arriving to beg
Friar Laurence's help, engages in double-edged wordplay with Paris.
Nor could she keep the lines where Juliet openly lies to her parents
about her new willingness to marry Paris, despite Regency audiences
having coped with them. An ideal Juliet could not speak lines that
made her seem too sexual or strategic. Theatre critic A. B. Walkley
got to the heart of the Victorian demand when he praised Mrs
Patrick Campbell's 1895 Juliet for being all 'naïve simplicity', adding:
'Even when the hot passion wells out from her heart in the balcony
scene she is absolutely naïve!'[44]

★

The Victorians didn't invent the trope of the unconsciously sexy child-woman. But they did really roll around in the fetishisation of the child whose beauty was both provocative and not hers to understand. This obsession drove visual culture. Depending on your viewpoint, Lewis Carroll's photographs of nude children are either an innocent aesthetic project or a packet of child pornography. As a postgraduate, I saw some of Dodgson's photographs in the Bodleian, reprinted in an old book on Victorian sexology. One shows eight-year-old Evelyn Hatch sprawled naked against a faux-pastoral backdrop, hands laced behind her head.[45] As in Edouard Manet's controversial 1863 *Olympia*, in which a naked prostitute gazes confrontationally at the viewer, little Evelyn's eyes are locked challengingly on the camera lens. Unlike in Manet's painting, Carroll posed Evelyn so that her genitals are just visible.

Carroll was one of a group of Victorian artists thus to depict the naked child. Paul Chabas made a career out of painting naked girls in works with titles like *The First Bath* or *Tender Morn*; Adolphe Bouguereau's *The Wet Cupid* (1891) shows an adolescent girl in mournful, vampy pose (with wings). Bruno Piglhein's *Christmas Morning* (c. 1890) feasts on a spreadeagled, naked toddler whose genitals are concealed by a toy soldier; Antonio Ugo's sculpture *Pubescit* (1900) shows a naked adolescent girl with developing breasts, seated with eyes closed and head raised. I find it hard to look at any of these without hate, but Carroll's photographs are, to me, most shocking. That said, Evelyn Hatch remained Carroll's friend until death, and for every family that refused Carroll permission to photograph their daughters nude, there was one that happily consented.

This popular desire for sexualised innocence reached the theatre, where adult audiences enjoyed plays with all-child casts, titillated by the (apparent) distinction between the salacious scripts and the innocent children who performed them. Unsurprisingly, several high-profile child actresses were stalked by paedophilic men.[46] Childishness was a boon for the adult Juliet; Mrs Patrick Campbell's Juliet 'danced like the daughter of Herodias' according to George Bernard Shaw.[47] Herodias's daughter is Salomé, the biblical princess whose dancing so aroused her stepfather King Herod that his sexual obsession led to the execution of John the Baptist. Victorian artists could not decide whether Salomé was an innocent little girl or a predatory temptress – her 'Dance of the Seven Veils', originating in Oscar Wilde's 1891 play, has become a byword for strip routines.

Like Salomé, Juliet is seen dancing in her father's house, and commentaries on the character stress her simultaneous innocence and provocation. Helena Faucit described her naïve sensuality: 'swaying to the rhythmic movement of the music, with unstudied grace, so noble, yet so childlike; looking for nothing, unconscious of admiring eyes, herself delighting only in the simple enjoying of the dance'.[48] Faucit was clear that it was Juliet's childishness that so appealed to Romeo, insisting that it was 'that passionate childlike loving [that] queens her in his sight, and makes him her slave forever'.[49] These Victorian strictures on Juliet's innocence some-times go implausibly far. Helena Modjeska insisted that the young lovers were 'unconscious of their passion', that Juliet had no 'sensu-ousness' and that they had sex only because of 'natural law', not desire. But there seems to have been a gulf between what these actresses wrote on paper and the intensely sexual moments they brought to their performances.

Despite objecting to 'naturalistic details' like 'a disarranged four-posted bed' and 'a dishevelled Juliet' to 'remind the audience what had just happened in Juliet's room' (i.e. the sexless sex act), it was Modjeska who reintroduced Romeo and Juliet's first onstage kiss three acts earlier.[50] In Shakespeare's text, Romeo and Juliet kiss not once but twice at the Capulets' party, the first time as the climax of the spoken sonnet that reveals their instant mutual attraction. Juliet 'grant[s]' their first kiss and explicitly invites the second (1.5.101–4), and then flirtatiously teases Romeo about his prowess: 'You kiss by th' book' (1.5.106). Decorous Georgian and early Victorian produc-tions – in the era of what Ellen Terry called 'fragile domestic hero-ines' – shortened the sonnet and downgraded the embrace to a chaste kiss on the hand. Modjeska, instead, brought back what her biographer called 'the electric touch of her lover's lips'.[51] She also made Juliet's death a sexual consummation, kissing Romeo as she died and deliberately impaling her abdomen upon his dagger (a move echoed by Mrs Patrick Campbell).

When Henry Irving kissed Ellen Terry onstage at the Lyceum in 1882, the world witnessed the real-life attraction of performers who were lovers behind the scenes. But for Ellen Terry, who began the ballroom scene not as a dancing sugar-plum fairy, but as a more realistic 'indifferent' adolescent forced to dance with Paris, the scene's greatest eroticism lay elsewhere.[52] The Terry–Irving production restored Rosaline, making Romeo a less idealised character who essentially gatecrashed the ball to stalk a girl who had told him no. Irving's Romeo was hopelessly chasing Rosaline when he spotted Juliet. As Terry recalled in her autobiography, 'Can I ever forget his face when in pursuit of *her* he saw *me*'.[53] Terry's copy of the play, now in a collection at Harvard, is full of her own notes detailing the intensity of Juliet's feelings: she 'loves him in a minute'; they 'look at each other all the while, can't help it'; she kisses Romeo after a 'tremor' and shows 'passion' on the balcony.[54] Nevertheless, it's clear how much of the attraction is to Irving as well as to Romeo. Terry even annotated the scenes in which Juliet didn't appear, describing Irving as 'quite tremendous' in the duel scene, and praising the rage and despair Irving showed when Romeo was banished from Juliet. One comment reads, poignantly and ecstatically, 'Oh, Henry!'[55] Irving's letters to his Juliet are similarly rhapsodic in the period; he writes as her 'own true love', calls her his 'darling wife' and signs himself her 'adoring lover husband'.[56] The Victorians might have praised Juliet's childishness, but they flocked to a production which revealed its leading actors' very grown-up passion.

*

Some women also found in the figure of Juliet the opportunity to experience something other than heterosexual love. The nineteenth century saw one extraordinary Romeo: the lesbian American actress Charlotte Cushman (1816–76). Her performances made *Romeo and Juliet*, that totem of heterosexual romance, resonate for queer women on both sides of the Atlantic. Cushman was the greatest American tragic actress of the nineteenth century, ending a four-decade career with the most spectacular farewell in American theatre history. She thrilled audiences on both sides of the Atlantic, and lived for several years as the centre of an artists' colony in Rome. Originally an acclaimed opera singer, she found her greatest Shakespearean success in the roles of Hamlet and, above all, Romeo. Her 'Harem (Scarem) of emancipated females' – so dubbed by a contemporary observer – with whom she lived and worked included numerous lovers and several long-term partners.[57]

Not only was Charlotte Cushman history's most famous female Romeo, she is probably the only Romeo since Garrick who consistently mattered more than their Juliet. Initially, Cushman played opposite her sister, Susan – they are immortalised in Staffordshire pottery – and despite what we might expect of 1840s mores, for most spectators the big scandal was Susan Cushman's ambiguous marital status.[58] Although one actor, George Vadenhoff, did call her cross-dressed performance 'monstrous', Charlotte's supporters claimed that it was 'solely on her sister's account' that she was playing a leading man, to bring her indigent sister safe professional opportunities.[59] Paradoxically, the fact that Charlotte was a woman allowed her to give a much more sexualised performance as Romeo than any man at that time. One critic said her 'amorous endearments' to Juliet were 'of so erotic a character that no man would have dared indulge in them' onstage.[60] In response, her London audience was 'roused to the wildest excitement'; when, several years later, Charlotte toured to Exeter, she 'ravished the house with wonderment'.[61]

Cushman's Romeo showed 'all the vehemence, the warmth of passion, the melancholy, the luxuriant imagination [. . .] of the Italian boy-lover' in a way no man would have been allowed to do. The theatre critic of the *Britannia* noted that Cushman's production 'would certainly outrage [. . .] a modern audience, were the performers of opposite sex'.[62] The *Mercury* critic quipped that after seeing Cushman's Romeo, women would find 'lovemaking as practiced by the other sex [. . .] a very stale, flat, and unprofitable affair'.[63] Amidst this melange of Victorian doublethink (a woman's wildly sexualised cross-dressed performance is fine because she is a woman) and journalistic ho-hoing ('Girls might fancy girls after this – lol @ girls'), Charlotte Cushman thrived as an enormously butch lesbian, at the centre of international expatriate gay drama that makes *The L Word's* shenanigans look tame.

The old myth of nineteenth-century lesbianism is that nobody knew it existed; that it never made it into the kind of homophobic legislation that scuppered Oscar Wilde because Queen Victoria didn't believe it was real. In fact, public perceptions especially

associated sex between women with actresses. Diarist Hester Lynch
Thrale noted in the 1790s that 'Mrs *Damor* a Lady much suspected
for liking her own Sex in a criminal Way' had fallen for the 'fine
comic Actress' Miss Farren, while Françoise Saucerotte (Madame
Raucoux), 'the famous actress on the Paris stage', was also rumoured
to sleep with women.[64] Nearly a century later, sexologist Havelock
Ellis would claim that 'the most elaborate excursions in the direction of Lesbos, are extremely common in theatres, both among
actresses, and even more, among chorus and ballet girls'.[65]

The theatre – and specifically Shakespeare – was always key to
Cushman's relationships with women. Her first girlfriend, Anne
Hampton Brewster, described having 'luxuriated' in Shakespeare
with Cushman, who was 'full of fascination' and left in her wake 'a
subtle perfume, the haunting of a melody; the faint memory of a
dream'. Anne wrote in her diary: 'never shall I love another as I
loved her'.[66] In her late twenties, Cushman had lovebombed the
Shakespearean actress and famous former Juliet Fanny Kemble;
Cushman wrote that she 'possesses me like enchantment', and
offered to help extricate her from an unhappy marriage to American
plantation-owner and enslaver Pierce Mease Butler. When
Cushman's girlfriends weren't filling newspapers with poetry in
Shakespearean iambic pentameter dedicated to her ('I know thou
art an altar where my lyre / May honourably yield its worship
chaunt,' gushed Eliza Cook in 1848), they were writing barely coded
novels featuring thinly disguised Cushmans ('Lord Charlie' in
Matilda M. Hays's *Adrienne Stanley*) as perfidious lovers.[67] Anna
Jameson, Fanny Kemble's confidante, introduced Cushman to
several of the literary women with whom she enjoyed passionate
friendships. Cushman promptly caused huge romantic jealousy
between two – Geraldine Jewsbury and Jane Carlyle – when the
former fell for Charlotte. Jane Carlyle, infuriated by Jewsbury's
'blaze of enthusiasm' for Cushman, wrote her an angry 'screed';
Jewsbury, meanwhile, wrote passionate letters to Charlotte, confessing that her own jealousy of Charlotte's current lover left her feeling like 'a wild cat [. . .] you have pained me more by your silence
than you at all know'.[68]

Cushman's circle, a polite biographical term for 'web of outra-
geous lesbian drama', has been extensively studied, and her

unparalleled success as Romeo has ensured her place in the pantheon of Victorian Shakespeare. But what did it mean to be Cushman's Juliet? Audaciously, after her sister left the stage, Cushman's many Juliets included her lover, Matilda M. Hayes, 'a brunette, tall, with a fine figure, and an interesting expressive face'.[69] In 1859, Cushman acted opposite beautiful teenager Mary Devlin, telling her younger lover Emma Crow that Devlin made 'such a pretty Juliet [. . .] that I am inclined to think I never acted it so well before', and wondering whether Emma would be 'very jealous' if she saw her as 'your darling's Juliet'.[70] Devlin would sign herself 'your Juliet' in correspondence with Cushman until her premature death at twenty-two.

When *Romeo and Juliet* has interested queer readers, it's usually because of the boys. Mercutio's twin obsessions – hating women and loving Romeo – drive comedy and tragedy in turn. When Tybalt confronts Mercutio as a substitute for Romeo, beginning the duel that leads to both their deaths, he makes the accusation 'thou consort'st with Romeo' – 'consort' could mean both associate with and have sex with (3.1.37).[71] Through the twentieth and twenty-first centuries, the boys from Verona have become queer icons. Leonard Whiting's 'beautiful' Romeo in Zeffirelli's 1968 film brought many gay fans to the cinema, with the *Los Angeles Advocate* praising him as 'perfection from head to toe'.[72] Playing a leather-trousered Mercutio for the RSC in 1983, Roger Allam channelled his own homoerotic memories of boarding school – 'emotional exchange, whether sexually expressed or not' via 'intense friendships' – while Baz Luhrmann's film presented Mercutio as a Black drag queen enamoured of Leonardo DiCaprio's unbelievably pretty Romeo.[73] Most queer readings of *Romeo and Juliet*, from academia to fanfiction, focus on Mercutio, and most same-sex adaptations are male/male.[74]

Juliet is an unlikely lesbian icon: she is definitely devoted to her man, and unlike other Shakespearean heroines, she doesn't cross-dress and no woman falls for her (unlike Viola or Rosalind). Nor does she devote herself to protecting a beloved female friend (unlike Beatrice or Paulina). But for Charlotte Cushman's queer female fans, being 'her Juliet' was a profoundly erotic idea. Martha Le Baron, infatuated with Cushman, 'could not help being very absurdly jealous of pretty Juliet when you drew her head against your bosom', and Cushman's own lover, Emma Crow, 'felt a thrill when in the balcony scene [. . .] Romeo returned again and again for a last embrace' and 'won more hearts than Juliet's'.[75] For these women, being Juliet meant not a straitened life and a premature death, banished from love and persecuted by parents, but the possibility of public yet exclusive and intimate passion with another woman, speaking the words of the author who defined nineteenth-century theatre on an internationally acclaimed stage.

The ways in which Romeo and Juliet typically resonates with queer experience, past and present, are overwhelmingly negative: secrecy, opposition, and the violent disjunction between society's expectations and personal desire. Even in fiction, queer stories often end with death, from deathbed clinches and suicide pacts in nineteenth-century fiction (I have given whole lectures called 'Bury Your Gays') to epoch-defining TV deaths like Ianto in Torchwood or Tara in Buffy. But for Charlotte Cushman and her circle, real-life Romeo and Juliet meant no men and no death. A woman didn't need to go onstage to be Cushman's 'Juliet' – in fact, friends would call Charlotte and her life partner, the sculptor Emma Stebbins, 'Romeo and her Juliet', even when Charlotte had effectively retired from the stage.[76]

Before the mid-nineteenth century, there was only one version of Shakespeare's play that dared to imagine Romeo and Juliet surviving: a 1776 German opera by Georg Benda. By the time Charlotte and Emma met, Benda's opera was long forgotten, with no successors – and yet here were Charlotte and Emma, living the dream. Shakespeare's final line, 'Juliet and her Romeo', had become the play's most portable quotation throughout the first two centuries of its existence. Now 'Romeo and her Juliet' were rewriting the story for themselves. Instead of a three-day relationship surrounded by violence and suicide, and conducted between barely acquainted children, Cushman and Stebbins were together for twenty-two years. A complicated twenty-two years, certainly – including Cushman's affair with Emma Crow, her eventual niece by marriage – but a relationship that endured in Rome, England and America.

In 1878, Stebbins became Cushman's first biographer, beginning the commemoration of America's greatest Shakespearean actress that would see Cushman celebrated in the Hall of Fame for Great Americans in New York City, the Charlotte Cushman Club in

Philadelphia and its philanthropic successor, the theatre-funding Charlotte Cushman Foundation. For decades, there was a Cushman Award for Lifetime Achievement in the Theatre (won by Angela Lansbury, Katharine Hepburn, and Ginger Rogers, among others), and there remains a bust in the Smithsonian, and a considerable amount of Shakespeare scholarship on Cushman. Both major twenty-first-century biographies of Cushman – Lisa Merrill's *When Romeo Was a Woman* (2000) and Tana Wojczuk's *Lady Romeo* (2022) – draw heavily on Stebbins's first discreet but adulatory memoir of the woman who 'had a mission to fulfil much higher and broader than she ever realised'.[77] In perhaps the most striking reversal of the Shakespearean play, we have the story of America's Romeo because 'her Juliet' survived her to write it.

In a way, that Juliet, the woman who survived her Romeo, is the most apt avatar for a century in which Juliet became a hero and a rebel.

*

The writers and actresses in this chapter were very different women, but they all paid tribute to Juliet's personal strength. When Ellen Terry gave her lectures on Shakespeare to 'packed houses of women', including numerous suffragette groups, she was keen to present Juliet and her fellow heroines as role models for the 'modern revolutionaries' before her, explicitly tying Shakespeare's women to the contemporary political moment.[78]

It was natural enough that these suffragists also began to imagine other fates for Juliet. Terry was at the centre of an artistic, pro-suffrage circle led by her daughter Edith Craig. Within this milieu, women aware of Terry's interpretations of Shakespeare were inspired to question the value of Romeo's passionate but destructive love, and to scrutinise the wider world in which Juliet lived, centring the play's female characters. One of Terry's acolytes, the Irish suffragist and playwright Clotilde Graves, wrote a *Romeo and Juliet* proto-fanfiction in which the lovers are estranged high-society cousins who meet at Lady Capp-Yewlett's ball at '10, Verona Gardens'. The Honourable Romeo Mont-Ague chucks Tighe Balt off Brighton Pier ('"Here is my card," said Romy to the policeman, as cool as any cucumber') and urges Juliet to elope 'down the fire escape'. But Juliet, due to marry her alternative 'Gallic wooer', hesitates between clandestine marriage and a veil with 'diamond sparks', and eventually decides she prefers her own reflection of 'bridal magnificence' decked out in her fiancé's jewels. She dumps Romeo, lives, and becomes a countess.[79]

The South African-born actress and suffragette Jess Dorynne had a daughter by Terry's son Edward Gordon Craig, who abandoned Dorynne before the baby's birth. Dorynne became temporarily dependent on morphia, condemning herself for having been 'a green fool of a girl', almost Juliet-like, who persisted in adoring a Romeo who had abandoned her: 'my heart hugs tight Love's corpse and cannot bury it'.[80] Terry welcomed Jess and Kitty to her home in Smallhythe, Kent, telling her son: 'I would rather <u>kill</u> you than see you grow <u>systematically</u> exacting & dishonourable to women'.[81] In print, Dorynne turned her attention to a variety of Shakespearean women in a book, which, although entitled *The True Ophelia*, is really more interested in Shakespeare's supporting roles. Her chapter on *Romeo and Juliet* is entitled 'The Insignificant Mother of Juliet' and is the earliest surviving Shakespeare criticism to take Lady Capulet seriously – she is seen not merely as 'swift and cruel as a hawk', but as a true 'tyrant'.[82]

The idea that the Capulets were bad parents was not new. Shakespeare, after all, establishes in his prologue that the lovers' parents cause their deaths, and has Prince Escalus reiterate it at the play's end. Most Victorian commentators had dismissed Lady Capulet contemptuously but briefly as 'a piece of cold, formal propriety'.[83] Dorynne, meanwhile, firmly tackled the text. She found in Lady Capulet a murderous proto-Lady Macbeth with 'no atmosphere of maternal tenderness' who is obsessively set on killing Romeo.[84] Although Victorian convention heavily cut Lady Capulet's role, reducing it, in Dorynne's words, to 'a part that no successful actress would dream of playing', Dorynne found in Shakespeare's original text a Lady Capulet who is 'the strongest character in the play!'[85]

She noted that while Lord Capulet says nothing at the scene of Tybalt and Mercutio's murders, neither responding to the deaths nor seeking justice from the prince, Lady Capulet causes a 'frantic outcry', publicly lying that 'some twenty' killed Tybalt on Romeo's command. Dorynne writes: '*it is Lady Capulet, only, who ever demands the death of Romeo, and is apparently determined to effect it by fair means or foul*'. Dorynne emphasised the sequence in Act 3, Scene 5, usually cut, in which Lady Capulet, 'as relentlessly fierce against Romeo as ever', plots before Juliet to commission poison for him, extending her pursuit of Romeo into the Mantuan underworld. Dorynne saw her behaving 'viperishly' as she abandoned her supposed grief for Tybalt; when Lady Capulet cheerfully announces a 'sudden day of joy' to Juliet (the forced marriage to Paris), it's less than twenty-four hours since she was 'enacting distracted grief [. . .] Finding, however, that it did not avail in obtaining the death of Romeo, she has not troubled to keep up even the faintest semblance of it'.[86]

Importantly, Dorynne used her portrait of a villainous, cold mother, 'obviously bored by her daughter's tears', to justify the aspects of Juliet's character that nineteenth- and early-twentieth-century society found most disagreeable – the same characteristics, perhaps, that caused Mary Cowden Clarke to exclude her from the gallery of role models she presented to readers of the *Girl's Own Paper*.[87] Dorynne observes that Juliet has 'again and again' been called 'sly and deceitful' for not admitting her marriage to Romeo to her mother when such a confession 'would have averted the tragedy'.[88] Dorynne could bring her lived experience to bear here: *she* had confessed an unmarried pregnancy to her mother, but, unlike Juliet, knew beforehand that her supportive 'mother _won't_ get angry'.[89] Instead, Dorynne claimed that 'Juliet makes attempts to put out cautious feelers to such a confession' when discussing Romeo with her mother, but finding Lady Capulet 'so bent upon achieving his death [. . .] her horrified daughter finds any confession of her marriage to him impossible'. After all, Dorynne argued, 'Juliet has been brought up to consider herself the absolute chattel of her arrogant mother'.[90]

Today, Jess Dorynne is almost forgotten as both an actress and a writer, but her rendition of Juliet as a victim of an intergenerational conflict with highly emotionally and psychologically culpable parents would come to define the character's status in the second half of the twentieth century. Dorynne's complaint that Lady Capulet 'utterly ignores her child's individuality' sounds closer to a work of 1960s child psychology than the conduct literature of

Dorynne's own childhood and adolescence, when the *Girl's Own Paper* vaunted 'a parent's Divine prerogative to teach, counsel, and rule their children', and condemned young women who – like Juliet and Jess Dorynne – entered relationships 'utterly unknown to their own mothers'.[91] Long before post-war Britain would encounter the teenager, the hoodlum and the 'generation gap', Dorynne discovered them all in the pages of Shakespeare's play.

Victorian actresses might have shied away from openly acknowledging a sexuality their society perceived as un-English, but they embraced Juliet's darkness as never before. The play became a vehicle for self-expression: Cushman's Romeo embodied the desire she felt for women, while Terry gave her Juliet a second life as a role model for 'modern revolutionaries'. The generation that came of age at the *fin de siècle* wanted a Juliet who spoke to their contemporary moment; they scrutinised the play in new ways. Clotilde Graves dared to question whether marriage to Paris could be a smart choice based on a woman's individual financial interests rather than eloping with a murderer; Jess Dorynne further decentred romance to look at Juliet's experiences with her mother. Where they saw in Juliet a terrible warning, it was not because the play punished her for filial disobedience or excessive passion, but because she suffered the consequences of a world that victimised young girls. Throughout the twentieth century that followed, Juliet's story would increasingly be made to speak to societal issues; in turn-of-the-century Britain, chief among those was the status of women.

Meanwhile, another country was using Juliet to tell a different kind of story: a story that took Juliet back through the history of her myth, to the source. In a new country, aspiring to become a new empire, Juliet would not be a suffragist but a saint, and the scene would be laid in fair Verona, northern Italy, with Il Duce rising to power.

Fair Verona

At the end of *Romeo and Juliet*, Juliet's father-in-law promises her father to erect 'her statue in pure gold' as a memorial (5.3.298). Today, in a crowded courtyard on Verona's Via Cappello, there is a statue in bronze. It's of a girl, very young, with a coronet and braided hair. Slender and downcast, she stands with her chin lowered and her left hand protectively curled beneath her collarbone, as if she might be cherishing something inside her palm. Standing contrapposto, she gathers her skirt in heavy folds beneath the fingers of her right hand. Her eyes express the blind, blank patience common to most statues, one sigh away from total resignation. Sometimes, while tourists gather and smile for selfies with her, she looks as if she is waiting, head inclined pensively towards the archway, to see Romeo drift in from Mantua. At night, when the courtyard eventually falls quiet, the lengthening shadows make her look frail. She is no longer poised and alert on her bronze rock, but seeming to hang in the air, bent with weariness.

Through the day, she has the face of a Botticelli Madonna, full of the sad virtue of a Renaissance funerary monument. But when the sun burns directly overhead, the light particularises her, makes her look bored and frustrated. Open beauty shades into determination around the lips and jaw. Shadows cast across her face empty those patient eyes into the hollows of a skull. Caught then in the courtyard's heat, with sun and shadow and tourists' breath all converging on her face, Juliet looks almost angry.

Juliet's dress has a tight bodice – only the thinnest seam indicates where the neckline begins. Her skirt falls in heavy folds, but the bodice wrinkles beneath her breasts, where her weight has shifted. It's difficult to tell whether the dress as originally cast had sleeves.

When I visit her in September 2019, it's as if Juliet is wearing a dress of gold. There's a burnished patina across her arms, breasts and body that resculpts her medieval gown into something far more daring; a Hollywood red-carpet number, with the crowd of tourists as cinema fans. Under the Veronese sun, Juliet shines like a heat map of all the ways tourists have groped and grabbed and caressed her: her right arm polished into anonymous perfection; her right breast glowing. I remember at eighteen seeing the smoothed foot of St Peter in the eponymous Basilica in Vatican City, Rome – moulded by hundreds of thousands of hands.

St Peter and Juliet – or rather, his foot and her breast – are part of a select but distinctly heterogeneous group of lucky bronze body parts. Across the globe, travellers consider it lucky to rub or touch the stomach of a semi-historical Chinese monk, Budai (the 'Laughing Buddha'); the arm and thigh of medieval Belgian military hero Everard t'Serclaes; and the toes of John Harvard, clergyman and college benefactor.[1] There are a few animals in the group, including Manhattan's *Charging Bull*, sculpted by Arturo di Modica, with its apparently lucky testicles, and the lucky snout of the *Porcellino* statue in Florence.[2] The only male human statue to be touched the same kind of sexualised way as Juliet's is that of French journalist 'Victor Noir', whose effigy lies in Paris's Père-Lachaise cemetery.[3] Jules Dalou's 1891 life-size bronze of Noir includes a prominent crotch, and superstition says that kissing his lips and rubbing his groin will enhance fertility and sexuality. Today, Noir's lips and groin are the only parts of him not covered in verdigris, thanks to visitors' enthusiasm.[4]

Lacking Noir's unlikely proportions, Juliet's breasts are clothed and unremarkable; this is a practice tied specifically to Juliet as a character, perhaps combining superstition with a fantasy of sexual access to Shakespeare's heroine. The statue's sisters in Munich ('Julia', situated beside the Rathaus, 1974) and Ningbo, China, (Lhingzhu Park, c. 2017) also have burnished right breasts from tourists' hands. The tourists who grope Juliet in Verona do so lavishly, posing for pictures. The flushed, excited faces of some suggest a thrill at transgression and taboo. One particularly distasteful image, shot for the British stock photography company Alamy, shows a man holding Juliet's breast while smiling in open-mouthed, breathless triumph for the camera on his selfie stick.[5] The shot's low angle makes him look as though he's actually swinging from Juliet's breast, hanging above some cavernous height as he pants into the camera. Groping the statue in this shot becomes a daredevil act; Juliet's sculpted body becomes part of the adventurer's terrain for the masculine traveller, who fakes a moment of athletic display as he holds the statue's breast.

That statue, today's statue, is a replacement: the 1970s original had to be replaced after public groping wore the breast away. One of the older tour guides tells me that tourists to Verona had become so enthusiastic – or aggressive – that they cracked Juliet's arm and made holes in her breast. Back in my Airbnb, I google the pictures. The images I find recall the nineteenth-century medical photographs I saw as a graduate student; before effective surgeries for breast cancer, women resorted to corrosive poultices that were meant to 'draw out' the tumours. The hole in Juliet's breast reminds me of the results: black salves that simply burned the breast away.

In researching the statue, I discover something else: when the Veronese tourist board removed the original for repair, it turned out to be full of love-notes and invocations. They had been forced through the holes caused by the over-zealous tourists. Lovers had filled her up with their hopes and dreams, reshaped her with their hands, and destroyed her in the process.

Touching a national hero, illustrious benefactor, or religious icon for luck all makes more sense than groping the breasts of a fictional teenager who died young. But this is Verona, where Juliet is simultaneously city heroine, golden goose, and secular saint. She is the source of the tourism that populates and energises the city, the enduring symbol of Veronese identity, and the talisman of semi-religious romance. To understand Juliet's legacy, you have to know her city, too.

When I visit Casa di Giulietta, the atmosphere of the courtyard crowd is raucous as well as romantic, extended families and student groups mingling with couples. A few visitors (typically Irish or East Asian) avert their faces from the groping. All nationalities, meanwhile, are enthusiastic about affixing a note to the walls of the archway joining street to house. These walls are covered with advice on family life and personal philosophies, as well as statements of fidelity. 'We will always be a loving family,' boast 'Lee, Kalyn, and Nolan'. Zeta tells Dimitri that her wish is to 'keep making you smile like this, because soulmates aren't only for lovers' on the reverse of a group travel train ticket. 'Steve and Jackie' celebrate 'True Romance. 25 years plus two Boys'. Instagram wisdom vies with lewd suggestions. Brand names – TopQuality, GruppoTravel, and, inevitably, McDonald's – peep through the chaos, and curling Post-its fade to the colour of parchment. Postcards and re-smoothed receipts are attached to the wall with chewing gum – 'Marcelo e Bruno' commemorate their love thanks to a wad of demi-foiled Trident gum – plasters and even the odd (clean, thank God) sanitary towel. It's somewhere between Parry's *A London Street Scene* (1835) and the wall of a school bathroom.

A house with gold awning opens from one side of the courtyard, its hoardings advertising a package called 'One Night As Juliet'. This begs the question of *which night* (snogging your enemy? Losing your virginity with the Nurse on watch? Faking your own death?). My focus group (schoolfriends on WhatsApp) reckon it's either an 'assisted suicide experience', or, equally troublingly, 'a sex LARP'. In fact, it's a sixteen-room B&B offering a variety of themed packages from the 'One Night' to a week's 'Honeymoon As Juliet'. Since Juliet's 'honeymoon' involved her murderous husband fleeing to exile and her parents immediately fixing her up for bigamy, this seems inauspicious. However, the rooms are beautiful, in a Google Translate sort of way ('Romantic Junior Luxury' and its stripper cousin, 'Luxury Precious'). Romeo and Juliet would doubtless have enjoyed a jacuzzi once they'd had it explained.[6]

A storey above ground level, two sides of the courtyard give way to a large terrace; beneath it is a vine-covered side entrance to the Teatro Nuovo, a nineteenth-century time capsule in swagged velvet and gold, seating nearly 900 people in Enrico Storari's auditorium. Facing the theatre is a gift shop selling *Romeo e Giulietta*-branded fridge magnets, phone covers, glasses cases, T-shirts and espresso cups. The logo evokes Baz Luhrmann's film title without actually incurring the wrath of copyright. The colour scheme is fixed: baby pink, hot pink, white, and scarlet. The profusion of rosy silicone is faintly reminiscent of a sex shop, although perhaps surprisingly, that is about the only direction in which souvenir construction hasn't gone, the presence of branded condoms highlighting the omission. A range of metal keyrings in the shape of Juliet's breast, coyly encircled with flowers, is as close as we get.

Most popular in the shop are the 'love locks': branded, heart-shaped padlocks, which couples can sign and lock to a gate or bridge. This is one of Verona's newer traditions; I assumed it was an import from Paris, where the Pont des Arts' railings have buckled under the weight of such padlocks, but in fact the practice dates from 1980s Hungary, when young lovers first fixed padlocks to a fence in the city of Pécs.[7] These couples marked their rebellion against Soviet repression of public romance by using a symbol of the countercultural punk movement: love as defiance of state control. So damaging are the architectural consequences that love locks and related graffiti are banned in Venice, an hour's train ride from Verona. However, despite successive attempts by the Veronese authorities, no one has controlled the practice here. The bricks, grates, and paintwork are covered in graffiti, posters – and padlocks. Only the vine-covered walls escape.

Folklorists call these massed love locks 'folk assemblages', a process of 'collaborative creation' where visitors add themselves to a romantic community.[8] Here, tourists embrace love locks – supposedly permanent and immovable – as an artefact through which to imitate the tenacity and immortality of the Shakespearean lovers. Scholars see love locks as being part of modern, secular pilgrimage rituals; they've even been compared to the wayside shrines that – appropriately – commemorate both violent death and the routes to holy destinations. Pilgrimage is fundamental to *Romeo and Juliet*, with Romeo addressing Juliet as 'saint', and his lips 'pilgrims' at her shrine. To follow the Juliet tourist trail is to become a pilgrim in more ways than one. Before Juliet's statue dominated the courtyard, an image of the Virgin Mary was there instead.[9] The virgin mother of God, conceived without sin, has been replaced by the passionate young wife whose breasts are available to purchase as keyrings in every souvenir shop. Juliet is a patron saint of money as well as sex in the Veronese canon.

Casa di Giulietta itself is a thirteenth-century house whose interior is eclectically decorated: there are eighteenth- and nineteenth-century prints, neo-medieval friezes, and Renaissance ceramics. Dotted around the public rooms is a series of damaged wooden books bearing quotations and stills from George Cukor's 1936 film version of the play.[10] A Victorian lithograph of Shakespeare, enlarged, gives him pursed lips and a lazy eye. One room houses two costumes and a bed, all recognisable from Zeffirelli's 1968 film, although none are labelled and the costumes look dusty. The small size of Olivia Hussey's gown reflects just how effectively they starved her. The bed is beautiful: walnut wood dressed with crisp linen, and the subject of many photographs. I hear one mother tell her daughter, 'Look, the *actual bed*'. The climax of the house tour is the opportunity to stand on the balcony overlooking the courtyard, imaginatively embodying Juliet for a few seconds or minutes. Parallel experiences can be found at other literary tourist destinations: you can lurch dramatically from a coffin in Hotel Castle Dracula, Transylvania, or grasp a trolley at London's King's Cross Station to try and run for the Hogwarts Express on Platform 9¾. Folklorists call these 'ostensive actions': mimetic enactments of the poses and behaviours that make up a narrative.[11] It's at the heart of historical re-enactments, cosplay, and the dance routines of Disneyland cast members. Lurking in the courtyard, I see Juliets recite speeches from the balcony, and take selfies. The practice is the same regardless of whether or not they have a Romeo: the ritual is about her, not him. They're recreating not the moment when Romeo steps out of the shadows, but the moments before, when Juliet communes with her imagined lover: a chance to be both the yearning girl and the audience member who knows that girl's love is requited. It's all the thrill of Shakespearean first love without the risk of tragedy.

Tour over, it's back down to the courtyard and – if you didn't manage it sooner – a pose with the new statue. The plinth shows four plaques:

Nero Costantini fecit 1969

Giulietta

La statua originale ora esposta all'interno
fu donata dal Lions Club nel 1972

Dono di Cattolica Assicurazioni dal 1995

Nero Costantini, a sculptor and portrait painter who found fame
in the 1930s, sculpted the first Juliet in 1969. Not inappropriately,
Costantini also created funerary sculptures and religious monuments – Juliet's face reappears on the Virgin Mary in Verona's
Cathedral of St Maria Assunta, now with a golden halo.[12] The
Juliet statue gave Costantini a legacy but no luck; he died suddenly
that August. The original statue was funded by the Verona Lions
Club, a branch of the (then all-male) international service organisation with strong local links to the Church. The replacement
statue was funded by the Catholic Insurance Agency, which also
sponsors Italy's rugby team. One of Italy's most powerful financi-
ers, the company prides itself on its Catholic values, and has a
specific interest in insuring religious bodies. The mix of the sacred,
the state, and the sexual sums up Juliet's myth in Verona. She is
the city's patron saint of love – a saint you can grope in public.
How did we get here?

*

I know something about literary pilgrimages. In high season, 3,000
visitors tour Shakespeare's Birthplace every day in my hometown
of Stratford-upon-Avon. The Royal Shakespeare Company manages
three theatres primarily dedicated to his plays. An annual proces-
sion of local dignitaries and schoolchildren commemorates
Shakespeare's birth and death on 23 April. Year-round, there is a
Shakespeare Hotel, and you can hire rowing boats named after
Shakespeare's heroines. Summer visitors can travel from
Birmingham on the steam-hauled Shakespeare Express, drink
Shakespeare-themed cocktails *al fresco* and observe street perform-
ers and living statues including a classic blanched Shakespeare's
Ghost (better known locally as Creepy Shakespeare).

The nearest equivalent to Stratford must be Haworth, the small
Yorkshire town made famous by the lives and deaths of the Brontë
sisters in its austere, graveyard-facing parsonage. Victoria Wood
once satirised Haworth in a sketch featuring a tour guide plugging
everything from 'Brontë video-games' to 'novelty tea-strainers'.
The sketch's title is 'Brontëburgers'; Stratford-upon-Avon once had
a real 'Judith Shakespeare Wimpy Bar'.[13] The Lake District thrives
on Wordsworth & Co; the National Trust curates the former homes

of writers from Beatrix Potter to George Bernard Shaw. One of my favourite London museums is the former home of a recently-married Charles Dickens and his wife; today, you can roam from kitchen to garret, via the bedroom where Dickens's teenage sister-in-law, Mary Hogarth, died in the author's arms.[14]

But fictional homes are far rarer. I now live and work in Oxford; when tourists visit the filming locations for *Harry Potter* or *Morse*, these are places they have seen onscreen, and their visits are a tribute to the actors as much as the characters. *Alice in Wonderland* may have been partly inspired by the architecture of Christ Church, where author Lewis Carroll was a tutor, but this is less interesting to tourists (and prospective students) than the fact that Christ Church's Hall and grand staircase were used as locations for Hogwarts in the Harry Potter films.[15] One bench in the Botanical Gardens commemorates the protagonists of Philip Pullman's *His Dark Materials*; one wall of Cardiff Bay's Mermaid Quay boardwalk is a dwindling (but still-curated) shrine to Ianto Jones, a fictional character from the BBC's *Doctor Who* spin-off series, *Torchwood*.[16] Far more extensive is London's Sherlock Holmes Museum, which commemorates its subject with impressive earnestness. A family tree hangs in one room; mocked-up props are presented as real artefacts from Holmes's career, and the commitment to verisimilitude is helped along by 'personal effects' taken from the 1984 Granada Television series. In front of the museum, a blue plaque above the door commemorates 'Sherlock Holmes | Consulting Detective | 1881–1904', emulating the English Heritage plaques identifying real historical personages.

Few characters have merited such close attention, combining biography, tourism, and heritage. That Sherlock Holmes does is perhaps not surprising. His source texts are numerous and (relatively) recent, he is located in a precise geographical area, and he visits several equally real locations. But step outside 221B Baker Street to view the plaque, and you're back amid the sandwich outlets, hotels, and luggage shops that dominate the area – and you also realise that the building supposedly marked 221B is actually 239. There may be a deerstalker in the Baker Street Tube mural, but Holmes must fight with Madame Tussaud's and the Planetarium for conceptual control of Marylebone Road.

Cults around characters have spiralled into small religions or 'fictive faiths', such as the Star Wars fans who claim 'Jedi' as their religion or the mid-2000s phenomenon of 'Snapewives', *Harry Potter* fans who constructed a mystical faith centred on the belief that they were married to the fictional character Severus Snape on the astral plane.[17] Such phenomena, however, lack the longevity and the geographically embedded nature of the Juliet cult: they have no 'Holy Land' beyond their source media. Hamlet – theatre's most famous character, and one who speaks more than three times as many lines as Juliet – is the focus of a certain amount of tourism at Kronborg Castle in Helsingør, Denmark, fictionalised as Elsinore. There have been films and theatre festivals there, but the castle website is also keen to stress the story of the legendary knight and national hero Holger Danske.[18]

Juliet's mythos exceeds that of all these characters. Today, she dominates Verona, which has become Italy's city of romance: not Romeo and Juliet as dynamic devoted duo, but Juliet alone. As well as Juliet's house, you can visit her supposed tomb, La Tomba di Giulietta, in the now-deconsecrated church of San Francesco al Corso. On my way there, I pass a café selling themed sandwiches: a 'Romeo' or a 'Giulietta', both of which contain ham, mozzarella, and tomato, except – mysteriously – the Romeo has cured ham and costs twenty cents more.[19] The café is the only place in Verona that thinks Romeo is worth more than Juliet – at the tomb, he is only mentioned (briefly) in the gift shop. Otherwise, he is significantly less important than the security lockers, the wedding room, and the signs for the loo. It is Juliet's tomb we crowd in to see, the strange, empty sarcophagus somewhere between a basin and a manger; it is Juliet's dead, beautiful body that's so strikingly absent. Two churches – the deconsecrated Church of St Francis and the Basilica San Zeno – have competing claims to the crypt where she was married. Verona has plenty more to offer engaged tourists – Castelvecchio, its medieval castle, and the spectacular Roman amphitheatre – but Juliet is the city's main attraction. Because of her, you can attend a different promenade production of the play every night of the week. Because of her, you can wear virtual-reality spectacles in a cellar and follow the story in eight languages across a digital performance in five damp rooms. You can buy sweets with Juliet's name on and have a civil wedding in the Fresco Museum adjacent to her tomb. You can pose on her balcony, or write her a letter.

It's all the more astonishing given that not only was Juliet Capulet fictional, but Shakespeare – unlike Arthur Conan Doyle, who lived and worked in the same city as his creation – never visited Italy. The evidence is all over Shakespeare's plays, in his atrocious knowledge of Italian geography. In his first play about Verona, the early effort *Two Gentlemen of Verona*, he gives the landlocked city a coast and has a character sail by boat from there to Milan – another landlocked city, 105 miles away along the Roman Via Gallica.[20] Other plays contain similar geographical howlers: 'Bohemia' in *The Winter's Tale*, modern-day Czechia, doesn't really have the depicted coast, and Delphi lies on the slopes of Mount Parnassus, rather than being an island.[21] Even when Shakespeare wrote about Venice, Italy's most cosmopolitan city, he only knew the basics. Gondolas, a Duke / Doge, and the Rialto bridge? Yes. The fact that Shylock, as a Venetian Jew, would have lived in the ghetto? No.[22] Shakespeare builds an impressionistic Italy, a Verona characterised by the ideas and legends that were filtering back to Britain at the end of the sixteenth century.

Just before Shakespeare created *Romeo and Juliet*, his friend and former collaborator Thomas Nashe addressed Italy in *Pierce Penniless* (1592) as 'the academy of manslaughter, the sporting place of murder, the apothecary shop of poison for all nations': a pretty good description of the play's violent, masculine Verona, with its brawling adolescents, its druggist friars and – in nearby Mantua – a literal 'apothecary shop of poison'.[23] Equally, the other half of Shakespeare's gendered vision – female seclusion and intense religiosity – also reflected early modern England's popular impression of life in the Veneto. Thomas Coryat, discussing the gentlewomen of neighbouring Venice, commented that you almost never *saw* them, except on the odd gondola excursion: Venetian men 'coope[d] up their wives alwaies within the walles of their houses', except for public religious events like 'the solemnization of a great marriage' or, less edifyingly, 'the Christning of a Jew'.[24] Juliet similarly ventures outside her parents' house only to receive the sacraments: confession, marriage, burial.

In fact, Shakespeare makes Verona even more restrictive for Juliet than his predecessors did. Brooke, his source, named Capulet's castle 'Freetown', anglicising Painter's earlier version, 'Villafranca' (named for a commune outside Verona, giving the text a spacious feel). 'Freetown' is only referred to in Shakespeare's unfree Verona by the Prince as 'old Freetown, our common judgement place', where he will meet Lord Montague (1.1.87–90).[25] Freetown, once Juliet's ancestral home, becomes for Shakespeare the site of a justice to which she will never have access. Romeo is free-ranging, evading his parents, lurking in a 'grove of sycamore' (1.1.108–9), and infiltrating his enemy's party. When exiled to Mantua, he is back within seventy-two hours. Juliet's parents have spent time in Mantua, too, during her babyhood (1.3.29); Lady Capulet has an ally there whom she considers enlisting to poison the banished Romeo (3.5.87–91). Juliet, meanwhile, is 'a stranger in the world' (1.2.7) – a world so unfree and so intensely religious that she has never seen her hometown's eligible aristocrats, only leaving her parents' house for church. No wonder she doesn't make it to Mantua. Also unsurprising, perhaps, is the fact that Romeo doesn't have the wit to accept Juliet's early offer to 'follow you, my lord, throughout the world'. Instead, the world has followed her to Verona.

For four centuries, travellers have visited Verona to discover Juliet: her house, her tomb, her city. At this point, it's important to remind ourselves once more – because Verona does its best to forget – that Juliet Capulet never existed. The first writer to mention a Giulietta was Luigi da Porto, author of the prose story *Historia novellamente ritrovata di due nobili amanti* ('Newly found story of two noble lovers', posthumously published in 1531), which anticipates many of the features of the English texts of Painter, Brooke, and – ultimately – Shakespeare.

Da Porto seems to have based his narrative of Romeo e Giulietta partly on an old Sienese tale, and partly, perhaps, on a thwarted love for his distant relative Lucina, to whom he dedicated the story.[26] However, Lucina was no Juliet; she survived to marry another man, and both Lucina and Da Porto were from Udine, 140 miles from Verona and close to the Slovenian border. Da Porto set his story in the early 1300s, when Verona was ruled by Bartolomeo della Scala, due to the latter's associations with Dante. Dante also depicted two feuding families, the Montecchi and Cappelletti, in the *Purgatorio* (6.106–7).[27] These were real historical factions in thirteenth- and fourteenth-century political rivalries, but while the Montecchi were based in Verona, the Cappelletti were from Cremona, sixty miles south-west. There is no record of any romantic tragedy between the children of the faction, or of any girl named Juliet.[28]

Da Porto's tale proved popular. In the early 1590s, Veronese gentleman Girolamo dalla Corte published the first *Istoria di Verona*, including the story of Giulietta Capuletti and Romeo Montecchi. Inspired by both his uncle Gerardo Boldiero's 1553 poem, written under the female pseudonym 'Clizia', and Da Porto's prose version, Dalla Corte also dated the lovers' deaths to 1303 and linked several real-life locations to the story.[29] The Friar, named as Friar Londardo da Reggio of the Minor Order of St Francis, marries and buries Juliet at San Francesco al Corso, the location that is visited today as her tomb.[30] Romeo murders Tybalt 'not far from the de Borsari gate, towards Castelvecchio': the only Veronese location *not* identified with Juliet in Dalla Corte's tale – and, perhaps not coincidentally, the only one the city does not commemorate today.[31]

Three minutes' walk from Casa Giulietta is the fortified Casa di Cagnolo Nogarola, house of the last heir of the medieval Nogarola family, who served the ruling Scaglieri dynasty in the 1300s. The fourteenth-century palazzo has a crenellated façade, a long balcony and a private courtyard. It's also identified as the home of Romeo and the Montagues, indicated both on the road sign ('Casa di Cagnolo Nogarola, detto [called] Romeo') and on a graffitied plaque quoting from Act 1 of the play. Nobody cares. Tourists barely pause before visiting the Gothic tabernacles of the Scaglieri tombs further down the road. The house remains in private hands, closed and not immortalised by souvenirs.[32]

Dalla Corte describes Romeo and Giulietta being buried in an above-ground tomb of *pietra vivia*, or bare stone.[33] He recalls seeing the tomb 'repeatedly' being used as a well-trough for poor Franciscan pupils, and being shown by his uncle a place in the wall from which this tomb – along with some ashes and bones – had been removed 'many years ago'.[34] Two hundred and fifty years later, the novelist Charles Dickens echoed Dalla Corte's description when he viewed the 'little tank, or water-trough', which a 'bright-eyed woman' identified as 'La tomba di Giulietta la sfortunáta' ('the unfortunate') in 1844. By this point, all associations with Romeo had been dropped.[35]

Sure enough, the sarcophagus you see today does look like a large, rough-hewn bathtub, weathered enough to have seen four and a half centuries of continuous pilgrimage.

Even aside from the fact that the lovers didn't exist, there's a big problem with the tomb. In 1726, John Breval visited Verona as part of a Grand Tour later recorded as one of the eighteenth century's most influential travelogues. By then approaching fifty, Breval had lived the life of a picaresque hero, expelled from his Cambridge fellowship for beating up his mistress's abusive husband. He had a short-lived army career before setting up as a pseudonymous writer of drama and verse. When not feuding with Alexander Pope, Breval was travelling tutor to George, Viscount Malpas, with whom he toured Europe. According to Malpas's brother-in-law Horace Walpole (a flamboyant Gothic novelist who became Breval's friend), Breval found time alongside his pedagogical duties to seduce a nun in Milan and marry her in Rome – none of which (unfortunately) makes it into his book. In Verona, Breval heard from his tour guide a story similar to that of Dalla Corte, including the tomb's rediscovery by workmen. Connecting it with Shakespeare's 'celebrated story of *Romeo and Juliet*', Breval visited San Francesco al Corso, but claimed that 'what became either of the Stone Chest or the Ashes that were in it, is what I never could learn', suggesting the sarcophagus had disappeared.[36] Other accounts of Verona in the decades preceding Breval's visit – including that of poet and Shakespeare adaptor John Dryden – fail to mention Juliet or the tomb.[37] This might indicate disinterest or ignorance, however unlikely with Dryden, but Breval's account asserts positively that the tomb is not there.

Did the same chest reappear after 1726? In 1793, when the well-connected English gentlewoman Mary Carter told her friend Lady Nelthorpe that she had 'been a pilgrimage to Juliet's tomb', she left open the question of what precisely she saw there.[38] The tomb Dickens saw in 1844 clearly had a similar shape to Dalla Corte's 'water-trough'. But there's another issue. In 1812, Lord Byron's friend John Cam Hobhouse stole a souvenir 'chip of red marble' from the tomb. Although the sarcophagus tourists see today is red, Dalla Corte merely described a tomb of *pietra viva* – bare stone – in 1594. Other sixteenth-century references to *pietra viva* clarify that

Dalla Corte's contemporaries and neighbours in the Veneto region typically use it to describe stone that's *white*.[39] Size also matters. Girolamo dalla Corte's account emphasises that the lovers shared one piece of *pietra viva*, the above-ground tomb he saw used at the well. Wealthy medieval Italians like Romeo and Juliet had an average height of 172cm (men) and 160cm (women) – not much shorter than today's Italians.[40] There is no way two bodies could possibly fit inside the sarcophagus now displayed at the tomb. Did Girolamo see a larger one?

This isn't a question of historical veracity: no real Romeo and Juliet lay – separately or together – in a Veronese tomb. Nor is it surprising to find gaps in the history of a four-century fake. What's important is not that the tomb may have disappeared, as averred by Breval, but that at some point between 1726 and 1793, when Lady Nelthorpe saw it, it was *brought back*. By 1812 at the latest, it was the tomb we see today. If so, this was arguably not triggered by any resurgence of the homegrown Italian myth – after Dalla Corte, the story was mentioned briefly within Italy in a handful of seventeenth-century poems, but there was no major new Italian work until the late 1800s – but by enthusiasm for Shakespeare's play.[41] Over the second half of the eighteenth century, *Romeo and Juliet* returned to Italy, initially in French adaptations, and then in Italian translations of the French. One, by Giuseppe Ramirez, was called *Le tombe de Verona* (*The Tombs of Verona*, 1789). Operas and operettas followed.[42] Simultaneously, the Grand Tour and the vogue for European travel were bringing British tourists to Verona – and with them, their homegrown enthusiasm for Shakespeare's heroine. These tourists wanted only one tomb. By the time Mary Carter visited in 1793, and as others including Byron, Hobhouse and Dickens followed her, Dalla Corte's joint burial had become 'Juliet's tomb', and, as Carter noted, a visit was a 'pilgrimage'.

Enthusiasm for visiting Juliet grew through the late eighteenth and early nineteenth centuries. Mary Shelley's account of the tomb begins with scepticism but ends in spiritualised reverie. She has 'little doubt' that Juliet 'lived and died', but thinks the tomb's location 'not likely'. Nevertheless, she is beguiled by the local colour, concluding that 'a garden, with its high antique walls, its Italian vegetation, and the blue sky, cloudless above – was a scene familiar to Juliet; and her spirit might hover here, even if her fair form was sepulchred elsewhere'.[43] Visitors' responses to the tomb were increasingly emotional. The actor William Macready, like Shelley, thought the tomb was probably 'fabulous' but 'stood like a fond and credulous pilgrim before [Juliet's] shrine', imagining her 'perfections'.[44]

Other travellers went further. Two nineteenth-century anecdotes circulated about women who actually climbed inside the tomb. French traveller Jacques Augustin Galiffe heard in 1816 the story of a lady who 'lay herself at full length in this tomb, like a monumental figure, with her hands piously crossed on her bosom'; however, since 'it is dangerous to tempt the devil, and especially in a monastery [. . .] a sudden gust of wind so disarranged her undefended garments, as to cause no slight confusion to herself, and some scandal to half a dozen male and female friends who accompanied her'.[45] By the mid-century, novelist William Harrison Ainsworth described a Juliet fan found 'half dead and in a state of ecstasy – in a white muslin morning dress and satin shoes – in the tomb itself'.[46] Both stories are about Englishwomen – and both, too, have a distinctly sexual element, from the dishevelled Georgian lady, suddenly exposed, to the Victorian girl's 'state of ecstasy', dressed in thin bridal white. That sex comes into this is not surprising; after all, both Capulet and Romeo imagine Death seducing Juliet. What the Englishwomen who climbed into the tomb reveal – especially Ainsworth's heroine, found in an ecstatic, 'near-dead' state – is the possibility of reclaiming Juliet's silent passivity as a consummation devoutly to be wished, a sexual surrender permissible by the national poet. Even if purely fictional – designed to ridicule Englishwomen as especially superstitious, sentimental and sexual – the stories associate Juliet with a powerful and aspirational emotional experience.

Today, plaques engraved with English and Italian quotations from the play build the emotional atmosphere around the tomb. Statues of Diana and Temperance, strongly resembling Costantini's Juliet and her Marian sisters, create a pantheon of female saints, preparing us for the beauty of a close encounter with the Capulet heroine. 'Here lies Juliet,' insists one plaque close to the crypt: all the plaques quote Romeo, in whose steps we walk as we approach the tomb, a 'pilgrim' at her 'shrine' (1.5.90–1). Shakespeare's play primes us for pilgrimage; Romeo's final pilgrimage, for his final kiss, is towards Juliet's tomb.

And then: nothing. Inside the crypt is an empty, heavily-chipped sarcophagus, without any of the ashes and bones Geraldo Boldiero saw, but with plenty of lumps gouged out of its edges. Barriers prevent either climbing into the sarcophagus or removing chunks from the stone in order to make souvenirs: a fashionable nineteenth-century practice that saw Napoleon's widow wear bracelets contain-ing stone from the tomb.[47] Byron, following Cam Hobhouse's example, also stole bits for his daughter and nieces.[48] The tomb is, indeed, more like a washing-trough, or perhaps a large bathtub, than anything else. Its emptiness is inevitable, but also – after the build-up – disturbing. Italy is a country that displays in its churches some of history's most famous human remains, many of them female. Seventy miles away, in Venice, tourists can see the silver-covered face and claw-like, skeletal feet of St Lucy in her chapel at San Geremia. Until 1955, you could scrutinise the rotting skull itself.[49] Tuscan pilgrims have St Zita of Lucca, whose flower-decked, open-mouthed skeleton leaves the Church of San Frediano each April to be touched by the pious.[50] Rome is full of holy female corpses, from the wax-covered Blessed Anna Maria Taigi, formida-ble despite her frilly white bonnet, to St Paula Frassinetti, whose corpse was washed in carbolic acid and looks exactly how you'd think.

Shrine-visiting in Italy is all about the presence: the leathery face; the phial of blood; the wax hand – cut away like St Vittoria's – to reveal the skeleton beneath; the nun's habit falling away from the tiny brown hands of St Rita of Cascia, mummified in her Umbrian tomb. The cult of saints' bodies is particularly crucial to Italian Catholicism, dating all the way back to Christianity's status as a persecuted religion in the first four centuries AD. In that period, Christians hid the bodies of their martyrs, carefully preserving them in catacombs.[51] After the Roman Emperor Constantine I converted to Christianity and passed the Edict of Milan in 313 AD, legalising the religion throughout the Empire, these corpses were brought to the surface. The exhumation of St Zita allegedly cured the blind, the paralysed, the infertile and the mute.[52] 'Martyria' – altars, then churches – were built around them, to preserve and honour the martyrs' bodies; even the dazzling St Peter's Basilica in Vatican City began as a tiny, secret oratory built over St Peter's subterranean grave. In 828 AD, two Venetian merchants stole the body of St Mark from Alexandria, over whose remains Venice then founded the Basilica and the eponymous square.

Hundreds of cults emerged around saints' bodily remains.[53] There was also a particular interest in mummifying female saints in Umbria and Tuscany, around the period when the Juliet legend emerged in Siena, before migrating to Verona.[54] Writer Elizabeth Harper explains that for centuries, until the late 1800s, ordinary Italian parish churches buried worshippers inside their church buildings rather than in cemeteries. In southern Italy, mummification was common. People lived and prayed close to the bodies of their dead ancestors. Today, Italy has more saints than any other nation, thanks in part to a tradition of forming cults around the beloved dead and campaigning for their canonisation. Historian Emily Guerry explains that there is 'something deeply ancient and site-specific' about the cults of saints' bodies; Harper adds that wild celebrations of a local patron saint can mean nothing to the next village or town. When so many Italian cities have holy corpses in coffins filled with lace, wax, bones, and silver, it's astonishing to remember that Juliet, Verona's patron saint of love, has an empty coffin at the centre of her city-sized shrine.

Perhaps it's easier that way. A far more recent icon, Eva Perón, First Lady of Argentina and official 'Spiritual Leader of the Nation', died in 1952; her embalmed corpse was hidden, brutalised, and temporarily stolen. The corpse was buried under a fake name in Milan in 1957, then exhumed in 1971 and flown to Madrid, where Juan Perón and his new wife displayed Eva in their dining room. Meanwhile, graffiti was appearing on Buenos Aires walls – *Where is the body of Eva Perón?* – and Péronist guerrillas had murdered an ex-president responsible for her corpse's disappearance.[55] In 1974, Eva Perón was repatriated, re-embalmed for a final time, and finally buried in Buenos Aires. The crypt's underground chamber is billed as 'capable of withstanding any bomb attack, even a nuclear one'; the multiple locks and alarms recall a maximum-security prison cell, not only for keeping others out but also for keeping Evita locked in. The design, say experts on Perón's legacy, 'reflects a fear that the body will disappear from the tomb and that the woman, or rather the myth of the woman, will reappear'.[56] Sacrilegious though the thought may seem, few things have caused more upheaval in the world than an empty tomb.

Verona is a city that tries to resurrect Juliet: in its statues, in its theatres, and in the persons of its romance-loving pilgrims, encouraged to pose on her balcony. Never mind that Juliet never existed. Never mind that if there were ever bones and ashes in the chest, they belonged to someone else entirely and were sluiced away in a hot sixteenth-century summer, in the washing-trough of the poor pupils of St Francesco. What remains is a sarcophagus empty of bones but full of mystery. No wonder some nineteenth-century travellers occasionally felt compelled to climb inside.

Visitors to Juliet's tomb are also participating in an alternative tradition. Those who study travel and exploration describe 'dark tourism': the practice of visiting sites of atrocities or disasters, ranging from the location of a single violent death to mass extermination.[57] Juliet's tomb is not only the site of her burial, but of her suicide. It may be fictitious, but arguably that only makes the practice of pilgrimage more bizarre. After all, many of the most horrific and disturbing sites visited by travellers are visited precisely because of the real atrocities they represent. I am discussing these sites of real suffering not because I want to imbue Juliet's fictitious death with an iota of these places' – and their victims' – tragedies, but because I think it throws one aspect of Juliet's tomb into stark relief.

Among the most difficult death-related locations to visit are the sites of Nazi death camps. These are rightly recognised as formative sites of moral learning and commemoration – for Jewish visitors, there's a powerful religious or familial element to the travel. For Gentiles, there's the cautionary and unforgettable evidence of where fascism has led. But other locations are far less didactic, associated with prurience or ghoulishness – the Hollywood tours of dead celebrities' homes, for instance, or the Jack the Ripper walks that visit the 1888 murder sites in Whitechapel, East London. Some sites of tragedy are highly developed: the footprint of the World Trade Center, now the 9/11 National Memorial Museum, is one of Manhattan's most-visited sites, with eight acres of landscaped memorial glades, waterfalls, and 11,000 square feet of museum space. Even before the redevelopment, Ground Zero was a sufficiently popular site that city authorities built a viewing platform on which tourists paid to spend thirty minutes viewing the wreckage, deeply offending relatives of those killed in the terrorist attack.[58] By contrast, the Northern Irish tourist board hesitates to promote tours of the Falls Road, the epicentre of conflicts between Irish republicans and the Royal Ulster Constabulary during the Troubles; nevertheless, tours are easily organised by phone or email.[59] Some sites reveal marginalised histories, while others are founded on misconception. The 1967 car crash death of actress and sex symbol Jayne Mansfield – one of the mid-century 'crash-and-burn blondes' whose glamorous careers ended in tragedy – became notorious enough to prompt several roadside memorials partly because of the urban legend that the accident decapitated Mansfield. In fact, her wig came off.[60]

If dark tourism sounds like a modern phenomenon, it isn't. Places of death and violence, such as gladiatorial arenas, catacombs, martyrdom sites, and the ruins of Pompeii, were all tourist destinations by the early 1800s, when Juliet's house and tomb were firm fixtures on the Italian Grand Tour. Visitors to Britain could also see the Tower of London, the shrine of Thomas à Becket, and Marie Tussaud's travelling exhibition of wax heads, modelled on newly-guillotined victims of the French Revolution. Today, many sites of atrocity are carefully curated and extensively interpreted, and visitor experiences are tightly controlled, but uncertainties and concerns about how to behave – and feel – persist. Long-term anxieties over appropriate behaviour at concentration camps led, in 2019, to official condemnation of photographs on the railway tracks at Auschwitz.[61] Visitors to the six Rwandan Genocide Memorials, commemorating the Rwandan Tutsi massacred by Rwandan militia in 1994, have described uncertainty about how to move through one of the starkest commemorations of conflict. The museum in Murambi includes displays of hundreds of murdered Rwandans' corpses. Partially decomposed, partially preserved in lime, the whitened and often visibly mutilated bodies are laid out on tables. Visitors often struggle to navigate the display. One described the 'discrepancy between her visitor group's behaviour, who repeatedly felt compelled to "pause" for respectful silent contemplation, and

the guide's rushing them on to see all the rooms [. . .] as if to emphasise the enormity and incomprehensibility of the scale of the tragedy'.[62] Just how long should visitors spend looking at each exhibit
remembering the dead? Even in Christian tourism, where contemplating the martyred or massacred is pretty central to the project –
no Catholic contemplating the feet of St Lucy or the eye sockets of
St Catherine would think they were enacting *dark tourism* – uncertainties abound. Aged eighteen, I shuffled through the Vatican
Grottoes to see the first of the final resting places of Pope John Paul
II. A few queue-loops before the grave, the nun waiting ahead of me
suddenly dropped to her knees in prayer. I waited. So did we all.
Behind me, the waiting crowd (many of them also nuns) grew
restive. After what length of time is it appropriate to queue-jump
the devoted?

Juliet's tomb does away with these doubts. She has no descendants to offend, no sensibilities to outrage, and apparently no prob-
lematic allies to cancel. The leading lady of the world's most prestigious playwright, she is the highest-culture answer to accusations
of prurience: the one dead teenage girl it's actually highbrow to
fancy. The statue-lined cloister, the shadowy vault, and the Latinate
tombstones provide you with the full spooky self-indulgence without any need to imagine a real child stabbing herself to death.

Gradually, though, Victorian travellers' enthusiasm for the tomb
waned – not for the concept of the grave, but its authenticity. By the
late nineteenth century, the now-damaged sarcophagus had been
moved underneath a portico, derided as 'a sort of cheap, two-storey
brick shed', and scepticism and distaste were reinforcing each
other.[63] Leading Shakespearean actress Mary Anderson described
the coffin as 'palpably spurious', but seems to have been more troubled by the 'disenchanting' leavings of other tourists.[64] One
American author found the sarcophagus 'really strikingly like a
large bathtub'.[65] English writer Grant Allen condemned tourists for
'weep[ing] over the sham tomb where Juliet never lay – the stone
coffin, in all probability, of some sleek provincial Roman magis-
trate'.[66] The house, too, was deteriorating; visitors found it in 'sad
decay', a 'third-rate Italian inn'.[67] Victorian tourists were openly
racist and classist in their response to the Veronese, disgusted by the
intrusion of contemporary poverty into their fantasy of the

aristocratic past. John Ruskin, who adored the architecture but hated the people, wrote with full Victorian bigotry of 'the vilest wretches of ape-faced children' he saw on Veronese streets; London journalist George Sala called the locals 'dirty, lazy, good-for-nothing'.[68] Dirt recurs: one 1877 American visitor recoiled from the 'two dirty, lounging men smoking in the shade of an angle of a staircase' outside the property, and from the 'slattern, sore-eyed woman with a baby in her arms, who came and asked alms of us'. Instead of a balcony, travellers found 'an old ruined window', and deplored not only the 'heap of rubbish' in the courtyard but 'the smell of garlic, too – faugh!'[69] On the street, 'dirty children swarm[ed] round the gaping tourists' of 1906.[70]

In 1894, the Veronese municipality purchased Juliet's tomb, followed by the house in the summer of 1905; the latter cost 7,500 lira.[71] Initially, nothing changed. Soon, however, the entire country would change beyond recognition.

★

The late nineteenth century was a terrible time for Verona. Successive Napoleonic and Austrian occupations had impoverished the city-state, which was 'pitiably neglected and dilapidated' by the time it joined the kingdom of Italy in 1866.[72] The struggle continued after unification, as the Italian banking system floundered; hunger was rife.[73] Victor Emmanuel III, who succeeded as king in 1900, was timid, scholarly, and an unmemorable public speaker who shied away from political conflict.[74] Benito Mussolini, meanwhile, was a charismatic schoolteacher-turned-journalist who became editor of the socialist newspaper *Avanti!* in his twenties. When the First World War broke out, Mussolini abandoned socialism's official policy of neutrality and strenuously supported the war as a means of achieving class revolution. By November 1914, he had his own newspaper, *Il Popolo d'Italia* ['The People of Italy'].[75]

War worsened conditions in Italy. Food and medicine shortages meant one in every five babies died in infancy.[76] As after unification, Italy, 'the least of the great powers', suffered terribly after 1918, with a rise in preventable deaths from malnutrition and malaria. The historian R. J. Bosworth spells out the effect on a rising generation of nationalists, writing that 'the killing fields of war trained

Fascists to be Fascists'.[77] Liberal parents saw their Nationalist sons flock to Mussolini.[78]

Mussolini became Italy's prime minister in 1922. His regime killed up to 3,000 political opponents, ended the Italian free press, and brutalised Libyans and Ethiopians as part of the 'almost constant warfare' that characterised his tenure.[79] Within Europe, Mussolini's fascism became the 'principal precursor and model for Nazism'.[80] The student would inspire the master: from 1938, Italy passed its own far-reaching anti-Semitic laws in imitation of Hitler, and willingly followed Germany into the Second World War. From April 1941, Italy occupied the region of Yugoslavia that is today central Slovenia, where Italian troops deported, brutalised and murdered thousands of Slovenians, including in Italian concentration camps. In 1942, one Italian soldier boasted in a letter home: 'We kill entire families every night, beating them to death or shooting them'.[81]

Verona loved the fascists. The Veronese were early adopters: by March 1921, there were 3,000 party members in the city, far more than the 1,480 in Rome and 500 in Florence.[82] When Italy surrendered to the Allies in 1943, the North remained a Nazi puppet state – the Saló Republic (RSI), still headed by Mussolini. So loyal to the fascist cause was Verona that the November 1943 congress to set out the RSI's ideology was held there, and its results were called the 'Verona Manifesto'.[83] One of the RSI's first actions was to declare Jews enemies of the nation, helping the Nazis deport around 7,000 Italian Jews to their camps and approximately 30,000 political prisoners to Mauthausen and Gusen.[84] At the same time, Nazi forces inside Italy massacred civilians who were part of the anti-fascist Resistance.[85]

Fascism repaid the Veronese people's love and loyalty, not only in the person of Il Duce – Mussolini told the Veronese Fascist Party: 'You know that I adore Verona' – but also at the level of city planning and cultural identity: the literal bricks and mortar of Verona's daily life and world-famous heritage.[86] In the 1920s and 1930s, fascist Italy encouraged ordinary cities to hearken back to their Renaissance heritage, idealising the thirteenth to fifteenth centuries as a time of military strength, political independence, and cultural glory. In this version of history, Renaissance Italy was nationally united, and ideologically and racially pure, rather than the reality of a smorgasbord

of warring city-states whose multicultural cosmopolitans – especially in Verona's closest neighbour, Venice – helped kick-start the
financial and artistic revolutions that created modern Europe. At its
most extreme, fascist Italy's version of history had as much to do
with fourteenth-century Italy as Disney's theme park Fantasyland
resembles actual Alpine villages.

Romeo e Giulietta gave Verona the perfect legend through which
to live out its fascist destiny: a medieval romance among the
Veronese nobility, refashioned by the wider European Renaissance
into the greatest love story ever told. For a regime that had an
uneasy relationship with the Vatican – wanting Il Duce rather than
Christ to be the country's spiritual leader – Juliet was the perfect
saint, belonging to the city rather than to the Church. The seeds of
fascist interest in Juliet had been sown in the Italian nationalist
movements of the very early twentieth century, when local poet
Vittorio Betteloni wrote Zulieta e Romeo (1906), a version of the
legend in Veronese dialect. Betteloni defended the 'cult' of Juliet as
'popular in its truest meaning, that is, known and dear to every citi-
zen of whatever class or condition'.[87] Juliet was part of 'national
memories', as important to emotional as to rational 'reasoning'.
Juliet was powerful because she inhabited the 'heart'. She had both
local and international significance, making Verona important to
the entire world.

Three decades later, the architect of Juliet's fascist re-imagining
was a local historian and committed fascist, Antonio Avena, the
director of Verona's civic museums from 1915 to 1955. Like many
Italian fascists, Avena had a lifelong obsession with Italy's glorious
past, writing his university thesis on the fourteenth-century poet
Francesco Petrarca. Italian schoolchildren are routinely taught that
the Italian Renaissance began in 1341, when Petrarch was crowned
Poet Laureate at Rome.[88] Avena pushed fascist-led renovations of
Verona, using a regional political bulletin for engineers to publish
his views.[89] Between 1924–6, Avena totally remodelled the fourteenth-century Veronese castle fortress Castelvecchio, creating
fantastical battlements and crenellations, and demolishing the
Napoleonic block built during the French occupation.[90] Next, he
turned his attention to the buildings connected with Verona's most
famous daughter.

Avena's inspiration came not only from his political ideology, but from a greater dream-maker than even Shakespeare, or Il Duce: Hollywood. For five years, American producer Irving Thalberg had been pestering MGM studio head Louis B. Mayer to make a film of *Romeo and Juliet*. Mayer was dubious – the Great Depression in the USA had forced austerity on film studios, and he also doubted that the general public wanted to see Shakespeare onscreen. Mayer eventually agreed only because MGM's competitors were planning a film of *A Midsummer Night's Dream*. A delighted Thalberg appointed George Cukor as director, and cast his own wife, thirty-four-year-old Norma Shearer, as Juliet. Leslie Howard (better known for his later role as Ashley in *Gone With the Wind*), aged forty-two, was Romeo. The elderly British actress Constance Collier became Shearer's acting coach. Two East Coast academics, William Strunk of Cornell, and John Tucker Murray of Harvard, were enlisted as Shakespearean advisors.[91] And the MGM team visited Verona; the city appointed Avena as the filmmakers' guide and assistant, with special mandate from Mussolini's Minister of Propaganda to smooth their path.[92] There's some irony in the Fascists scrambling to welcome a production so defined by Jewish talent: as well as Cukor (the child of Hungarian Jews), Mayer (born Lazar Meir in Ukraine), and Irving Thalberg (the son of Jewish immigrants to Brooklyn), Leslie Howard was officially Leslie Howard Steiner, of Jewish ancestry via both parents, while Norma Shearer had converted to Judaism to marry Thalberg.[93]

MGM's team took 2,769 photographs of Verona, from every possible angle. Cukor wanted to shoot the film there, but Mayer thought it was too expensive.[94] 'Fair Verona' was rebuilt on the MGM backlot. The crew also took inspiration from beyond Verona. Juliet's tomb design came from the Chapel of St Giacomo, an early Renaissance church in Vicovaro, north-east of Rome.[95] Juliet's balcony was based on the exterior pulpit of the cathedral in Prato. The Capulets' garden, visible below the balcony, was inspired both by the courtyard of Villa Pia – a sixteenth-century mansion standing behind the Vatican – and Villa Falconieri, home to the International Institute of Educational Cinematography.[96] The IECI had been created partly as a propaganda tool; its presidents were all prominent fascists.[97]

Despite everything, Mayer's initial foreboding about the project proved correct. *Romeo and Juliet*, then the most expensive film in Hollywood history, made a box-office loss of £922,000. In America, *Romeo and Juliet* was a flop. Not so in Verona. On 5 March 1937, the film received its European premiere to an adulatory and invited Veronese audience, including local fascist officials. The daily paper *L'Arena* rejoiced that 'the city of Verona had every right to be the first to host the two lovers returning home and is profoundly grateful to MGM executives for having acknowledged its wish and made it come true'.[98] Two days later, Avena opened an exhibition in Castelvecchio, curating costumes and pictures from the film.

Looking around the castle, Avena must have felt delighted. His own architectural confection of medieval and Renaissance pastiche now hosted an exhibition based on a film with a similarly freewheeling, picturesque spectacle. The film had fired his imagination. In 1936, after Hollywood visited Verona, Avena won approval for a plan to renovate Juliet's house. A slightly nervous Alfredo Barbacci, the superintendent in charge of the local Preservation Agency, had told the Ministry of Antiquities and Fine Arts that the work was purely stabilising, and would not 'alter the architectural lines in the least' – in other words, Casa Giulietta would not be another Castelvecchio, now with cinematic sparkle.

Unfortunately for Avena, work on the house in Via Cappello seems to have been delayed for several years.[99] Undeterred, he applied for money to renovate Juliet's tomb at San Francesco al Corso. The tomb's restoration had long been on the fascist agenda. Five years earlier, journalist Giulio Barella had written to Roberto Paribeni, director of the Ministry of Antiquities, complaining of the 'painful impressions' he'd experienced on witnessing the tomb's neglect: 'It seems to have been abandoned!'[100] Barella was the managing editor of *Il Popolo d'Italia*, which was then near the zenith of its popularity.

Avena first refurbished the road leading to San Francesco – the Via delle Franceschine – with stone benches, fountains, and decorative trees. The agricultural markets there were removed, and with them the sounds and smells of horses and cattle, which an American visitor had likened to a 'county fair-ground' in 1909.[101] Avena's plans for the convent seemed very conservative: restore the only extant chapel and repair the ruined cloister, where the lidless sarcophagus had laid beneath a portico since 1868. Almost as an afterthought, the plans mentioned renovating the complex's basement and adding a staircase to reach it: nothing odd about that. A year after *Romeo and Juliet* premiered in Verona, the city council – presumably agreeing that stairs between storeys were a sensible architectural innovation – awarded Avena 109,000 lira (well over £80,000 today).[102]

The plans absolutely did not mention *moving the tomb*.

The lidless red sarcophagus suddenly found itself in a brand-new historic crypt, fashioned from that conveniently refurbished cellar. The architecture couldn't quite run to the elaborate Gothic groin vault knocked up by MGM, but there was a vaulted ceiling, a freshly minted twelfth-century early Gothic window, and arched doors with occasional Romanesque details. As in Cukor's film, Juliet's tomb now rested on a plinth. There were fake tombstones and an antique oil lamp was fixed to the wall.[103] All this happened in the summer of 1938, while Verona was hastily preparing for a visit by Il Duce himself. His visit on 25–6 September saw a rapturous reception by nearly 47,000 Fascist Party members, whom Mussolini addressed as 'my Verona [. . .] militaristic, Fascist in soul until the end'. He paraded along Via Mazzini, which had become a shrine to fallen soldiers and the 'martyrs' of the fascist revolution, the glorious dead young men who were now key to fascist ideology.[104] It's not clear whether Mussolini visited the tomb, but one thing is certain: Verona was celebrating the legacy of its dead boys at the same time as Avena was building the cult of its most famous dead girl.

Although loyal fascists, the local preservationists weren't impressed by the changes to the tomb. Poor old Barbacci had already complained in June about Avena exceeding the brief, and in late October, Barbacci exploded. The crypt was 'a ridiculous fake', created to lend the illusion of 'historic credibility' to a place of which 'good taste and culture' could not possibly approve. But then, oddly, he subsided. Having thoroughly exonerated his own superintendency, he admitted that 'if an error had been made' in moving the tomb, 'another major one, *and this time of a psychological nature*, would be made by restoring the tomb to the place it previously occupied' (emphasis mine).[105] Barbacci was finally admitting that

Juliet's story was now about more than architectural or historical fact. The myth was more important; it was about the minds of the Veronese people. For a superintendent dedicated to historical integrity, it was an astonishing admission. The rest of the letter subsided into a grumble.

Despite Barbacci's retreat, the message to Avena was still: 'don't do it again'. Avena seems not to have heard. By 1940, still riffing on Cukor's Hollywood film, he had completely remodelled Via Cappello 23. As on the big screen, the Capulets' house now became a palace (smaller, admittedly, than that in the MGM backlot) combining elements from wholly different eras: sixteenth- and seventeenth-century furniture, twentieth-century frescoes in a neo-medieval style, and a second-floor hall with a double-columned, internal arcade. This imitated not only Francesco Hayez's *The Last Kiss of Romeo and Juliet* – a painting from 1823 – but, more immediately, the double-columned interior seen in the film's Prologue, where actors ranged themselves between pillars like the figures in a Renaissance portrait. Outside, Avena ripped terraces and shutters off the late-eighteenth-century façade. Plain square windows suddenly acquired Gothic trilobes sourced from medieval buildings demolished elsewhere in the city. An old ground-floor window was bricked up and replaced with a small Gothic tracery rose window, complete with rounded quatrefoil – the same shape used for a prominently featured fountain in Cukor's film. Walls that had never previously had merlons – the distinctive M-shaped crenellations now visible in Verona (and, oddly, at the Kremlin) – acquired them, just as they had on screen, as a backdrop to the Hollywood lovers' tryst. And finally, the new balcony arrived. It was the first the house had ever had; local tour guides had previously had to spin yarns about a third-floor *terrasse* jutting into the narrow street above the gatehouse, which (as tourists must have realised) would have been equally unsuitable for an heiress's bedroom and for a discreet midnight tryst.[106] Avena had watched Norma Shearer address Leslie Howard from an imitation pulpit, so Avena gave Juliet a medieval tomb. The marble balcony on which tourists pose today is actually another sarcophagus, lifted from the museum holdings at Castelvecchio; an early twentieth-century image circulating online purportedly shows it lying among museum detritus in the castle courtyard. Unsurprisingly, the local preservation agency went mad again, condemning this 'affastellamento di forme' – a shoddy jumbling of different historical periods. But Avena won, and the 'affastellamento' remained.[107]

Like many middle-management fascists, Avena kept his power and influence after the war. He continued as director of Verona's civic museum, witnessing in 1948 the beginning of a Shakespeare Festival he'd been agitating for since the 1930s. The first production (guess which play?) was designed by Pino Casarini, who had produced the faux-Renaissance frescoes for the Castelvecchio.[108] Avena finally resigned in 1955, and persisted as a researcher through the twelve years of his generously-pensioned retirement. His Juliet renovations persisted, too. Despite minor cosmetic updates in the 1990s, and the addition of a fresco museum in the tomb complex, both Casa di Giulietta and Tomba di Giulietta are very much as Antonio Avena last left them. Indeed, the addition of a 2002 permanent exhibit at the house, curating costumes and a prop bed from Franco Zeffirelli's 1968 film, is *precisely* what Avena would have wanted; he had tried unsuccessfully to make MGM agree to a permanent exhibition of costumes from the Cukor film, to be housed in exactly the same location that the Zeffirelli exhibit occupies today.

★

Historians have long noted that Italy has consistently avoided confronting its fascist past: the local silence over fascism's centrality to the Juliet myth is key. Fascists made the Juliet that tourists in Verona experience today. In 2010, Hollywood revisited her myth in another film, *Letters to Juliet*, a blandly likeable 'Chianti country' rom-com starring Amanda Seyfried. In the film, Seyfried's heroine reunites long-lost lovers and finds her own soulmate as one of the 'Secretaries of Juliet', the women who answer lovelorn romantics' letters to Juliet. This is a real-life custom, and it's also the invention of a fascist: Ettore Solimani.

Although usually described simply as a photographer and chauffeur, Ettore Solimani was also a loyal and long-standing soldier to Mussolini, part of a regime 'unrestrained in extolling the virtues of war and killing, [. . .] the essence of Fascist manhood'.[109] The most detailed biography of Solimani notes that he fought for Italy during the First World War, and again in 'the Libyan conflict'. Details of his service are scant, but this 'conflict' was in fact the so-called 'pacification campaign' of 1932, when Italian forces committed war crimes against the Libyans resisting Italian colonisation. Mussolini's troops used illegal chemical weapons, executed civilians en masse and committed ethnic cleansing against 100,000 Bedouins, who were forced into concentration camps in the east of the country. Forty thousand people died there. Later, Solimani served a 'voluntary year' in the Second Italo-Ethiopian War of 1935–7, where Italian war crimes included the mustard gas-laced bombing of British Red Cross hospitals, Ethiopian villages, and Egyptian ambulance units.

By 1937, Solimani was back in Verona and unemployed. Early in the year, the wife of the Prefect of Verona, Marcello Vaccari, had been appalled by the tomb's state of disrepair while on a girls' trip with friends. Vaccari rang the mayor, lawyer Alberto Donella, to express his displeasure. A custodian was quickly headhunted; Ettore got the job on the recommendation of an unnamed 'dear friend', and received the tomb's keys on 12 April, in the presence of leading local officials, including Avena. The speed of the headhunting shows what excellent fascist credentials Solimani must have had. Vaccari was no ordinary official: historian Matteo Millan calls him a 'particularly brutal and violent former *Ras*' among the '*squadristra* prefects'. The *Ras* were local leaders who controlled the *squadristi*, Mussolini's Blackshirt paramilitaries. Whoever Solimani's 'dear friend' was, he must have wielded considerable power in Veronese politics.

Solimani's wife and children moved into the apartment that came with the job; Solimani paid for forty rose bushes, and also trained doves to land on the female visitors. After Avena remodelled the crypt the following year, Solimani developed a sideline in photographing couples kissing across the sarcophagus, and designed a souvenir pin with the motto: 'If you love, believe in Juliet'. When he began answering letters that arrived at the tomb, Solimani told writers he was 'the custodian of [Juliet's] tomb and of her legend'. Later, he admitted to *Oggi* magazine that Juliet was 'the woman of my dreams', which Signora Solimani must have really appreciated. Her husband, though, had effected a touristic miracle.[110] Three decades earlier, travel books had described the tourists who left cards in the 'sham tomb' as 'misguided' and Juliet's existence as 'highly problematical'.[111] Now, when Solimani re-installed a guestbook there, it was signed by luminaries including Greta Garbo, Laurence Olivier, Maria Callas and the Duke of Windsor (the former Edward VIII).

The Friedmans, authors of the fullest English-language account of Solimani, call the advice he gave to letter-writers 'pragmatic'.[112] More accurately, he parroted fascist views, expounding Mussolini's belief in 'returning women to home and hearth, restoring patriarchal authority, and confining female destiny'.[113] Ostensibly, Juliet makes a very bad fascist icon. She defies and deceives her parents, and defends Romeo for murdering her cousin, the other scion of the Capulets' tree. In loving Romeo, she rejects her family's values and ruthless struggle for dominance in Verona. But there's another way to see Juliet: as the ultimate faithful wife, angrier with herself for departing from her own doctrine of Romeo's perfection than she is with him about the murder he has actually committed. Her faithfulness to Romeo carries her beyond life into a violent death: a model for any fanatical fascist woman learning to be true to her cause. Solimani, as advisor, blamed women for their unhappy marriages, telling one 'she must understand the love of her husband in all its purity, considering it the sole purpose of her existence'; after all, a good wife 'supports, tolerates, and makes the peace'.[114] Another wife is told not just to think of herself as the wife of her husband, but also as his 'advisor, sister, friend, and even mother'.[115] In marriage, 'the greatest responsibility for this happiness depends on the woman'.[116] Solimani encouraged a quasi-religious devotion to Juliet, promising that Juliet 'from her sky of love' would 'continue to protect' the faithful.[117]

The heady mix of Shakespearean imagery and Italian martyria makes requests for Juliet's intercession inevitable. Verona's churches, like those in most Italian cities, are filled with ex-votos and handwritten prayer requests. In 1896, leading Shakespearean actress Mary Anderson recalled in her memoirs that Juliet's damaged coffin was 'half filled with visiting-cards of English and American tourists'.[118] The earliest nineteenth-century photographs of the tomb show ex-votos, visiting cards and postcards left there, indicating some kind of supplicatory tradition even before full letter-writing began.

Initially, the evolution of letter-answering into Club Giulietta sounds like just another story of patriarchal power and regional pride. Solimani's contempt for the 'stupid little girls' who idolised older boys, for whom 'two smacks would have been a better cure', was balanced by a possessive conviction that only *he* deserved the perfect woman: 'I love Juliet [. . .] not like Romeo, but better'.[119] After Solimani retired in 1958, he was replaced as Juliet's amanuensis by 'the professor', journalist Gino Beltarimini. Beltarimini would only answer letters in Italian: 'If I had her reply in English or use the Cyrillic alphabet [. . .] it would no longer be Juliet. Juliet is from Verona, and it should already be considered an infringement if I use Italian. The fair-headed Capulet spoke, and wrote, in Veronese'.[120] The next writer, Giulio Tamassia, was headhunted by his friend, Alfred Meocci, Verona's 'cultural commissioner', just as Solimani had been tipped for his post by friends in local government. Tamassia had co-founded a members' club in Juliet's name, but banned female members because 'their presence would have impeded one of the principal topics of conversation': namely, women.[121] Beltarimini had founded *Vita Veronese*, a paper on local affairs; Tamassia's club emphasised 'problems related to the city's cultural life'.[122] Relations with the city varied; despite this vision of a Veronese rather than a Shakespearean Juliet, in the mid-1970s, the Protocol Office assigned Juliet's correspondence to the artistic director of the summer theatre festival, whose unnamed secretary replied as 'Secretary to Juliet' for several years before Tamassia took over again. Tamassia lost control of Juliet's mailbag once more in the mid-1990s, when Veronese officials wanted to reclaim her for the city; cultural affairs staff were told to answer letters in English, using Shakespearean phrases.

When Tamassia regained the mailbag in the late 1990s, he moved the Club back to a building he owned, and organised a festival to mark Juliet's birthday – not 31 July, the date given in Shakespeare's play, but 16 September, calculated using the Da Porto text and cross-referenced with papal calendar reforms. Naturally, the festival is medieval-themed: yet another fourteenth-century fantasy. Today, Tamassia's Club and the city are good friends: the council covers postage for the Club's outgoing post, and the Club di Giulietta writing paper, on which the Secretaries respond to the lovelorn, is sponsored by Cesari, Verona's leading winemakers.

The Club, finally, is where Juliet's Veronese story changes.

★

Asking Juliet for advice should be a terrible idea. She's a thirteen-year-old girl from four centuries ago, who met and married an equally clueless teenager in under twenty-four hours. Even Disney now acknowledges, as a central totem of its blockbuster *Frozen* franchise, that hasty stranger-love is a totally doomed idea.

Online discussion of the Secretaries, and the only book dedicated to the club, sweetly describe how Giulio Tamassia recruited a willing daughter, a middle-school teacher, a trained dancer and a young multilingual Mexican who'd come to Verona to learn Italian as the core of the first group of secretaries. Imagining the Secretaries and their successors today, I cynically pictured a sorority of shiny-haired, clear-skinned maidens. I thought of them dressed somewhere between evangelical Christians and Sweet Valley High, wielding fluff-topped pens as they consoled lonely hearts. In their downtime, I thought, the Secretaries probably rode bicycles on Instagram and saved inspirational quotations on Pinterest. They shared well-lit Airbnb rooms and did a lot of laughing with salads.

In fact, on a warm Veronese day in September 2019, the secretaries were one sensible Italian woman and, well, me.

The Juliet Club is a sunny office opening on to a quiet courtyard, a few streets from Via Cappello. The room mixes the medieval and the modern: stone walls and antique cabinets interspersed with IKEA furniture and a refectory table. A shabby-chic green trunk seems theatrical; dotted around the room are promotional materials for old productions and festivals. An immense cupboard stores yet-to-be-answered letters, sorted by language, as well as the branded writing paper. In the back are metal bookcases, archiving the answered letters. Although some letters are posted locally, in red postboxes beneath the inscription 'Juliet lives here, write to her!' others arrive from all over the world.

Each letter I answer is an unhappy Valentine. Their authors fall into three overlapping categories: unrequited, undeclared, and unfulfilled. *Should I tell him?* is a common question. *When will I meet him?* is another. 'Family relationships deter me from speaking loudly', confides one lonely Australian. Many ask, *should I leave him?*, and I wonder about the significance of choosing Juliet to ask that question: Juliet, who stayed faithful to her man even when he murdered a family member. Some have clearly written before, like the adorable high-schooler – five different inks, love-hearts over the 'i' in Juliet – who writes 'with a heavy heart' and without chill to update Juliet that her beloved has 'MOVED. Not to a different school but a different STATE'. She laments her 'heart is frozen', in red gel ink for impact. A shy girl confides of her Facebook correspondence that 'kissy emojis aren't uncommon'. Others write as if to a deity: 'Pray for me, Juliet'; 'Send me a sign'. This isn't uncommon: over the years, letter-writers have described being 'uplifted by a divine force, ready to help me and sustain me', as they testify to their faith in 'the purest of women [. . .] I know that it is possible for you to do anything'. They 'turn to [Juliet] with faith, as to a saint'.[123] The Club's official anthology, *Letters to Juliet*, has plenty of these: 'My mum says you will not answer me, but I trust you,' writes one Hungarian girl.[124] Others in the archive are endearingly quotidian: Mina, writing from Lombardy in 1972, tells Juliet, 'I care about you like a sister', while Natalina, from Brazil, sends her 'a huge, warm hug'.[125]

My job is to reply to each new letter and annotate it with a summary. 'Needs to end relationship with boyfriend' is written more than once. I worry this is not on-brand for Ms Capulet. It is also probably not strictly how Christ Church imagined me using my research funding, en route from archival work in Florence to a visiting fellowship in Venice. It's possible to find some of Juliet's previous advice online. Some of it is in character: women are generally advised to stand by their men, and on occasion the creepiest excesses of fedora-tipping, wounded-knight self-pity are praised as truly romantic. 'Christoph' from Germany describes an 'Angel of the Night [. . .] a female Jekyll and Hyde' who locks him in 'a prison of the mind' because 'even her way of walking was a temptation'. He is bafflingly told by Juliet that his 'wonderful ode' means he 'deserves to be loved and worshipped'.[126]

But a lot of the advice is sensible. Rather than enlisting your priest in a death-faking escape plot, lonely people are told to 'volunteer for a local or overseas charity' to help them meet 'kindred spirits'. At times, the advice comes close to that of the brisk yet mumsy strictures of the women's magazine (Make Friends With Shared Interests), which is probably the best advice there is. There's quite a lot of stuff about loving yourself first, which straddles the line between good psychology and Pinterest (see above), but overwhelmingly, what the Juliet Club tells you is much less about Juliet and more about the correspondents themselves.[127]

Halfway through one morning, I ask to see the weirdest letter they've got. Immediately, Elena Marchi, my new boss, produces an enormous scroll from 2013, topped with a Sharpie-annotated, black-and-white photographic collage of places relevant to the author's beloved: perfect as an exhibit in a particularly frightening crime drama. Parts of the scroll are stitched together with red thread. The contents are a ramble about some previous encounter with 'Romeo and Juliet', and the letter-writer's love for a filmmaker called Seamus. We all laugh nervously (I google 'Seamus AND filmmaker AND murder' a few minutes later).

By this point in my secretarial shift, I'm dehydrated, and my inspiration is dwindling. I've found myself resorting to self-care clichés repackaged with a certain pastoral briskness. The truth is, I can rail against a bad relationship, but I'm not sure how you find a good one. I'm certain it's a numbers game, but I also believe in soulmates. I once matchmade so successfully it got me a godson, but never since. Doomed marriages blossom once I've disparaged them; divorces always shock me. I'm good at bolstering the heart-broken undergraduate (saying an unfaithful rugby player has a 'weirdly long face' seems disproportionately cheering), and at talking the big talk about plentiful fish in the sea, but underneath I'm caught in the same shifty perplexity as everyone who's found love. *I dunno*, I want to write, to Morocco and Mexico and Spain. *I made enthusiastic bad choices, then joined OKCupid. This won't help you navigate interfaith dating in Rabat, but then nor will snogging an enemy at your dad's masked ball.* A good relationship can only be described in terms of the happiness it brings, and what's more insufferable? Besides, I'm meant to pass as a dead thirteen-year-old who talks in iambic pentameter, not a thirty-something lesbian who says 'my wife' a lot.

Suddenly, we're interrupted by Americans following a Juliet itinerary with their tour group. Among Americans in Verona, if you're not a tanned study-abroad girl pensively journaling in a $100 sundress, you're a tour group: headphoned, lanyarded, pleated at every possible opportunity. They read over my shoulder while Elena explains the Club mission. They pick up the letters, moving slowly round the tables. Elena asks them their advice to young lovers.

'Don't waste your young life rushing,' one man says, after reading aloud the lament of the lovelorn teenager. I'm on board with that.

'Get a puppy,' snorts a woman. I flinch.

'Become a lesbian,' says another, which I think is – on principle – good advice (her husband disagrees).

'There's no such thing as true love,' announces a man with blue-jean slacks hitched to just beneath his armpits. Various dentures and baseball caps agree.

'These are pathetic,' his wife says, turning the pages of the letters. 'So melodramatic.' There is a collective contemptuous sneer.

These Americans have flown halfway round the world, presumably at great expense (to say nothing of the premiums on khaki-coloured leisurewear), to visit a city whose *raison d'être* is romance, and now they're deriding it. Many of them are here with spouses; many of them wear wedding rings; several of them have crucifixes and ichthys fish round their necks or pinned to their multi-zipped gilets. And they're laughing at love. Not sympathetically or nostalgically, but cruelly. As if loneliness and longing and the desire to give love are stupid. The tourists tell me that to wade through this 'garbage', I must be very patient (patience and I were never formally introduced), and then they leave.

I am suddenly in a terrible temper, and I think, *at least those who write to Juliet want love*. Their letters have flown round the globe to describe the kind of passion that changes lives. They haven't risked deep-vein thrombosis, mosquitoes and sunburn just to scoff. And, unlike the tour group, the Juliet Club doesn't sneer at same-sex love. It celebrates it. One man writes wanting to 'keep himself loyal' and settle down with a boyfriend. Jonathan from France marvels that 'such a guy has fallen for someone so plain and boring'. The Club's anthology even includes a letter from 'Mercutio', complaining of unrequited love for a distracted best friend: 'You might know him, his name is Romeo Montague'. Aina confesses from Delhi: 'I am in love with a GIRL, and in India lesbians are never heard of'. Sweetest of all is 'S', from China, who says that her beloved girlfriend is a 'moon shining in the night'.

I realise that these writers sound more like Juliet than those who reply to them in her name. Juliet, after all, is hyperbolic and prepared to love endlessly, telling Romeo:

My bounty is as boundless as the sea
My love as deep. The more I give to thee,
The more I have, for both are infinite (2.2.133–5).

She knows what she wants: marriage, the happy-ever-after craved by those brave enough to ask for it. She asks for advice and intercession. And, like her correspondents, she passionately wants to believe in a higher power. Juliet's experiences of that higher power shed light on what kind of a confidante she makes.

For much of the play, the higher power on which Juliet relies for guidance is the Catholic Church, in the form of its sacraments of marriage and confession, and its ordained representative, Friar Laurence. But doubt creeps in. When confronted with the possibility of taking poison, she does what Romeo never does and believes the Friar may be capable of murder to save his career. She asks,

What if it be a poison which the friar
Subtly hath ministered to have me dead
Lest in this marriage he should be dishonoured? (4.3.23–5).

When she drinks the poison, it is not out of faith in the Friar, but as a toast to her husband: 'Romeo, Romeo, Romeo! Here's drink. I drink to thee' (4.3.67). When she wakes in the tomb, she discovers rapidly that she is no longer a wife but a widow – Romeo is gone. Once more, the consolations of religion are offered to her, both the immediate assistance of the Friar and life '[a]mong a sisterhood of holy nuns' (5.3.157). This makes sense for a Catholic whose world – until recently – has been so defined by her faith. But Juliet rejects both the convent and the friar.

Romeo sees death as an eternal embrace with Juliet; he vows to 'lie with her', and dies 'with a kiss' (5.3.120). Juliet finds in his dead body only another failure of masculine foresight; he's drunk all the poison, he's (yet again) left her no way out, nothing to 'help [her] after' (5.3.164). The Shakespeare scholar Katherine Duncan-Jones called this Juliet's 'desperate rage with, and tragic alienation from her young husband'.[128] I think it's also the culmination of Juliet's alienation from, and rage against, all the characters of the play.

Her mother and the Nurse have both failed her in different ways. A further five characters, all men, have also forced Juliet to this point. Three of them – Romeo, Paris, and Tybalt – lie dead around her. Friar Laurence has abandoned her. The forces of the city are noisily massing, and clearly she cannot endure a reunion with the fifth man, her father, who is already hastening to the tomb. Alone in the dark, she remembers the words with which she comforted herself in Act 3, Scene 5: 'Myself have power to die'. She picks up a dagger and stabs herself with it. She dies without a prayer, without a word for Romeo, and without any attempt to embrace him. What Juliet learns in *Romeo and Juliet* is that you cannot rely on anyone. Her only higher power is herself.

Perhaps this is what qualifies Juliet, even as a fiction, to comfort the lovesick. Not because she is one half of literature's greatest love affair, but because that love takes her to the worst and darkest places in the world. Buried alive, distraught in a corpse-filled darkness, and betrayed by everyone she's loved, she endures agony in those few wretched minutes in the family vault.

For Verona, Juliet's death is a martyrdom and her glory that of a saint. Her myth sells condom packets and espresso cups, and hides its fascist past in plain sight. That Italy's most romantic tourist experience is the product of fascism should give us pause. Fascism is only a phase of Juliet's Italian story: Franco Zeffirelli, director of the play's most successful film adaptation, fought fascism alongside Italian partisans and the British Army. But that Verona's fascist makeover was inspired by Hollywood indicates how powerfully film narratives shaped the fascist imagination. Today, as a new generation slowly begins to confront Italy's shameful past, there is a chance that the nature of its tourist municipalities could be refashioned too. But it's a chance that Verona is unlikely to take.

In Verona, reading the newspaper in a café after working at the Juliet Club, the political landscape becomes depressingly clear. Verona remains a stronghold for ultra-conservative anti-immigration political groups, such as the Lega party. Local activist and author Emmanuele Del Medico calls the resurgence of Italy's far-right the 'Veronification' of politics, where ultra-Catholicism and right-wing nostalgia chase the same fantasy of 'restor[ing] a lost order of the past'.[129] This past looks a lot like Avena's: as one political opponent opined, after the Lega successfully sponsored a council motion to oppose abortion and fund anti-choice measures, 'in Verona, they have gone back to the Middle Ages'.[130]

But at the same time, Verona's tourism – its commercial lifeblood – relies on everything the far-right hates: the immigrants who helped translate Tamassia's letters, and the cosmopolitanism of the tourists who flock to celebrate their love. Today, gay and lesbian couples can even marry on the balcony at Casa di Giulietta. Perhaps not every same-sex couple would want to celebrate their love on a Catholic sarcophagus wall-set created by a local fascist, but it's nice to think how much Avena would have hated it. The Lega, too: councillor Alberto Zelger called gays and lesbians 'a disaster'.[131] Paola Bonatelli, an LGBT rights activist in Verona, says that the city's fascist past and far-right present are tied together by a 'black thread', still winding through the city streets.[132]

Perhaps the black thread will go on winding itself around Via Cappello. But perhaps the answer is to be found in a different courtyard and the small, sunny atrium where, at Club di Giulietta, all desires are known, and from whose Juliets no secrets need be hidden. The Club's anthology celebrates eighteen-year-old Haley's love for 'a joyful girl named Avi' alongside happily married Marisol, commemorating '22 years of marriage' to 'Erney Bosque [. . .] a Man among men'.[133] The Veronese Juliet will answer all letters. Perhaps not every religious believer has the same certainty about their prayers.

An early feminist critic of Shakespeare, the English suffragette Nora Stransom, wrote in 1914 that Shakespeare had depicted women as 'need-filling creature[s] [. . .] what Shakespeare would like the woman-thing to be'.[134] Verona shows us the needs that Juliet goes on fulfilling: romantic, mystical, commercial, and nationalist.

For the letter-writers, Juliet is a confection of mysticism, magic, romance and compassion; she is as personal as a guardian angel, and as anonymous as a priest behind a grille. The digital age is changing tourism, but the Veronese cult of Juliet still relies on 'need-filling' women – the anonymous 'secretaries' of Club di Giulietta who volunteer their labour to ensure that Juliet goes on performing her role of mystical confidante through the decades. Veronese writers such as Geraldo Boldiero and his nephew Dalla Corte created the myth of her grave, but Shakespeare gave us the language to call her a saint. Catholic history makes the phenomenon of Juliet's cult of sainthood peculiarly Veronese and, at the same time, the multilingual messages on the walls of her courtyard and in her mailbag show us that Juliet's appeal is universal. Italians made her, but Verona reminds you as nowhere else that Juliet belongs to the world.

6

Society's Child

If Shakespeare hadn't understood teenagers, we wouldn't have *Romeo and Juliet*. His plays are full of generation gaps: Prince Hal partying in taverns while his kingly father frets; Richard II horrifying his uncles with his decadence; a host of rebellious daughters defying paternal strictures about marriage. Even though we think of the delinquent teenager as a post-war phenomenon, Shakespeare's loveliest late play, *The Winter's Tale*, sees one father describe male adolescence as lasting from 'ten to three-and-twenty' and being good for nothing but 'getting wenches with child, wronging the ancientry, stealing, fighting' (3.3.60–1). By the time the 1960s came, intergenerational conflicts had already shaped the first half of the twentieth century, from women's suffrage and the Bright Young Things to – most tragically – the trauma of two world wars. These wars rocked the deference of the maimed young for their elders and, in the aftermath, poverty further sharpened divisions. Meanwhile, new cultural spaces – the nightclub, the dance hall – imported American culture via jazz and, later, folk music. But much more was still to come.

Here is one version of that story. It's one in which Teen Culture – a procession of Causeless Rebels, Teddy boys, Mods, Rockers, Haight-Ashbury flower children, and 1968 revolutionaries, placard-waving or disaffected, dropping out or turning out, but always dressing, reading, playing, and loving contrary to their parents' ideals – takes centre-stage through the fifties and sixties. In December 1944, *Life* magazine introduced its readers to the 'teen-age girl'. With Judy Garland as its cover girl, *Life* offered a profile that stressed group identity and its signifiers: girls for whom 'the most important thing in the world is to be one of a crowd of other girls and to act and speak and dress exactly as they do [. . .] a world of sweaters and skirts and bobby sox and loafers, of hair worn long, of eye-glass rims painted red with nail polish, of high school boys not yet gone to war'. But *Life* also called this 'a lovely, gay, enthusiastic, funny and blissful society' (describing adolescence as 'blissful' makes you wonder if the writers of *Life* had ever *met* a teenage girl). *Life* claimed that the world of the teenager was one 'still devoted to parents who are pals even if they use the telephone too much'.[1]

Soon, *Life's* profile felt hopelessly out of date. In 1953, J. Edgar Hoover warned of 'an appalling increase in the number of crimes that will be committed by teenagers in the years ahead'.[2] In the UK, the *Daily Express* coined the phrase 'Teddy boy' to describe the emerging Edwardian-pastiche sartorial subculture, and anxiety rose about teenage gang violence and vandalism, some of which was explicitly racist, as when white Teddy boys attacked West Indian immigrants in the 1958 Nottingham and Notting Hill riots.[3]

On both sides of the Atlantic, a new wave of dramas explored juvenile delinquency, in films including *Cosh Boy* (1953), *The Wild One* (1953), *The Boys* (1962) and the iconic *Rebel Without a Cause* (1955). Beautiful masculine protagonists, violent or vulnerable, depraved or deprived (depending on your point of view), became avatars of the new male rebellion. In British theatres, the man of the hour was John Osborne's Jimmy Porter, the sneering, spiteful, apparently captivating hero of *Look Back in Anger* (1956). Kenneth Tynan, *Observer* theatre critic, was so enthralled that he compared Porter to Hamlet in 'his flair for introspection, his gift for ribald parody, his excoriating candour, his contempt for "phoneyness", his weakness for soliloquy and his desperate conviction that the time is out of joint'. He gushed: 'I doubt if I could love anyone who did not wish to see *Look Back in Anger*'.[4] Shelagh Delaney's play *A Taste of Honey* (1958) depicted Jo, a working-class white girl who, pregnant by her Black boyfriend, defies convention to raise the baby along-side her gay best friend. When Tony Richardson directed a 1961 film version, The Beatles re-recorded the title song for their first album, *Please Please Me* (1963).

The sixties swung. The English-speaking press looked on in disapproval of this youthful rebellion against parental authority and the role violence played therein. Over time, fear of working-class gangs of juvenile delinquents – in 1959, a poll found that Americans were more worried about juvenile crime than about *open-air atomic bomb testing* – shifted towards distaste for the 'love generation' of the late sixties.[5] These were the hippies, artists, and student activists who rejected institutional hate and prioritised solidarity over hierarchy, fighting for civil rights and peace. In the eyes of their elders, young people deployed both love and violence in the wrong ways, whether they were working class, or – thanks to the growth of higher education and student grants – newly middle class.

But here's the other story. Not everybody aged thirteen to nineteen actually found themselves living a radically different kind of life overnight. Not everyone was a Mod or Rocker in radical new fashions; girls' magazines are full of complaints from 'out-of-town groovers', readers who lived hundreds of miles from Carnaby Street or the King's Road and were never likely to glimpse either.[6] Even as the women's liberation movement expanded, teen girls' magazines published recruitment ads for the nursing profession captioned 'Nurses Make the Best Wives!'[7] And when the hippie counterculture came, for every girl wearing a flower in her hair on the way to San Francisco in 1968, there was a girl writing in to *Mirabelle* to criticise whatever John Lennon had most recently done to his hair (i.e. grow and give up washing it). 'Yeuck!' concluded Karen from Worcester.[8]

In the performing arts, barnstorming new plays and films were far harder on their women than their men. In *Look Back in Anger*, Jimmy Porter coercively controls his wife, and when she dares to leave him, the play punishes her with sterility. The heroine of *A Taste of Honey* ends up back in her mother's clutches, after the latter expels the gay man with whom she'd planned to raise the baby on her own terms. Longitudinal studies of teenage girls through the sixties and seventies found that girls' 'central preoccupation' was 'to get married and have children', and most post-war teenagers expected to work in jobs similar to those of their parents, and to live modestly.[9]

The gap between the media obsession with and the reality of new teen subcultures (and their sizes) was enormous. And despite the best efforts of teenage aspirants, the gap between the swinging culture of Soho-Chelsea-Manhattan and everyday adolescent life was equally so. About as huge a gap, in fact, as the distance between

Romeo and Juliet and real-life love. But that's the point: myth is omnipotent. The adage that 'if you can remember The Sixties, you weren't there' is true. It's true because 'there' was a revolving free-love party featuring Jean Shrimpton, Pattie Boyd, a Beatle and a Rolling Stone, making the London sound in an E-type Jaguar slouching towards Woodstock while being photographed by David Bailey in a club owned by the Krays. *Vogue* editor Diana Vreeland called it the 'Youthquake', and we still imagine we can feel its vibrations.

The 1960s saw two film adaptations of *Romeo and Juliet*: *West Side Story*, the 1957 musical and 1961 film inspired by reports of juvenile gang violence, and Zeffirelli's 1968 film *Romeo and Juliet*, marketed by Paramount as the adaptation for 'The Love Generation'. Juliet's story has always been about how cultures deal with the idea of the girl-woman, and in the 1950s and 1960s, that meant reckoning with the real and imaginary icons of teenage girlhood. No other Shakespearean heroine could have so embodied the contradictions of the era. Juliet is a revolutionary who rejects the wars and wishes of an older generation, but who rebels in pursuit of the most conservative goal: early, virginal, and passionately monogamous marriage. She is both a bystander, doomed by the murder her husband commits, and the instigator of the marriage that binds them. She is very much a rebel with a cause.

The two screen Juliets in this chapter were in some ways very different. Twenty-three-year-old Natalie Wood, who played Maria (*West Side Story*'s Puerto Rican Juliet), was a Russian-born Hollywood actress and former child star 'not eager to play another ingenue'; Zeffirelli's Juliet, Olivia Hussey, was a fifteen-year-old model and stage actress with little screen experience.[10] Hussey faced particularly misogynistic and troubling treatment by the film's production and press, as she was sold simultaneously to teen and adult audiences. Meanwhile, Wood as Maria was Hollywood's ultimate erotic girl-woman, completing an arc of teen cautionary tales that she'd begun in *Rebel Without a Cause*: desirable and reprehensible in equal measure.

But *West Side Story* and Zeffirelli's *Romeo and Juliet* emerged in a period characterised by another formative concern: the post-war desire to find *new* things to do with Shakespeare. This was a desire not limited to the teams behind *West Side Story* and Zeffirelli: new theatrical institutions and methods were proliferating on both sides of the Atlantic. In Britain, this meant the Royal Shakespeare Company (founded in 1961) and the National Theatre (founded in 1963, and based at the Old Vic until 1976). Both had ambitions to represent contemporary Britain, but both 'new' institutions had long, intermingled histories. Their governors included dynastic philanthropists; their stars, like John Gielgud, Laurence Olivier, and Peggy Ashcroft, had already been onstage for thirty years, and could tell tales of Henry Irving and Ellen Terry (Gielgud was her great-nephew).

When Franco Zeffirelli cast the young, then-little-known Judi Dench as his first Old Vic Juliet in 1960, rehearsal photographs show that he performed every pose and movement for her to copy. This new director, the 'volatile young Florentine' who fascinated the press, did as much rehearsal-room acting as any Victorian actor-manager dictating the performances of his supporting cast.[11] Meanwhile, Leonard Bernstein, composer of *West Side Story*, wrote in his copy of *Romeo and Juliet* that the play was 'an out and out plea for racial tolerance', implying a radical adaptation.[12] The quartet of *West Side Story*'s creators – Bernstein, Jerome Robbins, Arthur Laurents, and Stephen Sondheim – were all queer sons of Jewish immigrants, whose families had fled oppression in Eastern Europe.[13] They still cast most of their Sharks as white actors in muddy brown-face, with a lighter-skinned Juliet who avoided any *actual* spectacle of an interracial relationship on screen and stage.[14]

The creations and receptions of *West Side Story* and Zeffirelli's *Romeo and Juliet* reveal both the drive to stage *Romeo and Juliet* and the convulsions these adaptations caused in the 1950s and 60s. Both films were marketed and received as strikingly contemporary. But while Zeffirelli's film used authentic Italian locations, and he himself was likened to 'a Renaissance Veronese', *West Side Story* was the first modern *Romeo and Juliet* adaptation interested in the dramatic possibilities of a feud-filled play-world beyond the sixteenth century.[15] James N. Loehlin, the finest writer on post-war adaptations and performances of *Romeo and Juliet*, describes in his recap of Cold War productions of the play how '[i]n the latter half of the twentieth century, *Romeo and Juliet* was transformed, in production and perception, from a play about love into a play about hate'.[16]

I would argue that this began with *West Side Story* and continued into Zeffirelli's film. One was set in gang-ridden Manhattan, and the other in Renaissance Italy. Nevertheless, film critics recognised that despite the 'velvet doublets and striped hose' of Zeffirelli's film, the issues were as modern as those explored in *West Side Story*. The walls of Verona became 'the Berlin Wall', and the Montague–Capulet feud seemed 'as pointless to Romeo and Juliet as the Cold War does to many of today's children'.[17]

The 'play about hate' and Juliet's place in it were both shaped by the need to bear witness to the Cold War and the aftermath of the world wars. When we think of how the imaginative medium of theatre responded to the horror of the Second World War and the apparent imminence of nuclear apocalypse, we often turn to new plays like Beckett's *Waiting for Godot* (1953) or *Endgame* (1957): plays of blasted landscapes, absurdity, comfortless post-apocalyptic rooms, unnamed diseases and isolated men.

Masculinity is important. Both *West Side Story* and Zeffirelli's *Romeo and Juliet* sideline Juliet; one reason why is that both conceive of violent conflict as essentially masculine. This would persist – in her 2003 book *Regarding the Pain of Others*, Susan Sontag, after a lifetime of writing in and about warzones like Vietnam and Sarajevo (of which more in the next chapter), would write that 'War is a man's game [. . .] the killing machine has a gender, and it is male'.[18] Jan Kott, the great twentieth-century Polish political activist and Shakespeare critic – the only Shakespeare critic to assume his readers 'will at some point or other have been woken by the police in the middle of the night' – wrote of tragedy and the grotesque as becoming particularly potent when 'established values have been overthrown, and there is no appeal, to God, Nature, or History, from the tortures inflicted by the cruel world'.[19] Kott wrote that at the end of *King Lear*, all that remains is 'the earth – empty and bleeding'.[20] Kott was most interested in Shakespeare's tragedies of kingship or the 'amazing and modern' political problem play *Troilus and Cressida*.[21] He writes dismissively of Romeo and Juliet's love; he calls their dialogue together 'just a bird's love song'.[22] But I think Kott's description of *King Lear* actually gives us a clue as to why *Romeo and Juliet* was the right play to capture the imaginations of post-war cinemagoers – and why its specific story of love absolutely failing to conquer hate was the right romance for a bitter, post-Holocaust, Cold War world.

When I read Kott's description of 'the earth – empty and bleeding', I remember Lord Capulet. He describes Juliet in Act 1 as 'the hopeful lady of [his] earth' because 'earth has swallowed all my hopes but she' (1.2.14–5).[23] In Act 5, he sees how that daughter 'bleeds': the dagger's 'house/ Is empty [. . .],/ And it mis-sheathed in my daughter's bosom!' (5.3.201–4). At the end of *Romeo and Juliet*, it is Juliet that lies empty of life and futurity, bleeding, beside the unblemished Romeo, in the vault that has swallowed her kinsmen, her marriage, and all her hopes of a future. After the Second World War, the figure of the teenager, blazingly romantic and insisting on the possibility of rebellious love, became the symbol of the rising generation. *Romeo and Juliet* sees that possibility destroyed. In its final moments, it feels a lot like a post-apocalyptic play, as the survivors stumble out into a morning where the sun has failed to rise (5.3.305). Perhaps, too, we can read the end of the play as its own crisis of witnessing: the desperate reiteration of what the audience already knows, the production of documents, the scrambling for witnesses as the sun rises reluctantly over Verona. The Capulets and Montagues may try to reinscribe Romeo and Juliet as a celebrated, recognised, official married couple, with their 'statue[s] in pure gold' (5.3.298), but the Prince knows that he's dealing with anything but a love story. 'See what a scourge is laid upon your hate,' he tells them (5.3.291), and the parties leave the stage not for a love-in but for an official inquiry: 'Go hence to have more talk of these sad things/ Some shall be pardoned and some punished' (5.3.306–7). The Prince's vow to lead his subjects 'even to death' (5.3.216) indicates that the suffering is far from over. Lady Capulet is imagining her own 'sepulchre', Friar Laurence his execution. Punishment awaits.

★

In the winter of 1948, an American actor prepared to play Romeo for a class at The Actors Studio in New York. Newly founded by a trio of writers and directors – Elia Kazan, Cheryl Crawford and Bobby Lewis – the Studio taught 'method acting', in which actors endeavoured to identify totally with their characters, experiencing their emotions and drawing on their own pasts. The Studio's aspiring Romeo was struggling, and discussed his worries with the choreographer, Jerome Robbins, another member of the Studio. Robbins was thirty, and had recently won his first Tony Award for *High Button Shoes*. He had begun to co-direct as well as choreograph his shows. His musical *On the Town* (1944) had broken Broadway's colour bar for the first time, with a racially diverse chorus line. Robbins was also gay; in several versions of this anecdote, the actor who sought his help was his friend and sometime lover, Hollywood's Montgomery Clift. Robbins encouraged Clift to discover Romeo by modernising him, recreating him 'in terms of today' as part of 'the gangs of New York'. There were, he reminded Clift, many such gangs.[24]

Robbins's advice ended up changing his own life. By 6 January 1949, Robbins was on the phone to composer Leonard Bernstein, with whom he had worked on *On the Town*. Robbins proposed 'a noble idea: a modern version of "Romeo and Juliet" set in slums at the coincidence of Easter-Passover celebrations. Feelings run high between Jews and Catholics [. . .] Juliet is Jewish. Friar Laurence is a neighbourhood druggist. Street brawls, double death – it all fits'.[25] This Juliet shared the faith of Robbins and Bernstein – and of Arthur Laurents, the playwright and screenwriter (most recently on Hitchcock's *Rope*) with whom they met on 10 January.[26] Excitement followed; Bernstein engaged his agent for contractual negotiations on what was then entitled *Operation Capulet*.[27]

Robbins's first outline of the musical gave Juliet a detailed back-story. She is not an immigrant, but lives in Monticello, a New York state village 'where Jew and Gentile get along'. Juliet and her Romeo discuss the problem of 'in what church they could marry' – in this draft, their relationship is not only interracial but interfaith, an issue that *West Side Story* elides by matching a Puerto Rican with a Polish Catholic.[28] Her Jewish family features heavily, celebrating an English-language Seder onstage. Tybalt's onstage death was to coincide with the Seder's recollection of the last of the ten plagues of Egypt, the *Makkat Bechorot*, 'the death of the first born (which Tybalt is)'.[29] Robbins's Juliet instigates and endures open conflict with her family: 'She is a disgrace. She will go to the funeral that afternoon and leave for home immediately after'.[30] A wounded, fugitive Romeo hears

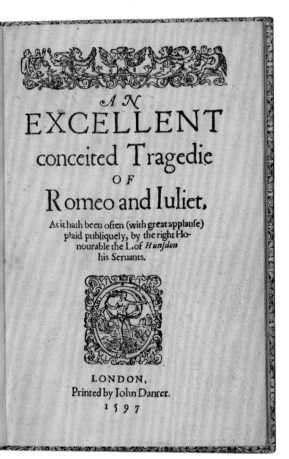

The title page of the first – messy and pirated – quarto of *Romeo and Juliet*, stressing the play's popularity. The printer, John Danter, was one of early modern England's great literary opportunists.

Boy-players, as pictured on the title page of William Alabaster's play *Roxana*.

Susannah Maria Cibber, opera goddess and vindicated wife:
Georgian England's great tragic Juliet. Painted by her brother.

David Garrick as Romeo and George Anne Bellamy as Juliet,
briefly reunited in Garrick's eighteenth-century rewrite.

Georgian London really leans into funeral and theatrical culture as mourners are invited to the obsequies of Mrs Rebecca Hale, April 1776.

Miss Fanny Kemble makes a demure Juliet in 'Fairburn's Portraits No. 21' (1837).

With Mary Ann Stirling as the Nurse, Ellen Terry, Victorian England's most beloved actress, makes her debut as Juliet at the Lyceum, 1882.

Window and Grove, photo.]

MISS ELLEN TERRY AND MRS. STIRLING IN
" ROMEO AND JULIET."

Charlotte Cushman: American superstar, lesbian icon, and the only Romeo ever to outshine a Juliet.

La Casa di Giulietta, Verona: statue by Constantini and balcony by Hollywood (via the imagination of Antonio Avena).

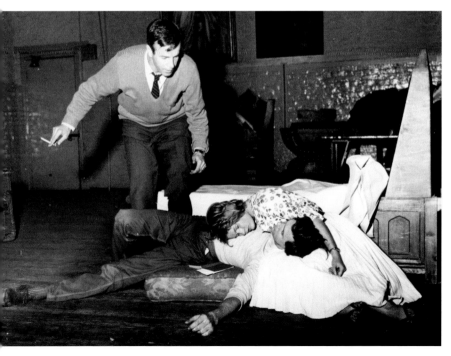

Franco Zeffirelli looms large in rehearsals with John Stride (Romeo) and Judi Dench (Juliet) at the Old Vic, 1960.

Richard Beymer and Natalie Wood as the
doomed lovers of *West Side Story* (1961).

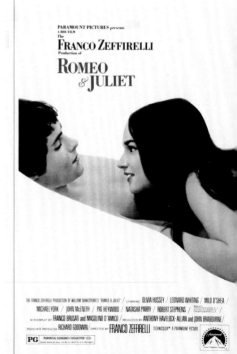

"STUNNING! BEAUTIFUL! GREAT
—SATURDAY REVIEW   —PLAYBOY   —NEWSWEEK
PERFECT! BREATHTAKING!
—BERNARD DREW GANNETT SYNDICATE   —MCCALL'S
PICTURE OF THE MONTH! A JOY!
—SEVENTEEN MAGAZINE   —N.Y. TIMES
BEAUTIFUL! PASSIONATE!"
—JUDITH CRIST NEW YORK MAGAZINE   —NEW YORKER

Paramount Pictures takes grea
pride and pleasure in presenting
to the American public the returr
of the greatest love story of all time

PARAMOUNT PICTURES presents
A BHE FILM
The
FRANCO ZEFFIRELLI
Production of
ROMEO
&JULIET

THE FRANCO ZEFFIRELLI PRODUCTION OF WILLIAM SHAKESPEARE'S "ROMEO & JULIET" / STARRING OLIVIA HUSSEY / LEONARD WHITING / MILO O'SHEA
MICHAEL YORK / JOHN McENERY / PAT HEYWOOD / NATASHA PARRY / ROBERT STEPHENS /
SCREENPLAY BY FRANCO BRUSATI and MASOLINO D'AMICO / PRODUCED BY ANTHONY HAVELOCK-ALLAN and JOHN BRABOURNE
ASSOCIATE PRODUCER RICHARD GOODWIN / DIRECTED BY FRANCO ZEFFIRELLI TECHNICOLOR® A PARAMOUNT PICTURE

PG PARENTAL GUIDANCE SUGGESTED

Paramount proudly presents
Leonard Whiting and Olivia
Hussey without their clothes
in this shot by Lord Snowdon
for Zeffirelli's film (1968).

Claire Danes is the angelic heroine of Baz Luhrmann's *Romeo + Juliet* (1996).

Admira Ismić and Boško Brkić, Sarajevo's star-crossed lovers.

Michael Byrne and Siân Phillips are late-in-life lovers whose
Verona is a care home (*Juliet and Her Romeo*, 2010).

Gwen Ffrangcon-Davies:
as Juliet, opposite
John Gielgud, in 1924;
and as a centenarian, 1991.

instead that she has drowned, and overdoses in Doc / Friar Laurence's basement. Defying her family and abandoning the return to Monticello, Juliet enters to find Romeo still alive. In a recognisable remix of eighteenth-century stage and operatic versions, the lovers enjoy an ecstatic, if brief, reunion before Romeo sickens. 'There is no hospital or doctor he can go to; there is no life for Juliet without him. She takes the rest of the pills and, almost happy that they are together, they lie down happily to die'.[31] This draft offered the strongest, most extensive backstory and character arc for Juliet, as a fully-fledged Jewish girl with a detailed home and family, who defies tradition and dies with her lover. But plans for *Operation Capulet* collapsed in April: Laurents was dismayed by Bernstein's wish for 'an almost purely poetic style', and Bernstein by the 'too-angry, too-bitchy, too-vulgar tone' of Laurents's contemporary script.[32]

A six-year hiatus ensued, until in July 1955, Arthur Laurents tried again. Fired up by the New York press's obsessive coverage of youth crime, he wrote to Bernstein: '[J]uvenile gang war news [. . .] is all over the papers every day [. . .] we have hit on an idea which is suddenly extremely topical, timely, and just plain hot'.[33] A month later, Bernstein and Laurents were at the Beverley Hills hotel, 'our legs dangling in the pool', as they reconceived the project with 'two teen-age gangs as the warring factions, one of them newly arrived Puerto Ricans, the other self-styled "Americans"'.[34] Robbins, when told, was thrilled.

The transition was indeed timely: there were now over 500,000 Puerto Rican New Yorkers, including Rita Moreno, the actress who would later play Anita in the *West Side Story* film. Like many, Moreno vividly remembers the racial abuse she endured as a child; one of her earliest memories was being called 'spic', the same ethnic slur that appears in *West Side Story*'s script.[35] Initially, this second draft still showed Juliet within her family, with their apartment a major location, and a family musical number with the Capulets 'singing and playing [guitar?] a gay, happy P. Rican type folk tune'. The plot gave the actress dramatic opportunities; when Detective Lieutenant Schrank enters the apartment to announce Tybalt's murder, 'the family doesn't understand English, and Juliet has to translate the horrible news'.[36] Stephen Sondheim joined the show as lyricist in early October 1955, meeting with Bernstein more than forty times

between November and the following February.[37] By now, the show
was called *Romeo*, a title it kept until at least summer 1956; eventually, in May 1957, auditions began for a show called *West Side Story*.[38]

Bernstein's notes indicate that Carol Lawrence, after a slightly
disappointing first audition ('not quite Maria'), was the only serious
contender for leading lady once auditions were underway.
Nevertheless, she had thirteen auditions before being paired with
Larry Kert, a Californian Jewish baritone who'd initially avoided
auditioning for Tony, because, as he told Sondheim, 'every day I
read in the paper you're looking for a six foot blond Polish tenor'.[39]
Lawrence and Kert adored each other. Meanwhile, hundreds audi-
tioned for chorus roles. Bernstein's notes on the unsuccessful
women are especially blunt, dismissing them as a 'great big zero',
'tallissimo' or, more than once, 'dog'.[40]

Rehearsals began on 24 June 1957.[41] Robbins created a rehearsal-
room bulletin board of cuttings documenting local violence,
captioning the murder of one local Puerto Rican gang member
with 'this is your life'.[42] Performers researched juvenile delinquency
and wrote character biographies. The two gangs became alienated
from each other; when Tony Mordente (A-Rab) began dating Chita
Rivera (Anita), Mordente's fellow Jets didn't speak to him for a
week.[43] The Washington first night was on 19 August, followed by
Bernstein's 25 August birthday, 'the Jewish version – a big party for
me, but the admission is one Israel bond'.[44] The Washington reception was adulatory: 'I never dreamed it could be like this,' Bernstein
wrote to his wife, 'reviews such as one would write for oneself'.[45]
Reviews of the Broadway opening (26 September) were more
mixed, but by late October the show was sold out to the end of
February, despite nightly walkouts.[46] Artists from Vera Lynn to
Sammy Davis Jr clamoured to record the show's numbers. The
original run lasted a highly respectable – if not extraordinary – 723
performances.[47]

For Robbins, the love story came second to the psychology of
male delinquency. But this was not unusual: those who most enjoyed
West Side Story also preferred the gangs to the lovers. Martha
Gelhorn, the great American war correspondent who had been the
only woman at D-Day and had seen the liberation of Dachau, found
West Side Story 'beautiful and terrifying [. . .] a sociological

document turned into art'. She had 'never heard or seen anything more frightening' than 'Cool', and saw in the gangs a 'mad obsession with nothing, the nerves insanely and constantly stretched – with no way to rest, no place to go; the emptiness of the undirected minds, whose only occupation could be violence and a terrible macabre playacting [. . .] it looks to me like doom, as much as these repeated H-bomb tests'.[48]

Even the show's detractors thought that 'almost everywhere the romance falls short of the gang warfare', with *Time* noting that 'the romance of Laurents' libretto catches rasping, inarticulate hate better than yearning, inarticulate love'.[49]

Speaking on camera from the rehearsal room, Robbins said that *West Side Story* was indeed not about love, but 'intolerance'. *West Side Story*'s creators added to Shakespeare's *Romeo and Juliet* a racial rationale for the 'ancient grudge' of the Capulets and the Montagues (1.0.3), and a sustained examination of the benefits of clan identity from the opening 'Jet Song': you're 'never alone'; you're 'well-protected'; you've 'got brothers around; you're a family man'.[50] The gangs are subject to a far more vindictive justice system; while Escalus equally criticises Capulet and Montague, Schrank offers to help the Jets assault the Sharks. Mercutio is Escalus's kinsman, friends by choice with Romeo but invited to the Capulet ball, but Riff – Mercutio's equivalent – is the Jets' leader.

Looking over the papers of Bernstein, Robbins and Laurents, it's clear how this intensifying focus on racial conflict and gang culture increasingly sidelined the play's Juliet, Maria. The mid-fifties drafts offered her one big scene. In a 1955 synopsis, Juliet is taunted as a 'dirty Puerto Rican', overdoses, and walks through a delirious dream-ballet before dying with Romeo on the boat where they planned to elope. In an October 1955 draft by Bernstein and Laurents, Juliet succumbs to poison while wearing a wedding veil and arranging mannequins for a mock wedding. When Romeo arrives, 'in her delirium, she thinks they are at least in their own world which has been transported to heaven'. What follows is the opposite of *West Side Story*'s final denouement: 'She sinks to the floor, he cradles her in his arms, they both start a reprise of their balcony song but never quite finish'. The musical ended in apotheosis: '[T]he walls disappear, the music soars upward and the audience swoons'. Robbins rejected the scenario as goofy, complaining that 'Juliet becomes Ophelia', but, more importantly, that Romeo was marginalised: 'I had to read the whole thing a couple of times to find out why Romeo dies'. Bernstein half-conceded the point: 'True. Maybe he doesn't – but we know he's doomed'. Evidently, this wasn't good enough for Robbins. Although two more 1956 drafts saw Juliet kill herself with dressmaking shears, leaving Romeo to summon the police ('Come and take me, come and take me too!'), ultimately his death, and not hers, would be the musical's last tragedy.[51] Despite his earlier objections, Robbins was also happy to leave Maria's fate unresolved, after Richard Rodgers had commented: 'She's dead already, after all this happens to her'.[52]

The importance of Juliet/Maria – a Monticello-born Jew who celebrated Passover; a Puerto Rican responsible for translating the news of her brother's death for her family; a Gothic heroine with a dream-ballet death scene – was steadily eclipsed, as the show evolved, by the real star of *West Side Story*: Maria's Romeo, Tony. After all, it was a discussion of Romeo that originally inspired Jerome Robbins to stage the show.

We know far less about Maria than any other version of Juliet. We learn that her father's nickname for her is 'Maruca' and that her mother is 'delicate-boned'.[53] She works in the bridal shop and has just arrived from Puerto Rico, joining elder brother Bernardo. In comparison, we know that Tony, baptised Anton, is the child of a Polish-born mother and a father who is (like many working-class Americans) extending his education at night school.[54] In both stage and film versions, the most developed relationship is not that of Maria and Tony, but that of Tony and Riff. We know that Tony's family has housed Riff for four and a half years; that Tony co-founded the Jets, and was a serious fighter in at least one rumble, where he 'saved [Baby John's] ever-loving neck'; that he is Baby John's hero; and that Anybodys, the Jets' despised and probably genderqueer tomboy, risks everything for him.[55] Jerome Robbins's notes on Tony stress the nuances of his character: he 'has a need for the magic' of gang life with Riff and depends on Riff 'as an anchor', his 'home base from childhood'. By comparison, Robbins's comments on Maria seem to be about reducing the character, asking 'Is Maria too strong?' upon meeting Tony. Does having her hear Anita's jokes 'hurt her innocence?'[56] Cheryl Crawford, the show's first producer, was right about Tony: 'in his character rests the kernel of the story'.[57] In the six weeks before *West Side Story* begins, Tony has abandoned the Jets to work as a delivery boy, precipitating the insecure Riff's desire for a rumble. During the month before the events of the show, he has had a strong premonition of a lifechanging event, not unlike Romeo's belief in '[s]ome consequence yet hanging in the stars' (1.4.108).[58] But unlike Romeo, Tony predicts 'something good': his meeting with Maria.

Tony's premonition gives him his first of two solos: 'Something's Coming', which was added to the show during rehearsals, specifically to develop Tony's character. His other solo, 'Maria', was reassigned from a 'spic song', in Bernstein's words, to a solo for the male lead, fundamentally reshaping the show.[59] While Tony's role is especially demanding for a non-opera role, Maria is a standard high soprano without a solo number of her own. Although Maria's survival at the play's end could signal her importance as a spokeswoman, she is very much the Horatio to Tony's dead Hamlet, or, appropriately given her musical canonisation ('Say it soft, and it's almost like praying'), the Mary to his Christ.[60] One Mike Cuomo, an ex-New York gang member, spotted the parallels when watching the film (in a group of other ex-gang members) for a documentary to mark *West Side Story*'s sixtieth anniversary, saying that Tony added a 'Christ aspect to the story [. . .] his death creates this reconciliation'.[61] In making Tony the centre of *West Side Story*'s tragedy, the show's creators were in step with the 'teen tragedy' pop genre – frequently banned songs, derived from prison ballads and folk tradition, in which one or both of a pair of star-crossed lovers died a violent death. Although there were *more* Dead Girl Songs, like Mark Dinning's 1959 US number one 'Teen Angel' or Johnny Cymbal's now-forgotten 1960 single 'The Water Was Red' (a shark attack, since you ask), the most influential teen tragedy songs, from 'Tell Laura I Love Her' (1960) to the Shangri-Las' iconic 'Leader of the Pack' (1964) and Bobbie Gentry's 'Ode to Billie Joe' (1967), have all been about Dead Boys. The musical moment should have been right for Maria to sing out her grief. Bernstein knew he'd failed to do Maria justice by depriving her of a final song after Tony's death, admitting that 'it cries out for music [. . .] I never got past six bars with it'.[62]

Not only did *West Side Story*'s creators ultimately give their Juliet fewer songs than their Romeo, they also took less interest in the ones they did create. Sondheim was embarrassed by his own lyrics for 'I Feel Pretty', and Laurents outright disliked the song; the two of them, accompanied by Jerome Robbins, would leave for coffee during run-throughs of 'One Hand, One Heart'.[63] *West Side Story* cuts several of Juliet's dramatic opportunities. The equivalent of her 'Gallop apace' soliloquy is 'Tonight', a sumptuous ensemble piece for most of the cast. There is no potion speech; instead, Maria's death is faked by proxy, when Anita dramatically announces that Chino has killed her as retaliation for the Jets' assault on her. Earlier versions of this scene originally gave Maria / Juliet more to do: the Juliet of 1949 faked her own suicide by drowning, while the first 1955 draft saw Juliet, not Anita, undergo the 'taunting scene where they bait her [for] being a dirty P. Rican'. This is, inevitably, the show's most upsetting sequence on stage or screen.[64]

Far from being '[t]wo households both alike in dignity' (1.0.1), the Jets are the default and the Sharks are the 'other'. While the Jets have backstories revealed during the show (Anybodys' sister is a prostitute; A-Rab's father is an alcoholic), the supporting Sharks are stock types, hardly individuated. Maria's Puerto Rican identity barely develops her characterisation. Her grasp of English is erratic, with Spanish idioms and more stilted dialogue ('One month have I been in this country [. . .] For what did my fine brother bring me here?') contrasting with the improbably complex lyrics of 'I Feel Pretty': 'The city should give me its key / A committee / Should be organised to honour me'.[65] Maria is also excluded from the show's two big displays of Puerto Rican identity through dance: 'Mambo', which she merely observes, and 'America', during which she is off-stage, also missing the Sharks' dissection of the double-edged immigrant experience. Maria's desire to assimilate, first as 'a young lady of America', and then as Tony's wife, indistinguishable from him ('I'm his, / And everything he is / I am, too' – a declaration Tony never makes) is one the show endorses.[66]

In production, Maria's heritage was seen as an acoustic problem, not an asset, with one early draft recommending that, since 'Juliet [. . .] has not been long in this country', they 'take the dramatic licence of eliminating all accents'.[67] Although it's hard to reconstruct how she sounded in dialogue, Carol Lawrence's singing accent is barely distinguishable from Larry Kert when they duet on the 1957 recording. Throughout *West Side Story*'s history, Maria has consistently looked more white-passing than other Shark girls – especially Anita. Carol Lawrence was Italian; Chita Rivera, as Anita, was the only Puerto Rican American woman in the original cast. In the 1961 film, Natalie Wood looks like a white Maria in a bit of tinted moisturiser; Rita Moreno, an authentically Puerto Rican Anita, was still given darkening make-up, and described the stock Shark cosmetics as 'a bucket of mud'.[68] Even in Steven Spielberg's 2021 remake of *West Side Story*, the actress playing Maria, Rachel Zegler, is of mixed Colombian and Polish descent, and identifies as 'a white Latina'.[69] Ariana DeBose, 'a Black queer woman' with mixed Puerto Rican and African American ancestry, plays Anita.[70]

Anita is the musical's equivalent of Shakespeare's Nurse, the play's older, sexually ribald woman. The Nurse recalls her husband's off-colour joke about toddler Juliet's future sex life (1.3.42–4) and adds plenty of her own about Paris and Juliet's wedding night (4.4.33–5). Anita is also sexually experienced, thanks to misdemeanours with ''Nardo in the balcony at the movies' and Bernardo's post-violence libido.[71] The repeated practice of casting darker-skinned Anitas against white-passing Marias invites the inference that Anita's sexual experience and Maria's innocence are somehow written into, or explained by, the colours of their faces. Tellingly, in a 1955 draft (working title: *GANG BANG*) where Juliet is Jewish, the plot depended on her being visually indistinguishable from the Gentile Montagues; Romeo and his gang read her as white.[72] When Irving Shulman published an authorised novelisation to tie-in with the film script in 1961, he went even further.

Shulman was a screenwriter and novelist who'd provided the first film treatment for *Rebel Without a Cause*. Like Robbins, Laurents, and Bernstein, he was a New York-born Jew fascinated by teenage street criminals. Shulman's *West Side Story* novel elaborates on the sex and violence of gang life, with the Jets assaulting gay men in Central Park, unruffled by the notion of raping women, and 'hat[ing] everything and everyone in their path'.[73] Nonetheless, he describes a Maria who 'want[s] to speak English as Americans did [. . .] She wanted so much to be an American', noting that her parents are 'so much younger, more self-assured, even better dressed' in New York than in Puerto Rico.[74]

Shulman's racialisation of Anita is even more blatant. She is hypersexualised and primitive, with 'dark, savage eyes that became brighter in the dark'; her hair is 'long, loose, and wild', while her lips appear 'full blown with passion'. In contrast, Maria will 'never have to shave her legs' and 'look[s] like the Madonna'.[75] When Tony sees Maria in her Communion dress, 'he nod[s] to approve of her dress which [is] white, beautiful, so different from anything worn by the other girls'.[76] Eager to improve her English, virginal, desperate to assimilate, and the antithesis of 'savage', hairy Anita, Maria is the novel's ideal white American bride.

It's deeply ironic that a show designed to 'plea[d] for racial tolerance' by depicting an interracial relationship should have worked so hard, through multiple incarnations, to make that relationship look anything but interracial. The Jets are in the majority and offer the first insult to the newly arrived Sharks; they are backed by a police officer who calls the Sharks 'trash', and they instigate the rumble that leads to two murders – yet the film blames its worst violence on the Puerto Ricans.[77] Bernardo kills first; Anita vengefully invents Maria's death to punish Tony after his gang mates assault her; and Chino murders Tony. Every major Puerto Rican character but Maria directly or inadvertently precipitates a death: whereas, as we saw in Chapter 1, Shakespeare's Romeo is the play's most violent character, killing twice. Bernstein and his co-creators may have understood *Romeo and Juliet* and *West Side Story* as pleas for racial tolerance, but it's a plea that fails.

That failure is one reason *West Side Story* is so spectacularly of its time. Its conclusion that an interracial relationship couldn't succeed was one American culture largely endorsed. Although American legislation had never explicitly prohibited marriage between white and Hispanic people, racist laws banning marriages between white people and Black, Asian, Native American and/or Filipino groups persisted in many Midwestern and Southern states well into the 1960s. Even after the landmark 1967 *Loving* v. *Virginia Supreme Court* case made such laws unenforceable, sixteen states kept them as symbolic parts of their constitutions. Alabama's constitution only removed the wording – 'The legislature shall never pass any law to authorize or legalize any marriage between any white person and a negro, or descendant of a negro' – in 2000, after a referendum. Forty per cent of voters opposed the change.[78]

Leonard Bernstein did not give Maria the final song for which her denouement 'cried out'. But as the decade wore on, he did amplify the voice of one 1960s Juliet. In 1965, fourteen-year-old New Jersey folk singer Janis Ian recorded 'Society's Child', a song that she wrote about a white schoolgirl in apparently star-crossed love with an African American boy.[79] Banned by many radio stations, the song missed chart success until Bernstein featured it as the part-one finale of his CBS documentary, *Inside Pop: The Rock Revolution*. Praising Ian's 'cool, nasty electric organ sound', 'astonishing key changes' and 'ambiguous cadences', he put her, and her song, on national television.[80]

On the video recording, the teenage Ian is pale, her guitar high in front of a white pinafore dress. She sings of maternal disapproval – 'Honey, he's not our kind' – and of hypocritical teachers whose self-congratulatory support for equality disappears when faced with a real interracial relationship. Her voice rises to a wail of imploring regret: 'They say I can't see you any more, baby'. There's a hint in the last verse of paradise postponed: 'When we're older, things may change.' Years later, Ian told a website, 'I don't think I made a conscious decision to have the girl cop out in the end; it just seemed like that would be the logical thing at my age, because how can you buck school and society and your parents, and make yourself an outcast forever?'[81] In the last lines of the song, the schoolgirl, unlike Juliet, chooses society over her lover, and claims the decision as her own: 'I don't wanna see you anymore, baby'. When Janis Ian performed the song onstage in Encino, California, she was threatened with violence from her audience. But the Juliet in 'Society's Child' rejects her Romeo – and lives. In the 1967 documentary, Bernstein, now grey-haired, listens to Ian from the stool of a grand piano, his eyes frequently shut. At the end of the song, he turns back to camera.

'It kills me,' he says.

★

When Franco Zeffirelli's theatre production of *Romeo and Juliet* hit
New York in 1962, veteran journalist John McClain timed his review
for Valentine's Day. Under the headline 'Love That New Love
Affair!' he praised the romance as 'fleeting and fiery' and the
'Montague-Capulet fussin'' as a 'big rumble' with 'the lusty sense-
lessness of two juvenile gangs'. 'Do you suppose,' asked McClain,
'Mr. Zeffirelli saw *West Side Story*?'[82]

Zeffirelli's first *Romeo and Juliet* opened in 1960 in London. I start
researching it in 2019, at the Fondazione Zeffirelli in Florence,
where the staff refer to him as 'Maestro', and where the air condi-
tioning has broken (when I martial my inadequate Italian to tell
them '*l'aria condizionata non funziona*', they say, 'Susanna is not
here', a non sequitur for which I am no match). In a beautiful
panelled room, even my eyeballs feel like they're sweating.

I'm uncomfortable about more than the heat. It's September.
Zeffirelli died in June, and Florence mourns. When I visit San
Miniato al Monte, a hilltop basilica run by Olivetan monks, I accidentally see Zeffirelli's vault, decorated with crisping wreaths and
new white roses. Zeffirelli got his name when a registrar misspelt
Zeffiretti ('little breezes'), the name Zeffirelli's mother invented for
her illegitimate son. Now *Fam. Franco Zeffirelli* ('the Franco Zeffirelli
family') is chiselled into the stone overlooking Florence's most
breathtaking view. That afternoon, I'm in search of neither Juliet
nor the director; I just want to eat sorbet (monk-made, delicious)
and look at art. I do both while worrying about Zeffirelli.

In a 2017 interview for the British Film Institute, the actor and
writer Bruce Robinson claimed that Zeffirelli made forcible, unwel-
come sexual advances to him when Robinson was twenty-two and
playing Zeffirelli's film Benvolio. Robinson fictionalised the assault
in his film *Withnail and I* (1987), with Zeffirelli as the predatory
Uncle Monty.[83] In January 2018, at the height of the #MeToo movement, American actor Johnathon Schaech alleged that Zeffirelli had
verbally and sexually abused him on the set of *Sparrow* (1993), an
experience Schaech called 'brutal' and a 'life theft'.[84] Schaech says
that after he spoke out, four men contacted him with similar allegations. Among them was former child actor Justin Vetrano. When
Vetrano was eighteen, he lived in the home of his agent, Ed Limato,
who was both his father's cousin and a friend of Zeffirelli. Vetrano

told Schaech that Zeffirelli, while also staying with Limato, assaulted Vetrano, destroying his career.[85] Zeffirelli was in his nineties and too ill to respond to the allegations, according to his son Pippo, who denied everything on his behalf. These accusations have never been investigated by police or tested in court. In his 1986 memoir, Zeffirelli revealed that during his childhood, he had been sexually abused by a priest, and that after the assault, that priest had begged the boy's forgiveness.[86] Such an experience would be no excuse for the behaviour Robinson, Schaech, and Vetrano allege; the fact that Zeffirelli insisted the priest's abuse hadn't harmed him might shed light on his attitude to sex and power. When I visit the Fondazione in 2019, boxes of personal effects arrive daily from Zeffirelli's house in Rome, and one day I think I spot Pippo among the Fondazione's staff. They are all still visibly upset at his death. I don't discuss Zeffirelli to rehabilitate him, but because this book is the story of Juliet, and every box of photographs the Fondazione staff brings shows how closely Zeffirelli shaped Juliet for his productions, his film, and twentieth-century culture.

The first photograph I find is of Judi Dench. She's twenty-three, she's Juliet, and she's dead. In blouse and voluminous skirt, she lies curled forwards with her head on John Stride's stomach, having collapsed there while cradling his head in her lap. It's the pose that recurs throughout all Zeffirelli's productions and, in a modified way, on film. In the photograph, Zeffirelli is leaning over the lovers. The 1960 photograph flash has blanched his face unnaturally white and cast his extended right arm in a horror-film shadow on the back wall (it being 1960, he's holding a lit cigarette out of harm's way). He looks part-explorer, part-voyeur. In another photograph, he's acting Romeo for the benefit of Dench and Stride. In a third, he's manipulating Olivia Hussey's head on the pillow as she feigns sleep in the bedroom scene. The black-and-white photography makes her look like a waxwork. A French magazine that published these pictures described him as 'comme un sculpteur', writing excitedly of his 'mains inspirées'. The caption was beneath another photograph of the sleeping Hussey/Juliet, shot so the camera foregrounds her barely covered fifteen-year-old cleavage. An English press cutting shows him lifting and scattering a smiling Hussey's long black hair. Youth, sexuality, plasticity, and beauty run through the photographs.

Cuttings for the Old Vic production and the film show how one became a blueprint for the other. Judi Dench and her New York replacement, Joanna Dunham, 'inched towards' Romeo 'deliberately and with passion aforethought', as Hussey would on screen.[87] Dench's Juliet had a 'beatnik heart' and was praised for 'scampering like a child and bubbling with excitement', seeming 'genuinely just fourteen years old'.[88] Later, she recalled that Zeffirelli made her 'concentrate upon the childish qualities of Juliet'.[89] One New York critic wrote approvingly of Dunham that 'her childishness makes her anguish no less real'.[90] Dench, Dunham, and Hussey existed in worlds steeped in rich Italian detail, simultaneously pungent and perfect. Costumes looked 'like a Renaissance fresco'; Dench recalled wearing the 'soft browns and ochres and gold and cream' that would characterise Hussey's film costumes, against a backdrop of set walls 'spattered [. . .] with dirty water to look like dog pee'.[91] The film used locations across Tuscany, Lazio, Umbria, and the Veneto.

Dench and Dunham's childish Juliets were nonetheless frank about their own desires. Zeffirelli's notes for the 1960 production fill the balcony scene with kissing; '1000 baci' to match 'A thousand times goodnight', and 'J. bacie R' or 'molti baci' filling the page's margins. Juliet is restless, 'correndo impaziente' (running, impatient), as she waits for the Nurse; embracing her pillow and unable to keep still as she anticipates her wedding night.[92] Sexuality defined both productions. Kenneth Tynan, who called the production 'a miracle [. . .] a revelation, even perhaps a revolution', had 'no doubt' that when Dench and Stride prolonged their post-coital parting, it was due to 'sheer, newly-wedded exhaustion', while critics speculated of Dunham that 'it is possible that the girl yearning on a balcony has not yearned with such explicit abandon before'.[93] Zeffirelli directed *Romeo and Juliet* as 'a fresh work with a passionate, dynamic story'; critics described the young lovers as 'bear-cubs'.[94] His 1964 Italian-language follow-up was 'un drama di teddy boys', with Anna Maria Guarnieri, his 'Giulietta in Blue-Jeans', exuding 'the amorous passion of her age – fourteen! – with the shamelessness of today's films'.[95]

In 1967, Zeffirelli announced the film casting for his young lovers, his two 'young animals' with 'classic beauty and yet a quality of today': Olivia Hussey and Leonard Whiting.[96] The promotional leaflet for his film insisted that Shakespeare 'was really writing a screenplay for the new generation'. The 'star-crossed lovers of Verona [. . .] could also be the love children of Haight-Ashbury and the East Village', added the leaflet, offering strong signals that the film would depict sexual liberation. Zeffirelli told *Look* magazine that 'I want this to be a young people's *Romeo and Juliet*'.[97] To that end, he'd already hoped to cast Paul McCartney, telling him: 'You look exactly how I see Romeo'. At some point, the Beatle had a date with fifteen-year-old Olivia Hussey, whom he 'quite fancied [. . .] she was gorgeous', and to whom he sent a telegram stating, 'You're a beautiful Juliet'. She responded, You'd make a great Romeo'. 'It was all very . . . [romantic swoon]'.[98] The nearest they came to being co-stars was when *Romeo and Juliet* and The Beatles both provided live segments for the June 1967 international television programme *Our World*, with Hussey as part of the Italian entry, and The Beatles as the British. Hussey's Romeo, Whiting, was a Cockney, not a Scouser – indeed, some snobbish reviewers found him 'torment-ingly Cockney, sapless in voice'. But the European press understood him as part of the Beatles aesthetic, *'un autentico "Ye-Ye"'*[99] (a term derived from rock-and-roll's 'yeah yeah yeah' refrain, which had been popularised in the French press three weeks before Lennon and McCartney began composing 'She Loves You (Yeah, Yeah, Yeah)' but was associated with them thereafter).

On film, Hussey's Juliet is energetic, skidding across the church floor to her wedding and to Friar Laurence's cell, and darting around the balcony. She upbraids Romeo with wide-eyed pudeur on 'What satisfaction canst thou have tonight?' and melts, charmed by his response. She is noisily amorous, shouting out her avowal of 'My bounty is as boundless as the sea', at an imprudent volume for night-time shenanigans with a blood-feud enemy, but with all the exulta-tion of requited first love. She is the happiest Juliet on film; until, that is, tragedy strikes and she is howling at her parents, and hurtling towards death in the tomb.

Before filming began, Hussey and Whiting posed for promo-tional photos that showed the pair kissing. Hussey wore school uniform – a costume from her role in *The Prime of Miss Jean Brodie*, not explained in the accompanying copy – clearly fetishising her youth. The *Daily Express* hoped Hussey and Whiting would become a couple, while by the premiere, the French press confidently reported that Leonard was '*fiancé d'Olivia dans la vie*'.[100] When the actors were photographed at a promotional visit to Juliet's tomb in Verona, the resulting image simultaneously resurrected Shakespeare's characters and had the feel of a honeymoon shot. Paramount's astonishing promotional reel for the film described them as 'the most talked-about teenagers in the world today', playing 'the most exciting lovers ever created [. . .] burning up with vitality, exuberant and playful'. As the stentorian mid-Atlantic voiceover rumblingly calls them 'part of the Love Generation', their hands touch, slightly soft-focus, on a rumpled pile of costumes.[101] Olivia is shown window-shopping for underwear in Carnaby Street's boutiques and bopping to the latest dances; an official profile verified that she 'loves dancing and music, particularly modern jazz, approves of mini-skirts and maxi-dresses, loves mod clothes [and] buys most of her dresses ready-made'; she is presented as a wholesome, hyper-feminine starlet who 'likes white particularly', wears 'no make-up except for mascara [. . .] and has always worn her hair long'.[102] In Paramount's film about the young cast, she and Whiting romp on camera, and the boys chuck each other prettily in and out of swimming pools.

Hussey was even linked with the future King Charles III. The then-Prince of Wales seemed highly taken with her at the Royal Command screening, talking to her throughout dinner ('*avec des attentions particulières*', according to *Paris-Match*) and dancing with her afterwards. The world press was divided as to whether it had been the waltz, *le jerk* – a swaying, arm-swinging, rules-free twist – or *il frug*, the Italian name for a vigorous, stylised, hip-bopping dance riffed on by choreographer Bob Fosse in the 1969 film *Sweet Charity*.[103]

In the winter of 1968, teen magazine *Mirabelle* serialised the film over five weeks in an illustrated comic-strip style punctuated by film stills. Juliet was the narrator. Part one opened with a sketch of Hussey in-role, and a speech: 'Five hundred years ago we lived and loved and yet . . . . . . [sic] ours is not a story of yesterday, but forever. It is your story and the story of all the lovers who have ever been'.[104] This is as good as the writing gets (everyone says, 'Oh, my darling! My darling!' a lot), but it was a shrewd move. Seven years earlier, young couples had responded to *West Side Story* with the same intensity of recognition. As one young Italian American, whose father 'in a four-room apartment, did not speak to me for six years' over her Puerto Rican boyfriend, described the 1961 film: 'It *was* our story [. . .] I can remember the movie theatre, I can remember the row we sat in'.[105]

Paramount clearly wanted young girls to identify with both Hussey and Juliet. As part of the *Mirabelle* tie-in, fans were offered the chance to 'win a Juliet dress': a cream, red, and black mini-skirted mix of Hussey's own 'high-Mod gear' aesthetic and pastiche Elizabethan details including 'Renaissance style ruched collar and sleeves'. Even the dress's manufacture mixed old and new. Harbro, a rising Mod fashion house, constructed it in Sekers fabric; Sekers, used in the 1950s by Dior and Cardin, and for the Ascot scene in *My Fair Lady*, had since diversified into furnishing fabrics, and was in its last days as a textile house for fashion. But even as the dress supposedly let girls dress like Juliet, it toned down one fashion choice from the film. Short the dress might have been, but the ruff and striped yoke ensured that Hussey's low onscreen necklines were not replicated for *Mirabelle*'s adolescent readership; girls could dress like Juliet, but they mustn't go too far.

Hussey's identification with the character was passionate and absolute: 'I feel very close to Juliet [. . .] understand all her motives and feelings. I would be able to kill myself for love'.[106] Interview quotes stress a dreamy, adolescent instability: 'I do daydream a lot. Sometimes I laugh and then the next minute I'm in tears – and I don't know why'.[107] Despite Zeffirelli's tendency to demonstrate how scenes should be acted, and despite being dismissed by some critics as giving 'very much a director's performance', Hussey recalls in her autobiography brokering a power balance from the beginning. She successfully suggested to Zeffirelli her 'modus operandi': 'Why not just let me do it my way, and if you don't like it you can tell me?'[108]

The central controversy of Zeffirelli's film was the nude scene between Romeo and Juliet that was introduced into Act 3, Scene 5: Romeo's departure for banishment after the couple's wedding night. Across his whole career, Shakespeare only wrote two explicitly post-coital scenes, and this is the first. Two ardent and newly married children bemoan and dispute the shortness of the night, and then part in secrecy and danger. In *Troilus and Cressida*, written seven years later in 1602, Shakespeare once again places his lovers in a warzone, in opposing tribes, but they are unmarried, and the Nurse is onstage as Pandarus, Cressida's matchmaking, semi-pimp of an uncle, who intervenes to mock Cressida's loss of virginity ('How go maidenheads?', 4.2.25). What's striking about these love scenes is how pessimistic and pensive they are, and how threatened with violence. Romeo tries to comfort Juliet with promises of letters and 'sweet discourses in our time to come' ('One day we'll look back on this and laugh', essentially) but then she has a vision of him as 'dead in the bottom of a tomb' (3.5.53–6). Soldiers enter the stage to search for Troilus. Neither couple sees each other alive again.

Sex in Shakespeare is fraught with violence. Throughout the canon, allegations of infidelity see husbands plot to kill their wives (*The Winter's Tale*, *Cymbeline*) and, in tragedies, they succeed (*Othello*). Premarital sex nearly gets a man killed in *Measure for Measure* (c. 1603–4); in the same play, a leading politician tries to rape a young nun. She escapes only by substituting that politician's discarded fiancée, entrapping him with his conjugal obligations. Jokes about venereal disease abound throughout the canon. But in his early career, leading up to *Romeo and Juliet*, Shakespeare was a playwright especially preoccupied with rape and sexual coercion. Both his early narrative poems, *Venus and Adonis* (1593) and *The Rape of Lucrece* (1594), deal with this, the latter culminating in the suicide of Lucrece. *Titus Andronicus* sees another young woman not only raped but mutilated, as Lavinia's tongue is cut out to silence her. The possibility of rape pervades Shakespeare's early comedies: Proteus threatens to rape Silvia in *Two Gentlemen of Verona* (c. 1589–93) and bitterly regrets it (5.4); Demetrius angrily threatens Helena with violent 'mischief' in *A Midsummer Night's Dream* (2.1.237).

During the early 1590s, Shakespeare began writing his sonnets, many of which are frankly vicious in their depiction of desire and betrayal. Perhaps the angriest, Sonnet 129, begins with the assertion that sex is a shameful waste of vital life-force: 'Th'expense of spirit in a waste of shame/ Is lust in action'. Lust is violent: 'perjured, murd'rous, bloody, full of blame/ Savage, extreme, rude, cruel, not to trust', and sex is not worth it: 'a very woe / Before, a joy proposed; behind, a dream'. Sexual regret is key to Shakespeare's one other morning-after scene, where Cressida tells Troilus:

You men will never tarry,
O foolish Cressid, I might have still held off,
And then you would have tarried (4.2.18–20).

Since the early twentieth century, *Troilus and Cressida* has been called a 'problem play'; Cressida is its 'problem'. Traded to the enemy camp, she pragmatically entertains the attentions of one of the occupying soldiers, breaking Troilus's heart. Cressida betrays Troilus and both survive. Juliet and Romeo have no sexual regrets and no such betrayal – they stay faithful and die for it. The world of *Romeo and Juliet* does not celebrate love. Shakespeare begins Act 1, Scene 1 of what's become the most famous romance in literature not with love but with a rape joke: the Capulet servant Sampson boasts to his colleague that he will rape the Montague women as well as fighting their men (1.1.14–20). Even without the Prologue, thanks to Sampson, we would know that sex in Verona is inseparable from danger, and the lovers' idyll cannot last.

The first quarto of *Romeo and Juliet*, the shorter 1597 version, sheds light on this parting scene. The unusually detailed stage directions are probably a record of the stage business performed by Elizabethan casts, rather than only Shakespeare's instructions. According to this quarto, the lovers begin the scene 'at the window'. This would have been a raised gallery or window in the early modern theatre, from which Romeo must descend by rope ladder, remaining visible to the audience for his final dialogue with Juliet.[109] Unless the entire Capulet family and Nurse then have their seismic, life-altering row on that little platform, Juliet presumably also descends, via a staircase, to an area of the stage that represents her bedroom. For the sake of both audience decorum and the plot, this bedroom was, for centuries, not one that showed evidence of recent sex, or even a bed: even the pioneering Victorian actresses of Chapter 4 objected to showing 'a disarranged bed'.[110] The twentieth century had brought beds into the scene, but little suggestion of what had gone on within them. Of George Cukor's 1936 film, critic

H. R. Coursen notes: 'On the dawn of Romeo's departure from Juliet's chamber, the lovers are clothed as if about to make a dog-sled run for the South Pole'.[111] The one couple with potential for truly rumpled bedlinen – Laurence Olivier and Vivien Leigh, then-lovers exchanging unhinged letters explaining how feral they were for each other – somehow managed to lack onstage lust.[112] Their 1940 production began the morning-after scene with the lovers on Juliet's bed, but critics found the performances antiseptic, saying Olivier 'talked as though he was brushing his teeth'.[113]

Zeffirelli's decision to film his two teenage leads nude fascinated and outraged the critics of 1968. Before it was released, one critic claimed the film had 'turned out X Certificate stuff'.[114] In fact, the lesser A Certificate was awarded – even taking into account both the nudity and the display of corpses in the Capulet vault, according to BBFC secretary John Trevelyan.[115] Few reviewers really disapproved; approbation, meanwhile, divided fascinatingly into two camps. There were those who admitted that the nude scene was there to arouse and that it had worked, and those who dressed up their drooling as a Considered Aesthetic Defence of High Culture.[116] In one camp was Françoise Giraud for *L'Express*, enjoying '*la chaude aventure d'un garçon de 17 ans et d'une fille de 14 ans*', and the *Los Angeles Advocate*, who found Leonard Whiting 'perfection from head to toe'.[117] In the other camp was breathless over-compensation: 'Nothing could be more chaste,' protested the *Evening Standard*.[118] *Newsweek*'s Thomas Gordon Plate praised the film for depicting 'kids who know what love is all about: it's grabbing, kissing, chasing, having, holding – it's touching [. . .] In bed they are two naked children reaching out for love [. . .] two children of God'.[119]

If, like me, you're starting to feel a bit queasy, I refer you, with delight, to one A. R. Thurlwell, and his letter to the London *Evening News*. Thurlwell (tragically otherwise lost to history) defended the bedroom scene as 'completely devoid' of the 'often sordid sex and passion with which many of the public are oh, so bored, and yet which is continually slapped in our faces like wet cod'.[120] Evocative.

Interviewed by the *Daily Sketch* in late February 1968, Hussey sounds unabashed about the filming: 'We played it absolutely stark-ers. The technicians were sweethearts. As soon as Franco was ready to film, they would all turn away, and the older ones used to take their hats off as if they were in church. They made it very sweet for me'.[121] This was the party line. Travelling back in time, the truth was much more complicated. In an interview recorded alongside Whiting, four months earlier, soon after shooting the nude scene, her poise falters. Softly, Hussey admits to trepidation – 'I was dreading it' – but recovers as she says, 'We did it gradually, and nobody was allowed to watch'. Whiting, although also visibly embarrassed, is protective; when the American interviewer tells them a paper describes it as 'chaste', he cuts in: 'Well, the paper didn't know [. . .] it was only shot the other day, how were they to know?', and Hussey laughs, confidence restored.[122]

Given Hussey's age, the scene would never be shot today. Natalie Portman, Baz Luhrmann's original fourteen-year-old Juliet for his 1996 film, was recast when her love scenes with DiCaprio 'looked as if he were molesting her'; seventeen-year-old Claire Danes replaced her.[123] In Zeffirelli's love scene, Whiting appears fully nude from the back and had to wear 'flesh-coloured tape' to prevent any 'unwanted shadows' from his genitals (or, indeed, cod-like slapping).[124] But on rewatching Zeffirelli's nude scene, two things become clear. First, that Hussey's gratuitous underage nudity serves no other function than to titillate. Second, we only see her topless on screen; Hussey did not need to be fully naked for filming. While the hat-doffing 'crew of older Italian gentlemen' behaved with 'total class', Hussey admitted in her autobiography that another, unnamed crew member, 'a "dirty old man"', tried to 'sneak his way onto the set'.[125] Hussey's autobiography and contemporary press reports imply that she was under sexual, emotional, and physical pressure throughout production and promotion of the film. Although the teenage Hussey claimed to have known about the nude scene 'from the audition', Hussey's autobiography reveals that the first she knew was when a make-up artist arrived 'to make [her] up from top to toe', leading to a 'panic attack'.[126] The actor playing her father, the forty-nine-year-old Paul Hardwick, 'got drunk' at a dinner hosted by Zeffirelli, and told the underage Hussey, '"Frankly, Olivia, I would just love to fuck you," in front of Sir Laurence Olivier, Dame Maggie Smith, and Robert Stephens.' Their reactions are not recorded.[127]

Hussey was also pressured to lose weight, recalling in her autobiography that she spent a week on diet pills that left her 'insanely hyper and strung out' until her furious mother banned the medication.[128] The pills were a secret, but beyond that, Hussey openly discussed the professional push to starve her. She told one interviewer of a 'sly joke' where 'everybody' told her that 'if I gain any weight, [Zeffirelli] is going to have me locked in a room for a week and beaten by Nazi doctors. And I believe it! I have to be awfully careful about my diet. I love spaghetti and potatoes and butter and bread [. . .] But I weigh about a hundred pounds now and I'm not supposed to gain any'.[129] Interviewed for another magazine, producer Anthony Havelock-Allan applauded Whiting for not letting Hussey eat ice cream.[130] What shocks me is not the cruelty, but the openness of the studio's fatphobia. In 1968, Hussey's weight was included in the film's promotional leaflet, distributed at cinemas (one critic still called her 'slightly plump').[131] Hussey's weight loss during filming had been dramatic. One of the first scenes shot, in early summer, was that of Romeo and Juliet's marriage (Act 2, Scene 6), where Hussey hurtles into Whiting's arms in a cloud of dusty lilac silk. When she kisses Whiting or appears in profile, you can see that she still has cheeks and a curve to her chin. By the filmed interview of October 1967, the light is bouncing off every bone in her face. It's not surprising that Romeo and Juliet marked the beginning of Hussey's descent into anorexia, as she 'began to hate her body' and saw food as 'the enemy'.[132]

It's doubly painful because fifteen-year-old Hussey had originally celebrated playing Juliet, given the discrepancy between her appearance and the traditional view of Juliet with 'long blonde hair and blue eyes'.[133] Her 'last competitor' at audition had been an 'ethereal, pale blonde girl'.[134] But again, her body was controlled by others. While other young stars frolicked in the sun, Hussey was kept shaded in 'a huge, floppy hat', caftans, and – in the promotional reel by Paramount – a vast orange and yellow towel, because, as she put it, 'Juliet has to be white'.[135] With an Argentinian father, Hussey is in fact of mixed British and Latinx heritage, as the South American press joyfully pointed out. In 1961, the white Natalie Wood had been made up to look like a fair-skinned Latina as Maria; now, in 1968, a mixed Latina actress was being covered up to look like a white Juliet.

But even as Hussey was praised for her 'oval-faced ivory-skinned beauty', Zeffirelli also exoticised and sexualised her, talking lasciviously of her 'profile of deceptive purity and a certain down-to-earth coarseness', which he knowingly attributed to her 'deepish husky voice that still carries a trace of a South American accent'.[136] She allegedly preferred 'rough English boys rather than polite Italian types'.[137] For a delighted world press, she was simultaneously a 'femme-enfant' who 'still had the rounded limbs of childhood' and a 'beauty' who was 'very open to expressing purity one second, a pre-sexual knowingness the next'.[138] Ivory-skinned and 'la joven argentina', 'pre-sexual' and knowing, kissing in her school uniform but coveting thigh-high boots, Hussey was the dimpled, laughing It girl for 1968.[139] She was equally capable of a sudden, gurgling laugh and of coolly telling a disapproving journalist that plenty of fifteen-year-old girls smoked, just like her.[140] Zeffirelli called her 'Boobs O'Mina' and gave her unusually low necklines in her costumes; a German promotional poster captured her naked but for a bedsheet, smiling and stretching her arms longingly towards the viewer.[141]

The official Paramount poster for the US release is basically soft porn, with an apparently nude Hussey crawling up, or quite possibly down, the body of the supine Whiting, shot by Lord Snowdon on a white bed that blends into the poster. The contrast between the Paramount message and the pull quotes from reviews is telling. Paramount pompously 'takes great pride and pleasure in presenting to the American public the return of the greatest love story of all time', nobly offering a prestigious cultural artefact for the benefit of a discerning public. Above Snowdon's nudes and Paramount's smugness, the gasps of the reviewers – 'Passionate!' 'Perfect!' 'Beautiful!' 'Breathtaking!' – in all their ejaculatory punchiness, belong more to a sexploitation film, and make it clear we're looking at a sex scene first and foremost. His eyes are downcast, his face soft; she is bright-eyed, with lips parted, her teeth showing. She gazes at him, urgent and excited. This is the Hussey presented to the media as not only 'extroverted, aggressive, full of impulses [. . .] sure of herself' but sexually demanding. She is also still underage.

Zeffirelli's film was chosen for a Royal Command Performance, where Prince Philip reassured a nervous Whiting 'by reminding him of the Confucian philosophy: "When rape is inevitable, lie back and enjoy it!"' – an anecdote that nicely epitomises the terrible sexual culture of 1968 as well as anything could. Hussey, looking drawn and fragile in the Pathé footage, was so frightened she wet herself onstage.[142] Her Juliet had gained a nude scene but lost many of her lines. There was no 'Gallop apace' speech and no pre-potion soliloquy; thanks to the latter cut, Hussey had fewer opportunities than the average nineteenth-century actress, for whom the 'potion scene' was the play's climax. The scene in which Hussey had first asserted her right to 'try it [her] way' with Zeffirelli, in which she 'first meets Lord Paris' in a green-and-gold dress, is nowhere in the film; presumably another cut.[143] Zeffirelli justified cutting the potion soliloquy, the speech that had won Hussey the role at the final audition, on the grounds that its inclusion would 'steal the movie', disrupting the 'balance' Zeffirelli said he wanted.[144] In fact, Zeffirelli's film centred on the men. David Robinson of the *Financial Times* noted that 'Zeffirelli uses men as Busby Berkeley's musicals used girls [. . .] Verona is full of Apollos with Denmark St. hairdos'.[145] There were sly remarks about 'assertive codpieces' and accusations of 'a softly homosexual' lens that manifested in 'a kind of Greek attention lavished on Romeo in the bedroom scene'.[146] This attention, however 'Greek', also appealed to women; when interviewed by the *Evening News*, Mrs Doris Hurt of Wivelsfield Road, Saltesdean, commented that she 'liked the strongness of the man's body'.[147] The film was, as Robinson noted, 'a boy show'.[148]

The 1960s couldn't accommodate Juliet as a strong heroine. It's clearest of all in *Mirabelle*, the girls' magazine that serialised the film in pictures over November and early December 1968. Juliet tells the reader: 'Ours is not a story of yesterday, but forever. It is your story [. . .] for me it started that night of my first ball'.[149] You would expect Juliet to become the protagonist; instead, the magazine follows Zeffirelli's lead and emphasises Romeo. *Mirabelle*'s Juliet is a passive, clingy waif, totally unlike Shakespeare's strategic, decisive heroine. She's 'so nervous' before the ball and convinced of her own inadequacy before Romeo, 'who probably didn't even notice me'.[150] Romeo is almost creepily over-confident ('my hands will touch your own and you will be mine forever' is very Hammer Horror), while Juliet begs him to stay – 'Don't leave me yet, please!'[151] Although she raises the idea of marriage, she immediately desponds, asking, 'What's the use? Our families would never let us marry!' She leaves Romeo to devise a cunning plan.[152] On Zeffirelli's screen, Juliet skids into her beloved's arms and starts snogging. In *Mirabelle*, a suave Romeo takes charge of a tottering bride: 'Gently he led me to his childhood teacher and friend Friar Laurence'.[153] When a pragmatic Romeo wants a head start to Mantua, she detains him with hysterics, wailing, 'Oh Romeo, I can't lose you already!'[154]

Mirabelle, like other teenage magazines of the time, favoured strong and decisive heroes over pugnacious heroines. Their pages are full of Rays, Steves, and Brians chastising their womenfolk: 'We could get married right away [. . .] if you'd give up your grand plans for tomorrow' (Edna obeys).[155] Recasting Romeo as the driving force of the lovers' affair reveals how radical Shakespeare's text actually was compared to the love stories being offered to young women in the 1960s. *Mirabelle*'s Juliet might have ended by insisting that she and Romeo 'live together in the hearts and on the lips of all true lovers', the most eternal of magazine romances, but the bulk of those magazines made it clear that female agency, let alone rebellion, got you nowhere.[156]

In the vein of Arthur Brooke's barracking 1560s preface, 1960s problem pages warned girls against disobeying their parents, and also against the excitement of 'forbidden' love, a category that included the slightest discrepancy in educational prospects, let alone race or faith. In the same week that *Mirabelle* serialised part one of *Romeo and Juliet*, readers were treated to 'the tender story of Susan and Harry', rent asunder by the insuperable barrier of her university degree ('Because all my brains, all my cleverness, can't teach me how to make you say you love me . . . as I love you').[157] When 'Life With Kathy', *Petticoat*'s 1968 serial about a flat share, raises the possibility of an interfaith marriage between Jewish Pam and her Gentile boyfriend, the characters are abruptly dropped without resolving the storyline.[158] A 'real-life' study of elopement, one solution that might have saved Shakespeare's lovers, parades dire consequences, from life in a caravan to juvenile courts, and sees pregnant heroines forced to wait defiantly for their eighteenth birthdays and marriage.[159] If the films of the 1960s had been more interested in Romeo than Juliet, the magazines read by would-be Juliets were determined to warn their readers off aspirations to a star-crossed love.

*

West Side Story and Zeffirelli's *Romeo and Juliet* continue to shape the world's understandings of 'the greatest love story ever told'. There have been well over 40,000 stage productions of *West Side Story*, as far afield as Johannesburg, Manila, Tel Aviv and Sydney.[160] Cher did a one-woman version, because of course she did. Zeffirelli's film, meanwhile, having been originally banned in Ontario, and remaining censored by conservative US districts well into the 1980s, is now a standard resource in schools and universities for teaching the play.[161] It is the subject of a permanent installation and exhibition at the Fondazione Zeffirelli, and costumes from the film are displayed at Veronese tourist sites. Both films have their own social media accounts, and Hussey's Juliet has been immortalised as a one-sixth size collectible doll in South Korea, even thinner and paler than the original.[162]

West Side Story and the Zeffirelli film apportion blame for the violence differently. In *West Side Story*, the protagonists' parents are unseen, and the 'generation gap' is between an inept, racist legal system and disenfranchised young men. In *Romeo and Juliet*, the parents are present and cruel, but the emphasis is still on their offspring; the critics who so assiduously labelled the lovers 'a pair of delightful flower children' scarcely commented on their elders.[163] The film's publicity encouraged teenagers to take ownership of *Romeo and Juliet*, a trend that persisted for the rest of the twentieth century.

Nevertheless, post-war, *Romeo and Juliet* became a story less about boy meeting girl than about that boy in the context of his gang. Shakespeare's Juliet, in her agency and volubility, jars with the romance narratives of the 1960s. For filmmakers, the things Juliet says became almost the least interesting aspect of the play. Even in the age of supposed sexual revolution and women's liberation, there persisted a directorial reluctance to trust Juliet with the most dramatic moments of her theatrical arc: her wedding-night and potion soliloquies. This persisted in Baz Luhrmann's *Romeo + Juliet* (1996), which updated *West Side Story*'s Manhattan teen culture for a nineties 'Verona Beach', and used the same Shakespearean language and youth-conscious casting as Zeffirelli. Like his predecessors, Luhrmann also heavily cut his Juliet. Like Natalie Wood, Clare Danes was already a star. Luhrmann praised her for having 'the poise and maturity of a thirty-year-old' and being able to play Juliet as 'a very smart, active character. *She* decides to get married, *she* resolves to take the sleeping potion, *she* really drives the piece'.[164] Despite the justice of this interpretation, Danes retained only a few lines from Juliet's 'Gallop apace' soliloquy, and three from the potions speech.

Although a better verse-speaker than her co-star Leonardo DiCaprio, what mattered more was how Danes looked against the mythic, 'multicultural borderland' of Luhrmann's Verona Beach, a landscape that is variously 'Miami, California, Mexico'.[165] The Marian iconography of *West Side Story*, with its heroine whose name is 'almost like praying', lingers in Luhrmann's Juliet-bedroom and in her party costume as a white-winged angel.[166] Whiteness, as in *West Side Story* and Zeffirelli's *Romeo and Juliet*, is key to Clare Danes's Juliet. Although the Capulet household aesthetic is Latinised kitsch and the Capulet parents are named 'Fulgencio' and 'Gloria', Danes is unquestionably another ideal-ised, angelicised, white Juliet.

Ultimately, the film's production and reception centred on teen idol Leonardo DiCaprio, 'the hottest property in Hollywood'.[167] DiCaprio dominated not only the popular media coverage and fandom – where he was the subject of such memorably named sites as 'Totally Decapitated' – but also scholarship on the film. The Shakespeare scholar Barbara Hodgdon theorised him as 'appealing to the precarious liminality of early to late adolescents [. . .] a *tabula rasa* onto which fans project the romance of identity', playing Romeo as 'a quintessential Greek boy-god', and 'a polysexual figure, equally attractive to young women and gay and straight men'.[168] DiCaprio himself described Romeo to *Mizz* magazine, briefly but no less justly, as 'a really horny guy'.[169] Concluded Hodgdon, 'If this be postmodernism, give me excess of it.'[170] The next twenty-five years would oblige.

DiCaprio went on to star in *Titanic* (1997), aptly described by Hodgdon as '*Romeo and Juliet*, with three hours of water'. In *Titanic*, the Christ-like fate of *West Side Story*'s Tony is amplified by having DiCaprio's Jack deliberately sacrifice himself so that Kate Winslet's Rose can escape hypothermia on a debatably capacious floating door. Rose then lived a full life of acting, equestrianism, travel and motherhood before dying peacefully as a centenarian, and enjoying a posthumous romantic reunion with Jack and all the *Titanic* dead. This vision of the afterlife recalls the lovers' apotheosis at the end of Prokofiev's 1935 ballet *Romeo and Juliet*, but also realises Laurents and Bernstein's October 1955 plan for the original *West Side Story*: 'the walls disappear, the music soars upward and the audience swoons'.

Pop culture re-imaginings of Juliet still negotiate the legacy of the 1960s. In 2008, Taylor Swift's 'Love Story' made Juliet alternately strong and a damsel in distress, encouraging Romeo: 'Don't be afraid, we'll make it out of this mess,' but begging him 'take me somewhere we can be alone'.[171] Like *Mirabelle*'s passive Juliet, Swift's heroine is begging Romeo not to leave and 'cryin' on the staircase'. Unlike *Mirabelle*'s Romeo, though, Swift's hero talks to her father, unlocking for Juliet the prize of patient femininity: permission to 'go pick out a white dress'.[172] Unlike *Mirabelle*, instead of speaking from her grave, Taylor Swift's survivor Juliet looks back *with him* at their romance, many years later. This lets Swift's lovers fulfil the promise naively made by Shakespeare's Romeo: 'all these woes shall serve / For sweet discourses in our times to come' (3.5.52–3). Unlike the teen tragedy-pop of the early 1960s, in Swift's song-world, nobody has to die. Unlike Janis Ian's 'Society's Child', Swift's Juliet doesn't choose society over her lover – but only because society, as embodied by her dad and Romeo, makes it possible for her to have both.

Swift is happy for Juliet to be a victim rescued by men, but just as the adolescent Victorian readers of the *Girl's Own Paper* turned on Juliet for her apparent passivity and cowardice, less conservative post-Swift adaptations have tended to treat Juliet harshly. Chicago improv troupe Second City's 2010 YouTube hit *Sassy Gay Friend* saw a camp interlocutor warn Juliet to 'slow down, crazy!' and haranguing her as 'an idiot. You took a roofie from a priest'.[173] In trying to create a strong, admirable heroine within *Romeo and Juliet*, Karen Maine's film *Rosaline* (2022) abandons Juliet altogether for Rosaline, an acerbic woman scorned. In a wise-cracking performance, Kaitlyn Dever sabotages then saves the relationship of a teenage dirtbag Romeo and a twittering Juliet, the latter a dim-witted, starry-eyed princess who gabs about her feelings. In this millennial schema,

Rosaline is the cool girl, Juliet, the basic bitch. Where post-war adaptations led in simplifying and sidelining Shakespeare's rebellious Juliet, these sneering revisionists have followed.

The 1960s Juliet, whether she sang and danced like Wood's Maria, or ran and shouted like Hussey on screen, ended up with less to say than her predecessors had a century earlier. Where the nineteenth century had created multiple star Juliets and only one star Romeo (a woman), these twentieth-century adaptations' homosocial, homoerotic aesthetics sidelined their heroines to write tragedies of masculine violence. Their emphasis on gang tribalism over romance had consequences for Juliet, and for *Romeo and Juliet*, for the rest of the twentieth century.

In the 1960s, Juliet, alongside her Romeo, became 'Society's Child' against a backdrop of civil rights activism, Cold War hostilities, and gang war. As societies around the world moved from ancient grudge to new mutinies through the new millennium, the resulting violence would create more new Juliets and her Romeos in fiction – and fact – than ever before.

Across The Barricades

The popularity of *West Side Story*, and critical readings of Zeffirelli's film as a comment on the Cold War, sparked a vogue for adaptations of *Romeo and Juliet* set in conflict zones. From fictional gang wars in New York City to real-life military struggles around the world, Shakespeare's play quickly became a kind of shorthand in both art and media. Real-life lovers from opposing groups were dubbed 'Romeo and Juliet' by the international press. Fiction writers wanting to explore relationships made taboo by sectarian violence reached for the trope of 'star-crossed lovers'. How these adaptations both upheld and departed from Shakespeare's plot has consequences for Juliet's character; when the young woman dubbed a 'Juliet' is a real-life victim of violence, those consequences can be deadly.

Among the prose fictions inspired by *Romeo and Juliet*, the most influential – a kind of blueprint for the genre – is Joan Lingard's 1970s 'Kevin and Sadie' series, a sequence of five novels aimed at teenagers. The second novel, the 1972 best-seller *Across the Barricades*, sees Catholic Kevin and Protestant Sadie rekindle their childhood attraction as teenagers in Belfast.

But while *Romeo and Juliet* begins with 'Two households both alike in dignity' and ends with two dead lovers, *Across the Barricades* does neither. The British occupy the Irish; Lingard downplays the inequality of this, and, further, presents the Northern Irish police (PSNI) as courteous and reasonable ('No one will ever tell us anything', laments one peace-loving British soldier).[1] The villains of the tale are all Catholic thugs. Kevin's mother is an unhappy prisoner of Catholic patriarchy, frustrated that 'all she ever saw [. . .] was this street of brick terraced houses and the main road beyond where she did her shopping'.[2] The Protestant narrative that Catholic girls are doomed not to have 'decent' lives prevails: 'She's a Mick and she'll probably have twelve kids'.[3] The 'dignity', or rather the 'indignity', of Catholic womanhood is constantly stressed.[4] As in *West Side Story*, assimilation is the only answer. But unlike in *West Side Story*, it is Romeo (Kevin), and not Juliet (Sadie), who must abandon his loyalties to elope with her to (Protestant, British) London, which is presented as a place of liberation. As in Shakespeare, it is Lingard's Juliet who first suggests elopement; unlike Shakespeare, Lingard's heroine gets the chance to carry out her idea, not 'follow[ing] my lord' but making him scramble after her. Lingard's appropriation of Shakespeare also fundamentally bypasses one of the Prologue's key claims: that the familial feud, the 'ancient grudge', can be solved by the 'children's end' (1.0.3–11). Lingard presents the religious conflict in Northern Ireland as irrec-oncilable – but also gives her lovers the chance to live.

When I mention on Twitter that I'm reading *Across the Barricades* for this book, the joyful reminiscences come rushing in. Within the resulting thread, I learn that Joan Lingard's Kevin and Sadie novels were so popular that libraries across the island of Ireland kept them at the issue desk for easy access, sometimes with waiting lists of borrowers. *Across the Barricades* became a British GCSE coursework text by the late 1980s, positioning it for direct comparison with *Romeo and Juliet*.[5] The novels also made their way on to a school curriculum in Drammen, Norway, and the writer Rebecca Mills even recalls enjoying them, aged twelve, in a Sierra Leone library, where they resonated with the contemporary unrest in Freetown.[6]

Lingard's successors in the fiction marketplace include Dorit Rabinyan, author of *All the Rivers* (2014), which was banned by Israel's Ministry of Education for its depiction of an Israeli/Palestinian love affair.[7] More famous is Malorie Blackman's *Noughts and Crosses* series (2001–21), a spectacularly successful speculative history in which powerful Black Crosses disenfranchise white noughts. As authors, Rabinyan and Blackman depart from Lingard in each killing off their Romeo figures – perhaps in an echo of *West Side Story*'s murder of Tony. But, unlike *West Side Story*, and like Lingard, both Rabinyan and Blackman assign their male lover to the more disenfranchised group. Like Lingard, too, the conflicts (historical or imaginary) are left unresolved at the ends of the novels. All these books are set in unequal conflicts; inequality has been a fundamental aspect of *Romeo and Juliet* adaptations, but wasn't a feature of the original relationship. Transposing Shakespeare's feud into an unequal conflict ostensibly allows the audience to imagine peace and love. But it also allows some audience members, faced with a representation of a real-life conflict about which they might have pre-existing views, to make an easy decision about which family, Montague or Capulet, is 'bad', whose 'fault' it is. *Romeo and Juliet* doesn't give us that luxury. Equally, when the real-life struggle is a patently unequal one, Shakespeare's even-handedness allows other members to dismiss the conflict as one with an equal degree of fault on both sides, which is inaccurate and offensive. In both scenarios, it's a reductive strategy that means audiences can avoid thinking deeply about either the real-life violence – or Shakespeare.

The direct use of the play as a teaching tool ought to avoid some of these pitfalls, but the key work on the subject, Tom Sperlinger's teaching memoir *Romeo and Juliet in Palestine*, ultimately tells its own cautionary tale. Sperlinger asks his Muslim students to imagine a Gazan version of *Romeo and Juliet*, and notes that 'if it were an Israeli/Palestinian conflict, the ending would have to change because the Montagues and Capulets would never join hands'.[8] Sperlinger is teaching English Literature at Al-Quds University in Abu Dis, which is a Palestinian village under Israeli control. The students can just about imagine a future for the couple in exile, but the location is a problem; when Sperlinger suggests Gaza, he's greeted with 'general laughter'.[9]

Two moments in *Romeo and Juliet in Palestine* are particularly disquieting. One is the conclusion that Sperlinger no longer sees *Romeo and Juliet* as a love story, based on the lovers' first dialogue in the balcony scene. Romeo's declares that 'with love's light wings did I o'erperch these walls'. This is the play's most exuberant metaphor for love overcoming difficulties in an almost supernatural, airborne fashion; the fantastical coincidence of him finding Juliet is explained away because Cupid has lent him wings. So far, so romantic, but Sperlinger muses on Juliet's warning reply to Romeo that 'if they [her kinsmen] do see thee, they will murder thee'. He argues that

'You could read Juliet's words, like Romeo's, as teenage hyperbole. But now I think she is in earnest'.[10]

Why would Juliet's words ever be seen as hyperbole? And why does recognising *Romeo and Juliet* as a play about violence – one that begins with threats of murder and rape, includes six deaths, and sees 'gentle Romeo' kill twice – preclude recognising the romance? Why wouldn't Juliet be in earnest? Is it impossible to see her as a clear-eyed commentator on her situation because she is also a teenage girl in love? I think this dismissal of Juliet inherits from the post-war belief that if the play is primarily about conflict, it is no longer about its heroine.

Another uneasy moment comes when Sperlinger's students are plotting their Palestinian rewrite. The students desperately want the lovers to live, demanding, 'Give it a happy ending!' and 'roar[ing]' for the couple to 'escape into exile'. Sperlinger tries to dissuade them: 'If Romeo and Juliet live, I suggested, the Montagues and the Capulets can't be reconciled'.[11]

The adaptation Sperlinger commissions from his students is not merely an interesting artistic thought-experiment. It is an adaptation of the students' own real lives, evinced by the unnamed female Muslim student who, when someone suggests the combination of an Israeli Romeo and a Palestinian Juliet, confirms 'that happens a lot'.[12] Sperlinger's students want their Romeo and Juliet, whose identities are based on their own, to live beyond the violent interfaith conflict that positions them as 'star-crossed'. In telling them that if *this* 'Romeo and Juliet live [. . .] the Montagues and Capulets can't be reconciled', Sperlinger implies that the lovers' deaths, in ending the conflict, are not only necessary but *sufficient*. This seems like a valid comment in the context of the play: the prologue tells us that only the death of children can foment parental reconciliation, even if Capulet's claim to Paris that ''tis not hard, I think / For men so old as we to keep the peace' (1.2.2–3), and his hospitable tolerance of Romeo as a 'well-governed youth' suggest other possibilities (1.5.62–5). But in the Abu Dis classroom, where Sperlinger deliberately blurs the boundaries between fact and fiction, this is a dangerous assumption. This implication – that young lovers can unite their families by dying, but not by living – lingers not only in fictional adaptations of *Romeo and Juliet*, but in real-world love stories on to which the names of Shakespeare's lovers have been projected.

★

Referring to real-life lovers as 'Romeo and Juliet' is not new. Victorian newspapers ascribed the label to a succession of tragedies. In 1860, they reported the gruesome details of a suicide pact in Cienfuegos as 'quite a romantic and melancholy affair' under the heading 'A Romeo and Juliet in Cuba'.[13] The *Worcestershire Chronicle* described a murderous feud in a Loire Valley village as 'reviv[ing]' the 'old-world tragedy in which the Montagues and Capulets played a prominent part'.[14] In 1894, several papers syndicated the *Daily Chronicle*'s report on the suicide of a young Warsaw woman at the funeral of 'Makoffsky', a man who had also died by poison, as that of 'Romeo and Juliet in real life'.[15] The moniker allowed newspapers to gloss snippets of overseas scandal – the details of the suicides, including notes, types of poison, funerals, and other gruesome details – with a high literary tone, thanks to association with the national poet. Editors willingly ignored major differences between real-life events and the plot attached to the names of Shakespeare's lovers. The Cienfuegos couple took strychnine in coffee together due to one-sided opposition from his family. The girl told her family she had taken poison; the boy survived. The Loire Valley case saw the murder of one family's son after the discovery of a secret relationship. This was followed by his killers' imprisonment, and the local domination of his family's clan. 'Makoffsky' was the young woman's rejected suitor, with no surrounding feud.

As consumption of mass media intensified through the twentieth century and into the twenty-first, narratives of real-life Romeos and Juliets have been written and circulated with ever-increasing fervour – particularly thanks to war correspondence, photojournalism, and the internet. The real-life stories of three particular couples were consumed and re-consumed all round the world, and, in the case of one couple, it was actually the fact that they had become a story, and the narrative pleasure they afforded one reader, that allowed them to survive.

Of those three cases, two date from the early 1990s and one from the 2010s. Diarmuid Shields and Julie Statham were a young couple from Northern Ireland, planning to become engaged on Diarmuid's twenty-first birthday. Like Lingard's lovers, they had grown up during the Troubles, but unlike Kevin and Sadie, both were Catholics. On 3 January 1993, the Ulster Volunteer Force, a banned Unionist paramilitary group, murdered twenty-year-old Diarmuid alongside his father in the family home behind the Shields' shop in County Tyrone. Laurence Maguire, 'director of operations' for UVF's 'mid-Ulster unit', shot Diarmuid and his father Patrick Shields dead in the family kitchen, allegedly in the presence of UVF commander 'Rat King' Billy Wright.[16] Over a thousand mourners attended the father and son's joint funeral.[17] Julie, a student at Queen's University Belfast, killed herself a month later. Father Denis Faul, Julie's priest, dubbed them 'Romeo and Juliet', and said that Julie had 'died of a broken heart'.[18] On Valentine's Day 1993, the international press followed suit with headlines about a 'Modern-Day Romeo and Juliet'.[19] The French media revisited the story in a 2014 documentary, again making the link.[20]

In 1990s Bosnia, Boško Brkić and Admira Ismić, both in their twenties, had been together since school. He was an Orthodox Christian Bosnian Serb and she a Bosnian Muslim, or Bosniak. During the Bosnian War (1992–5) and the Siege of Sarajevo, Boško and Admira attempted to leave their besieged, majority-Muslim neighbourhood for the Serb-controlled quarter of Grbavica. Snipers shot and killed the lovers on 19 May 1993 on the [then-named] Vrbanja Bridge. Boško was killed instantly; Admira took ten to fifteen minutes to die, having crawled to Boško's body and embraced him. Mark H. Milstein, an American photojournalist, photographed their bodies. Kurt Schork, who wrote the first media dispatch, didn't call them 'Romeo and Juliet' but the connection was swiftly made.[21] A documentary, the Emmy-nominated *Romeo and Juliet in Sarajevo* (1994), ensured three decades of media attention.[22] Their murder site and graves are now part of the Sarajevan tourist trail.[23]

Mohammad Ali and Zakia grew up on neighbouring potato farms in a village near the Hindu Kush Mountains in Afghanistan. He was a Shi'a Muslim and a member of the Hazara minority, and she was a Tajik and a Sunni. In an Afghan echo of the balcony scene, Ali wooed Zakia by sneaking into the walled garden of her home and reciting song lyrics to her as she lay on the flat roof.[24] Denied permission to marry, they eloped. Zakia was threatened with death by her family, who tried to have her legally removed from the women's shelter to which she had fled to avoid an honour killing; Ali was also briefly imprisoned on a false charge of kidnap, then released. Zakia and Ali's months on the run from both her family and the Afghan police were documented by the Afghan media, to whom Zakia became a hero, and by *New York Times* Kabul bureau chief Rod Nordland. Nordland would also recount the story in his book *The Lovers*, subtitled 'Afghanistan's Romeo and Juliet'. Zakia and Ali, with their daughter Ruqia, eventually got permission to emigrate to America in 2016. Documentary-makers, journalists and authors all drew on the language and paratexts of Shakespeare's play: Nordland's book even begins with a 'Dramatis Personae' and the same speech by Romeo, about 'stony walls' failing to 'hold love out', used by Sperlinger in his final chapter.

Beyond the fact that all these young couples were in love against a backdrop of political violence, there are fundamental differences between each story and the plot of *Romeo and Juliet*. All three couples were in long-term relationships, and only Zakia and Ali faced familial disapproval. Julie's relationship with Diarmuid, like that of Admira's with Boško, had the enthusiastic approval of both families. Julie's father found Diarmuid a 'nice boy', 'very friendly' and 'quiet', while Admira's father reflected on Boško, 'after a time, I started to love him'.[25]

Although each relationship was affected by violence, the contexts varied wildly. In Northern Ireland, so pervasive is the idea that Diarmuid and Julie were an interfaith couple, a real-life Kevin and Sadie loving 'across the barricades', that Liam Kennedy – a historian of the Troubles and Julie's Queens University Belfast professor – wrote: 'He was from the Catholic tribe, she from the Protestant'.[26] In fact, both were part of the same County Tyrone Catholic community.

Conversely, Admira and Boško were from different ethnic and faith groups, but had been raised 'without thinking about religion or nationality' in cosmopolitan, pre-war Sarajevo.[27] Admira was not raised to regard Boško as her 'great enemy'; her Muslim family had 'many mixed marriages', and her father sang in a Catholic choir. Boško's mother loved Admira and 'didn't regard her as different'.[28] As part of the break-up of Yugoslavia, the Socialist Republic of

Bosnia and Herzegovina declared independence after a referendum, which Serbs within Bosnia largely rejected. Serbian President Slobodan Milošević supported Serb Democratic politician Radovan Karadžić and the Yugoslavian army in a series of violent conflicts that saw the Bosnian Serb Army commit genocide against Muslims.

The enmity between Zakia and Ali's families began not with a feud but with wider sectarian conflicts in Afghanistan. Although Zakia and Ali grew up in the same village and spoke the same language (Dari), they came from different indigenous groups and Islamic sects. The Tajiks, Zakia's community, are Afghanistan's second-largest and second-most-powerful ethnic group, ethnically Iranian and more routinely urbanised than other Afghan ethnicities. Like more than three quarters of worldwide Muslims, she is also a Sunni. The Shi'a Hazaras, the smaller group to which Ali belongs, face prejudice from many people in Afghanistan (the Taliban and Al Qaeda hate them most of all). Historically, they've been particularly vulnerable to persecution and land-grabs. Bamiyan, Zakia and Ali's province, is immediately between majority-Tajik and majority-Hazara territories, in the east of Afghanistan's impoverished, resource-poor central region. Although Hazaras are typically less privileged than Tajiks, Ali's family were slightly better off financially. When Zakia and Ali eloped and married in secret, the Tajik status of Zakia's family enabled them to bribe the police and judiciary to arrest Ali and persecute Zakia.[29] The lovers faced opposition not from both families, but from Zakia's family, in collusion with the state.

And there are other key differences in their stories, including the way they each ended. Julie Statham killed herself after Diarmuid's murder, while Juliet does so after Romeo's suicide. Admira was murdered alongside Boško, having chosen to leave their neighbourhood with him – as opposed to Juliet, stuck behind in Verona. While Admira and Boško's joint grave, first just outside Sarajevo in Lukavica's Serbian cemetery and then in the Lion cemetery in Sarajevo, has become a monument of the kind envisaged by the Montagues and Capulets, Julie and Diarmuid were buried separately, 'several miles' apart.[30] Zakia and Ali are still alive, and in the United States.

Given the gulfs between life and art, why do we apply such an ill-fitting fictional frame to real experiences? As in the Victorian era, connecting these tragedies with Shakespeare ascribes prestige to the often irresponsible reporting of gruesome and violent stories, as if Shakespeare is far seemlier. Coverage of Julie Statham's suicide, both in 1993 and in the 2013 documentary, dwelt on Julie's final hours, the method of her suicide, and the appearance of her corpse as found by her father – details that best-practice guidelines agree should not be publicised, given the increased likelihood of suicide contagion when methods, images, and romanticised narratives are disseminated.[31] Photographer Mark H. Milstein's image of Boško and Admira's corpses provided important evidence of their murders, but NBC's televised description of how those corpses were partially eaten by 'hungry dogs and cats' during the eight days they spent 'in the heat, on the streets' is gratuitous.[32]

Ali and Zakia, mercifully, survived, but Nordland surrounds their biography with a plethora of details about honour killings and the terrible deaths of other Afghan 'star-crossed' lovers, like Layla and Waheed, a Pashtun/Tajik couple who killed themselves with poison in the tragically mistaken belief they had been caught at a police checkpoint in Kunduz city, or Munira and Farhad, a Sunni/Shi'a couple who asphyxiated in a shipping container.[33] My account of these stories is a summary; Nordland's catalogue goes beyond providing vital context for foreign readers and becomes a gallery of death that is both prurient and oddly desensitising. Desensitising because Nordland betrays himself when he considers the possibility that his (fervent) efforts to save Ali and Zakia will fail – a possibility he admits he facilitated by 'shining [. . .] an unhelpful light of publicity upon them'. Photographer Diego Ibarra Sanchez photographed the couple in a situation that risked them being 'captured there and then [. . .] because one of us had been too journalistically eager for yet another piece of the story'.[34] A government PR advisor in Kabul complained that both Husu Banu Ghazanfar, the then-Minister of Women's Affairs, and President Karzai were unhappy – Karzai 'especially unhappy' – that Nordland had 'made a Romeo-and-Juliet story out of this'.[35] A love story was 'wrong' in a country that was 'officially anti-romantic', and it especially endangered Zakia when her Tajik family was leveraging the authorities' support. In places where women are disproportionately the victims of so-called 'honour killings' and 'honour'-based abuse, international media stories about unsanctioned relationships could be deadly.[36] But even as Nordland expressed anxiety about causing Zakia and Ali's deaths, he described them in terms of narrative banality. If Zakia and Ali had been murdered or killed themselves, they would have become 'just another typical Afghan love story after all'.[37]

Susan Sontag was right when she described exceptional images of violent death as pornographic. But they're nothing new. Broken bodies are fundamental to the history of Western art: the Passion, the Rape of the Sabine Women, Saint Sebastian, the images that Georges Bataille described as 'at the same time ecstatic and intolerable'.[38] An obsession with the horrible reaches into the highest places of our culture. Sontag recalls the philosopher Edmund Burke, musing on the sublime and concluding: 'We have a degree of delight, and that no small one, in the real misfortunes and pains of others'.[39] Burke's belief that people enjoy the sight of 'some uncommon and grievous calamity' is reflected in cars slowing at crash sites, or the phenomenon of 'shock websites' that collate images of autopsies, violent deaths, terrorism, and medical crises. When the title 'Romeo and Juliet' is used to add romance and respectability to graphic imagery (visual or written) of violent death, this risks creating 'trauma porn', art that exploits marginalised people purely for the fascinated titillation such images can bring, and which is sometimes defended on the grounds of 'raising awareness'. This merely creates 'trauma porn that wears a social justice fig leaf', in the words of Mexican-American writer Myriam Gurba.[40] Coleridge's eighteenth-century 'sensibility' has been succeeded by a comfortable delusion that the recirculation and reiteration of traumatic images is the same as advocacy.

But of course, Shakespeare is also obsessed with the gratuitous and gory. Early modern drama knew all about 'uncommon and grievous calamity' and its sexual potential. Isabella in *Measure for Measure*, willing to wear 'the impression of keen whips [. . .] as rubies' (2.4.99), is both a martyr dying for Christ and 'so erotic', as Juliet Stevenson, who played Isabella for the Royal Shakespeare Company in 1983, notes.[41] Elsewhere, Shakespeare's language encourages his audiences to scrutinise violated bodies in *Titus Andronicus* and *The Rape of Lucrece*. In *Romeo and Juliet*, specifically, Capulet encourages Paris – and us – to see Juliet's apparently dead body as 'deflowered by' Death himself (4.4.65). Even after we've seen the suicides of Romeo and Juliet unfold in real time, other characters call our attention to bodily details of the scene onstage, where 'the ground is bloody'. The Chief Watchman stresses that she's 'bleeding, warm' and 'newly dead' (5.3.171–4) – he presumably touches her to obtain this datum, a macabre thought – while Capulet calls his wife to 'look how our daughter bleeds!' (5.3.201) from a wound from Romeo's dagger. Recasting real-life victims as Shakespearean characters should remind us how exploitative and violent Shakespeare is himself. When newspapers describe tabloid scurrility as resembling a Shakespearean plot, they're not disguising sensational coverage as art – they're just following Shakespeare's lead.

*

Another reason for linking real-life violence to Shakespeare is the ideological burden that British politics currently places on pedagogy. *Romeo and Juliet* is consistently the most popular choice of set Shakespeare text both at British GCSE and in American high schools. As well as teaching *Romeo and Juliet* for literary-critical purposes, English Literature teachers in the UK are now called upon to teach the play, and all curriculum texts, in a way that actively promotes 'British values' in everyday life. Since 2011, the Conservative government has described these values as democracy, the rule of law, individual liberty, mutual respect and tolerance of those with different faiths and beliefs.[42] One Sussex comprehensive uses *Romeo and Juliet* to teach the rule of law and 'causes and consequences of criminal activity', while a Catholic academy promotes 'democracy' through *Romeo and Juliet*'s illustration of 'how civil unrest causes problems'.[43] One syllabus for a Pupil Referral Unit describes how *Romeo and Juliet* teaches 'the depths that humans can sink to through rash judgements and poor choices or being at odds with a regime' (re: individual liberty) and the consequences of 'acts of revenge, taking the law into our own hands' (re: the rule of law).[44]

Certainly, advocates of fiction have long claimed that its moral influence can make us better people in our day-to-day lives. In *A Defence of Poetry* (c. 1580), Elizabethan England's most important piece of literary criticism, courtier and poet Philip Sidney argued

that poetry was full of 'virtue-breeding delightfulness', while tragedy 'maketh kings fear to be tyrant'.[45] Even comedy, in its depiction
of 'private and domestical matters', could instruct. 'Nothing', Sidney
argued, could 'more open [a man's] eyes than to find his own actions
contemptibly set forth' in literature. But today, the idea that literature should be relevant to real life and have real-world application is
encoded in law. Across the UK, several school documents also
mention the play alongside the highly controversial PREVENT strategy. PREVENT is a part of the UK government's counter-terrorism
scheme, in which public bodies – including schools – must monitor
and report anyone vulnerable to the 'risks of radicalisation'.[46]

Despite the government's demand that *Romeo and Juliet* be related
to 'daily life', there's no official guidance on the dangers of teaching
plays containing suicide and murder. Nor, ironically, does a policy
demanding teachers scrutinise their pupils for signs of 'extremism'
include watching for students in obsessive or dangerous relationships. Nearly everyone in *Romeo and Juliet* has 'extreme' views on
love and marriage. The teachers with whom I spoke for this chapter,
all of whom prefer to remain anonymous, expressed frustration
that the play was being used as a tool for teaching government-
ordained values, let alone as a reasonable arena in which to watch
students for signs of extremism.

Simultaneously, students often share a 'common desire' for the
literary texts they study to be 'relatable' to their own lives and experiences.[47] It's easy to see the positives in this: a greater diversity of
writers and texts, and of performers when those texts are staged.
Baz Luhrmann's 1996 *Romeo + Juliet*, still popular thirty years on,
made aesthetic choices that strongly emphasised relatability and
familiarity: contemporary clothing, the inclusion of modern-day
technology, and the recasting of the Chorus who speaks the
Prologue (otherwise the play's least naturalistic element) as an
American newscaster, identical in appearance to those shown every
day on 1990s TV. But, for some critics, 'relatability' is a synonym for
reader passivity. Seen strictly as a literary-critical evaluation, 'relatability' is uselessly subjective because it is, as author and editor
Rebecca Onion puts it, 'shorthand masquerading as description';
nobody can evaluate an argument for 'relatability' without first-
hand experience of the person making it.[48]

'Relatability' becomes even trickier with historical distance. At my own university, most BA English undergraduates study Anglophone writing from about 800 AD to the present day. The first millennia of that literature, with few exceptions, assumes an ubiquity and intensity of Christian practice that is totally unrelatable to most twenty-first-century students. A lot of literature is fantastically strange on first reading – Mercutio's 'Queen Mab' speech, John Donne wanting to be ravished by God, *Finnegans Wake*, Kafka's *Metamorphosis*, *Wuthering Heights*, or Richard Crashaw's yen to be breastfed by Jesus – and the strangeness offers the opportunity vicariously to expand our own experience into the unfamiliar.

But at the same time, most of us are kept reading by moments of affinity. Aged twenty and in the viscera of a bad break-up, I felt sure Geoffrey Chaucer had been prophesying my exact situation in *Troilus and Criseyde* (c. 1380s) when Troilus bewailed his inability to 'unloven yow a quarter of a day!' ('yow' being Criseyde). Chaucer follows up with the line: 'In cursed tyme I born was, weylaway!', which also seemed applicable.[49] Alan Bennett describes the occurrence eloquently in *The History Boys*:

> The best moments in reading are when you come across something – a thought, a feeling, a way of looking at things – which you had thought special and particular to you. Now here it is, set down by someone else, a person you have never met, someone even who is long dead. And it is as if a hand has come out and taken yours.[50]

I'm keen to avoid knee-jerk snobbery about the terms in which young people articulate their enjoyment of art. As well as being pedagogically sanctioned, 'relatability' is part of Shakespeare's enduring popularity. Shakespeare's greatest fans have long discussed him in terms of his universality. As a Stratford-born former employee of both the Shakespeare Birthplace Trust and Royal Shakespeare Company (like my parents before me in the latter case), with three degrees in literature and a career based largely on talking about Shakespeare's works, I find Shakespeare universally applicable – but my universe is unusually Shakespeare-shaped. Claims for Shakespeare's universality sometimes mean that the fan sees the values or qualities they find in Shakespeare, usually their own, *as universal*, or believes they should be. This is reinforced by the 'What Shakespeare can teach us about COVID/Brexit/the Wagatha Christie libel trial' articles that inevitably appear at moments of cultural stress. Nevertheless, if seventy-six per cent of the Chinese population still finds Shakespeare relevant, if Mandela drew on the playwright's words in prison on Robben Island, if *Hamlet* can enthral audiences in Micronesia with little tradition of performed drama, then he resonates very widely indeed.[51]

For good or ill, we are in a literary climate that tries to bridge the gap between literature and real life. The real-life cases of Diarmuid and Julie, Boško and Admira, and Ali and Zakia unite elements of Shakespeare's *Romeo and Juliet* that are ideal for media consumption. One is very general: a strong narrative. Professor of cognitive science Mark Turner argues that we enjoy narrative because our brains are essentially literary, because '[n]arrative imagining – story – is the fundamental instrument of thought'. We need a storyteller's imagination, Turner argues, for the basic ways we anticipate the future, making plans and explaining our lives.[52] Aristotle located the pleasure of narratives in 'their imitation of life and their rhythm'.[53] Narrative consoles because it is 'linked to desire [. . .] a desire to know: we want to discover secrets, to know the end, to find the truth'.[54] Superimposing literature on life can create that truth. Shakespeare scholar David Francis Taylor looks at how satirists have drawn on Shakespeare to comprehend violent and frightening realities; by likening them to Shakespeare, they 'borrow syntax and plots through which a seemingly incomprehensible event might be understood'.[55]

Literary tragedy is pleasurable, because of and not in spite of the distress it induces. From 2014 to 2018, I was part of a group that tested audience response to tragedy at the University of Oxford. We discovered that watching tragedy actually releases endorphins, the body's homegrown opiates that improve our pain tolerance, even if the tragedy was so harrowing that, on the face of it, we wouldn't say we'd enjoyed it. Tragedies also make us feel more bonded to those around us; they're good for us *and* good for society.[56]

We survive real-life tragedies by narrativising them. Joan Didion describes modern humanity as seeking 'the sermon in the suicide,

[. . .] the social or moral lesson in the murder of five'.[57] Prince Escalus is right there, 400 years ahead of her, interpreting Romeo and Juliet's deaths to their fathers: 'See what a scourge is laid upon your hate/ That heaven finds means to kill your joys with love' (5.3.290–1). In reconciliation and rich memorials to commemorate their children, Capulet and Montague also fulfil our desire for 'something good' to come out of a tragedy. This framing is visible in press coverage of Julie Statham's death, which documented in detail her mother's subsequent successful campaign to fund a bereavement counselling centre in County Tyrone. Julie had sought counselling in Belfast, but an appointment was only offered the morning after her death.[58]

Escalus's rewriting of the lovers' suicides as divinely ordained, echoed by Capulet's description of them as 'poor sacrifices of our enmity' (5.3.303), strikingly sidesteps the theological ramifications of suicides for practising Catholics. Similarly, Julie Statham's suicide was rewritten by her own priest, Father Denis Faul, as death 'of a broken heart', and by others as essentially a second UVF murder.[59] One journalist invoked the narrative of 'another tragic Shakespearean heroine, Ophelia', to further diminish Julie's agency in her own death.[60] When she drowns, Ophelia's demise is 'doubtful' as regards how 'witting' or deliberate her drowning was (5.1.8–10; 187). Julie Statham left an entire folder of suicide notes, letters, poems and an anonymous newspaper tribute to Diarmuid, but comparisons to both Juliet and Ophelia reduce her to a character in a media narrative, not the author of her own story.[61]

Allowing us to experience these real-life narratives as fictions gives us the luxury of sensibility without the responsibility of intervention. Infuriated by the evils of the transatlantic slave trade at the end of the eighteenth century, the poet and abolitionist Samuel Taylor Coleridge railed at the average reader's ability to consume sugar picked by enslaved Africans 'even while she is weeping over the refined sorrows of Werter or Clementina', the suffering protagonists in contemporary novels.[62] The 'sorrows' of drama demand no action; in the theatre, the success of traditional Western drama depends on the audience *not* intervening to alter the content of the performance. Likening the Troubles, the Bosnian War and the endemic inter-ethnic conflicts of Afghanistan to the Shakespearean feud makes dangerous assumptions about those wars. It implies that they are trivial, unjustified and fought between evenly equipped partisans enthusiastic for continued combat. Comparing these factions to Montagues and Capulets also implies that the entrenched conflicts *could* – and indeed might – yet be solved instantly by individual choice, as when the belligerent patriarchs end the 'ancient grudge' in the play's final scene. Projecting the Capulet–Montague feud on to the real-life conflicts also obscures the fact that lasting peace is always a collective process.

In 2014, Nordland's first article about Zakia and Ali began: 'She is his Juliet and he is her Romeo' under the headline 'Two star-crossed Afghans cling to love'. He admitted later that as he wrote it, he saw it primarily as a 'great story, though sad, and with a follow-up that was a death foretold', since 'the next and final article would be about how the girl's family came one night' and murdered her.[63] He expected this familiar story would be ephemeral: 'We would all be outraged and then turn the page'.[64] His use of the *Romeo and Juliet* moniker was picked as part of that 'foretelling'. The most dangerous consequence of seeing real-life people and events as the characters in *Romeo and Juliet* is seeing them as pre-destined to die, just as naming enslaved Africans after doomed Shakespearean characters enabled British enslavers to ignore their own culpability in the Africans' real, avoidable suffering. Calling Zakia and Ali 'Romeo and Juliet' allowed readers to make essentially comfortable assumptions about the lovers' fates.

As well as sweeping away the specificities of individual political and racial identities, the way these narratives are reported can minimise the importance of gender. In these retellings, each pair of lovers becomes not only indivisible but indistinguishable from each other, both victims described by commentators as passively 'caught up in' a conflict with which they have nothing to do. To be 'caught up in' – to become unwittingly embroiled or entangled in some situation – is a relative neologism, dating from the last century. But a closer reading of the present cases reveals histories in which each partner, however much in love, experiences the world in ways radically differently from their beloved.

Ironically, this is something the modern couples do share with Shakespeare's lovers and the play itself: Juliet's experience is defined by being a woman surrounded by patriarchy and patriarchal violence, in which Romeo is profoundly involved. Juliet dies because of bad luck, but also because of a series of bad decisions made by men: Romeo kills Tybalt, which leads to his banishment; her father emotionally abuses her and accelerates her forced, bigamous marriage. These events prompt Friar Laurence's chaotic and ultimately derailed plan, the failure of which sees Romeo murder Paris and kill himself. If the 'two houses' are alike in resources, the lovers are not, and Shakespeare acknowledges that in the (often cut) prologue to Act 2, describing Juliet 'as much in love, her means much less' than Romeo's (2.0.11). The 'real-life Juliets' are equally subject to the particular consequences of their identities.

Admira died because Boško's black-market activities brought him to the attention of the local Muslim police, necessitating his rapid departure. Boško's gangster friend Ismet 'Ćelo' Bajramović, the 'Godfather of Sarajevo' who 'controlled most of Sarajevo's drugs trade', supposedly concocted a plan to see them safely cross the bridge.[65] Although he had previously safely traded Boško's mother for Serbians wishing to return, his apparent plan to evacuate Boško and Admira went fatally wrong.[66] Even had they survived the bridge, Boško was travelling to safety and Admira was not; she was moving to a region where she was explicitly in danger of genocide. Six of her relatives had already been killed.[67]

In Afghanistan, Ali was briefly arrested at the behest of Zakia's family, and threatened with violence, much as Lady Capulet plots to murder Romeo. But it was Zakia who spent months in a shelter she experienced as a prison, because it was Zakia whom her family relentlessly and explicitly wanted to kill. The reason Ali's family was more accepting was largely because Ali was their son, not their daughter; perhaps this, too, is why Romeo leaves his father a letter while Juliet maintains her silence. It was Zakia whose parents cursed and disowned her. It was also Zakia who, after denying her father and refusing all traditional ideas of Afghan womanhood for a man supposedly that father's opposite, was expected by Ali to uphold the same patriarchal pattern.[68] In coverage of the pair, Ali frequently seems selfish and unreasonable (as readers pointed out, sometimes unpleasantly, via Nordland's Facebook page).[69] He wanted 'complete obedience to himself when he had insisted that Zakia reject obedience to her father'.[70] Given money for flights out of Afghanistan, Ali wanted to re-appropriate the money and take the heavily pregnant Zakia on a dangerous road journey back to Bamiyan, telling her: 'If you are my wife, then come with me'.[71]

Reading of Zakia and Ali's marital battles reminds me how little we see of Romeo and Juliet together; Shakespeare scholar Hester Lees-Jeffries points out that, by early modern standards, Romeo and Juliet 'do not have a marriage', merely a brief courtship and wedding. We never see Juliet managing a household or Romeo disciplining their children.[72] It seems odd to ask how they would problem-solve, when they are constantly beset by problems but they tackle everything via mediators, their actions largely dictated by Friar Laurence. Would Juliet's willingness to rebel against her father and her family, and her ability to strategically deceive both her parents and the Nurse, also have made her, like Zakia, a more rebarbative wife than Romeo expected? Had the young lovers' marriage been revealed, might Lord Capulet have warned Romeo, as Desdemona's father Brabantio does Othello, 'She has deceived her father, and may thee' (1.3.288)?

In Nordland's book, one exchange between Zakia and Ali tellingly rewrites Romeo and Juliet's moment of balcony-scene fantasy. Realising that 'Tis almost morning', Juliet is torn between her desire for Romeo to leave safely and her desire to recall him. She compares herself to a bird-owner

Who lets it hop a little from her hand
Like a poor prisoner in his twisted gyves
And with a silk thread plucks it back again
So loving-jealous of his liberty (2.1.221–4).

It is a sado-masochistic fantasy in which Romeo is the 'poor prisoner' and Juliet not merely his 'loving-jealous' owner, but a 'wanton'.[73] In the first quarto of the play, the wanton is female – her hand – carrying the connotations of a sexually promiscuous woman, the pampered courtesan with a menagerie; and 'wanton' has sexual connotations when the Nurse sees the 'wanton blood' in Juliet's cheeks at the prospect of her wedding.[74] By the second quarto, the wanton is male, letting the bird hop from 'his hand'; 'wanton' could also mean an unruly child, a schoolboy.[75] Whether Juliet imagines herself as a promiscuous woman or a mischievous schoolboy-esque tomboy, Romeo submits to her enthusiastically – 'I would I were thy bird' – with Juliet acknowledging, 'Sweet, so would I, / Yet I should kill thee with much cherishing' (2.1.225–6). Juliet recognises the danger of keeping Romeo her 'poor prisoner', rehearsing for their second, final parting when Romeo, having again ecstatically submitted to the idea of remaining in Verona at Juliet's will, declares: 'Come, death, and welcome; Juliet wills it so' (3.5.24). Juliet is the one to face the truth, that 'More light and light it grows' and he must go (3.5.35). Then, as now, she puts safe limits on their shared fantasies, recognising their peril as well as their pleasure.

In Afghanistan, in Bamiyan, Ali kept caged quails – literal and not metaphorical birds. After marrying Zakia, he teasingly asked her why she had fallen in love with him: guessing it was because of 'watching him playing with his quails'. She admitted, 'I never liked the birds [. . .] Why do you keep them in cages? They have wings – they should fly. Why don't you let them go?' A 'bit shocked', Ali explained, 'Because I love them'.[76] Something he saw as desirable and endearing, she saw as cruel. That which was cruel in Zakia's eyes was central to Ali's conception of love. Compared to Romeo and Juliet's symbiotic fantasy, it feels like a fundamental mismatch.

In Julie Statham's case, both she and Diarmuid were innocent victims of the vicious Loyalist violence inflicted on the Shields family – but the neat delineation of Montagues and Capulets implied by the *Romeo and Juliet* frame obscures the situation's complexity. One IRA historian, Ed Moloney, describes Patrick Shields – Diarmuid's father – as an IRA member during the 1970s who had left long before 1993. However, Moloney also alleges that Shields remained a close contact of Kevin Mallon, a Tyrone IRA leader 'dedicated to physical force' and 'one of the most formidable and daring IRA figures of the century'.[77] Kenneth Maginnis, then a local Ulster Unionist MP, insists that in 1993 Patrick Shields was still an IRA 'soldier and an intelligence officer', and a 'very dangerous man' whose shop was the 'centre of an intelligence cell'.[78] The republican priest Father Denis Faul, who buried Julie and was Shields's 'close personal friend', became a kind of Friar Laurence analogue in the minds of the international press. Again, this simplifies his position. Faul was, despite his public criticism of IRA violence, regarded as a 'provo priest' by the British establishment and considered 'offensively sectarian' even by Mary McAleese, Ireland's (Catholic) president from 1997 to 2011.[79] At the time Patrick and Diarmuid were murdered, Faul was well-known for having been Catholic chaplain to republican prisoners at the Maze prison (although for some republicans, he was 'the person responsible for breaking' the 1981 strike). He was also known as a conduit to the IRA in peace talks, and as a civil rights activist who had exposed British torture of republican internees.[80]

If the UVF and the British government shared Maginnis's view of Patrick Shields and his networks, it's possible that they saw in twenty-year-old Diarmuid a fellow IRA activist. Diarmuid had cut off his studies at an English university and got a job at a local heritage centre, sharing his father's passion for indigenous Irish culture.[81] Ultimately, the young lovers' deaths were co-opted to further, rather than end, the conflict that surrounded them. Frédéric Tonolli's documentary on the case was filmed in 2013, fifteen years after the Good Friday agreement, and twenty years after Diarmuid and Julie's death: the film nonetheless makes the agreement and the two deaths seem simultaneous and very recent, largely thanks to the intensity of political and personal feeling. Thus, rather than seeing in Diarmuid's murder and Julie's suicide an argument for reconciliation, republican former Deputy First Minister for Northern Ireland Seamus Mallon specifically cited them as reasons not to reconcile, saying he would be doing a disservice to them if he were to 'reconcile with the people who took their lives away'. Rather than *Romeo and Juliet* illuminating Diarmuid and Julie's story, their deaths illuminate the play. As a lens on *Romeo and Juliet*, the documentary's juxtaposition of Mallon with scenes from the Good Friday Agreement reminds us that the Montague–Capulet reconciliation is bordered by the Prince's warning that 'Some shall be pardoned and some punished' (5.3.307). As in April 1998, if there is amnesty between the belligerents, there is no amnesty granted by the authorities.

The label 'Romeo and Juliet' is in some ways intended as a compliment, a statement of the lovers' mutual intensity and commitment to their relationship, and as a sign they belong in a historical canon of great romances. We cannot be sure what

Diarmuid and Julie, or Boško and Admira, would have made of the 'Romeo and Juliet' label, but Boško and Admira's families strenuously reject it. They cite their loving support for the couple and each other; Rada, Boško's mother, lived with Admira's parents after her apartment was shelled. Admira refused to marry Boško for fear their mixed marriage, like many wartime unions at Sarajevo's city hall, would be used as propaganda, becoming, in Admira's own words, an 'international media event'. It thus seems likely she might have resisted her commodification as Sarajevo's Juliet, and to the many commercial tours that run today, cashing in on the 'Romeo and Juliet Bridge' and a trip to the lovers' graves.[82]

Although Nordland gave Zakia and Ali escape money, and his book helped them acquire a life-saving visa, their website stresses that the lovers receive no money from his articles or the book, which has been published in ten languages across (at a conservative estimate) twenty-six editions. The couple are not mentioned in Nordland's acknowledgements. One thing that Zakia and Julie's identification as Juliet should alert us to is that, just as the fictional Juliet has been commemorated far more widely than her Romeo, Zakia and Julie's images have similarly been exploited far more than their partners.

Despite Nordland's book's plural title, *The Lovers*, and the 'Afghanistan's Romeo and Juliet' subtitle that adorns the American, Bulgarian, Czech, Italian, and Slovak translations, several of these editions show only Zakia on the cover.[83] The most popular image is a head-and-shoulders portrait, with Zakia's downtrodden gaze turned towards the left of the frame. Her expression is frustrated, enigmatic, unhappy; her set jaw suggests determination, while her eyes are lost in private thought. Her purple hijab has slipped back to reveal some of her dark hair. The photograph is cropped from a larger *New York Times* image showing Zakia in a bare room at the women's shelter, beneath a staircase, clearly a resentful prisoner.[84]

The cover of the French edition of *The Lovers*, *Un amour interdit* (*A Forbidden Love*), shows only Zakia's scarf-fringed face, staring challengingly into the camera, in extreme close-up.[85] With one green eye illuminated, Zakia's image also strikingly recalls *Afghan Girl* (1984), Steve McCurry's portrait of green-eyed Pashtun refugee Sharbat Gula, which appeared on the cover of *National Geographic*.[86]

The images of both twelve-year-old Sharbat and Zakia epitomise the way Western media simultaneously sexualises Afghan women while affirming their status as victims. The book cover belongs to what Adam Talib has identified as a tradition of 'exotic, orientalising marketing technique[s]', or what Marcia Lynx Qualey, a Cairo-based writer, calls the 'saving Muslim women' genre.[87] Although Zakia *feels* the forbidden love, the cover design makes Zakia the 'forbidden love' object, implying that it is her race that makes her 'forbidden'. 'If they separate us, I will die' (*'S'ils nous séparent, je mourrai'*) is printed in capitals beneath her face. The statement of devoted desperation is far more typical of Ali than of Zakia, but the placement attributes it to her: the passionate, 'forbidden' woman looking out of a darkness that is simultaneously repressive and mysterious, who cannot live without her man.

Nordland's own commentary on Zakia's appearance swings from an ethnographer's ambivalence – 'Afghans find her beautiful' – to astonished, clichéd praise: her smile 'could illuminate her face', which 'enhances her attractiveness'. At one point in the book, Zakia is sitting for photographs and Nordland claims that '[e]very interaction between photographer and subject is a kind of seduction', adding that Zakia 'seemed to like' being photographed. His implication is uncomfortable at best and is in no way substantiated by Zakia herself. But the moment acts as a pivot; suddenly, in Nordland's eyes, Zakia becomes 'a beautiful woman'.[88]

In interviews, Nordland described Zakia as having, like Juliet, 'a real strength of character' and a 'spark of independence', crediting her with the extraordinary events documented in *The Lovers*.[89] But it is only later in the marriage that Nordland sees her 'emerge, finally, as much more fully realized a person than she had previously seemed', and he notes that Zakia's children, not her, 'will be the ones who will realise Zakia's human potential'.[90] The author colludes with Ali and his father Anwar to lie to Zakia about the date of the couple's departure date to the US, in case she tries to arrange a last meeting with her family, who might kill her.[91] All this is double-edged; the exploitation by a white journalist was the price of Zakia's US visa. Rae Lynn Schwartz-DuPre notes that images of subjugated Afghan women have helped to create the 'Afghan Alibi' for Western interventions of all kinds.[92] But it was that intervention, and the power of Nordland's narrative, that removed her and her daughter (the couple had two daughters as of 2018) from a country routinely ranked the worst in the world in which to be a woman. An unnamed reader with White House connections waived the customary asylum requirements because they wanted the lovers' story to have a happy ending. Today, Zakia and her daughters are not in a country once again ruled by the Taliban. Meanwhile, Sharbat Gula, *National Geographic*'s 'Afghan Girl', had to be evacuated to Italy after the Taliban's return espe-cially endangered prominent Afghan women, above all those who – like Gula – had perceived links with America.[93] Zakia, a contro-versial 'hero to every young Afghan woman', had become notori-ous, 'the most recognisable female face on the Afghan airwaves'; Gula's danger would also have been hers.[94]

★

In the aftermath of Diarmuid and Julie's deaths, rather than images of the couple together, or of Diarmuid, the newspapers printed close-ups of Julie in extreme distress at Diarmuid's funeral, and tele-vision footage showed her weeping on her father's shoulder. These are painfully intrusive shots, some showing Julie staring straight at the camera in baffled, tearful outrage. When the (British) *Evening Herald* covered her funeral, beneath the headline 'Tearful goodbye to tragic love girl', they used a profile shot of Julie at Diarmuid's grave, distraught, clutching a white handkerchief to her lips.[95] On the page, the photograph is arranged so that Julie's gaze falls, across a column of text, on to the later image of her parents at her coffin – it's as if she's spectating her own death.

Julie Statham was the ideal dead girl: the beautiful white teen-ager, with her 'superb blonde hair', cast in the Shakespearean role to which whiteness remained so important.[96] She was 'poor wee Julie', in the words of Father Faul: devastated, devoted and easily compared, in her 'distracted behaviour' to Shakespeare's 'distraught' Juliet. 'In Dungannon,' the *Irish Independent* said, unforgivably, after Julie had killed herself, 'many agree Julie is better off'.[97] This despite the fact that Julie had sought bereavement counselling, signed up for future university seminars, and taken steps to protect her academic future: efforts suggesting that alongside her misery was a desire to live.[98] This is not the behaviour of Juliet, or of Ophelia. Julie wrote a loving, nuanced memorial to Diarmuid in the pages of the *Dungannon Courier*, relating how some found him 'difficult to get along with [. . .] he had friends, yet they were kept at a distance. He found it hard to trust people with his feelings. He was afraid of hurt. Yet what he did not realise is just how much he meant to so many people.'[99] Julie, meanwhile, became a tokenised 'suicide girl' to the press.[100]

In Shakespeare's play, the Montague–Capulet feud is exceptional. The Prince makes it clear that only they 'distur[b] the quiet of our streets', with weapons 'cankered with peace' – rusted through lack of use. Conversely, the couples in this chapter were part of far larger conflicts, and, as Sontag notes, 'the pity and disgust' their oppression inspires 'should not distract [. . .] from asking what pictures, whose cruelties, whose deaths are not being shown'.[101] 'Juliet' is a moniker only awarded to girls who, regardless of fate, are young, attractive, and seemingly apolitical: women who defy their background, faith, or family, but only for their man. The tradition of dubbing couples 'Romeo and Juliet' not only erases the lovers' individuality, but by definition only memorialises requited, heterosexual lovers, excluding single people, the elderly, or anyone who doesn't fit this narrative. Witness how Sarajevo's Vrbanja Bridge is now known internationally as the 'Romeo and Juliet' bridge, rather than by its official name of 'Suada and Olga Bridge', after Bosniak Suada Dilberović and Croat Olga Sučić, the peace protesters shot by Serbian snipers as the Sarajevo siege's first victims.

Ali and Zakia had never heard of *Romeo and Juliet* until Nordland explained it to them; they had their own literary tradition of tragic romances by Persian poet Nizami Ganjavi, author of *Layla Majnun*. Qays becomes a madman, or 'Majnun', for love of Layla, whose father forces her to marry elsewhere. She dies of love for Qays, who then perishes at her grave. *Layla Majnun* provided the plot of the only film Ali had seen. This, alongside other Ganjavi narratives, and the Persian love stories that circulated secretly among Zakia and her girlfriends, were more than adequate for them in making sense of their story. The addition of *Romeo and Juliet*, which Nordland presents as evidence that '[e]very great love must be doomed to experience its happy endings in some afterlife', only encouraged the idea of suicide; Ali 'especially liked the ending'. He told Nordland his 'ambition' was 'the same' as Romeo's: to die with Zakia.[102]

Ultimately, *Romeo and Juliet* is the wrong referent for these couples because Shakespeare's fictional conflict *ends*. In the Capulet tomb, we're told that the discussion will continue 'hence', but Montague and Capulet are reconciled, and there is the certainty of a 'glooming peace'. This is not the experience of those who survive the real-life 'Romeo and Juliet' experiences. Maggie (Margaret) Shields, Diarmuid's sister, described her ongoing, visceral 'fear. You don't normally lose somebody and you have a fear afterwards'. Brigid, his mother, confirmed the family 'were terrified' after the murders. They fled their Verona, Coalisland, and felt unable even to revisit their home: 'If we were driving past it, I wouldn't even look over. I'd just pretend it's not there'.[103] Twenty years after Julie Statham's suicide, her father Paul described the loss of his 'honeymoon baby' as 'hell, that's just what it is'.[104] Boško and Admira's families have sometimes found the press demand to retell their story – feed the romantic narrative – traumatic. Admira's sister said in 2008: 'That is our tragedy and each time when we talk about it, it is like we are going through it again'.[105] When Zijo Ismić, Admira's father, did speak to CNN in 2012, he said it was as if Admira's death had 'happened yesterday'.[106] Zakia and Ali continue to live in the US. Sources I spoke with indicated they want privacy. Although their celebrity as 'Afghanistan's Romeo and Juliet' might well attract continued philanthropic assistance, it is not a story they want to keep telling. It is, after all, a story that could have killed as well as saved them.

Although retelling a couple's story as that of a 'real-life *Romeo and Juliet*' does nothing to end or prevent conflict, productions of *Romeo and Juliet* set in or staged by communities in conflict can be useful on a local, even individual, level. There is anecdotal evidence of school projects benefitting schoolchildren who are encouraged to consider the play's violence along very familiar sectarian lines, as when a Glaswegian school dressed the Montagues and Capulets as (Protestant) Rangers fans and (Catholic) Celtic supporters to expose 'the lunacy of factionalism'.[107] But it's not inevitable. In 1994, Jerusalem's Khan Theatre and Ramallah's Al-Kasaba Theatre collaborated on a Hebrew- and Arabic-language production with a

Palestinian Romeo (Khalifa Natour) and Israeli Juliet (Orna Katz). Despite the directors' aims of 'remind[ing] all that the cost of hatred between fathers is the death of their children', the production had little political valency. According to Freddy Rokem of Tel Aviv University, the show reproduced existing inequalities by making Hebrew the dominant language and by being staged in a hall owned by the Israeli Electric Corporation, during a time of power cuts for Palestinians. The tone was not radical but 'nice', neither 'danger-ous' nor 'dangering' but merely a 'polite handshake of official recognition' for the peace process.[108]

Above all, in these cases, we don't need Shakespeare to tell the stories of Julie, Admira, and Zakia. We have their own words. They are often difficult to read – Julie's father could not open the folder of her writing until two decades after his daughter's death.[109] Admira's love letters to Boško are unbearable as much for their love of home as of him: 'My dear love, Sarajevo at night is the most beautiful thing in the world. I guess I could live somewhere else but only if I must, or if I'm forced. Just a little beat of time is left until we are together'.[110] Zakia, too, speaks eloquently of her love and loss: 'I am happy because I am together with him [. . .] where I should be and should have been, with him'.[111] But she recognises, in perhaps the greatest blow to the Romeo-and-Juliet myth, that he should not have persuaded her to elope. It was 'not a good thing. It is a bad thing, because we cannot live together freely'.[112] Ali remains more reso-lutely romantic, advising a man in difficult love to 'do something to win her heart and to live a happy life'. Zakia hopes that 'If I were killed, and not here with [Ruqia], I hope our daughter would grow up to learn where to go, and where not to go, and that she should be educated'.[113] Her priorities are no longer romantic: Shakespeare's Juliet never gets as far as contending with motherhood.

★

As I write up this chapter, the Twitter thread on Lingard's novels grows. I receive more than 500 messages of happy nostalgia, includ-ing the contributions of Lingard's own daughter. And then, suddenly, someone criticises an East Belfast bookseller for being a loyalist, and in the resulting sectarian row invokes the tragic and controversial death of a mixed-race Catholic child, Noah Donohoe, who drowned in a Belfast storm drain in 2020. The thread stops, and with it, the stories of Lingard's readers. Perhaps the time for Kevin and Sadie has passed. After all, *Derry Girls*, Lisa McGee's hit television comedy about teenage Catholics in mid-nineties Derry, gently mocks Lingard's novels throughout the series. It begins in the pilot, when heroine Erin's mum thinks Macaulay Culkin (then seeking emancipation from his parents) is some Protestant who Erin met 'at that stupid scheme [. . .] "Friends Across The Barricades"'. It continues through the series two opener (also called 'Across the Barricade'), where Catholic and Protestant teenagers meet and spectacularly fail to obtain, in Michelle's words, 'a piece of that fine Protestant ass'. The satire culminates in McGee's tie-in book for the series, modelled on Erin's diary. It sees Erin rejoice that she's written 'an absolutely brilliant' Shakespearean adaptation, in which 'and this is the genius bit . . . Romeo is a Catholic and Juliet is a Protestant. It's just SO original and groundbreaking'.[114] The joke is that the idea, like all Erin's literary efforts, is a hopeless cliché.

In Northern Irish literature, at least, a new generation of 'star-crossed' narratives is here – and is more hopeful. Sue Divin, author of *Guard Your Heart* (2021), updates Lingard's Protestant-girl, Catholic-boy premise with characters born on the day of the Good Friday Agreement. Iona's police officer father apologises to Catholic Aidan for his prejudice, and the young lovers agree to attend Queen's University Belfast and complete the Camino together. Some of Lingard's idealisations of the British are reversed in Divin's novel; this time, the affable Catholics are busy organising fundraisers for Syrian refugees, while the Protestants are ignorant, violent, and thuggish. Iona, a devout Protestant throughout the novel, also has an improbably flexible approach to religion in its final pages, when she takes Communion in a Catholic church: a particularly odd concession since Aidan, throughout the novel, stresses his unbelief.

There seems to be no two-faith solution available in fiction. But there is a welcome appetite for hope. It's not a new appetite – Georg Benda's 1776 opera *Romeo und Julie* saw Juliet awaken before Romeo poisoned himself, and the parents joyfully reconcile – but it is a highly creative, metatheatrical one. It's in the audiences who flock to *& Juliet* (2019), a jukebox musical in which Juliet eschews suicide for a journey of self-realisation and Britney Spears solos,

culminating in a reconciliation with Romeo, whom Shakespeare
has helpfully resurrected. It shows up most joyfully in Ryan North's
wonderful book *Romeo And/Or Juliet* (2016), a 'chooseable-path'
adventure in which readers can play as one of several characters,
mingling play-worlds across the Shakespeare canon and following
storylines in which the lovers don't meet, where Juliet is a body-
builder, where the reader is murdered by Montagues, or where
Romeo and Juliet survive in Mantua with the blessing of a respectful Paris.[115]

None of these literary efforts affects the sufferings of real-life
Juliets and their Romeos, but they do help to unpick and unravel the
trope of 'star-crossed lovers', and the idea of tragic destiny that
encourages us to read individual suffering as preordained, and individual death as literary experience. On shutting the final pages of
Guard Your Heart, leaving the fictional Aidan and Iona sunning themselves in Santiago, it's heart-warming to hope that, for some real-life
lovers, life might begin imitating art, some day soon.[116]

We won't get there by recasting real-life tragedies as across-the-
barricade romances. To do so perpetuates exploitative and irresponsible reportage, above all of women's experiences. Ironically,
though, while these adaptations romanticise and over-simplify the
real-life histories, they usefully draw attention to the play's jagged
edges. In Zakia and Ali's marital struggles, we reflect on Juliet and
Romeo's inability to make decisions together, without interventions, and the regrets Juliet might ultimately have felt. Ali's ongoing
relationship with his father, contrasted with Zakia's total loss of her
family of origin, reminds us of the characters' last decisions about
their parents. Romeo leaves a long letter for his father, confessing
everything; Juliet not only maintains her silence, but stabs herself
rather than reunite with her family. In the violence of Boško's asso-
ciates, we are reminded of the consequences that the play's network
of male violence has for Juliet. In Julie's nuanced mourning for
Diarmuid, and the press's romanticisation of her suicide, we're
reminded that Juliet doesn't eulogise Romeo; she calls him a 'churl'.

In the late twentieth century, *Romeo and Juliet* became a 'play
about hate'; it is also, strikingly, a play about power. While she is
alive, Juliet is endlessly eloquent; after she is dead, men tell her story.
Romeo's words are at least relayed through his letter and the

corroboration of Balthasar and Paris's Page. From the self-pitying Friar Laurence and his snivelling offer to 'let my old life/ Be sacrificed, some hour before his time' (5.3.266–7) we get the briefest and most uncharitable glimpse of Juliet. She disappears in two lines, a madwoman 'too desperate' to hear reason, who sacrilegiously 'did violence on herself' rather than listen to the kind Friar Laurence's counsel (5.3.263–4). With the Nurse offstage too, no one speaks up for Juliet. None of the women in this chapter could control how they were represented. Perhaps this is the quality they and Juliet truly share.

By The Time She Understands Her

'By the time an actress understands Juliet, she's too old to play her'. This theatrical adage, sometimes misattributed to Ellen Terry, and extant for at least the last 120 years, blends two flavours of ageism with a misogyny topping. If younger actresses are ignorant, the old ones are haggard; all actresses, it seems, must disappoint.

Shakespeare certainly stresses Juliet's youth; we've seen how he departed from Painter and Brooke to make his heroine a shockingly-juvenile thirteen. Does this mean the actress who plays her must be a teenager? The films of Franco Zeffirelli, Baz Luhrmann, and Julian Fellowes are certainly premised on the idea that very young actresses are best placed to interpret her. The ubiquity of *Romeo and Juliet* on exam syllabi implies that on some level, teenagers of all genders can be made to 'understand' not just Shakespeare's first tragic heroine, but the whole play. In terms of experiential understanding – the wisdom that, the adage implies, can only come with a mature perspective – it's striking that Juliet's own lived experiences, of teenage love, arguments with parents, and disappointment in formerly-treasured confidantes, are all experiences that most people gain early in their lives.

The passage of time might give performers a global perspective – sympathy for the Capulet parents or caution about Romeo – but this is more about 'understanding' the play, rather than the character of Juliet. The saying also implies that the later interpretation is always the right one: that 'understanding' Juliet means reaching a fixed destination to which an actress can only travel over time. If tracing Juliet's lives and afterlives proves anything, it's that Juliet has been protean – all things to all people, and radically different things depending on time and context. If so, the actress faced with this adage simply cannot win.

Juliet isn't the only Shakespearean character who has been deemed in some way unplayable. Cleopatra must be a 'lass unparalleled' (5.2.305), have an appearance that 'beggar[s] all description' (2.2.197), be in possession of a sex appeal that 'makes hungry/ Where most she satisfies'. She must be constantly changeable: 'Age cannot wither her, nor custom stale/ Her infinite variety' (2.2.233–6). She offers a challenge to human casting directors. If Victorian actresses were keen to blame their early failures as Juliet on being nice English misses rather than precocious Mediterranean hussies, they flocked to explain that they couldn't play Cleopatra because of all the North African sluttery. Sarah Siddons said it memorably, claiming she would 'hate herself, if she should play the part as it ought to be played'.[1]

Anti-theatricalists have suggested Lear is too unassailable to be attempted – but it is more flattering to blame a failed performance on a role's epic emotional and philosophical heights than the short shelf life of pretty young actresses. There are also more pragmatic quips about Lear and the inverse correlation between actorly character insight and the muscle mass required for carrying Cordelia. Patrick Stewart suggests actors should play Lear twice, 'once when you are young and strong enough to carry Cordelia, and once when you are old enough to know what the part's about'.[2] In practice several actors have succeeded as Lear while elderly and seriously ill: Olivier won an Emmy in the role at seventy-five, suffering 'an endless series of illnesses', including the degenerative muscle disorder dermatomyositis. David Ryall was a heartbreaking Lear while enduring chemotherapy and memory loss, unable to carry his daughter, Charlie Ryall, as Cordelia.[3] Three decades after playing Lear at Stratford, Michael Redgrave reprised the reunion scene with Cordelia while suffering from Parkinson's – the deeply moving footage formed part of his son Corin's documentary about him.[4] At the opposite end of the age scale, while some who saw the twenty-seven-year-old John Gielgud play Lear in 1931 'hoped to be alive in twenty years' to see him reprise it, Gielgud was still praised by several journalists for a 'magnificent performance' and being 'almost as great as the elements'. A young Lear can have a second chance.[5] Today, a Juliet cannot.

★

Between 1967 and 1968, Bernard Braden – the Canadian actor and interviewer who shamed Olivia Hussey for smoking – also filmed a series of eight monthly interviews with his own daughter, the eighteen-year-old aspiring actress Kim Braden. In one piece of footage shot on 22 March 1968, the younger Braden, wearing a blue dress and white pussy-bow blouse, has recently seen Zeffirelli's *Romeo and Juliet*. In her well-heeled, debbish, slightly transatlantic tones, she describes the film as 'quite frankly [. . .] beautiful', but objects to Olivia Hussey's 'very sweet and charming and kind' performance. Braden thinks Juliet must instead have had a 'nasty [. . .] funny little mind' to doubt Friar Laurence in the potion scene. But one quality Braden does applaud is the youth of both Hussey and Whiting – the deaths were 'really, really sad' *because* 'they were both so young'. In comparison, Braden cited the apparently insuperable problem with the Juliet of Peggy Ashcroft. 'You know she's fifty', Braden claims, meaning that 'when she dies, you don't feel sad, because you really know she's just an actress'.[6] Ashcroft's age means her performance is unmoving.

There is a parallel moment early in the Paramount trailer for the Zeffirelli film. The voiceover describes how the lovers have 'always' been played by 'established stars [. . .] at the peak of their maturity'. As the teenage cast romps, Leonard Whiting says, 'I heard that Sarah Bernhardt played Juliet with a wooden leg, over the age of fifty'. An unseen actress says 'You're joking,' and the youngsters laugh in horrified disbelief.[7] More recently, Lolita Chakrabarti's 2012 play *Red Velvet* – a biopic of African American actor Ira Aldridge – strikes a related note. Facing hostility for his race and the perceived violence of his performance as Othello, Aldridge complains that 'no one bats an eye when grandma plays Juliet', or 'we all applaud the East End drunk as the warrior Moor'.[8] The scene equates the two: the visibly drunk actor in blackface is as abominable and inauthentic as an older Juliet, especially in comparison to Aldridge's modern performance style.

But there is a problem with all these anecdotes. When the teenage Kim Braden was critiquing Peggy Ashcroft in 1968, Ashcroft hadn't played Juliet since 1935, when she'd been twenty-eight. Sarah Bernhardt never played Juliet (she was a fifty-year-old Hamlet). While 'the East End' drunk in *Red Velvet* is Edmund

Kean, whose collapse catalyses Chakrabarti's play's plot, there was no 'grandma' Juliet, because in 1833 there hadn't been an older Juliet on the stage for twenty years. Even then, thirty-two-year-old Sarah Bartley had, in 1803, been decried for having developed 'an insufferable sing-song' delivery rather than being applauded.[9] In fact, the Regency London stage specialised in younger Juliets: twenty-three-year-old Eliza O'Neill, twenty-year-old Fanny Kemble, and nineteen-year-old Helena Faucit. Like Braden's ancient Peggy Ashcroft, or the Zeffirelli cast's laughable Bernhardt, the 'grandma Juliet' – totally inadequate but still applauded by a mob of philistines – has never existed. She is not merely a theatrical myth, but a bogeyman. What is it that makes her so frightening? The ageist aphorism that began this chapter merits a second look. Even in its criticism of the two denigrated contenders for the role, the younger and the older, it is the older actress who is deemed artistically capable of a great performance, if only she could look the part.

Performance culture presents an older Juliet as a Juliet out of time, because in an ageist society, innocence, ecstatic love, and virginity are laughable rather than desirable in all but very young women. Fictional depictions are typically much kinder to older men than older women – just as there is no female equivalent of 'silver fox', there is no male equivalent of the phrase 'mutton dressed as lamb'.

Culture dictates that middle-aged or later-in-life passion should not reflect Juliet's abandon, but rather the smouldering, sultry, worldly-wise sexuality of Cleopatra. Even then, critics evince relief when the 'lass unparallel'd' is reduced from sex symbol to frail, fallen old woman. A review in the *Birmingham Post* in 1992 described how Claire Higgins's Cleopatra '*finally* abandoned her wigs' (emphasis mine) to reveal 'her head cropped like a poor soldier'; the critic's simile here imagines a Cleopatra forcibly shaved, demoted, and made to toe the line.[10] When Frances de la Tour played the same role in 1999, the conservative *Daily Telegraph* critic Charles Spencer was relieved that – after a production in which he'd had to watch Mark Antony give Cleopatra oral sex – de la Tour's 'Cleopatra [was] finally revealed as a hideous, Norma Desmond-like crone'.[11] *Don't worry*, these reviews say, *she's not really middle-aged and sexy, she'll get her comeuppance.* The onstage collapse usually occurs after Antony's death, as though her appeal was predicated on his presence. The reference to Norma Desmond is important: the heroine of *Sunset Boulevard* (1950), Norma Desmond is a sexually rapacious and ultimately murderous ageing actress, deluded about both her talent and desirability.[12]

Ageing or unsuccessful actors certainly come in for their fair share of cultural criticism. There is 'Sir', the volatile, homophobic, chauvinist actor-manager in Ronald Harwood's *The Dresser* (1980), for example, or the deluded Withnail dreaming of *Hamlet* in Bruce Robinson's film *Withnail and I* (1987). But 'Sir' in *The Dresser*, as Ryan Gilbey notes, is allowed to be both 'grand and pitiful'. Withnail, in his final, garbled, rain-soaked recitation of *Hamlet*'s 'What a piece of work is a man' speech, reveals genuine, if wasted, talent, and is an object of sympathy rather than repulsion.[13] The older female performer is far more freighted with narratives of desperation, predation, and inadequacy. There is the enigmatic, diseased Princess Halm-Eberstein, Daniel Deronda's opera diva mother, who rejects him for her career in *Daniel Deronda* (1876); or the faded actress Irina Arkadina in Chekhov's *The Seagull* (1895), who loses her lover to the ingenue, aspirant performer Nina. Both women are also conspicuous failures as mothers: the Princess abandons Daniel Deronda, while Arkadina humiliates and fails to appreciate her own son, who kills himself at the play's end.

In modern-day Britain, despite national pride in a handful of world-famous octogenarian dames with still-mobile faces, the performing arts are manifestly ageist and sexist. Even in the documentary most celebrating older actresses, Roger Michell's *Nothing Like a Dame*, the Dames Judi Dench, Maggie Smith, Joan Plowright, and Eileen Atkins report their own experiences of ageism – and the difficulty for Smith, Plowright, and Atkins of getting work that 'Judi Dench hasn't already got her paws on'.[14] Given the profiles and international fame of each, their complaints reflect the incredibly limited opportunities for older actresses. Dame Harriet Walter, a few years their junior, has recently excelled in male Shakespearean roles, but the existence of the 'Acting Your Age' campaign (2018– present), demanding better representation for actresses over forty-five, indicates how uncommon this is.[15]

This ageism, an employability gap accompanying the longevity gap, isn't a new problem – actress Gwen Ffrangcon-Davies told John Gielgud in a 1989 documentary that she 'regretted not being able to act as long as I would have liked, not like you' – but it is intensifying. The average age for female BAFTA nominees has dropped from fifty-two to thirty-two since 2000, while for men it's only gone from forty-eight to forty-five.[16] Ffrangcon-Davies, who remained devoted to Shakespeare as 'master poet' for a century, ultimately concluded that the best roles for older women were beyond Shakespeare. Gielgud – Ffrangcon-Davies's 1924 Romeo – had promised to recast her as Juliet, but chose Peggy Ashcroft for a 1935 revival. Ffrangcon-Davies's partner, Marda Vanne, confessed to her diary that although Ffrangcon-Davies felt 'like a shrivelled acorn' at the betrayal, she was 'so courageous in sorrow that I go into the lavatory to cry for her in private'.[17] In 1962, aged seventy-one, Ffrangcon-Davies said that her recent role as the morphine-addicted mother Mary in the first British production of Eugene O'Neill's *Long Day's Journey into Night* 'is to the older actress what Juliet is to the younger actress' because it's 'got everything in it' and is 'most lovely'.[18]

If cross-gender performance is increasingly an option for older actresses, cross-*age* performance certainly isn't. While a handful of Shakespearean roles – Lady Capulet, Beatrice, *Twelfth Night*'s Maria – are frequently cast older than the texts suggest, critical enthusiasm for this practice is limited to casting middle-aged, rather than truly *older* performers. Carol Chillington Rutter applauded fifty-nine-year-old Zoë Wanamaker as Beatrice for being 'thick in the waist and lumpy with emotional scar tissue'.[19] But when Sean O'Connor and Tom Morris adapted *Romeo and Juliet* as a love tragedy of old age, the *Sunday Times*'s Jane Edwardes struck a particularly scathing note against creating a precedent: 'What next? Vanessa Redgrave as Little Orphan Annie?'[20]

Is this aversion authentically Shakespearean? Like most aspects of his biography, it's difficult to infer the playwright's personal attitude to older women. There were certainly some in his family circle. Shakespeare's own mother and two of her sisters, Margaret and Joan, lived into their seventies, the latter involved in a property dispute against William and his parents. A maternal great aunt, Elizabeth Conway Arden, died aged eighty-five in 1597.[21] Across the Shakespearean canon, it's notable how many Shakespearean fools, beyond those actually labelled 'Clown' or 'Fool', are old fools, and male: Polonius, Holofernes, and Justices Shallow and Slender in *Henry IV Part 2*. His older men are thwarted in their pursuit of wives (Gremio in *The Taming of the Shrew*) or in the control of their daughters (Shylock, Capulet, or Egeus in *A Midsummer Night's Dream*). In tragedy, their serious misunderstandings of themselves and others leads to their destruction, as in the cases of Lear and Gloucester. Nevertheless, Shakespeare's older men also confound expectations: there are military heroes like Old Talbot in *Henry VI Part 1*, Old Siward in *Macbeth*, and Belarius, the rugged forester of *Cymbeline*. Prospero, the usurped Duke of Milan, is so supernaturally powerful that he boasts of raising the dead in *The Tempest*. Old men are loyal counsellors – such as Gonzago in *The Tempest* or the saintly Adam in *As You Like It* – or prophets with political and spiritual insight – in *Richard II*, John of Gaunt and the Bishop of Carlisle both deliver devastatingly accurate assessments of their realms' presents and futures.

Although the most sexually desirable of Shakespeare's female characters, Cleopatra, is middle-aged, and the Countess of Rousillon is an adored surrogate mother, Shakespeare's older women are usually presented negatively. They are frequently associated with violent conflict: Volumnia in *Coriolanus* is a tiger mother who brings about her son's death as well as her own, while the militant Margaret ages across the *Henry VI* plays into the disenfranchised, cursing beldame of *Richard III*. If likeable, Shakespearean older women are often bawdy, as with Mistress Quickly, Doll Tearsheet, or Juliet's Nurse, who jokes incessantly about sex. Their sexuality is frequently also mercenary, as with the Old Lady in *Henry VIII*, who would cheerfully sell her body for the crown: 'three-pence [. . .] would hire me/ Old as I am, to quean it' (where 'quean' means 'prostitute' and puns on 'queen', 2.3.36–7). At best, older women are consolation prizes: Hortensio in *The Taming of the Shrew* marries a widow only when definitively dumped by the nubile Bianca. Aside from Cleopatra, women have a short sexual shelf life; Viola agrees pensively with Orsino in *Twelfth Night* that a woman's beauty 'being once displayed/ Doth fall that very hour' (2.4.35–6). Nonetheless, Shakespeare's attitude to older women is perhaps milder than those of his contemporaries. In Marlowe's *Dido, Queen of Carthage,* the Nurse's desire for 'a husband, or else a lover' is presented as comic: 'Fourscore is but a girl's age, love is sweet'.[22] When the playwright Thomas Croote wanted to describe a very elderly woman in his 1578 play *All for Money,* he specified that she should look 'evil favoured like an old woman'; the two were obviously equivalent.[23]

Romeo and Juliet is uniquely preoccupied with Juliet's specific calendar age, and, accordingly, her youth. Other Shakespearean characters celebrate birthdays – in *Julius Caesar, Antony and Cleopatra,* and *Pericles* – but only Juliet gets a specific calendar date. Her father's initial emphasis on patience and delay – 'Let two more summers wither in their pride / Ere we may think her ripe to be a bride' (1.2.10–11) – belies the fact that this is a play-world in which people age fast. Lady Capulet is twenty-seven or -eight at most, but finds her 'old age' summoned to a 'sepulchre' by Juliet's death (5.3.205–6). Although the Nurse is often played by an elderly actress, frequently to conclude her Shakespearean career, the Nurse gave birth to Susan, her now-dead daughter, at the same time Lady Capulet did Juliet – i.e. fourteen years before the play's events – making the character probably no older than fifty.[24] Youth and age can seem mutable and contested in the play; during the ball scene, Capulet and his elderly cousin disagree over the age of a friend's son, who is barely an adult in Capulet's imagination, but thirty according to his cousin (1.5.30–8). And although Capulet chastises Tybalt in derogatory terms for youth, 'goodman boy' and 'saucy boy' (1.5.73–9), age in the play is more usually an insult. In the very first scene, Lady Capulet mocks her husband for calling for his sword when she thinks he's better suited to 'a crutch' – this ageism is the sole point in which Juliet resembles her mother (1.1.63). Impatient for the Nurse's news of Romeo, she is briefly and almost viciously unkind about her:

Had she affections and warm youthful blood,
She would be as swift in motion as a ball; [. . .]
But old folks, many feign as they were dead;
Unwieldy, slow, heavy and pale as lead (2.4.12–17).

For Romeo, the idea of being 'old' is similarly negative. When demanding to know how Juliet has responded to the news that he's

murdered Tybalt, his question is: 'Doth she not think me an *old*
murderer' (3.3.93, emphasis mine), as though the adjective would
intensify his crime. The feverish desire of youth to overtake death
can be glimpsed throughout the play's language. The prologue to
Act 2 describes Romeo's transition from Rosaline to Juliet through
the metaphor of 'old desire' being on his 'deathbed' while 'young
affection gapes to be his heir' (2.0.1–2). Even the silent ball guests
are enlisted, as the Nurse identifies one not by his name but as 'the
son and heir of old Tiberio' (1.5.125). The nameless son's identity is
bound up with anticipating his father's death.

Everything, then, is stacked against the older Juliet: theatrical
myths of past embarrassments, discrimination in casting, an ageist
and misogynist aversion to the spectacle of older women in love,
and a contempt for age that's woven into the language of
Shakespeare's playtext. Nevertheless, since 2000, two stage adaptations have reimagined the lovers as older couples, remixing the text:
Ben Power's *A Tender Thing* (2009) and Tom Morris and Sean
O'Connor's *Juliet and Her Romeo* (2010). The former is set at the end
of the lovers' long marriage, and the latter sees them meet in a care
home. Rather than full-blown feuds, *Juliet and Her Romeo* has a class
difference – Juliet is in a private ward, Romeo on the NHS. *A Tender
Thing*, meanwhile, is about age-related disability and the terminally
ill Juliet's request that Romeo assist her suicide. Both are more
about death than love; even *Juliet and Her Romeo,* in which the couple
are newly in love, evinced only the passion of 'little, chaste, tight-
lipped kisses' in its opening production.[25] While both adaptations
do give older performers a chance to play the lovers, it's notable that
this only happens within play-worlds where the most tragic thing is
old age itself. When Shakespeare's violent feud is equated with age
and illness, it's hard not to think that ageism is woven into the fabric
of the adaptations.

There is, nonetheless, an alternative history of the successful
older Juliet – one that doesn't rely on rewrites, and doesn't derive its
tragedy from the shock of Juliet not looking thirteen. Despite the
spectres that haunted Kim Braden, Zeffirelli's cast and Chakrabarti's
Ira Aldridge, over the past century, many notable Juliets have found
great success in the role well into middle age – not as ingenues, but
as powerful performers, able both to 'understand' Juliet and

evidently to look enough like her for their appreciative audiences. In fact, rather than being inadequate 'grandma Juliets', older performers have frequently used Juliet either to triumphantly conclude or to regenerate their careers.

Mary Anderson de Navarro, having retired from the stage aged thirty-one upon her 1890 marriage, returned in 1903 for fundraising readings of the balcony scene. Reviewers noted that 'Fifteen years [. . .] have taken nothing whatever from her youthful beauty'; she made Juliet 'glow with tender love' and achieved, 'as of old, a great triumph'.[26] During the First World War, by then in her mid-fifties, Anderson acted scenes from the play (this time in full costume) in Worcestershire, Liverpool and London, 'without being made up or seeking recourse to stage art', and was 'still a great tragedienne, still beautiful and charming', who 'thrilled her audience' with her 'youthful spontaneity'.[27] Julia Sothern, who had played Juliet as a novice in the 1880s, found her greatest success in the role from 1905, opposite E. A. Sothern, with whom she acted throughout her forties; she was still a successful Broadway Juliet in 1913, aged fifty. Aged sixty-five, Nellie Melba sang Act 2 of Gounod's *Roméo et Juliette* for her '*soirée d'adieu*' at Covent Garden in 1926, receiving 'a tremendous ovation' as her 'girlish voice still cas[t] that marvellous illusion of youth'.[28]

Ballet is, perhaps inevitably, an even more ageist art form. While writing this chapter, I was entertained by a Tumblr post contrasting a retiring ballerina who 'has worked a long career and has earned her rest' at thirty-one with the excitement in opera over 'a promising young bass!!! [. . .] all wide eyed and bushy tailed!! we're excited to see where his career will go' who is forty-seven.[29] Nevertheless, both Margot Fonteyn and Alessandra Ferri enjoyed great success as Juliet in Kenneth MacMillan's ballet: Fonteyn aged forty-six in 1965, and Ferri all the way from the age of nineteen to fifty-three. Dancers describe MacMillan's Juliet as less physically but more emotionally demanding than other canonical roles such as Odette, the heroine of *Swan Lake*. Ferri chose to reprise Juliet at fifty-three because she 'wanted to make sure that I enjoy my life to the last moment', and she was acclaimed for it.[30] Julie Kent, principal ballet dancer with the American Ballet Theatre from 1993 to 2015, chose MacMillan's Juliet as her farewell role, aged forty-five, claiming Juliet is especially transformative for the older dancer because of her focus on the future, on the possibility of love transforming pain: 'You are so in tune with the possibility of what is to come, and how beautiful that is'. Kent concludes, 'that feeling is eternal. That feeling is still so fresh, and it makes you feel forever young'.[31] These ballerinas' words indicate the psychological appeal of Juliet as a role, and the importance of emotional identification as well as physical ability.

Not only have older Juliets succeeded in theatre, opera, and ballet, but some have even been seen as especially youthful while concealing their age. Gwen Ffrangcon-Davies was 'nearly crazy with joy' to play Juliet in Birmingham in 1922, and then in London opposite John Gielgud in 1924.[32] She was known as the 'child Juliet', physically diminutive and slight, with a wig of long red plaits. She was, in fact, thirty-three. The besotted *Daily Graphic* critic S. P. B. Mais noted approvingly that: 'Usually the Juliet of the stage is either lovely and can't act, or a skilled actress, too mature in years or girth to satisfy our physical senses' – some vintage 1920s body-shaming to boot. Mais also sent Ffrangcon-Davies a truly unhinged letter, 'written in a train at white heat', in which he 'want[ed] to thank God for you [. . .] above all for playing the part as Shakespeare saw it [. . .] with a completely unsophisticated child's abandon [. . .] it is your youth that makes your performance so memorable', complaining that he felt 'like a prostitute in selling [his] initials to a newspaper' in which he could write only calm praise.[33] Mais's 'white heat' shows how erotic he found Juliet, at least partly because he was convinced by her performance of youth.

As Ffrangcon-Davies noted, sixty years later: 'in those days, an actress's age was her own private business [. . .] everybody thought I was about eighteen [. . .] I didn't undeceive them'.[34] Ffrangcon-Davies's reticence reveals both the theatre's ageism and, in her case, the irrelevance of calendar age to reception when the former is unknown. Even Mais, her most besotted admirer, felt that either 'girth' (weight or bodily changes) or the simple fact of 'years' could preclude success; Ffrangcon-Davies proved him wrong.

It is time to reappraise the idea that an actress's birth certificate is a fatal impediment to playing Juliet. Theatre is full of ongoing conversations about performer diversity, and the need for more inclusive casting processes in terms of sex, gender identity, race, and disability – especially in canonical roles. In Shakespeare, non-traditional casting along the lines of gender or race is common, from the pioneering work of companies like Talawa to the all-female Donmar trilogy directed by Phyllida Lloyd, along with increasingly diverse casts elsewhere. Actors with visible disabilities are also appearing more frequently onstage – in the summer of 2022, Arthur Hughes, who has radial dysplasia, performed as *Richard III* for the RSC. Anyone who tracks casting patterns knows that they have sometimes reinforced racial stereotypes – a Black actor may find himself shunted into violent, militaristic roles, such as Hotspur, or cast as the supportive confidant of a white leading man (Banquo, Horatio), while actresses of colour are disproportionately cast as prostitutes and servants. East Asian actors in particular remain under-represented in all forms of mainstream theatre. It's also still the case that some theatre critics do make bigoted complaints when a production is 'garishly diverse' – as the *Sunday Times*'s John Dugdale did of Erica Whyman's *Romeo and Juliet*, which featured the British South Asian actor Bally Gill as Romeo, and the non-binary actor Charlie Josephine as Mercutio.[35] If I were a twenty-something actor in pursuit of a lucrative and interesting career, I'd still rather be a slender, white, cisgender, able-bodied boy (preferably pretty and an RP speaker) than anything else. But progress, although fitful, is occurring.

Sex, gender reassignment, race and disability are all protected characteristics under the UK Equality Act: so, too, is age.[36] Equity, the UK union for creative practitioners, notes that actors should not be asked for their 'actual age' in auditions, except when casting children or for the advertising of age-restricted products.[37] Nevertheless, as in other creative professions, opportunities for 'emerging' talent (such as bursaries or mentoring) are frequently aimed at the under-twenty-fives, as if the emergence of talent and financial hardship both end at twenty-six. Alessandra Ferri points out that it is identifying with and experiencing the 'feeling' of Juliet that ignited the role for her once again at fifty-three. We accept, now, that you need not be flaxen-haired, white, and male to play Hamlet – after all, it's about inhabiting and communicating the emotions of the character, through voice and performance. Searching for Juliet need not mean a trawl through drama-school showcases or ingenues' headshots. 'New talent' need not mean young.

Archival materials show us just how compelling an older Juliet can be. Rachel Kempson played Juliet aged twenty-two in 1932 at the newly built Stratford Memorial Theatre. In 1996, she revisited the role of Juliet, almost incidentally, in the documentary made by her son, Corin, about his father, Michael Redgrave, who had died a decade earlier.[38] The documentary features Kempson being gently led to the stage of what was by then the Royal Shakespeare Theatre. She is white-haired and slightly lopsided, bright-eyed, elegant, and a little deaf.

Seated upstage, occasionally prompted by Corin, Kempson delivers Juliet's potion speech. She speaks slightly to Corin, but primarily to the empty theatre, which feels full as she engages the unseen audience. It is not just a theatrical curiosity, but a moving and memorable performance. Kempson's Juliet is, more than any I have seen, grieving. Her performance comes from a place of incredible loss. When Kempson says, 'My dismal scene I needs must act *alone*', we remember that this is a Juliet whose mother, father, and Nurse have all let her down. Her husband, too, although Juliet will not articulate that – we have already seen, in Act 3, Scene 2, her rigid determination not to reproach him for murdering Tybalt. Nevertheless, it's hard to believe a Juliet of such reflective sorrow is unaware. Occasionally Kempson interrupts herself to gloss the props she is miming, telling her son, 'That's the knife', as if her skilful gestures – above all, the infinite care with which she bids it, 'Lie thou there' – could permit any doubt.

That Kempson gives the whole speech seated makes the power of her voice all the more striking: its flexibility, modulation, and the control she gives even the nightmare of 'dash out my desperate brains'. Her 'Stay, Tybalt, stay!' isn't a horror-film heroine's scream, but a plea to a phantom that Juliet believes might still contain something of the cousin who loved her. In other performances, I've seen the speech delivered impetuously or hysterically, with both the possibility of death and 'hideous fears' of the tomb seeming as lurid as the terrors of a ghost train, and about as dangerous. Kempson's Juliet accepts her own death as a realistic, imminent possibility. She avers, 'Romeo, I come,' not as a fanatic without doubts, but in sad remembrance of why she's making the sacrifice.

Gwen Ffrangcon-Davies reprised her Juliet several times on the radio, including in her 1988 *Desert Island Discs* episode, in which she performed part of the balcony scene, recalling it as a 'dream fulfilled'.[39] That same year, her friend Nigel Hawthorne interviewed her for *Gwen – A Juliet Remembered*, an Emmy Award-winning television documentary in which she discussed her roles, and taught a masterclass featuring four drama-school students who each performed a speech by Juliet.

Ffrangcon-Davies was by now ninety-seven, with red hair, horn-rimmed spectacles and pearls, and a variety of outfits, from patterned kaftans to a kind of Elizabethan and vaguely piratical garb. In the masterclass, all four students had a pretty tough time of it; as Ffrangcon-Davies's biographer said, her feedback was given 'very lovingly', but was 'demolition work, and needfully so'.[40] The chief interest of the masterclass, as in *Desert Island Discs*, is in Ffrangcon-Davies's demonstration of her own interpretation. In discussing the balcony scene, Ffrangcon-Davies delivered 'Take all myself' not rashly or in an infatuated rush, but with full under-standing of the enormity of Juliet's sacrifice – a sacrifice she never-theless makes blissfully. Ffrangcon-Davies was a much *happier* Juliet than her balcony scene debutante, the National Youth Theatre's Kathy Owen, who played the scene intently, almost angrily. Owen's Juliet was intensely self-critical, and full of regret about the situa-tion – reasonable enough, given the danger of Juliet's predicament, and the inadvertence of her confession. Ffrangcon-Davies encour-aged her instead to think about 'the fantastic meeting' that precedes the balcony scene: 'He has KISSED you, with a kiss that jolly well nearly stops your heart'. This, and not the hopelessness of the situ-ation, predominates. Juliet is 'bewitched'. Rather than emphasising her frustration, Ffrangcon-Davies's Juliet enjoys the pleasures of confession, 'in a maze of this exquisite love'. In 'Gallop apace', Ffrangcon-Davies is very frank about Juliet's anticipation of sex: 'She knows what she's in for, the Nurse has told her all about it [. . .] she's ardent and willing and a little frightened'. Begging for Friar Laurence's assistance, Juliet is 'as near demented as makes no matter [. . .] underneath is a kind of dementia'. The emotional extremity contrasts with what, in Ffrangcon-Davies's delivery, becomes the humility of Juliet's ambition: to be 'an unstained wife'.

Conversely, in the potion scene, Ffrangcon-Davies stresses Juliet's hesitation. Rather than performing a continuous soliloquy, we see that Juliet *intends* to take the potion almost immediately, constantly moving to taste the phial, but is beset by her fears. After the 'dementia' of the previous speech, this is a white-knuckled Juliet who has been desperately repressing her 'breathlessness, panic' during the final encounter with her mother, when she makes the barbed and 'devastating remark' that her wedding is 'this so sudden business'. Having refused to 'let on to anybody at all that everything is not perfectly in order', Ffrangcon-Davies describes a unique degree of relief in feeling the potion kick in, and a very deliberate closing of the curtains 'so they'll think she's fallen asleep and died'.

Comparing four inexperienced actresses balancing the demands of live and filmed performance with the insights of the beloved nonagenarian critiquing them will never favour the former. Ffrangcon-Davies was drawing on a lifetime's insight. One of the students remembered decades later that, while Ffrangcon-Davies's style was 'big, out to the gods and theatrical', it was 'absolutely rooted in truth so it didn't matter'. Twentieth- and twenty-first-century culture dwells on older people losing confidence and self-esteem with age: what's perhaps most striking about Ffrangcon-Davies is her urge to give the *younger* performers the confidence she manifestly still feels. Encouraging Emma Conway, the performer of 'Gallop apace', she insists: 'Give yourself time [. . .] it is you whose business it is to hold the audience; *they'll listen to whatever you give them*'. Her conviction of the young actresses' onstage authority is a radical one, given how junior these performers are.

Rewatching Kempson and Ffrangcon-Davies's performances, it's striking that they are both also far more consciously romantic than the younger actresses, whether performing the role or discussing it. Kempson has a sweet anecdote about being 'madly' in love with her Romeo, John Wyse, while Ffrangcon-Davies overflows with Juliet's 'delirious' experience of first love. Watching footage of the two actresses brought back memories of the rather jaded tour group I'd met in Verona, with their disdain for love and letters to Juliet. The power of the older actresses' celebration of love and the tourists' cynicism shows the latter need not prevail.

*

Today, *Romeo and Juliet* has become firmly the property of young people – and as an academic whose business is to recruit, teach and nurture university students, they are a demographic with whom I spend much professional time. Initiatives for widening access to my university, or strengthening its links with the surrounding community, tend to the focus on the same demographic – as do, of course, many of the theatre industry's initiatives for discovering and nurturing talent. It's ironic that Shakespeare, achieving theatrical success in his late twenties, would by then have been too old for many twenty-first-century schemes for 'emerging' creative talent.

One striking exception is the Oxford Playhouse, a producing theatre that has stood on Beaumont Street, opposite the Ashmolean Museum, since 1938. As well as educational programmes for schoolchildren and students, the theatre has an 'Adult Company' for amateur actors over the age of twenty-six, pre-matinée discussion groups for theatre fans, dementia-friendly performances, and, during the coronavirus pandemic, a Tea Talks system of befriending calls and creative exchange for later-in-life Oxfordshire residents. This makes the Playhouse a haven for Oxford's older theatre enthusiasts – and, as it turns out, for me.

In the spring of 2022, I meet with groups of older people who've agreed to discuss the play with me. I want to know what they think of Juliet. Arranging this has been slightly fraught – I had to apply for funding, and conduct an ethics application, which was expertly supported by the University, but was also processed in a format more suited to medical research than a lively chat about Shakespeare. Because the Playhouse's historic building boasts neither lift nor stairlift, we need to meet downstairs, near the bar – competing in volume with a coffee machine, passing traffic and schoolchildren lining up outside. I begin the first session nervous about non-attendance, non-enjoyment, trigger warnings, and/or an error with the consent forms. I began my grant application convinced everything was going to be fine; I grew up in Stratford-upon-Avon, after all, a place rich in older Shakespeare fans, many of whom are brimming with opinions referencing a variety of productions, all staged before my birth. But in the half hour before my first Playhouse workshop, which I spend at a tea party with some of the participants, I am convinced the whole thing is a mistake, and (despite my three negative COVID tests and the cheerful masklessness of all assembled) that even if it does go well, I will probably accidentally kill someone with plague.

As it turns out, I needn't have worried. The participants generally treat my consent forms as a kind of bureaucratic neurosis afflicting The Young, but are otherwise generous, insightful, and extremely forthcoming. Their backgrounds and enthusiasms are various; a retired psychiatrist chats to a poet who used to run a carpet-cleaning business. Some are Shakespeare fans and others prefer ballet. Some are married and some single. Two of the loveliest ladies are widowed neighbours from the same sheltered housing. One gentleman is able to join us because his wife, who has dementia, attends a day centre on the relevant morning. Two other ladies are retired actresses with tales of repertory theatre and – like Kempson – crushes on their Romeos. Together, we explore the lovers' first meeting, the balcony scene, Juliet's rejection by her parents, and the lovers' fates. I'm keen to know how Shakespeare's thirteen-year-old heroine, and her love story, look from where they're standing.

Certainly, my workshop participants evince some scepticism about the intensity of Juliet's feeling. Peter calls it an 'infatuation', while Ellen feels that it doesn't 'ring true' after knowing Romeo so briefly. While deploring the Capulets' incuriosity about their daughter's rejection of Paris, the wonderful Olive, ninety-three, says that what's missing is 'any understanding [of] why Juliet is behaving as she is'. And they are sympathetic about the intensity of the Capulets' hurt, as well as that of their daughter. Peter, speaking as the father of two daughters, empathises with the feeling that 'the best possible thing is to look after them well'. As a group, what sets them apart from younger students with whom I've worked is their interest in the Capulets' own, apparently loveless, marriage – something the workshop participants acknowledge also wouldn't have interested them as much in youth. Most participants feel their responses have changed more broadly, too, with age. Ellen and Olive recall, as schoolgirls, admiring Juliet hugely for defying her father: Ellen because her own 'authoritarian upbringing' would have made such an act impossible. Kim Braden, interviewed in 1968, had been similarly incredulous at 'the way [Hussey's Juliet] answers her father and screams at him', an interesting insight given that she was speaking to her own father at the time. Similarly, Olive remembers thinking 'bully for you!' when Juliet defied her parents, more struck by that rebellion than anything else in the play. Now her primary emotion is pity for a heroine who is essentially a trapped child. All present feel that there are probably many Juliets in British society whose parents still deny their rights to self-determination. Ellen would advise a present-day Juliet to live her life, get out of her parents' house, and see the world.

From what I've written, you'd be forgiven for thinking that the familial dynamics chez Capulet intrigued the workshop participants more than the romance itself. Although Peter is markedly the most pragmatic about the Nurse's views on Paris and Juliet's potential bigamy, most of those present feel strongly that Juliet has 'no good options', and the Nurse, who loves her, has chosen a strategy that would, if followed, keep Juliet alive. When I ask the participants whether Juliet is right to stand by Romeo after he murders her cousin, Andrew says – regretfully, not unkindly – that she's made her bed and must lie in it. But the one point on which everyone present agrees is the one that can sometimes seem most improbable: love at first sight. Andrew fell in love with his wife the moment he saw her. Jean volunteers that she saw her husband for the first time when she was thirteen, when he sang in the church choir. She describes the sensation as that of feeling 'an inner light'. They've been married for half a century. Maggie calls the play a 'pure love story', and all of them are beguiled by the romance of the balcony scene; the two former actresses, Avril and Anita, read it particularly beautifully, drawing out the tenderness, romance and almost mysticism of the scene (it should also be noted that Olive makes a completely fantastic Nurse and ought to be cast as such immediately). At the same time, they're enthusiastic about the various adaptations they've seen – and the possibility of the text shifting further as time passes. Andrew, the resident poet, thinks the story will 'keep evolving' and become 'less straight'; he is enthusiastic about changing the ending, and shares several lively poems on the play, composed alongside the workshops.

The power of the older actresses in this chapter shows we should look again at theatrical myths of 'grandma Juliets' and older actresses who played Juliet for 'too long'. Shakespeare's text is of sufficient complexity to reward the sustained attention that comes from revisiting a role, or remaining with it longer. As Ffrangcon-Davies noted in the *Omnibus* documentary, 'I have seen things since I've been doing this again'. With all the performers in this chapter, whether in archive footage or my workshop participants, their interpretations of the roles brought out, as never before, how high the stakes are for Romeo and Juliet. Ffrangcon-Davies's self-giving Juliet on the balcony and Kempson's Juliet, contemplating her possible death, both thoroughly understood the sacrifices they were making. Less exclusively preoccupied with the lovers than most undergraduate audiences, my workshop participants brought the entire play to equal life. Despite the contemporary cultural tendency to associate older people with more conservative views of the text, the workshop participants were enthusiastic about different adaptations and the possibilities of a text evolving over time. All were markedly accomplished at verse-speaking, whether or not they'd acted before.

Alessandra Ferri, speaking of her last Juliet, said that she saw the advantages of being an older performer as the ability 'not to perform, but to be present. Just to *be*. To be present with the whole of yourself. It's an inner faith I'm talking about'. She urged younger performers: 'Don't be afraid of strength, force, sexuality'.[41] As with Ffrangcon-Davies advising younger actresses that the audience 'will listen to whatever you give them [. . .] Don't be afraid', there is a contrast between the confidence of older performers and the inhibition of Kim Braden, who confessed in interview that she got 'a bit embarrassed' when called upon to portray extremities of emotion. That confidence is essential for Juliet, who, in the shortest life, lives out the most dramatic extremities of love, despair, anger and terror. Theatrical culture is constantly pushing the boundaries regarding the casting of marginalised actors in the widest variety of parts. That must include older actors. Like her creator, Juliet is not of an age but for all time.

Epilogue

Over four centuries, the life and death of Juliet Capulet has held up a mirror if not to nature, then to society, and its changing attitudes to young women in love. The eighteenth century recast her as a death-driven maiden, full of suffering and sensibility, while the British Caribbean created a spectacle of enslaved women renamed as romantic objects. These women were given a facsimile of identity that bound them to a culture not their own, their enslavers using a prestigious literary narrative to disguise their experiences of exploitation. In the Victorian era, Juliet's nature and how to embody it became a question of national identity as society debated the differences between English and 'Mediterranean' womanhood, and the limits of onstage sexuality. At the same time, disparate women's voices towards the end of the century – the young, the indignant, the politically aware – began to question the value of the play's central romance, and to recognise that no relationship exists in a vacuum.

Going to Verona and researching that city's history showed me how a celebration of a woman's love could become the propaganda tool of a totalitarian regime, used to indoctrinate locals and visitors with a narrow, artificial view of love – and local history. Whether in *West Side Story* or the real-life 'across the barricade' tragedies of Chapter 7, the twentieth century presented Juliet as victim of – and often less important than – the male violence that dominates her life. Post-war incarnations of Juliet, such as *West Side Story*'s Maria and Zeffirelli's Renaissance teenager, saw Juliet's body scrutinised. Speaking heavily cut lines and spotlit by a fascinated, critical world media, the Juliet these actresses had to embody was based on thinness, whiteness and silence. Hussey's Juliet became an icon for teenage girls struggling with authoritarian parents and an ostensibly swinging, actually stagnant society. But as war correspondents covering sectarian violence in Northern Ireland, Eastern Europe and Afghanistan began to dub young women in those conflicts 'Juliet', the character had even more direct consequences for how we talk about young women in love, in danger, and in death. Juliets have been abused in the name of art and money, from Jenny Cibber at the hands of her odious father to Olivia Hussey, starved and sexually exploited on Zeffirelli's set. Misogyny and objectification run through Juliet's afterlives, romanticising dead girls and encouraging us to read all rebellious girls – and Juliet *is* a rebel – as destined for an aesthetically pleasing tragedy.

At the same time, in Juliet's history, wherever you look, there are signs of a public willing to tolerate more diverse interpreters and interpretations of the role than we might expect. You see it in Susannah Cibber's triumphant return to the stage after her divorce, and in Rachael Baptiste, the Black Irish singer who succeeded in eighteenth-century Lancashire, and in Charlotte Cushman and her lovers, who showed that the greatest love story ever told could be lived by two women in and out of the Victorian theatre. In Verona, a city ruled by the far-right, and in a 'Juliet Club' that originally banned women, correspondents now celebrate LGBTQ and interracial love in a way that Ettore Solimani, Juliet's first caretaker, could never have tolerated. Lived experience has long been important to Juliet, from Helena Faucit bringing her Christian faith to guide her Juliet into the darkness of the tomb, to Ellen Terry rapturously recalling her private romance with Henry Irving, so briefly and brilliantly public when they met each night as lovers onstage in the Capulets' ballroom. Some of the most radical readings of the play I've encountered came from my workshops with older people: poems altering the play's end, or suggestions that Juliet should indeed run away from Verona – by herself.

I finish writing this book on an autumnal afternoon in my new office at Magdalen: the college where I first had the idea of writing about Juliet, and to which, four years later, I've returned. Still in bubble wrap, awaiting the expert attentions of our maintenance team, who will hoist it aloft and hang it from a nineteenth-century picture rail, is a framed print of a painting by the American artist

James Christensen.[1] It depicts a plethora of characters from Shakespeare's plays, grouped in and around a ruined castle tower, which itself arises from a stormy sea. For years this poster hung on my parents' wall, and now it hangs on mine.

This poster is how I learned the names of Shakespeare's characters. There are Macbeth's witches, hunched over a cauldron, and Richard III slinking malevolently towards a castle. Prospero commands the storm, while a withered and ragged Caliban clings to his legs. A remorseful Othello holds Desdemona. Titania and Bottom, my first favourites, sit in a fairy bower at the top of the castle, where the ruined battlements are now overgrown and green. I learned the symbolism of other images later – the verses on trees were Orlando's, and the forest Arden, from *As You Like It*. A snake in a Roman helmet meant *Antony and Cleopatra*. The naked man counting gold in a cave (perilously close to waves, in Christensen's version) was Timon, and the toga / dagger scene was *Julius Caesar*.

All these I know by heart. But now, in my office, I peel back a bit of the wrap from the poster, just to reacquaint myself with another familiar face. Juliet. She's on a balcony at the right of the painting, glittering with jewels, a red rose in her fingertips and her eyes gently shut.

Even when I was very little, I couldn't see myself as Juliet. I decided I preferred the other girl in the painting, another woman Christensen places on a balcony; she's arguing with an unseen spectator, her hair is ginger, and she has wild, dark eyes. Her colours are bright while Juliet's are soft tints, and after thirty years I'm still not sure whether she's Beatrice from *Much Ado* or Katherine, the eponymous *Shrew*. Nonetheless, it's Juliet I've looked at longest.

The rose, I've learned, is a nod to a piece of Victorian stage business. If Juliet's appearance in the painting resembles that of any actress, it's Rebecca Saire, the fourteen-year-old leading lady of the BBC Shakespeare series, as she looked around the time Christensen completed the painting. Christensen dresses his Juliet very traditionally: a medieval fantasy in full-sleeved gold and baby blue.

In writing this book, I've formed cynical explanations for why the mythic appeal of Juliet endures. She's the rebellious heroine whose daring either delights or unnerves us, but whose thwarting reassures us that the world doesn't really have to change; pursuing our desires so recklessly can only end badly. She offers us a spectacle of nubile femininity that it's acceptable to lust after in her life and in her death. The tragedy that destroys her is so arbitrary and specific that, if we choose, we can dismiss it entirely – the feud is a pointless one, not like *our* necessary, well-founded biases. She perpetuates the toxic idea that love should hurt, should struggle, that the most meant-to-be relationships are ones hated by everyone else in your life. In unswerving fidelity to her flawed and murderous man, she offers the most conservative ideal of what a wife should be; in defying her autocratic father, she has much to offer young women disenchanted with the patriarchy.

I think all of the above is true. I hold it in tension with the fact that Juliet Capulet is the first great Shakespearean heroine: perhaps his most amazing tragic heroine, because Shakespeare created a new type of tragedy to accommodate her. It is a tragedy about power and how power plays out in love, violence, and family, rather than at the top of a state. This isn't a tragedy about the downfall of a king; nobody in the play is more important than Juliet.

I keep coming back to Christensen's Juliet, the first Juliet I ever saw, with her closed eyes and rose, standing on the balcony at dusk.

She isn't looking for Romeo; she's certainly thinking of him, given the text. But the impression of the moment isn't one of yearning but of bliss: a single ecstatic moment in the starlight, communing with the night and love and her own young beauty. This, ultimately, is the appeal of Juliet: to feel that possibility, that rapture, in the absolute conviction of first love, and in the exultation that comes from being very young and very happy in defiance of all circumstances. Even knowing as we do – and Juliet does not – what follows, that rhapsody is what keeps us coming back.

Writing any biography, even of the most well-known, real-life subject, requires imagination. We cannot know all the details of our subject's life, let alone their mind; perhaps we come to life-writing in the first place because something in our subject made us imagine more about them, or because we wanted to find out why their life and times caught the imagination of those who succeeded them. When the subject of a biography is fictional, imagination plays a greater role: greatest of all when the subject is a theatrical character, brought alive specifically and explicitly by the imaginations of every actor or actress who ever played her, and by every director, writer, journalist, tour guide, traveller, or scholar who's been concerned with bringing her story to the world. I think that if you're searching for Juliet, for Shakespeare, or for any of the meanings of his plays, the best place to find them is onstage, where a new Juliet is found in each encounter with the play in performance. Every biography is an imagined life; drama, in the writing and the acting, is about imagining what it is like to be someone, and then embodying them for the world.

Writing this book, I've been confronted again and again by the power and beauty of Shakespeare's writing. At the same time, though, I know Juliet is much more than what we find on the page. She shifts and changes as the world changes, and as we change – the Juliet we find at thirteen is not the Juliet we find at thirty, or sixty, or ninety-three. Her story continues to teach us much about injustice, family, and violence. But ultimately, she manages to be both personal and universal, not because of the tragedy she endures, but because she embodies love. And there is nothing more personal – or more universal – than love.

Acknowledgements

To everyone listed in these pages: thank you for helping me write this book. I had a wonderful time and it's because of you. The munificence of Christ Church and Sir Michael Moritz first brought me and my students to the Fondazione Zeffirelli in Florence, paving the way for much of what followed. Thanks also to the Fondazione Giorgio Cini in Venice, for my visiting fellowship there, and to The Oxford Research Centre in the Humanities (TORCH) and the Oxford Playhouse, whose generosity enabled my adventures in this book's last chapter.

Much of *Searching for Juliet* was written as a Fellow at Christ Church during four lively and pandemic-punctuated years. I owe an especial debt to Mishtooni Bose and Sarah Foot for their mentoring there, and to the equally brilliant Katie Mennis and Katie Noble whose superb teaching kept our students in the safest hands during my sabbatical. James Allison, Sarah Bloch-Budzier, Ciara Kennefick, David Laws, Richard Rutherford, and Robert Vilain listened to me and made me laugh. I completed this book at Magdalen, which welcomed me and 'the Juliet book' with open arms – thanks to Kate Bennett, Robert Douglas-Fairhurst, Holly Finn, Chris Garland, Simon Horobin, Dinah Rose, and Katie Taylor-O'Connor for their friendship and for a beautiful place in which to finish *Searching for Juliet*. Archivists and librarians around the world made this book possible during Covid: thank you to Gabriel Sewell and Cristina Neagu at Christ Church; Mariaelisa Nannini of the Fondazione Zeffirelli; Paul Allen Somerfeld at the Library of Congress; and the teams at the Bodleian Library, British Library, British Film Institute, the Dungannon Tourist Information Centre, and the Armagh Heritage Library. Beth Sedgwick of the Oxford Playhouse and Ruth

Moore of TORCH brought this book's last chapter to life, and introduced me to its stars: Andrew, Anita, Avril, Ellen, Helen, Jean, Maggie, Olive, Peter, Simon, and those who wished to remain anonymous. You are all delightful.

Many other friends and colleagues, near and far, lent their expertise with generosity and insight, especially Robert Cashmore, Simone Chess, Lucy Fleming, Hélène Marquié, Marc Mulholland, Caitlyn Neilson, Alex Pryce, and Madeleine Seinberg; to Tim Thompson for a memorable tutorial on *rigor mortis*; and to Marie Douada, Emily Guerry, Elizabeth Harper, and Anne M. Thériault for their knowledge of holy corpses. For permission to quote their tweets about Joan Lingard, I am grateful to Kersten England, Sarah Louise Cleary, and Rebecca Mills. Laura Tisdall and Laura Harrison guided me through histories of the 1960s, to my lasting delight. Another band of friends became 'Team Italy': heartfelt thanks to Elena Bonacini for translations; to Emmanuella Tandello and Richard Cooper for advice on Italian histories and geographies; and to Matteo Millan and Rebecca Rolfe for information on Fascist Italy. Lucy Rayfield was an invaluable research assistant and translator, without whom Veronese dialect would have remained a mystery. David Landau and Henry Tann both made me very welcome in Venice. My thanks also to the teachers who spoke confidentially about their experiences of Tory educational policy, and to an anonymous colleague in the British Army.

Among many Shakespeareans who've helped this book on the way, Hester Lees-Jeffries, Laurie Maguire, Emma Smith, David Francis Taylor, and Bart van Es continue to amaze me with their patience, generosity, and insight. No praise is too great, and they have all my gratitude and affection. Many students have enriched my thinking and tolerated my habit of relating everything to *Romeo and Juliet*: as well as those mentioned elsewhere in these pages, they include Abigail Allan, Ethan Andrews, Seren Atkinson, Honor Brocklebank-Fowler, Joori Byun, Megan Chester, Maisie Corkhill, Florrie Crass, Cai Donoghue, Tilly Fawcett, Liv Fugger, Emma Gasson, Leilah Greening, Solly Hardwick, Emily Hassan, Angus Irving, Nicole Jashapara, Anouska Levy, Shona McEvoy, Stepan Mysko von Schultze, Caitlin O'Sullivan, Craig Paterson, Nicholas Phipps, Mia Portman, Hannah-Sarah Selig, Ella Tournes, and Laura Wilson.

The brilliant Georgina Capel is the agent I always dreamed of having. I owe her and her amazing team, Rachel Conway, Irene Baldoni, Philippa Brewster, Simon Shaps, and Polly Halladay, so much – you believed in this book from the beginning and made it a thousand times better. Juliet Brooke: perfect name, perfect editor. Thanks for wanting my book, and also for introducing me to the extraordinary Charlotte Humphery, proof that lightning strikes twice at Carmelite House. Claire Potter and Marissa Koors were their brilliant counterparts across the Atlantic: thank you for your patience, wit, and general rightness. I'm so grateful to everyone at Hodder, Sceptre, Basic Books, and Seal Press, especially Maria Garbutt-Lucero, Holly Knox, Tara O'Sullivan, Melissa Raymond, Will Speed, Liz Wetzel, and Ellie Wheeldon.

Thank you also to Sheenagh Bloomfield, Emma Elobeid, Alicia Fautley Lefebvre, Jessie Goetzinger, Jenny Hao Randall, Ellie Keel, Lucy McDonnell Naidoo, and John-Mark Philo for their solidarity, hospitality, and good humour while I was writing this. Gareth Russell lit the way and advised me with all his wit and astuteness, despite a thousand other commitments. Jay Gilbert co-founded a magazine with me, provided moral and technical support, and found me the bit about Paul McCartney.

My wonderful parents, Pam and Alastair Duncan, and my brilliant wife, Emily Oliver, have lived with, read, encouraged, started, and finished this book alongside me. Thank you for everything. *Searching for Juliet* is for you, with all my love.

Notes

Introduction

1. All quotations from the play, unless otherwise specified, are taken from: Gary Taylor, John Jowett, Terri Bourus, and Gabriel Egan (eds), *Romeo and Juliet* in *The New Oxford Shakespeare: Modern Critical Edition* (Oxford: Oxford University Press, 2016).
2. 'Romeo, n.', entry in *Oxford English Dictionary* (hereafter *OED*).
3. Nicole Prunster (trans.), *Romeo and Juliet before Shakespeare* (Toronto: Centre for Reformation and Renaissance Studies, 2000), 3.
4. Ivor Brown, 'Romeo and Juliet', *Observer* (1 December 1935), 15.
5. Richard Driscoll, Keith E. Davis, and Milton E. Lipetz, 'Parental Interference and Romantic Love: The Romeo and Juliet Effect', *Journal of Personality and Social Psychology* 24.1 (1972), 1–10.
6. Colleen H. Sinclair, Kristina B. Hood, and Brittany L. Wright, 'Revisiting the Romeo and Juliet Effect: Reexamining the Links Between Social Network Opinions and Romantic Relationship Outcomes', *Social Psychology* 45.3 (May 2014), 170–8.
7. Susan Forward, *Toxic In-Laws: Loving Strategies for Protecting Your Marriage* (New York: Harper Perennial, 2002); Terri Apter, *What Do You Want from Me?: Learning to Get Along with In-Laws* (New York: W. W. Norton & Company, 2009); r/JUSTNOMIL ('Just No, Mother In Law'), *Reddit* (2020) (reddit.com/r/JUSTNOMIL/, accessed 22 October 2022).
8. *OED*; John Lyly, *Euphues* (London: Gabriel Cawood, 1580), Bv.
9. Philip Sidney, *Sir P.S. his Astrophel and Stella* [1580s] (London: John Danter, 1591).

Chapter 1: Shakespeare's First Tragic Heroine

1. Aficionados of the British Library and the UL in Cambridge are welcome to disagree. Don't @ me.
2. Richard Baker, quoted in R. C. Bald, *John Donne* (Oxford: Oxford University Press, 1970), 72.
3. Francis Meres, *Palladis Tamia: Wit's Treasury (1598): Scholar's Facsimiles* (New York, 1978), 47v–48r.

4. Francis Meres, *Palladis Tamia* (London: Cuthbert Burbie, 1598), 286v; Charles Nicholl, 'Marlowe [Marley], Christopher' *Oxford Dictionary of National Biography* (2004).

5. John Stow, *The Annales of England faithfully collected out of the most autenticall authors* (London: Ralfe Newbury, 1600), 1276–8.

6. Henry's mother, Mary Boleyn, was not only Anne Boleyn's sister, but the King's former mistress; her eldest son bore his name.

7. Bart van Es, *Shakespeare in Company* (Oxford: Oxford University Press, 2013), 103–4. By 1604, Shakespeare would sell malt, and own 107 acres of land in Stratford's environs. See: 'Shakespeare Documented', Folger Library (shakespearedocumented.folger.edu/, accessed 1 May 2020).

8. If all this sounds pleasingly utopian, it should be remembered that Shakespeare immediately used the profits to become a massive landowner, landlord and moneylender. He was nothing if not financially shrewd.

9. Anon., *The Problemes of Aristotle* (Edinburgh: s.n., 1595), C5v; Anon., *The Office of Christian Parents* (Cambridge: s.n., 1616), L1r; NHS, 'Early or delayed puberty' (nhs.uk/conditions/early-or-delayed-puberty/, accessed 29 October 2022).

10. Henry Cuffe, *The Differences of the Ages of Man's Life* (London: Martin Cleare, 1607), 131r–v.

11. Jonathan Bate and Eric Rasmussen (eds), *William Shakespeare: Complete Works* (Basingstoke: Macmillan, 2008), 217.

12. Katherine Duncan-Jones, 'Grudge Fudged', *Times Literary Supplement* (20 October 2000), 19.

13. Emily Ross, 'Ripe to Be a Bride? Marriage Age in *Romeo and Juliet*', *JJPC* 19.3 (2011), 145–59.

14. *Calendar of State Papers Spanish*, vol. 1, 176, quoted in Maria Perry, *Sisters to the King* (London: André Deutsch, 2002), 28.

15. Susanna Shakespeare was baptised on 26 May 1583.

16. Lena Cowen Orlin, *The Private Life of William Shakespeare* (Oxford: Oxford University Press, 2020), p.159.

17. 'MSS 19 – The "Platt" (or Plot) of The Second Part of the Seven Deadly Sins 1612–1626', Henslowe-Alleyn Papers, Archive of Dulwich College, London.

18. David Kathman, 'Reconsidering *The Seven Deadly Sins*', *Early Theatre* 7.1 (2004), 13–44.

19. R. Mark Benbow, 'Dutton and Goffe versus Broughton: a disputed contract for plays in the 1570s', *Records of Early English Drama* 6.2 (1981), 3–9.

20. Michael Shapiro, 'Patronage and the companies of boy actors' in Paul Westfield White and Suzanne R. Westfall (eds), *Shakespeare and Theatrical Patronage in Early Modern England* (Cambridge: Cambridge University Press, 2002), 272–94.

21. Kathman, 'Reconsidering *The Seven Deadly Sins*', 19–20; David Scott Kastan (ed.), *King Henry IV, Part 1* (London: Bloomsbury, 2002), 79.

22. E. A. J. Honigmann and Susan Brock, *Playhouse Wills, 1558–1642* (Manchester: Manchester University Press, 1993), 71.

23. Aside from my identifications of Gough as Rosaline, Hermia, and Juliet, Gough is listed as Aspatia and Philomele in the backstage plot of *2 Seven Deadly Sins*. *Sins* consisted of three playlets on *Envy, Sloth,* and *Lechery* – Tereus's rape of his sister-in-law Philomele, from Ovid's *Metamorphoses*. Richard Burbage played Tereus in *Lechery*, and playing his wife, Procne, was Alexander Cooke. Alexander Cooke also played Videna, the leading female role in *Sloth*, with Gough-as-Aspatia supporting him. Critic Richard Dutton claims that this shows Cooke had 'the pick of female roles', suggesting he eclipsed Gough but Philomele, the victim of Tereus's rape, would have been a more demanding role than Procne, and is certainly more important in the Ovidian original. Crucially, Philomele is Procne's younger sister, and Aspatia is a childless young woman, contrasted with Videna, the mother of grown-up sons.

24. Honigmann and Brock, *Playhouse Wills*, 72–4.

25. Anne (b. 1603), Elizabeth (b. 1605), Nicholas (b. 1608), Dorothy (1610–12) and Alexander (1614–55). Nicholas, the Goughs' eldest son, shared his name with Nicholas Tooley (1583–1623), another former boy-player and a successful adult actor, who had been close to Elizabeth Phillips's brother, Augustine, who left Tooley twenty shillings in his will.

26. James Wright, *Historia Histrionica* (London: s.n., 1699), C1r; Martin White (ed.), *The Roman Actor* (Manchester: Manchester University Press, 2007), 221.

27. Shakespeare d. 1616; Burbage d. 1619; Phillips d. 1605; Kemp d. 1603; Pope d. 1603; Cooke d. 1614; Tooley d. 1623.

28. Andrew Gurr, 'The Date and Expected Venue of *Romeo and Juliet*' in Stanley Wells (ed.), *Shakespeare Survey 49* (Cambridge: Cambridge University Press, 1996), 15–26.

29. Claire Bourne and Jason Scott-Warren, '"Thy unvalued Booke": John Milton's Copy of the Shakespeare First Folio', *Milton Quarterly* 56.1–2 (2023).

30. Robert Allott, *England's Parnassus* (London: N.L., C.B. and T.H, 1600); John Bodenham, *Bel-vedére* (London: Hugh Alley, 1600).

31. John Marston, *The Scourge of Villainie* (London: John Buzbie, 1598), pages unnum.

32. John Marston, *Jacke Drums Entertainment* (London: Richard Olive, 1601).

33. Henry Porter, *The pleasant historie of the two angrie women of Abington* (London: Edward Allde, 1599), Gr–H2v.

34. *MS Sancroft 29*, Bodleian Library, Oxford 88; *MS ER82/1/21*, Shakespeare Birthplace Trust, Stratford-upon-Avon, fo. 1r.

35. *A common place book* (c. 1622–5), *MS. Eng. misc. d.28*, Bodleian Library, Oxford, 359.

36. Thomas Heywood, *An Apologie for Actors* (London: Nicholas Okes, 1612), G4r.

37. Colin Burrow (ed.), *The Oxford Shakespeare: The Complete Sonnets and Poems* (Oxford: Oxford University Press, 2002), 355–6.

38. Thomas Prujean, 'Love's Looking-Glasse', *Aurorata* (London: Hugh Perry, 1644), pages unnum.

39. Leonard Digges, 'To the Memorie of the deceased Authour Maister W. Shakespeare', *Mr. William Shakespeares Comedies, Histories & Tragedies* [First Folio], Bodleian Arch. G c.7.

40. Quoted in Emma Smith, *Shakespeare's First Folio: Four Centuries of an Iconic Book* (Oxford: Oxford University Press, 2016), 75–7.

41. Ibid.

42. Martin Wiggins and Catherine Richardson (eds), *British Drama 1533–1642: A Catalogue, Vol. 3, 1590–1597* (Oxford: Oxford University Press, 2013), 987.

43. Gilbert Swinhoe, *The Tragedy of the Unhappy Fair Irene* (London: J. Place, 1658), 30.

44. Richard Goodridge, 'To the Authour', in Jacques Ferrand, *Erotomania* (Oxford: Edward Forrest, 1640).

45. Andrew Gurr, 'Introduction' in J. R. Mulrayne (ed.), *The Spanish Tragedy* (London: A&C Black, 2014), vii.

Chapter 2: Everybody Loves a Dead Girl

1. Letter from Henry Jackson to 'G.P.' (September 1610), Corpus Christi Fulman Papers, X. 83r–84v.

2. Edgar Allan Poe, 'The Philosophy of Composition', *Graham's Magazine* (April 1846), 163.

3. The Fashion Law, 'Why Do Ads and Editorials Depicting Violence Happen in Fashion?', *The Fashion Law* (4 October 2017), (thefashionlaw. com/why-ads-editorials-depicting-violence-keep-happening/, accessed 1 September 2021).

4. Katie Hosmer, 'Fantasizing About the Perfect Elegant Death', *My Modern Met* (20 May 2013), (mymodernmet.com/izima-kaoru-land-scape-with-a-corpse/, accessed 2 September 2018).

5. Rebecca Solnit, *Recollections of My Non-Existence* (London: Granta, 2020), 4.

6. Alice Bolin, *Dead Girls* (New York: HarperCollins, 2018), 16.

7. Solnit, *Recollections of My Non-Existence*, 50.

8. Oliver Goldsmith, *The Vicar of Wakefield* [1766] (London: John Van Voorst, 1842), 210.

9. Thomas Hardy, *Tess of the D'Urbervilles* (Oxford: Oxford University Press, 1989), 539.

10. Sarah Kane, *4.48 Psychosis* (1999).

11. See: John Lahr, *Prick Up Your Ears: The Biography of Joe Orton* (London: Allen Lane, 1978).

12. R. Mai and J. Rutka, 'The Irony of Being Oscar: The Legendary Life and Death of Oscar Wilde', *Journal of Otolaryngology* 29.4 (August 2000), 239–43.

13. Annabel Mehran (photog.) and Annette Lamothe-Ramos (stylist), 'Last Words', *Vice* (June 2013); see Jenna Sauers, 'Vice Published a Fashion Spread of Female Suicides', *Jezebel* (17 June 2013), (jezebel.com/vice-published-a-fashion-spread-of-female-writer-suicid-513888861, accessed 1 September 2020).

14. George Frederic Watts, *Found Drowned* (1849–50), oil on canvas, 213 x 120 cm, Watts Gallery, Compton, Surrey.

15. See: Emma Stirrup, 'Time Concertinaed at the Altar of Saint Cecilia in Trastevere' in Dorigen Caldwell and Lesley Caldwell (eds), *Rome: Continuing Encounters Between Past and Present* (Oxford: Ashgate, 2011), 57–78; Stefano Maderno, *St. Cecilia* (1600), marble, Saint Cecilia in Trastevere, Rome.

16. Philippe Ariès, *Western Attitudes Towards Death: From the Middle Ages to the Present* (Baltimore: Johns Hopkins University Press, 1975), 57.

17. For a brilliant discussion of the 'maiden', see Judith M. Bennett, 'Death and the Maiden', *Journal of Medieval and Early Modern Studies* 42.2 (2012), 269–305.

18. Davenant claimed to have been conceived in the building that now houses Oxford's Pizza Express. Mary Edmond, 'Davenant [D'Avenant], Sir William (1606–1668)', *DNB* (8 October 2009), (oxforddnb.com, accessed 1 October 2020); Stephen Orgel, *Imagining Shakespeare: A History of Texts and Visions* (London: Palgrave, 2003), 77.

19. Gilli Bush-Bailey, *Treading the Bawds: Actresses and Playwrights on the Late Stuart Stage* (Manchester: Manchester University Press, 2006), 27–8.

20. Samuel Pepys, diary entry dated 23 May 1660, *Pepys Diary* (pepysdiary.com/diary/1660/05/23/, accessed 1 October 2020).

21. Secretaries of State: State Papers Domestic, Charles II, *Manuscript SP29/8/1*, National Archives, Kew; Bush-Bailey, *Treading the Bawds*, 11.

22. Bush-Bailey, *Treading the Bawds*, 27–8.

23. Thomas Jordan, 'I Come, unknown to any of the rest' (1660), reprinted in Fiona Ritchie, *Women and Shakespeare in the Eighteenth Century* (Cambridge: Cambridge University Press, 2014), 4.

24. Gary Taylor, *Reinventing Shakespeare* (New York: Weidenfeld & Nicolson, 1989), 11.

25. Pepys, diary entry dated 1 April 1662, *Pepys Diary* (pepysdiary.com/diary/1662/04/01/, accessed 1 October 202).

26. John Downes, *Roscius Anglicanus* (London: s.n., 1708), 22.

27. Thomas Otway, *The History and Fall of Caius Marius* (London: Thomas Flesher, 1680), 63.

28. Otway, *Caius Marius*, 64.

29. Luigi da Porto, *Historia novellamente ritrovata di due nobili amanti* (Venice: s.n., 1531).

30. Theophilus Cibber, *Romeo and Juliet, A Tragedy, Revis'd, and Alter'd from Shakespeare* [1744] (London: C. Corbett, 1748), 2, 62–3.

31. George Anne Bellamy, *An Apology for the Life of George Anne Bellamy*, 5th edn (London: J. Bell, 1786), II.84–6.

32. Elaine M. McGirr, *Partial Histories: A Reappraisal of Colley Cibber* (Basingstoke: Palgrave Macmillan, 2016), 111.

33. Theophilus Cibber, *A Serio-Comic Apology for the Life of Mr Theophilus Cibber* (Dublin: A. Long, 1748), 43.

34. Anon., *See and Seem Blind* (London: 1732), 13; Elaine M. McGirr, '"What's in a name?": *Romeo and Juliet* and the Cibber Brand', *Shakespeare* 14.4 (2018), 399–412; Wade Soule, 'Cibber'.

35. Francis Truelove, *The Comforts of Matrimony* (London: s.n., 1739), 15.

36. Cibber, *Romeo and Juliet*, 95.

37. Anon., *The Tryal of a Cause for Criminal Conversation* (London: T. Trott, 1739), 14–15.

38. Anon. (but probably Henry Fielding), *An Apology for the Life of Mr T---- C-----, Comedian* (London: J. Mechell, 1740).

39. Anon., 'Pistol's a Cuckold, or Adultery in Fashion' (London: s.n., 1738).

40. Thomas Davies, *Memoirs of the Life of David Garrick* (London: s.n., 1780), 2.110–11.

41. McGirr, 'What's in a Name?', 400.

42. Jenny played Prince Arthur throughout February 1745 and for the last time on 4 April, at a benefit for (guess who?!) her father. (See: london-stagedatabase.uoregon.edu/event.php?id=22747, accessed 1 October 2020).

43. *Apology for the Life of Mr T---- C-----*, 125.

44. Theophilus Cibber, *Four Original Letters* (London: T. Read, 1739), 35.

45. Joseph C. Roach, *Cities of the Dead*, 54.

46. Anon., 'London', *Daily Post* (26 January 1733), 1.

47. 'Philodramatus', 'A Proposal for the Better Regulation of the Stage', *Weekly Miscellany* (27 January 1738), 1–2.

48. David Garrick, letter to Somerset Draper (16 September 1744), quoted Lohelin (ed.), *Romeo and Juliet*, 11.

49. Quoted in McGirr, 'What's in a Name?', 404; *Daily Advertiser* (12 September 1744), 2.

50. Theophilus Cibber, 'Epilogue' in Cibber, *Romeo and Juliet*, 87.

51. John Hill, *The Actor* (London: R. Griffiths, 1750), 134–5.

52. Charlotte Charke, *Narrative of the Life of Mrs Charlotte Charke*, ed. Robert M. Rehder (Abingdon: Routledge, 2016), 165.

53. 'Marriage Bond and Allegation for William Ellis and Jane Cibber, Aldenham, Hertfordshire' (28 February 1761), *London and Surrey Marriage Bonds and Allegations 1597–1921*, DL/A/D/005/MS10091/103. 178; 188; Kenneth F. Gibbs (transcrib.) and William Brigg (ed.), *The Parish Registers of Aldenham, Hertfordshire, 1559–1669, with Appendix* (St Alban's, Gibbs and Bamforth, 1902), 178–9; 188.

54. Anon., marginal note (6 November 1762) to the will of Colley Cibber (12 December 1757), PROB 11/834/297, National Archives, Kew. See

also Helene Koon, *Colley Cibber: A Biography* (Kentucky: Kentucky University Press, 2014), 219n.

55. George C. Braham, 'The Genesis of David Garrick's *Romeo and Juliet*', *Shakespeare Quarterly* 35.2 (1984), 170–9; 173–4.

56. McGirr, 'What's in a Name?', 400–1.

57. *OED* entry for 'balcony, n.' (accessed 1 October 2020); Thomas Coryat, *Coryat's Crudities* [1611] (Glasgow: J. MacLehose & Sons, 1905), 1.307.

58. David Garrick, *Romeo and Juliet* (London: J. and R. Tonson, 1753), 38.

59. William Hazlitt, *Characters of Shakespeare's Plays* (London: John Templeman, 1838), 143.

60. James N. Loehlin (ed.), *Romeo and Juliet (Shakespeare in Production)* (Cambridge: Cambridge University Press, 2002), 15.

61. Quoted in Phillip H. Highfill, Kalman A. Burnim, and Edward A. Langhans (eds), *A Biographical Dictionary of Actors* (Carbondale, Il: Southern Illinois University Press, 1978), 22.

62. Bellamy, *Apology*, 2.118–21; Arthur Murphy, *The Life of David Garrick, Esq.* (Dublin: Brett Smith, 1801), 100.

63. Leslie Ritchie, 'Pox on Both Your Houses: The Battle of the Romeos', *Eighteenth-Century Fiction* 27.3–4 (Spring–Summer 2015), 373–93; 382.

64. Peter Thomson, *The Cambridge Introduction to English Theatre 1660–1900* (Cambridge: Cambridge University Press, 2006), 75–6.

65. David J. Goldby, 'Arne, Thomas Augustine (1710–1778)', *DNB* (23 September 2004) (oxford.dnb.com, accessed 1 October 2020); *Gentleman's Advertiser* (September 1750), 427; Charles Haywood, 'William Boyce's: "Solemn Dirge" in Garrick's Romeo and Juliet Production of 1750', *Shakespeare Quarterly* 11.2 (Spring 1960), 173–87; 174.

66. Tate Wilkinson, *Memoirs of His Own Life* (York: Wilson, Spence, and Mawman, 1790), 4.154; Christob Mylius, diary entry dated 23 October 1753, quoted in John Alexander Kelly, *German Visitors to English Theatres* (Princeton: Princeton University Press, 1936), 24–5.

67. Garrick, *Romeo and Juliet*, 57; Arne, 'Solemn Dirge' (1750), quoted in Haywood, 'William Boyce's "Solemn Dirge"', 175.

68. Playbill for *Romeo and Juliet* (Theatre Royal Drury Lane, 1 October 1750); see Haywood, 'William Boyce's "Solemn Dirge"', 177.

69. See: Frederick Kielmansegge, *Diary of a Journey to England* [1762] (London: Longmans, Green & Co., 1902), 221–2.

70. Garrick, *Romeo and Juliet*, 57.

71. Ibid.

72. Charles Wyndham used it as late as 1875; Loehlin (ed.), *Romeo and Juliet*, 15.

73. *Monthly Mirror* (November 1797), 293 (londonstagedatabase.uoregon.edu/event.php?id=50965, accessed 13 July 2022).

74. See: Kielmansegge, *Diary*, 221–2.

75. Francis Gentleman, *The Dramatic Censor* (London: J. Bell, 1770), 185–6.

76. Arthur Colby Sprague, *Shakespeare and the Actors* [1948] (Cambridge, MA: Harvard University Press, 2013), 305.

77. Ralph Houlbrooke, *Death, Religion, and the Family in England, 1480–1750* (Oxford: Oxford University Press, 2000), 280–1.

78. Letter from Horace Walpole to Horace Mann (24 December 1741), in John Wright (ed.), *Letters of Horace Walpole* (Philadelphia: Lea & Blanchard, 1842), 201–6; 204. Houlbrooke, *Death*, 280.

79. Houlbrooke, *Death*, 280.

80. Terry Friedman, *The Eighteenth Century Church in Britain* (New Haven, CT: Yale University Press, 2011), 185.

81. Jacques Chereau (artist), Noël-Nicolas Coypel (engraver), invitation to accompany the funeral procession of John Boyfield on 22 October (1747), E.864-1939, V&A Museum, London.

82. Anon., engraved invitation to the funeral of Mrs Rebecca Hale on 20 April (1776), E.235-1963, V&A Museum, London.

83. Houlbrooke, *Death*, 286.

84. Robert Campbell, *The London Tradesmen* (London: T. Gardner, 1747), 729–50.

85. Teerapa Pirohakul, *The English Funeral in the Long Eighteenth Century*, unpublished PhD thesis (London: LSE, 2015), 190.

86. Hervey, *Meditation Among the Tombs* [1745], quoted in Jack G. Voller (ed.), *The Graveyard School* (Richmond, VA: Valancourt Books, 2015), 99.

87. Samuel Richardson, *Clarissa* [1748] (Dublin, 1792), 7.359–60.

88. Richardson, *Clarissa*, 8.100, 106.

89. Ibid, 8.162.

90. Ibid, 8.133.

91. Anon., 'Here unentombed van Butchell's consort lies' in C.J.S. Thompson, *The Quacks of Old London* (London: Brentano's, 1928), 323–4.

92. See: Jessie Dobson, 'Some Eighteenth Century Experiments in Embalming', *Journal of the History of Medicine* (October 1953), 431–41.

93. See: Samuel Taylor Coleridge, 'The Monk. A Romance', *Critical Review* (February 1797), 194–200.

94. Anon., 'London. Thursday, Jan. 28th' *Reading Mercury* (1 February 1779), 2.

95. Anon., 'Yesterday, about one o'clock [. . .]' *General Advertiser* (2 February 1779), 3.

96. 'Spranger & Ann Barry', *Westminster Abbey* (2020) (westminster-abbey. org/abbey-commemorations/commemorations/spranger-ann-barry, accessed 12 October 2020); 'Susanna Cibber', *Westminster Abbey* (2020) (westminster-abbey.org/abbey-commemorations/commemorations/ susanna-cibber, accessed 19 October 2020).

97. Michael Burden, 'Shakespeare and opera' in Fiona McGill and Peter Sabor (eds), *Shakespeare in the Eighteenth Century* (Cambridge: Cambridge University Press, 2012), 204–24; 216.

98. Richard Erkens, 'The Earliest *Romeo and Juliet* Operas: The Happy Lovers of Johann Gottfried Schwanberger (1773) and Georg Anton Benda (1776)' in Maria Ida Biggi and Michele Girardi (eds), *Shakespeare*

All'Opera: Riscritture e Alletestimenti di 'Romeo e Giulietta' (Bari: edizioni di pagina, 2018), 15–32; 19.

99. Niccolò Antonio Zingarelli, *Romeo and Giulietta* [1796] (New York: E. M. Murden, 1826), 46; Vincenzo Bellini (music) and Felice Romani (libretto), *I capuleti e I Montecchi* [1830] ed. Dario Zanotti *Libretti di Opera* 105 (June 2006), 27–8 (Vaccai also used this libretto); Charles Gounod, *Roméo et Juliette* [1867], in 'Romeo et Juliette', *Opéra L'Avant scene* 41 (May–June 1982), 64–5.

100. Robert Wise and Jerome Robbins (dirs), *West Side Story* (Mirisch Pictures/Seven Arts Productions, 1961), 152 mins; Raymond Knapp, *The American Musical and the Formation of National Identity* (Princeton: Princeton University Press, 2006), 211.

101. Loehlin (ed.), *Romeo and Juliet*, 242.

102. Baz Luhrmann (dir.), *William Shakespeare's Romeo + Juliet* (Bazmark Productions, 1996), 120 mins; Carlo Carlei (dir.), Julian Fellowes (screenplay), *Romeo & Juliet* (Echo Lake Entertainment/Swarovski Entertainment, 2013), 118 mins.

Chapter 3: Country Marks

1. Richard B. Allen, *European Slave Trading in the Indian Ocean, 1500–1850* (Ohio: Ohio University Press, 2015), 27.

2. Kirk Smock, *Guyana* (Chalfont St Peter: Bradt, 2008), 7.

3. Chris Jeppesen, 'East meets West: Exploring the Connections Between the East India Company and the Caribbean', *Centre for the Study of the Legacies of British Slavery* (University College London, 31 May 2013), (lbsatucl.wordpress.com/2013/05/31/east-meets-west-exploring-the-connections-between-the-east-india-company-and-the-caribbean, accessed 19 October 2020).

4. Samuel Taylor Coleridge, 'On the Slave Trade', *The Watchman* (25 March 1796), 130–40; 139.

5. 'Britain and the Slave Trade', *The National Archives* (2020) (national-archives.gov.uk/slavery/pdf/britain-and-the-trade.pdf, accessed 19 October 2020).

6. Richard Jenkins, *Memoirs of the Bristol Stage* (Bristol: W.H. Somerton, 1826), 70–1.

7. David Richardson (ed.), *Bristol, Africa, and the Eighteenth-century Slave Trade to America, Vol. 3: The Years of Decline 1746–1769*, Bristol Records Society Publications Vol. XLII (1991), (bris.ac.uk/Depts/History/bristolrecordsociety/publications/brs42.pdf), 201, 209; David Richardson, *The Bristol Slave Traders: A Collective Portrait*, Bristol Records Society (1985), (bris.ac.uk/Depts/History/bristolrecordsociety/publications/bha060.pdf), 29.

8. David Garrick, 'Prologue for the Opening of the Bristol Theatre' in *The Poetical Works of David Garrick, Esq.* (London: George Kearsley, 1785), 1.213–4.

9. 'Former British Colonial Dependencies, Slave Registers, 1813–1834', *Ancestry* (2020), (ancestry.co.uk/search/collections/1129, accessed 19 October 2020).

10. See Margaret Williamson, 'Africa or Old Rome? Jamaican Slave Naming Revisited', *Slavery & Abolition* 38 (2017), 117–34; Peter Kolchin, *American Slavery* (London: Penguin, 1995), 141.

11. Olaudah Equiano, *The Life of Olaudah Equiano* [1789] (Boston: Isaac Knapp, 1837), 56–7.

12. Justin Kaplan and Anne Bernays, *The Language of Names* (New York: Touchstone, 1999), 77.

13. Iman Makeba Laversuch, 'Runaway Slave Names Recaptured: An Investigation of the Personal First Names of Fugitive Slaves Advertised in the Virginia Gazette Between 1736 and 1776', *Names* 54 (2006), 331–62; 344.

14. For more on hypocoristic names, see: Williamson, 'Africa or old Rome?'.

15. Ancestry, 'Former British Colonial Dependencies, Slave Registers, 1813–1834'.

16. 'Juliet' is not as uniquely Shakespearean a name as e.g. Hamlet, Romeo, or Othello – but although in circulation in mainland Britain, its relative rareness in UK parish records indicates that it was disproportionately prevalent in enslaved populations.

17. Carlton Estate Records, St James, Jamaica (1817), *Office of Registry of Colonial Slaves and Slave Compensation Commission: Records*, Class T 71, Piece Number 203, National Archives, UK; Ancestry, 'Former British Colonial Dependencies, Slave Registers, 1813–1834'.

18. Juliet, b. 1758 in the Caribbean: Albany Sugar Estate Records, Westmoreland, Jamaica (1817), *Office of Registry of Colonial Slaves and Slave Compensation Commission: Records*, Class T71, Piece Number 178; Juliet, b. 1768 in Africa: unnamed estate, Westmoreland, Jamaica (1817), *Office of Registry of Colonial Slaves and Slave Compensation Commission: Records*, Class T71, Piece Number 178; Juliet b. 1773 in the Caribbean, New Hope Sugar Estate Records, Westmoreland, Jamaica (1817), *Office of Registry of Colonial Slaves and Slave Compensation Commission: Records*, Class T71, Piece Number 178.

19. 'John Campbell of New Hope', *Centre for the Study of the Legacies of British Slavery* (University College London, 31 May 2013), (ucl.ac.uk/lbs/person/view/2146634980)

20. Return of slaves including 'Old Juliet' (b. 1737, Africa), 'Othello' (b. 1737, Africa), and 'Polidore' (b. 1734, Africa), Carlton Estate Records, St James, Jamaica (1817).

21. Return of slaves including 'Juliat' (b. 1764, Africa), 'Oronoco' (b. 1764, Africa), 'Yorick' (b. 1774, Africa), 'Juliet' (b. 1777, Caribbean), 'Hamlet' (b. 1801, Caribbean), 'Romeo' (b. 1811, Caribbean), Horatio (b. 1816, Caribbean) for the Lowlands Estate, St Andrew's, Tobago (1819), *Office of Registry of Colonial Slaves and Slave Compensation Commission: Records*, Class T71, Piece Number 462.

22. 'Elphinstone Piggott', *Centre for the Study of the Legacies of British Slavery* (University College London, 2020), (ucl.ac.uk/lbs/person/view/2146633464, accessed 25 October 2020).

23. Return of slaves including 'Romeo' (c. 1768, Africa – c. 1823, Jamaica), 'Juliet' (c. 1778, Africa – c. 1823, Jamaica) for Lancaster, Trelawney, Jamaica (1823), *Office of Registry of Colonial Slaves and Slave Compensation Commission: Records*, Class T71, Piece Number 234.

24. 'Thomas Pepper Thompson', *Centre for the Study of the Legacies of British Slavery* (University College London, 2020), (ucl.ac.uk/lbs/person/view/2146642371, accessed 25 October 2020); June Badeni, 'Meynell [*née* Thompson], Alice Christiana Gertrude (1847–1922), *DNB* (7 January 2016), (oxforddnb.com/view/10.1093/ref:odnb/9780198614128.001.0001/odnb-9780198614128-e-35008, accessed 25 October 2020).

25. Return of slaves including 'Juliet' (b. 1819, Jamaica) and 'Romeo' (b. 1818, Jamaica) enslaved by John Alexander in St Ann's, Jamaica (1820), *Office of Registry of Colonial Slaves and Slave Compensation Commission: Records*, Class T71, Piece Number 44.

26. Laversuch, 'Runaway Slave Names Recaptured', 344.

27. Ibid.

28. Equiano, *The Life of Olaudah Equiano*, 115–6.

29. John Ferdinand Dalziel Smyth, *A Tour in the United States of America* (London: G. Robinson, 1784), II.184.

30. bell hooks, quoted in Rachel A. Feinstein, *When Rape Was Legal* (Oxford: Taylor & Francis, 2018), 40.

31. Harriet Jacobs, *Incidents in the Life of a Slave Girl* (Boston: s.n., 1861), 79–80.

32. 'Slave Narrative of Sam and Louisa Everett', *Federal Writers' Project, 1936–38* (8 October 1936), 3. Digital Commons, University of South Florida (digitalcommons.usf.edu/formerly_enslaved_narratives/5, accessed 30 October 2022).

33. 'Hilliard Yellerday (A Slave Story)', *North Carolina Slave Narratives* (23 October 1937), (northcarolinaslavenarratives.wordpress.com/north-carolina-slave-narratives-2/yellerday-hilliard/, accessed 25 October 2020).

34. Jacobs, *Incidents*, 119.

35. Feinstein, *When Rape Was Legal*, 22.

36. Return of slaves including 'Juliet Vincent' (b. 1777, Africa), 'Juliet Arguille' (b. 1777, Africa), 'Juliet R' (b. 1799, Caribbean), 'Romeo' (b. 1797, Caribbean), 'Polydore' (b. 1783, Caribbean), 'Grandison' (b. 1798, Caribbean), Orange Hill Estate, St Vincent (1817), *Office of Registry of Colonial Slaves and Slave Compensation Commission: Records*, Class T71, Piece Number 493.

37. Return of slaves including 'Juliet' (b. 1782, Caribbean), 'Ophelia' (b. 1772, Africa), 'Isabella' (b. 1811, Caribbean), 'Isabella' (b. 1777, Africa), 'Orlando' (b. 1779, Africa), 'Hamlet' (b. 1777, Africa), 'Cato' (b. 1772,

Africa), 'Pompey' (b. 1807, 1807) enslaved by Samuel Barrett in St James, Jamaica (1817), *Office of Registry of Colonial Slaves and Slave Compensation Commission: Records*, Class T71, Piece Number 203.

38. 'Samuel Barrett Moulton Barrett MP', Centre for the Study of the Legacies of British Slavery (University College London, 2020) (ucl. ac.uk/lbs/person/view/21376, accessed 3 November 2020).

39. Return of slaves including 'Juliet' (b. 1805, Caribbean), 'Ophelia' (b. 1811, Caribbean), 'Cordelia' (b. 1798, Caribbean), 'Hamlet' (b. 1791, Caribbean), 'Swift' (b. 1777, Africa) and 'Pope' (b. 1757, Africa), Trelawney, Jamaica (1817), *Office of Registry of Colonial Slaves and Slave Compensation Commission: Records*; Class T 71, Piece Number 224; 'George Cunningham', *Centre for the Study of the Legacies of British Slavery* (University College London, 2020), (ucl.ac.uk/lbs/person/view/17894, accessed 3 November 2020).

40. 'The Coburg Theatre', *The Times* (11 October 1825), 2; *Figaro in London* (6 April 1833), 56.

41. John Jackson, *The History of the Scottish Stage* (Edinburgh: Hill and Robinson, 1793), 350–1.

42. Return of slaves including 'Juliette' (b. 1824, Mauritius), Port Lewis, Mauritius (1832), *Office of Registry of Colonial Slaves and Slave Compensation Commission: Records*; Class T 71, Piece Number 634.

43. Return of slaves including 'Juliette Suzanne' (b. 1819, Mauritius), Port Lewis, Mauritius (1832), *Office of Registry of Colonial Slaves and Slave Compensation Commission: Records*; Class T 71; Piece Number 633.

44. Return of slaves, including 'Juliet' (b. 1783, Africa) for New Forest estate, Berbice (1819), *Office of Registry of Colonial Slaves and Slave Compensation Commission: Records*, Class T71, Piece Number 438.

45. Katrina H. B. Keefer, 'Marked by Fire: Brands, Slavery, and Identity', *Slavery & Abolition* 40.4 (2019), 659–81.

46. Ibid.

47. Return of slaves including 'Juliet' (b. 1793, Africa), Berbice, *Office of Registry of Colonial Slaves and Slave Compensation Commission: Records*; Class T 71, Piece Number 438.

48. *Federal Gazette* (8 November 1796) and *Federal Gazette* (3 June 1809).

49. Return of slaves including 'Juliet' (b. 1769, Africa; d. 30 April 1819, Westmoreland, Jamaica), Jerusalem Estate, Westmoreland, Jamaica (1820), *Office of Registry of Colonial Slaves and Slave Compensation Commission: Records*; Class T 71, Piece Number 179.

50. Return of slaves including 'Juliet Sawers' (b. 1768, Africa, d. 1820, Hanover, Jamaica), *Office of Registry of Colonial Slaves and Slave Compensation Commission: Records*; Class T 71, Piece Number 191.

51. Zachary Macaulay, *Negro Slavery* (London: Hatchard & Son, 1823), 48–53.

52. Return of slaves including 'Juliette Denise' (1824–32, Mauritius), Port

Lewis, Mauritius, *Office of Registry of Colonial Slaves and Slave Compensation Commission: Records*; Class T 71, Piece Number 630. Little is known about the Ferrier family, but they seem to have been a powerful group of enslavers.

53. Slavery continued in the territories of the East India Company, Ceylon (modern-day Sri Lanka) and St Helena.

54. Adam Hochschild, *Bury the Chains: Prophets and Rebels in the Fight to Free an Empire's Slaves* (Boston: Mariner, 2005), 79–83.

Chapter 4: Her Southern Temperament

1. 'Brady, Francis Bridgford', *Principal Probate Registry / Index of Wills and Registrations* (London: Crown Copyright, 1981), H16.

2. Letter from F. B. Brady to the Librarian, Christ Church (24 November 1977), F. B. Brady Collection, Christ Church.

3. Robert Louis Stevenson, 'A Penny Plain and Twopence Coloured', in *Memories and Portraits* [1887] (London: T. Nelson, 1924), 203–16; 205.

4. Queen Victoria, diary entry dated 8 April 1837, Princess Beatrice's transcripts, 1.7.

5. Queen Victoria, diary entry dated 20 January 1839, Lord Esher's transcripts, 9.243–4.

6. Queen Victoria, diary entry dated 26 March 1840, Beatrice 9.165–6.

7. Queen Victoria, diary entry dated 26 January 1846, Beatrice 21.40–1; Queen Victoria, diary entry dated 1 December 1859, Beatrice 48.73–4.

8. See Queen Victoria, diary entry dated 6 October 1888 (Beatrice 88.88–90), and diary entries dated 18 November 1880 (Beatrice 73.84–5), 24 September 1884 (Beatrice 80.67–8), 9 October 1888 (Beatrice 88.92), 20 September 1892 (Beatrice 96.67–8), 27 June 1898 (Beatrice 107.203–foldout), 14 July 1898 (Beatrice 108.21–3) and others.

9. Queen Victoria, diary entry dated 22 February 1855 (Beatrice 39.117–20).

10. Mary Cowden Clarke, 'Juliet, the White Dove of Verona' in *The Girlhood of Shakespeare's Heroines* [1850] (London: J. M. Dent & Co., 1907), II.308–408; Anna Jameson, *Characteristics of Women* [hereafter *Shakespeare's Heroines*] (New York: Ottley, 1837), 93–4.

11. 'Our Prize Competition', *Girl's Own Paper* (10 March 1888), 380–3.

12. John Russell Brown (ed.), *Shakespeare Handbooks: Macbeth* (Basingstoke: Palgrave Macmillan, 2005), 21; Jacky Bratton, *The Making of the West End Stage* (Cambridge: Cambridge University Press, 2011), 4; Joseph Donohue (ed.), *Cambridge History of British Theatre* (Cambridge: Cambridge University Press, 2004), II.254.

13. Madge Kendal, *Dramatic Opinions* (London: privately printed, 1890), 31.

14. Quoted in Mrs Patrick Campbell, *My Life and Some Letters* (London: Hutchinson & Co., 1928), 33.

15. Arthur Wing Pinero, *The Second Mrs Tanqueray* [1893] in *Pinero: Three Plays* (London: Methuen, 1985), 78–184; 87.

16. Matthew Arnold, 'The French Play in London', *The Nineteenth Century* 6 (1879), 228–43; 243.
17. Madge Kendal, *Dame Madge Kendal by Herself* (1933), 5.
18. Carlisle, Carol J, 'Faucit, Helen [*real name* Helena Faucit Saville or Savill; *married name* Helena Martin, Lady Martin] (1814–1898)', *DNB* (2004), (doi.org/10.1093/ref:odnb/9200, accessed 31 October 2022).
19. Beth Holmgren, *Starring Madame Modjeska* (Bloomington, IN: Indiana University Press, 2012), 25, 106.
20. 'Scrutator', 'A Polish Juliet', *Truth* (31 March 1881), 15.
21. 'The Stroller', *Sporting Life* (10 May 1893), 8.
22. W. G. Robertson, *Life Was Worth Living* (London: Harper & Bros, 1931), 149. See: *Madame Tussaud & Sons Exhibition* (London: c. 1905), 20, repr. Chris Mullen, *VTS* archive (fulltable.com/vts/t/ta/mt.htm, accessed 2 January 2021).
23. I am indebted to Seren Atkinson for her knowledge of Wightwick.
24. F. W. Fairholt, MS account of his visit to Shakespeare's Birthplace (29 August 1839); Walter Savage Landor, 'The Sale of Shakespeare's House', *Examiner* (24 July 1847), both quoted in Julia Thomas's excellent *Shakespeare's Shrine* (Philadelphia: University of Pennsylvania Press, 2012), 18.
25. Earthenware transfer-printed mug with blue enamel (1800 to 1850), 127 x 86 mm, V&A 3650-1901, London; mantel clock, drum-shaped movement inset into bronze rockwork with an ormolu figure of Shakespeare (1840), 395 x 312 x 105 mm, NT 514785, Anglesey Abbey, Cambridgeshire.
26. Edward Dowden, *Shakspere* (London: Henry S. King, 1875), 403.
27. John Ruskin, 'Of Queen's Gardens' [1864] in Tyas Cook and Wedderburn (eds), *Works of John Ruskin* (Cambridge: Cambridge University Press, 2010), VIII.109–44; 113–4.
28. Mary Cowden Clarke, 'Shakespeare as the Girl's Friend', *Girl's Own Paper* (4 June 1887), 562–4.
29. Jameson, *Shakespeare's Heroines*, 26.
30. Jameson, *Shakespeare's Heroines*, 113, 95.
31. Cowden Clarke, 'The White Dove of Verona', 406; Jameson, *Shakespeare's Heroines*, 95.
32. Helen Faucit, 'Juliet', *On Some of Shakespeare's Female Characters* [1885] (London: William Blackwood & Sons, 1905), 83–155; 133, 116.
33. Ellen Terry, Christopher St John (ed.), *Four Lectures on Shakespeare* (London: 1932), 138.
34. Anon., 'Verona', *The Christian Lady's Magazine* (December 1837), 543–6; 544.
35. C. H. Williamson, 'A Lay Sermon', *Wesleyan Methodist Magazine* (October 1898), 764–6.
36. Arthur MacDonald, 'Statistics of Child Suicide', *American Statistical Association* (March 1907), 260–4.
37. See: John Stokes, *In the Nineties* (Hemel Hempstead: Harvest Wheatsheaf, 1989), 115–44. For varyingly lurid accounts of lovers who died together in the face of parental opposition, see: 'The Romantic Suicide of Lovers

Near Birmingham', *Derby Daily Telegraph* (6 June 1887), 4; 'Suffolk Lovers Die Together', *Derby Daily Telegraph* (9 September 1895), 4; 'Lovers Drowned Together' (in fact four lovers and two drownings), *Shields Daily Gazette* (27 July 1900), 3. On a spate of lovers drowning while deliberately tied together, see: 'Imitative Suicide', *Sunderland Daily Echo* (18 February 1893), 4.

38. Jameson Torr Altemus, *Helena Modjeska* (New York: J. S. Ogilvie, 1883), 124–33.

39. 'Romeo and Juliet at the Court', *Era* (2 April 1881), 7.

40. Faucit, 'Juliet', 110–11.

41. Helena Faucit, MS annotations to promptbook of *Romeo and Juliet* (c. 1836–45), Folger Library (Rom 8), 55–7.

42. Helena Modjeska, *Memories and Impressions of Helena Modjeska* (New York: B. Blom, 1910), 122.

43. Mary Anderson de Navarro, *A Few Memories* (New York: Harper & Bros, 1896), 23, 46.

44. Walkley, quoted in Campbell, *My Life and Some Letters*, 103.

45. 'Lewis Carroll' (photog.) and Anne Lydia Bond (colorist), 'Evelyn Hatch' (29 July 1879), photograph, *Wikipedia* (wikipedia.org/wiki/Evelyn_Hatch#/media/File:Hatch,_Evelyn_(Lewis_Carroll,_29.07.1879).jpg).

46. Sophie Duncan, *Shakespeare's Women and the Fin de Siècle* (Oxford: Oxford University Press, 2016), 107–8.

47. Shaw, 'Romeo and Juliet', *Saturday Review* (28 September 1895), 409–10.

48. Faucit, 'Juliet', 141.

49. Ibid, 149.

50. Modjeska, *Memories and Impressions*, 129–30.

51. Altemus, *Helena Modjeska*, 125.

52. Ellen Terry, MS annotation to 1882 promptbook of *Romeo and Juliet* (London: Chiswick Press, 1882), 13v, Harvester Microform 1974 microfilm of TS Promptbook, SH154.348, British Library.

53. Ellen Terry, *The Story of My Life* (London: Hutchinson & Co., 1908), 214.

54. Terry, MS promptbook annotations, 15r *et al.*

55. Terry, MS promptbook annotations, 39r; 44r.

56. Letter from Irving to Terry (c. January 1882) and letter from Irving to Terry (c. January 1882), 1–2, 2, both in THM/384/6/4, V&A Museum, London.

57. Quoted in Lisa Merrill, *When Romeo Was a Woman* (Ann Arbor, MI: University of Michigan Press, 2000), 171.

58. George Fletcher, *Studies of Shakespeare* (London: Longman *et al.*, 1847), 380.

59. Fletcher, *Studies of Shakespeare*, 380; Mary Howitt, 'The Miss Cushmans', *People's Journal* (18 July 1846), 30.

60. John Coleman, *Fifty Years of an Actor's Life* (New York: James Pott & Co., 1904), 2.363; Westland Marston, *Our Recent Actors* (Boston: Roberts Brothers, 1888), 76.

61. 'Exeter Theatre', *Western Times* (14 October 1848), 5.

62. J. M. W., 1846 review of Cushman, in James Shapiro (ed.), *Shakespeare in America* (New York: Library of America, 2014), 56–9.

63. *Mercury* (18 January 1847), quoted in Merrill, 155.

64. Hester Lynch Thrale, diary entries dated 17 June 1790 and 9 December 1795, reprinted in Alison Oram and Annmarie Turnbull (eds), *The Lesbian History Sourcebook* (London: Routledge, 2002), 58–9.

65. Havelock Ellis, *Sexual Inversion* [1896] (London: Springer, 2007), 164.

66. Anne Hampton Brewster, diary entry dated 18 February 1849, Anne Hampton Brewster Papers, Library Company of Philadelphia, quoted in Merrill, 57–9.

67. Eliza Cook, 'Poetical Dedication of a Volume', *Hampshire Advertiser* (25 November 1848), 7.

68. Letter from Jane Carlyle to Jeannie Walsh (19 January 1846), *Carlyle Letters Online* (carlyleletters.dukeupress.edu/volume/20/lt-18460119-JWC-JW-01, accessed 31 October 2022); letter from Geraldine Jewsbury to Charlotte Cushman (n.d.), Charlotte Cushman Papers 11: 3449–50 (archivalgossip.com/collection/items/show/338, accessed 31 October 2022).

69. 'Exeter Theatre', *Western Times*, 5.

70. Letter from Cushman to Emma Crow (15 November 1860), quoted in Merrill, 129–30.

71. See: Catherine Belsey, *Romeo and Juliet* (London: Bloomsbury, 2014), 153–4.

72. J. R., 'Zeffirelli's "Romeo" – Fresh, Alive, Young', *Los Angeles Advocate* (January 1969), 11.

73. Roger Allam, 'Mercutio from *Romeo and Juliet*' in Russell Jackson and Robert Smallwood (eds), *Players of Shakespeare* 2 (Cambridge: Cambridge University Press 1988), 107–19; 109.

74. Stage productions include Joe Calarco's *Shakespeare's R&J* (2003), Nick Bagnall's *Romeo and Julius* (Liverpool Everyman, 2017), and Rachel Garnet's *Starcrossed* (2018). Films include Eytan Fox's *The Bubble* (2006) and Alan Brown's *Private Romeo* (2011).

75. Undated letter from Martha Le Baron to Cushman, Charlotte Cushman Papers 16, Library of Congress, quoted in Merrill, 129; Emma Crow Cushman, 'Charlotte Cushman: A Memory', Charlotte Cushman Papers 15: 4019–36, Library of Congress, quoted in Merrill, 206.

76. Letter from Kate Field to Emma Crow (10 July 1860), Charlotte Cushman Papers 11: 3300–01, Library of Congress.

77. Emma Stebbins, *Charlotte Cushman* (Boston: Houghton, Osgood & Co., 1879), 12.

78. Duncan, *Shakespeare's Women*, 219; Ellen Terry, untitled MS lecture draft on Shakespeare's heroines, British Library Loan, MS. 125/31/1, f.3.

79. Clotilde Graves, 'O' Both Your Houses', *Gentlewoman* (25 January 1913), 101–2.

80. Letters from Dorynne to Craig, quoted in Michael Holroyd, *A Strange Eventful History* (London: Chatto & Windus, 2008), 309.

81. Letter from Terry to Edward Gordon Craig (3 September 1899), in Katharine Cockin (ed.), *Collected Letters of Ellen Terry* (Abingdon: Routledge, 2016), 4.49–51.

82. Anon., [Jess Dorynne], *The True Ophelia: And Other Studies of Shakespeare's Women* (London: Sidgwick & Jackson, Ltd, 1913), 70, 73.

83. Faucit, 'Juliet', 139.

84. Dorynne, *True Ophelia*, 73.

85. Ibid, 67, 73.

86. Ibid, 81–3.

87. Ibid, 87.

88. Ibid, 67.

89. Letter from Terry to Gordon Craig (22 August 1899) in Cockin (ed.), *Collected Letters*, 4.40–2; 41.

90. Dorynne, *True Ophelia*, 81–2.

91. 'Honour Thy Father and Thy Mother', *Girl's Own Paper* 6, no. 250 (October 11, 1884), 22–3, and no. 257 (November 29, 1884), 139–40.

Chapter 5: Fair Verona

1. Judith Miller, *Miller's Antiques Handbook* (London: Octopus Books, 2017), 117; Arthur Frommer, *A Masterpiece Called Belgium* (Brussels: Sabena, 1984), 89; Juan Siliezar, 'Big Statue on Campus', *Harvard Gazette* (4 September 2019), (news.harvard.edu/gazette/story/2019/09/iconic-john-harvard-statue-is-the-star-of-the-yard, accessed 9 March 2021).

2. Tao Tao Holmes, 'Tourists Love to Rub the Bronze Balls of Wall Street's Charging Bull Statue. Why?', *Atlas Obscura* (19 January 2016), (atlasobscura.com/articles/tourists-love-to-rub-the-bronze-balls-of-wall-streets-charging-bull-statue-why, accessed 9 March 2021); Jane Fortune, *To Florence Con Amore* (Florence: B'gruppo, 2011), 135.

3. Yvan Salmon (1848–70).

4. Marina Emelyanova-Griva, 'La tombe de Victor Noir au cimitière du Père-Lachaise', *Archives de sciences sociales des religions* 149 (2010), 89–108.

5. Evgenij Parilov, 'Selfie photo of man holding statue of Juliet chest in Verona Italy, smiling and laughing' (15 March 2019), Alamy Archive, 2ANRP03.

6. 'One Night As Juliet', Il Sogno di Giulietta, Via Cappello 23, 3721 Verona.

7. Ceri Houlbrook, *Unlocking the Love-Lock* (Oxford: Berghahn, 2021), 16.

8. Houlbrook, *Unlocking*, 6–7.

9. Theodore Child, *Summer Holidays* (New York: Harper & Bros, 1889), 158–9.

10. Cukor, George (dir.), *Romeo and Juliet* (USA: MGM, 1936), 125 mins, black and white.

11. Houlbrook, *Unlocking*, 19.

12. Image of 'Statue of the Assumption – Verona, S. Maria Assunta [by Nereo Costantini]', *Archivio Scultura Veronese* (2019) (archivio-scultura-veronese.org/portfolio-items/nereo-costantini/#prettyPhoto, accessed 14 March 2021).

13. Victoria Wood, 'Bronteburgers', *Up to You, Porky!* (London: Methuen, 1985), 17.

14. Charles Dickens Museum, 48 Doughty Street, London, WC1N 2LX.

15. BBC News, 'Harry Potter Fans Boost Oxford Christ Church Cathedral', *BBC* (25 March 2012) (bbc.co.uk/news/uk-england-oxfordshire-17434129, accessed 15 March 2021).

16. Anna Lewis, 'The Woman Who Looks After a Decade-old Shrine to a Fictional Sci-fi Character in Cardiff Bay', *Wales Online* (27 January 2020) (walesonline.co.uk/whats-on/whats-on-news/ianto-shrine-torchwood-cardiff-bay-17636862, accessed 14 March 2021).

17. Houlbrook, *Unlocking*, 19; Zoe Alderton, '"Snape Wives" and "Snapeism": A Fiction-Based Religion within the Harry Potter Fandom', *Religions* 5.1 (2014), 219–67.

18. 'Holger Danske', *Kronborg Castle* (2020) (kongeligeslotte.dk/en/palaces-and-gardens/kronborg-castle/explore-kronborg-castle/holger-danske.html, accessed 14 March 2021).

19. 'Buoono', Via Anfiteatro 6c, 37121, Verona.

20. I am indebted to Richard Cooper for his knowledge of Renaissance Italy's roads.

21. See: *Winter's Tale* (3.3.2) et al.

22. *Merchant* (2.8.8, 2.8.5 onwards, 1.3.16 and 3.1.1).

23. Thomas Nashe, *Pierce Penniless's Supplication to the Devil* [1592] (London: Shakespeare Society, 1842), 34.

24. Thomas Coryat, *Coryat's Crudities* [1611], in Andrew Hadfield (ed.), *Amazons, Savages, and Machiavels* (Oxford: Oxford University Press, 2001), 52–63.

25. See: Ewan Fernie, *Shakespeare for Freedom* (Cambridge: Cambridge University Press, 2017), 80–112.

26. Luigi da Porto, *Historia*, in Nicole Prunster (ed.), *Romeo and Juliet Before Shakespeare* (Toronto: Centre for Reformation and Renaissance Studies, 2000), 27.

27. Prunster, *Romeo and Juliet*, 8–11. Dante met both Bartolomeo and his younger brother Francesco, dedicating his *Paradiso* to Francesco.

28. Robert M. Durling and Robert L. Martinez (eds), *The Divine Comedy of Dante Alighieri: Volume 2: Purgatorio* (Oxford: Oxford University Press, 2003), 108n.

29. Girolamo dalla Corte, *L'Istoria di Verona* (Verona: Girolamo Discepolo, 1594), I.589–95.

30. Ibid, I.591.

31. Ibid, I.592.

32. Via Arche Scagliere 2, 37121 Verona.

33. Dalla Corte, *L'Istoria*, I.594.

34. Ibid.

35. Charles Dickens, *Pictures from Italy* (London: Bradbury & Evans, 1846), 121–2.

36. John Breval, *Remarks on Several Parts of Europe* (London: Bernard Lintot, 1726), II.103–4.

37. See: Gilbert Burnet, *Some Letters Containing an Account of What Seemed Most Remarkable in Switzerland, Italy, &c* (Amsterdam: Abraham Ascher, 1687), 109–11; William Acton, *A New Journal of Italy* (London: Richard Baldwin, 1691), 68–9; Nicola J. Watson, 'At Juliet's Tomb: Anglophone Travel-Writing and Shakespeare's Verona, 1814–1914' in Bigliazzi and Calvi (eds), *Shakespeare, Romeo and Juliet, and Civic Life* (Oxford: Routledge, 2015), 224–37; 227.

38. Letter from Mary Carter to Charlotte, Lady Nelthorpe (17 October 1793) in Frances Mary Nelthorpe (ed.), *Mrs Mary Carter's Letters* (London: Clayton & Co., 1860), 5–9; 9.

39. In 1568, Giorgio Vasari (1511–74), a painter and writer, wrote of *bronzo da Verona* (white Venetian limestone, used for sculptures) as '*quella pietra viva e bianca*': Vasari, Giorgio, *Le vite de' piu eccellenti pittori, scultori, e architettori, 3 vols* (Florence: Appresso i Giunti, 1568), III.518. In 1594, the year Dalla Corte published, Venetian nobleman Francesco Tiepolo (1555–1614) used the *pietra viva* to describe the white Rovigno stone that he wanted in his family chapel: '*piera viva da Rovignio de mar bianca, che imiti il marmo*', Tiepolo, quoted in Emma Jones, *The Business of Sculpture in Venice 1525–1625*, unpublished DPhil thesis (Cambridge), 2016, I.122n.

40. Giuseppe Vercellotti, Sam D. Stout, Rosa Boano, and Paul W. Sciulli, 'Intrapopulation Variation in Stature and Body Proportions: Social Status and Sex Differences in an Italian Medieval Population (Trino Vercellese, VC)', *American Journal of Physical Anthropology* 145.2 (June 2011), 203–14; Nicole M. Weiss, Giuseppe Vercellotti, Rosa Boano, Marilena Girotti, and Sam D. Stout, 'Body Size and Social Status in Medieval Alba (Cuneo), Italy', *American Journal of Physical Anthropology* 168.3 (March 2019), 595–605.

41. See, for example: Antonio Gaza, *Catena historiale Veronese* (Verona: Francesco Rossi, 1653), I.12.

42. Vincenza Minutella, *Reclaiming Romeo and Juliet: Italian Translations for Page, Stage, and Screen* (Amsterdam: Rodopi, 2013), 63–7.

43. Mary Shelley, *Rambles in Germany and Italy* (London: Edward Moxon, 1844), 76.

44. William Macready, *Macready's Reminiscences* (London: Macmillan & Co., 1875), 76.

45. Jacques Galiffe, *Italy and Its Inhabitants* (London: John Murray, 1820), I.90.

46. William Harrison Ainsworth, 'Artistic Travel', *New Monthly Magazine* 113 (1858), 253–63; 258.

47. Watson, 'At Juliet's Tomb', 230.
48. Letter from Byron to Moore (6 November 1816) in Thomas Moore (ed.), *Life of Lord Byron* (London: John Murray, 1854), III.305–9; 309.
49. 'The Sanctuary', *Santuario di Lucia* (2020) (santuariodilucia.it/en/project/sanctuary, accessed 1 March 2021).
50. Annetta Black, 'The Incorruptible St. Zita', *Atlas Obscura* (2021) (atlasobscura.com/places/incorruptible-st-zita, accessed 1 March 2021).
51. I am indebted to Emily Guerry, Elizabeth Harper and Marie Douada for their expertise on saints.
52. Heather Pringle, *The Mummy Congress* (New York: Hyperion, 2001), 248.
53. Ibid, 247.
54. Ibid, 255–6, 261.
55. Linda Pressly, 'The 20-year Odyssey of Eva Peron's Body', BBC Radio 4 (26 July 2016) (bbc.co.uk/news/magazine-18616380, accessed 1 March 2021).
56. Nicholas Fraser and Marysa Navarro, *Evita* (New York: W. W. Norton, 1996), 192.
57. For further definition, see: P. R. Stone, 'A Dark Tourism Spectrum: Towards a Typology of Death and Macabre Related Tourist Sites, Attractions and Exhibitions', *Tourism: An Interdisciplinary International Journal* 52.2 (2006), 145–60; A. V. Seaton, 'Guided by the Dark: From Thanatopsis to Thanatourism', *International Journal of Heritage Studies* 2.4 (1996), 234–44.
58. BBC News, 'Outrage at Ground Zero Visitor Platform', *BBC* (17 January 2002) (news.bbc.co.uk/1/hi/world/americas/1766687.stm, accessed 1 March 2021).
59. Maria Teresa Simone-Charteris, Stephen W. Boyd, and Amy Burns, 'The Contribution of Dark Tourism to Place Identity in Northern Ireland', in Leanne White and Elspeth Frew (eds), *Dark Tourism and Place Identity* (Oxford: Routledge, 2016), 60–78.
60. Gary Best, 'Dark Detours: Celebrity Car Crash Deaths and Trajectories of Place' in White and Frew (eds), *Dark Tourism*, 202–16; 207–8; Howard Lake, 'Jump on in, You're in Safe Hands: Flash-Frames from the Automobile Cargo Bay Experience' in Mikita Brottman (ed.), *Car Crash Culture* (New York: Palgrave, 2001), 45–72.
61. @AuschwitzMuseum, 'When you come to @AuschwitzMuseum remember[. . .]', Twitter (12pm, 20 March 2019) (twitter.com/AuschwitzMuseum/status/1108337507660451841, accessed 1 March 2021).
62. Peter Hohenhaus, 'Commemorating and Commodifying the Rwandan Genocide: Memorial Sites in a Politically Difficult Context' in White and Frew (eds), *Dark Tourism*, 142–54; 153.
63. Anon., 'Visiting the Tomb of the Capulets', *The Methodists* (28 April 1877), 11.
64. Mary Anderson de Navarro, *A Few Memories* (New York: Harper & Bros, 1896), 168–9.

65. Elize Lathrop, *Sunny Days in Italy* (New York: James Pott & Co., 1907), 315.

66. Grant Allen, *European Tour* (New York: Dodd, Mead, 1909), 61.

67. Rebecca Moore, 'A Month in Italy', *The Woman's Journal* (23 January 1892), 2; 'Visiting the Tomb of the Capulets', 11.

68. Letter from Ruskin to Charles Eliot Norton (21 June 1869) in John Lewis Bradley and Ian Ousby (eds), *The Correspondence of John Ruskin and Charles Eliot Norton* (Cambridge: Cambridge University Press, 1987), 141–3; George Sala, *Rome and Venice, with Other Wanderings in Italy* (London: Tinsley, 1869), 16.

69. 'Visiting the Tomb of the Capulets', 11.

70. Lathrop, *Sunny Days in Italy*, 48.

71. Silvia Bigliazzi and Lisanna Calvi, 'Producing a (R&)Jspace: Discursive and Social Practices in Verona' in Bigliazzi and Calvi (eds), *Shakespeare, Romeo and Juliet, and Civic Life*, 238–59; 243–5.

72. See: Caroline Webb, *Visitors to Verona* (London: I.B. Tauris, 2017), 197 and 56.

73. R. J. B. Bosworth, *Mussolini's Italy* (London: Penguin, 2005), 41–2.

74. Ibid, 44.

75. Ibid, 53.

76. Ibid, 37.

77. Ibid, 37, 60.

78. Ibid, 48.

79. Ibid, 2.

80. Robert Gordon, *The Holocaust in Italian Culture* (Stanford: Stanford University Press, 2012), 11.

81. Quoted in Rory Carroll, 'Italy's Bloody Secret', *Guardian* (25 June 2001) (theguardian.com/education/2001/jun/25/artsandhumanities.higher-education, accessed 31 October 2022).

82. Bosworth, *Mussolini's Italy*, 43.

83. Henrich August Winkler, *The Age of Catastrophe: A History of the West 1914–1945* (New Haven, CT: Yale University Press, 2015), 802–4.

84. Bosworth, *Mussolini's Italy*, 3; Gordon, *The Holocaust in Italian Culture*, 6.

85. Ibid, 10–11.

86. Mabel Berezin, *The Making of the Fascist Self* (New York: Cornell UP, 2018), 143.

87. Vittorio Betteloni, quoted in Bigliazzi and Calvi, 'Producing a (R&) Jspace', 256.

88. Maria D'Anniballe Williams, *Urban Space in Fascist Verona: Contested Grounds for Mass Spectacle, Tourism, and the Architectural Past*, unpublished doctoral dissertation (University of Pittsburgh, 2011), 66.

89. Bigliazzi and Calvi, 'Producing a (R&)Jspace', 245.

90. Maria D'Anniballe, 'Recreating the Past: The Controversies Surrounding the Refashioning of the Medieval Castle of Castelvecchio in Verona under the Fascist Regime', *Athanor* 28 (2010) (journals.flvc.org/

athanor/article/view/126691/126244, accessed 1 March 2021); D'Anniballe Williams, *Urban Space*, 67–9.

91. D'Anniballe Williams, *Urban Space*, 81–23.

92. Ibid, 20–2.

93. Jonathan Kuntz, 'Cukor, George (07 July 1899–24 January 1983)', *American National Biography* (hereafter *ANB*) (1999) (doi.org/10.1093/anb/9780198606697.article.1800264, accessed 1 March 2021); James I. Deutsch, 'Mayer, Louis Burt (1885? – 29 October 1957), motion picture producer', *ANB* (1999), (doi.org/10.1093/anb/9780198606697.article.1800809, accessed 1 March 2021); David B. Green, 'This Day in Jewish History', *Haaretz* (14 September 2014) (haaretz.com/jewish/. premium-hollywoods-boy-wonder-producer-dies-1.5264475, accessed 1 March 2021); J. Parker, rev. K. D. Reynolds, 'Howard, Leslie [real name Leslie Howard Steiner] (1893–1943), actor and film director', *DNB* (23 September 2004) (oxforddnb.com/view/10.1093, accessed 1 March 2021); David Max Eichhorn and Immanuel Jakobovits, 'Shall Jews Missionize?' in Laurence J. Epstein (ed.), *Readings on Conversion to Judaism* (Northvale, NJ: Jason Aronson Inc., 1995), 131–50.

94. D'Anniballe Williams, *Urban Space*, 84.

95. *L'Arena* (5 March 1937), 4.

96. Juan Antonio Ramirez, *Architecture for the Screen* (Jefferson, NC: McFarland, 2004), 145; James Yoch, *Landscaping the American Dream* (New York: H. N. Abrams, 1989), 100.

97. Zoë Druick, 'The International Educational Cinematograph Institute, Reactionary Modernism, and the Formation of Film Studies', *Revue Canadienne D'Étudies Cinématographiques* 16.1 (2007), 80–97.

98. *L'Arena* (27 February 1937), 3, quoted in D'Anniballe Williams, *Urban Space*, 89.

99. Letter from Alfredo Barbacci to Direzione Generale delle Antichità e Belle Arti (5 March 1936), Archivio Soprintendenza Beni Architettonici e Paesaggio (ASBAPVr), f. 91/163, Verona.

100. Letter from Giulio Barella to Roberto Paribeni (24 April 1933), *Belle Arti* II (2934–40), b. 352, quoted in D'Anniballe Williams, *Urban Space*, 98.

101. Caroline Atwater Mason, *The Spell of Italy* (Boston: L. C. Page & Company 1909), 311.

102. 'Estratto di deliberazione podestarile' (20 April 1938), ASBAPVr, f. 91/163, quoted in D'Anniballe Williams, *Urban Space*, 96.

103. See: Lise and Ceil Friedman, *Letters to Juliet* (New York: Stewart, Tabori, and Chang, 2006), 37.

104. Carlo Manzini, *Il Duce a Verona (dal 1905 al 1938)* (Verona: C.E. Albarelli-Marchesetti, 1938), 72–8. D'Anniballe Williams, *Urban Space*, 102, 107.

105. Letter from Alfredo Barbacci to Marcello Vaccari (27 October 1938), ASBAPVr, f. 91–3.

106. Elize Lathrop, *Where Shakespeare Set His Stage* (New York: Haskell House, 1906), 42.

107. Quoted in Maristella Vecchiato, 'Antonio Avena ricostruttore e la Regia Soprintendenza ai Monumenti di Verona' in Paola Marini (ed.), *Medioevo ideale e Medioevo reale nella cultura urbana: Antonio Avena e la Verona del primo Novecento* (Verona: Assessorato alla cultura, 2003), 115.

108. D'Anniballe Williams, *Urban Space*, 135–9.

109. Bosworth, *Mussolini's Italy*, 3.

110. Friedman and Friedman, *Letters to Juliet*, 47–52.

111. Allen, *European Tour*, 61.

112. Friedman and Friedman, *Letters to Juliet*, 54.

113. Victoria de Grazia, *How Fascism Ruled Women* (Oakland, CA: University of California Press, 1992), 1.

114. Undated letter from Ettore Solimani to Catherine Lansing, quoted in *Letters to Juliet*, 60.

115. Solimani, quoted in *Letters to Juliet*, 56.

116. Letter from Solimani to Lansing, quoted in *Letters to Juliet*, 60.

117. Solimani, quoted in *Letters to Juliet*, 57.

118. Navarro, *A Few Memories*, 168–9.

119. Solimani, quoted in *Letters to Juliet*, 65.

120. Gino Beltarimini, interviewed in *Familiglia Cristiana* (1972), quoted in *Letters to Juliet*, 88.

121. Tamassia, quoted in *Letters to Juliet*, 101–2.

122. Ibid.

123. Undated letter (from a French nineteen-year-old), quoted in *Letters to Juliet*, 7; undated letter from French girl, quoted in *Letters to Juliet*, 62.

124. Undated letter from Réka, Hungary, quoted in Giulio Tamassia, *Dear Juliet: Letters from the Lovestruck and Lovelorn to Shakespeare's Juliet in Verona* (San Francisco: Chronicle Books, 2019), 137.

125. Letter from Mina S. (Lodi, Italy, 1972), reprinted in *Letters to Juliet*, 92–3; 93; Letter from Natalina, Brazil, quoted in Tamassia, *Dear Juliet*, 57.

126. Undated letter from Christoph, Germany and reply from Juliet, reprinted in *Dear Juliet*, 68–71.

127. Tamassia, *Dear Juliet*, 103.

128. Katherine Duncan-Jones, '"O Happy Dagger": The Autonomy of Shakespeare's Juliet', *Notes and Queries* 45.3 (September 1998).

129. Claudia Torrisi, 'How Verona Became a "Model City" for Far-right and Ultra-Catholic Alliances', *Open Democracy* (31 January 2019) (opendemocracy.net / en / 5050 / verona-model-city-far-right-ultra-catholic-alliances/, accessed 1 April 2021).

130. Alvise Armellini, 'Forget Romeo and Juliet: Verona is Italy's Religious Right Stronghold', *DPA International* (1 November 2018) (dpa-international.com / topic / forget-romeo-juliet-verona-italy-religious-right-stronghold, accessed 1 April 2021).

131. Domenico Camodeca, 'Congresso Famiglie, capogruppo Lega si dimette: No a Verona culla del Medioevo', *Blastingnews Italia* (16 March

2019) (it.blastingnews.com/politica/2019/03/congresso-famiglie-capogruppo
-lega-si-dimette-no-a-verona-culla-del-medioevo-002872045.html, accessed
2 April 2021).

132. Quoted in Torrisi, 'How Verona Became a "Model City"'.

133. Letter from Haley, quoted in *Dear Juliet*, 18; letter from Marisol, quoted
in *Dear Juliet*, 28.

134. Nora Stransom, 'The Woman in Shakespeare's Plays', *Englishwoman*
(April 1914), 198–205.

Chapter 6: Society's Child

1. Nina Leen, 'Teen-Age Girls: They Live in a Wonderful World of Their
Own', *Time* (11 December 1944), 91–9.

2. Quoted in Derek Thompson, 'A Brief History of Teenagers', *Saturday
Evening Post* (13 February 2018) (saturdayeveningpost.com/2018/02/
brief-history-teenagers, accessed 31 October 2022).

3. Melanie Tebbutt, *Making Youth: A History of Youth in Modern Britain*
(London: Macmillan, 2016), 96–7; Benjamin Bowling, *Violent Racism:
Victimisation, Policing, and Social Context* (Oxford: Oxford University
Press, 1999), 30–1.

4. Kenneth Tynan, 'Jimmy Porter, Prince of Scum', *Observer* [13 May
1956], repr. *Guardian* (15 May 2011) (theguardian.com/news/2011/
may/15/archive-1956-kenneth-tynan-john-osborne, accessed 31 October
2022).

5. James Gilbert, *A Cycle of Outrage: America's Reaction to the Juvenile
Delinquent in the 1950s* (New York: Oxford University Press, 1988), 63.

6. Trilby Lane, 'Happy News', *Mirabelle* (30 November 1968), 17.

7. 'Nurses Make the Best Wives!', *19 Magazine* (March 1968), 14.

8. Karen Johnston, 'In a Word!', *Mirabelle* (14 December 1968), 2.

9. Laura Tisdall, '"What a Difference It Was to Be a Woman and Not a
Teenager": Adolescent Girls' Conceptions of Adulthood in 1960s and
1970s Britain', *Gender and History* 34.2 (22 June 2021), 495–513.

10. Suzanne Finstad, *Natasha: The Biography of Natalie Wood* (London:
Arrow, 2002), 363.

11. Joseph Hurley, 'The Old Vic's Master', *New York Herald Tribune* (11
February 1962), newspaper cutting, Fondazione Franco Zeffirelli (hereafter FFZ).

12. Leonard Bernstein, MS annotation to p. 3 of George Kittredge (ed.),
Romeo and Juliet (Boston: Ginn & Co., 1940), Leonard Bernstein
Collection, Box 73, Folder 9, Library of Congress, Washington DC
(digitised at loc.gov/exhibits/westsidestory/westsidestory-exhibit.
html#objo1).

13. Misha Berson, *Something's Coming, Something Good: West Side Story and
the American Imagination* (Milwaukee: Applause Theatre and Cinema
Books, 2011), 17.

14. Rita Moreno, quoted in Lynette Rice, 'West Side Story at 60: An Oral History of the Film's Shocking Oscar Triumph', *Entertainment Weekly* (9 April 2021) (ew.com/awards/oscars/west-side-story-flashback-george-chakiris-rita-moreno/, accessed 31 October 2022).

15. Richard P. Cooke, 'The Old Vic in Verona', *Wall Street Journal* (15 February 1962), press cutting, FFZ.

16. Loehlin (ed.), *Romeo and Juliet*, 66.

17. Felix Barker, 'The Very Beautiful Murder of Romeo and Juliet', undated press cuttings, Box C.194, FFZ; Thomas Gordon Plate, 'The Teen-agers of Verona', *Newsweek* (14 October 1968), Box C.194/2, FFZ.

18. Susan Sontag, *Regarding the Pain of Others* (New York: Picador, 2003), 8.

19. Jan Kott, *Shakespeare Our Contemporary* [1966] (New York: W. W. Norton, 1974), 10, 141.

20. Ibid, 147.

21. Ibid, 85, 75.

22. Ibid, 80.

23. Several editors feel that these rather repetitive lines, only printed in the second quarto, were Shakespearean false starts that erroneously made their way from manuscript to print. In 3.5, Capulet rages: 'Wife, we scarce thought us blest/ That God had lent us but this only child.' OUP editors feel this precludes the idea that Juliet ever had siblings. I disagree (children may have been stillborn and buried accordingly), but in any case, the lines have been printed and performed throughout the play's history.

24. Berson, *Something's Coming*, 20–1.

25. Bernstein, diary entry retrospectively dated 6 January 1949, quoted in Berson, *Something's Coming*, 22.

26. Nigel Simeone (ed.), *The Leonard Bernstein Letters* (hereafter *LB Letters*) (New Haven, CT: Yale University Press, 2013), 250n.

27. Letter from Leonard Bernstein to Howard Hoyt (8 February 1949) in *LB Letters*, 250–1.

28. Jerome Robbins, 'Outline "Romeo and Juliet"', undated typescript in attrib. Leonard Bernstein, *West Side Story Scene and Musical Sequence Outlines, Draft Scripts, Song Lists, Lyrics* ([incorrectly dated to] 1955 [whole bundle actually c. 1949–57]), Leonard Bernstein Collection, Library of Congress, Box/Folder 73/10, 2.

29. Robbins, 'Outline "Romeo and Juliet"', 3.

30. Ibid, 4.

31. Ibid, 5.

32. Letter from Arthur Laurents to Bernstein (April 1949), *LB Letters*, 252–4.

33. Letter from Laurents to Bernstein (19 July 1955), *LB Letters* 342–3.

34. Leonard Bernstein, 'Excerpts from a West Side Log', *Playbill* (30 September 1947), 47–8.

35. Rita Moreno, in Ursula Macfarlane (dir.), *West Side Stories – The Making of a Classic* (17 January 2017), BBC2, 60 mins.

36. Untitled typescript outline with MS annotations by Bernstein (c. 1955), in attrib. Leonard Bernstein, *West Side Story Scene and Musical Sequence Outlines, Draft Scripts, Song Lists, Lyrics* ([incorrectly dated to] 1955 [whole bundle actually c. 1949–57]), Leonard Bernstein Collection, Library of Congress, Box/Folder 73/10, 12.

37. *LB Letters*, 356n.

38. Letter from Leonard Bernstein to David Diamond (25 May 1956), *LB Letters*, 352.

39. Macfarlane (dir.), *West Side Stories*, BBC2.

40. Leonard Bernstein, MS note to typescript 'WEST SIDE STORY | AUDITIONS – Tuesday, May 7, 1957' in *West Side Story [Notes Re Auditions, Casting, and Orchestra]* (c. May 1957), Leonard Bernstein Collection, Library of Congress, Box/Folder 75/5, 1; 29.

41. Macfarlane (dir.), *West Side Stories*, BBC2.

42. Berson, *Something's Coming*, 69–70.

43. Ibid, 72–3.

44. Leonard Bernstein to Felicia Bernstein (15 August 1957), *LB Letters*, 371–2.

45. Leonard Bernstein to Felicia Bernstein (23 August 1957), Leonard Bernstein Collection, Box/Folder 5, 1–2, Library of Congress (loc.gov/resource/lbcorr.00065.0/?sp=1, accessed 2 February 2022).

46. *LB Letters* 380n–85; Berson, *Something's Coming*, 5.

47. *LB Letters* 385; Berson, *Something's Coming*, 2.

48. Martha Gelhorn to Bernstein (4 July 1958), *LB Letters*, 402–6.

49. Anon., 'Theatre – New Musical in Manhattan', *Time* (7 October 1957) (content.time.com/time/subscriber/article/0,33009,809976,00.html, accessed 5 March 2022).

50. Arthur Laurents, Leonard Bernstein, and Stephen Sondheim, *West Side Story* (New York: Random House, 1958), 13.

51. Arthur Laurents, three early libretti for *West Side Story* (January and March 1956), quoted in Geoffrey Block, *Enchanted Evenings: The Broadway Musical from Show Boat to Sondheim* (Oxford: Oxford University Press, 2004), 258–9.

52. Richard Rodgers, quoted in Elizabeth A. Wells, *West Side Story: Cultural Perspectives on an American Musical* (Plymouth: The Scarecrow Press, 2011), 44.

53. Laurents, Bernstein, Sondheim, *West Side Story*, 40 and 79.

54. Ibid, 49.

55. Ibid, 18, 12 and 141.

56. Jerome Robbins, untitled MS notes (c. 1957), Jerome Robbins Dance Division, Box 85, Folder 5, New York Public Library.

57. Undated typescript letter from Cheryl Crawford to Arthur Laurents (early 1957). Cheryl Crawford Papers, Box 83, Folder 4, Billy Rose Theatre Division, New York Public Library.

58. Bernstein, Laurents, Sondheim, *West Side Story*, 19.

59. Leonard Bernstein to Burton Bernstein (29 October 1955), *LB Letters* 349–50.
60. Bernstein, Laurents, Sondheim, *West Side Story*, 143.
61. Mike Cuomo, quoted in Macfarlane (dir.), *West Side Stories*, BBC2.
62. Quoted in Humphrey Burton, *Leonard Bernstein* (London: Faber & Faber, 1994), 75.
63. Berson, *Something's Coming*, 103–5.
64. Arthur Laurents, typescript outline for 'Romeo and Juliet' (1949) and untitled typescript outline (c. 1955), both in Leonard Bernstein Collection Box/Folder 73/10, Library of Congress.
65. Bernstein, Laurents, Sondheim, *West Side Story*, 24 and 100.
66. Ibid, 27 and 126.
67. 'Romeo' undated typescript (c. 1955), in attrib. Bernstein, Leonard, *West Side Story Scene and Musical Sequence Outlines*, 14, Leonard Bernstein Collection, Box/Folder 73/10, Library of Congress.
68. Moreno, quoted in Rice, '*West Side Story* at 60'.
69. Rachel Zegler, int. in Michael Schneider (prod.), *Variety Award Circuit Podcast* (14 January 2022) (variety.com/2022/film/awards/rachel-zegler-west-side-story-shazam-2-podcast-1235154905/).
70. Simon Button, 'The Star of Donna Summer's Musical on Speaking up for Queer Women of Colour', *Gay Times* (October 2018) (gaytimes.co.uk/originals/the-star-of-donna-summers-musical-on-speaking-up-for-queer-women-of-colour, accessed 31 October 2022).
71. Bernstein, Laurents, Sondheim, *West Side Story*, 24 and 75.
72. Bernstein, Laurents, 'GANG BANG' (c. summer 1957), in attrib. Bernstein, *West Side Story Scene and Musical Sequence Outlines*, 36, Leonard Bernstein Collection, Box/Folder 73/10, Library of Congress.
73. Irving Shulman, *West Side Story* [1961] (London: W.H. Allen & Co., 1987), 7–8, 12.
74. Ibid, 28–9.
75. Ibid, 57–61.
76. Ibid, 72.
77. Bernstein, Laurents, Sondheim, *West Side Story*, 6.
78. Wayne Flint, *Alabama in the Twentieth Century* (Tuscaloosa, AL: University of Alabama Press, 2004), 369–70.
79. Janis Ian, *Society's Child* (New York: Penguin, 2009), xv.
80. Bernstein, in David Oppenheim (prod.), *Inside Pop: The Rock Revolution* (25 April 1967), CBS.
81. Carl Wiser, 'Janis Ian', *Songfacts* (14 March 2003) (songfacts.com/blog/interviews/janis-ian, accessed 31 October 2022).
82. John McClain, 'Love That New Love Affair!', *Journal American* (14 February 1962), press cutting, FFZ.
83. Bruce Robinson, int. Justin Johnson, '*Withnail and I* 30 years on', BFI, YouTube (22 September 2017) (youtu.be/WxcGoEzoIOk?t=820, accessed 31 October 2022).

84. Johnathon Schaech, 'Actor Johnathon Schaech: I Was Molested by Director Franco Zeffirelli', *People* (11 January 2018) (people.com/movies/johnathon-schaech-molested-franco-zeffirelli/, accessed 31 October 2022).

85. Rebecca Keegan, 'The Dark Side of Franco Zeffirelli', *Hollywood Reporter* (18 June 2019) (hollywoodreporter.com/movies/movie-news/franco-zeffirelli-abuse-accusers-speak-1219298/, accessed 31 October 2022).

86. Franco Zeffirelli, *An Autobiography* (London: Weidenfeld & Nicolson, 1986).

87. Walter Kerr, 'First Night Report', *New York Herald Tribune* (14 February 1962), n.p, FFZ.

88. Clive Barnes, 'An Italian gives Juliet a beatnik heart', unattributed cutting, FFZ.

89. Peter Ansorge, 'Judi Dench', unattributed magazine cutting (c. 1968), FFZ.

90. McClain, 'Love That New Love Affair!'.

91. Julian Curry, *Judi Dench on Juliet* (London: Nick Hern Books, 2010).

92. Zeffirelli, MS notes to ring-bound notebook script of *Romeo and Juliet* (c. 1960), 39; 57–8; 73–4, in *Materiali preparatori* for *Romeo and Juliet*, FFZ.

93. Kenneth Tynan, 'The Straight Answer', *Observer* (9 October 1960), n.p.; Kerr, 'First Night Report', FFZ.

94. Howard Taubman, 'Old Vic Lessons' (1962), unattributed cutting; Kerr, 'First Night Report', FFZ.

95. Raul Radice, 'Romeo e Giulietta', *Corriere Della Sera* (Milan, 6 July 1964), n.p., FFZ; 'Anon., 'Anna Maria Guarnieri Giulietta in Blue-Jeans', *Noi Donne* (Rome, 23 October 1965), cover image, FFZ; B. Poirot-Delpech, 'Roméo et Juliette', *Le Monde* (15 June 1965), n.p., FFZ.

96. Anon., 'High Hopes of Teenage Romeo and Juliet', *Sydney Daily Telegraph* (10 September 1967), n.p.

97. Anon., 'A New Romeo & Juliet', *Look* (1 October 1967), n.p., Box 194.2, FFZ.

98. Paul Noyer, *Conversations with McCartney* (London: Random House, 2015), 154.

99. John Coleman, 'Little Stars', *New Statesman* (8 March 1968), n.p., FFZ; Anon., 'Los Problemas Modernos de Romeo y Julieta', *Actualidad Española* (7 October 1967), n.p., FFZ.

100. James Thomas, 'Romeo Is My Kind of Boy, Says Juliet . . .', *Daily Express* (26 May 1967), 3; Anon., 'Le prince Charles: play-boy pour Juliette', *Paris-Match* (16 March 1968), 129.

101. Paramount, *The Teen-Age Lovers of Verona* (1968), black and white, 5 mins.

102. *Royal Film Performance 1968* programme (4 March 1968), 73–4.

103. 'Le prince Charles: play-boy pour Juliette'; Laura Berry, 'Una Giovanissima attrice preoccupa la Regina Elisabetta' (1968), cutting, Folder 194/1, FFZ. My thanks to Jennifer Yee and Hélène Marquié.

104. Anon., 'Romeo and Juliette', *Mirabelle* (9 November 1968), 6–8.

105. Vita, quoted in Macfarlane (dir.), *West Side Stories*, BBC2.

106. Edward Miller, 'Love Is the Sweetest Thing', *Seventeen* (January 1968), 83, 104, 126.

107. Anon., 'A Romantic Heroine', *The Times* (4 March 1968), 7.

108. Olivia Hussey, *The Girl on the Balcony* (New York: Kensington, 2018), 55.

109. *An Excellent Conceited Tragedie of Romeo and Juliet* (London: John Danter, 1597), sig. G3, British Library C.34.k.55.

110. Helen Faucit, 'Juliet', *On Some of Shakespeare's Female Characters* [1885] (London: William Blackwood & Sons, 1905), 83–155.

111. H. R. Coursen, *Shakespeare in Production: Whose History?* (Athens, OH: Ohio University Press, 1996), 49.

112. Hannah Ellis-Petersen, 'Laurence Olivier's Steamy Love Letters to Vivien Leigh', *Guardian* (2 February 2015) (theguardian.com/stage/2015/feb/02/laurence-olivier-vivien-leigh-love-letters, accessed 1 February 2022).

113. Anon., 'Old & New Play in Manhattan', *Time* (20 May 1940), 69.

114. Anon., 'Zeffirelli with His X Certificate Stars', *Town* (January 1968), n.p., FFZ.

115. Letter from John Trevelyan to the BBFC (1968), quoted in 'Romeo and Juliet (1968)', *BBFC* (bbfc.co.uk/education/case-studies/romeo-and-juliet-1968, accessed 1 October 2022).

116. Anon., 'Film Review', *Daily Variety* (11 March 1968), n.p., photocopied cutting, FFZ.

117. Giroud, Françoise, 'God Save the Queen', *L'Express* (11 March 1968), n.p., FFZ; J. R., 'Zeffirelli's "Romeo"', 11.

118. Anon., 'Censor's "A" for Romeo angers Zeffirelli', *Evening Standard* (5 March 1968), n.p., FFZ.

119. Thomas Gordon Plate, 'The Teen-agers of Verona', *Newsweek* (14 October 1968), n.p., 194/2, FFZ.

120. Letter from A. R. Thurlwell to the editor, *Evening News* (13 March 1968), n.p., FFZ.

121. Fergus Cashin, 'The Other Face of Juliet', *Daily Sketch* (28 February 1968), n.p., FFZ.

122. Bernard Braden (dir.), 'Then and Now: Leonard Whiting and Olivia Hussey ([25 October] 1967)', BFI, YouTube (20 April 2016) (youtube.com/watch?v=XDv-iV1gFg0, accessed 1 May 2022).

123. James Dickerson, *Natalie Portman: Queen of Hearts* (Toronto: ECW Press, 2002), 96.

124. Hussey, *Girl on the Balcony*, 77.

125. Ibid.

126. Braden (dir.), 'Then and Now: Leonard Whiting and Olivia Hussey ([25 October] 1967)'; Hussey, *Girl on the Balcony*, 76–7.

127. Hussey, *Girl on the Balcony*, 70.

128. Ibid, 42.

129. Miller, 'Love Is the Sweetest Thing', 83, 104, 126.

130. @romeoandjuliet50th, Anne Austin, 'Dream Lovers', *Fabulous 208* (2

December 1967), Instagram, 24 February 2022 (instagram.com/p/CaYMTfwr3pO/, accessed 2 May 2022).

131. Ron Thompson, 'Royal Film Gamble by Zeffirelli Pays Off', *Sheffield Morning Telegraph* (5 March 1968), n.p., FFZ.

132. Hussey, *Girl on the Balcony*, 41–2.

133. David Wigg, 'Olivia Likes Rude Romeos', *Evening News* (16 February 1968), n.p., FFZ.

134. Hussey, *Girl on the Balcony*, 35.

135. Miller, 'Love Is the Sweetest Thing', 83, 104, 126.

136. Felix Barker, 'The Very Beautiful Murder of Romeo and Juliet', unattributed cutting, C.194, FFZ; Cashin, 'The Other Face of Juliet', n.p.

137. Ibid.

138. Louis Chavet, 'Roméo et Juliette', *Figaro* (no date, 1967), n.p., Box C.194, FFZ; Anon., 'Enfin Roméo et Juliette ont leur âge', *France-Soir* (24 September 1967), 5D, Box C.194, FFZ; John Coleman, 'Little Stars', *New Statesman* (8 March 1968), n.p., FFZ.

139. José Dominiani, 'Romeo y Julieta ante la reina', *Back to Back* (21 April 1968), 37–9.

140. Braden (dir.), 'Then and Now: Leonard Whiting and Olivia Hussey ([25 October] 1967)'.

141. Hussey, *Girl on the Balcony*, 57; @romeoandjulieth5oth, 'Romeo und Julia' promotional poster (1968), Instagram, (19 February 2022) (instagram.com/p/CaJFzCjLSa7/, accessed 1 May 2022).

142. Hussey, *Girl on the Balcony*, 90.

143. Ibid, 74.

144. Ibid, 75.

145. David Robinson, 'Apollos of Verona', *Financial Times* (8 March 1968), n.p.

146. Anon., 'Screen: Zeffirelli's "Romeo and Juliet"', *New York Times* (9 October 1968), n.p., Box 194/2, FFZ.

147. Anon., 'Juliet, We Think You're Wonderful', *Evening News* (14 March 1968), n.p., FFZ.

148. David Robinson, 'Apollos of Verona', *Financial Times* (8 March 1968), 28.

149. 'Romeo and Juliet', *Mirabelle* (9 November 1968), 6.

150. Ellen Terry, *The Story of My Life* (London: Hutchinson & Co., 1908), 214; 'Romeo and Juliet', *Mirabelle* (9 November 1968), 6–7.

151. Ibid, 8.

152. 'Romeo and Juliet', *Mirabelle* (16 November 1968), 10–11.

153. 'Romeo and Juliet', *Mirabelle* (23 November 1968), 6.

154. 'Romeo and Juliet', *Mirabelle* (30 November 1968), 8.

155. Anon., 'Tomorrow Is Today', *Romeo* (6 January 1968), 1–3.

156. 'Romeo and Juliet', *Mirabelle* (14 December 1968), 11.

157. 'Without You', *Mirabelle* (9 November 1968), 22.

158. 'Life With Kathy' in *Petticoat* (24 February 1968), 13; (2 March 1968), 12;

(9 March 1968), 43; (16 March 1968), 12; (30 March 1968), 14; (13 April 1968), 17; (4 May 1968), 10.

159. Jenny Campbell, 'Elopement', *Petticoat* (9 March 1968), 22–3.

160. Berson, *Something's Coming*, 3.

161. NCAC, 'Censorship: Part 3 (1936–2003)', Michigan State University, Microfilm Reel 124, Gale Document no. BJYLRQ329186608.

162. @romeoandjuliet6oth, Olivia Hussey doll by South Korean company '357partment', Instagram (7 August 2021) (instagram.com/p/CSREyYKso47/, accessed 10 May 2022).

163. Ian Christie, 'Too Young to Be in Love', *Daily Express* (5 March 1968), n.p., FFZ.

164. Shasta Darlington, 'Yo! Romeo!', *Los Angeles Times* (21 July 1996) (latimes.com/archives/la-xpm-1996-07-21-ca-26269-story.html, accessed 9 May 2022).

165. Barbara Hodgdon, 'William Shakespeare's Romeo + Juliet: *Everything's Nice in America?*' in Alexander, Catherine (ed.), *Shakespeare and Politics* (Cambridge: Cambridge University Press, 2004), 247–62.

166. Shulman, *West Side Story*, 61.

167. Jenny Peters, 'Shakespeare's Mister', *More* (26 March 1997), 46–7.

168. Hodgdon, 'William Shakespeare's Romeo + Juliet', 251–2.

169. George Spencer, 'Romeo Is a Really Horny Guy', *Mizz* (26 March 1997), 8–9.

170. Hodgdon, 'William Shakespeare's Romeo + Juliet', 250.

171. Taylor Swift, 'Love Story', *Fearless*, Big Machine Records, 2014.

172. A disclaimer: I love the whole song, second only to 'All Too Well', which I adore with such upstate nostalgia that, within six bars, I am also Jake Gyllenhaal's ex-girlfriend.

173. Second City, 'Sassy Gay Friend – Romeo & Juliet', YouTube (8 March 2010) (youtube.com/watch?v=lwnFE_NpMsE, accessed 4 November 2022).

Chapter 7: Across the Barricades

1. Joan Lingard, *Across the Barricades* (London: Penguin, 2016), 21.

2. Ibid, 22–3.

3. Ibid, 16; 35.

4. Ibid, 163–4.

5. Kathryn Rix (@KathrynRix), 'We wrote an essay [. . .]', Twitter (26 April 2022), (twitter.com/KathrynRix/status/1518965821506215942).

6. Sarah Louise Cleary (@sarahlou_iorua), 'Required reading [. . .]', Twitter (27 April 2022), (twitter.com/sarahlou_iorua/status/1519411328821170185) and private correspondence with the author; Rebecca Mills (@doombiscuits), 'Twelvish, 1994ish [. . .]', Twitter (26 April 2022), (twitter.com/doombiscuits/status/1519020306786103302).

7. Dorit Rabinyan, trans. Jessica Cohen, *All the Rivers* [2014] (London:

Random House, 2017); Michelle Zaurov, 'Interview: Dorit Rabinyan', *Jewish Book Council* (31 July 2017) (jewishbookcouncil.org/pb-daily/interview-dorit-rabinyan).

8. Tom Sperlinger, *Romeo and Juliet in Palestine* (London: Zero Books, 2015), 3.

9. Ibid.

10. Ibid, 142.

11. Ibid, 3.

12. Ibid.

13. Anon., 'A Romeo and Juliet in Cuba', *Hartlepool Free Press* (14 April 1860), 2.

14. Anon., 'A Modern Romeo and Juliet', *Worcestershire Chronicle* (12 July 1890), 8; Anon., 'Romeo and Juliet in Real Life', *South Wales Daily News* (24 April 1894), 5.

15. Anon., 'Romeo and Juliet in Modern Life', *South Wales Daily News* (7 August 1893), 6.

16. Anon., 'Godfather of Loyalist Death Squads Given Life Sentences', *Irish Independent* (17 June 1994), 5; Stephen Gordon, 'Life and Times of King Rat', *Sunday Life* (28 December 1997), 6–7.

17. 'Callous Murders', *Dungannon Courier* (6 January 1993), 1.

18. Dominic Cunningham, 'UVF Victim's Bride-to-be Found Dead', *Irish Independent* (3 February 1993), 7.

19. Paul Majendie (Reuters), 'Irish Grieve for Modern-Day Romeo and Juliet', *Los Angeles Times* (14 February 1993) (latimes.com/archives/la-xpm-1993-02-14-mn-129-story.html, accessed 31 October 2022).

20. Frédéric Tonolli (dir.), 'Belfast, mon amour', *La case du siècle* (TV5: 5 October 2014), 52 mins.

21. Mark H. Milstein, 'Romeo and Juliet in Sarajevo' (19 May 1993), *Northfoto* (21 May 2009) (flickr.com/photos/northfoto/3588896797, accessed 31 October 2022); Kurt Schork, 'Kurt Schork's Signature Dispatch from the Siege of Sarajevo' (23 May 1993) *KS Memorial* (ksmemorial.com/romeo.htm, accessed 31 October 2022).

22. John Zaritsky (dir.), *Romeo and Juliet in Sarajevo*, *Frontline* (PBS/CBC/NFB/WDR: 10 May 1994), 90 mins.

23. Y. Z., 'Sarajevo's Romeo and Juliet: A Red Rose on the Grave', *Sarajevo Times* (19 May 2015) (sarajevotimes.com/sarajevos-romeo-and-juliet-a-red-rose-on-the-grave-as-a-symbol-of-great-love/, accessed 31 October 2002); *Sondor Travel*, 'Romeo and Juliet Tour Sarajevo' (2022) (sondor-travel.com/tour-item/romeo-and-juliet-tour-sarajevo, accessed 31 October 2022); 'Romeo and Juliet Bridge', *Tripadvisor* (2022) (tripadvisor.co.uk/Attraction_Review-g294450-d447587-Reviews-Romeo_and_Juliet_Bridge-Sarajevo_Sarajevo_Canton_Federation_of_Bosnia_and_Herzegov.html, accessed 31 October 2022).

24. Nordland, *The Lovers*, 38.

25. Paul Statham in Tonolli (dir.), 'Belfast, mon amour'; Zijo Ismić in Zaritsky (dir.), *Romeo and Juliet in Sarajevo*.

26. Liam Kennedy, *Who Was Responsible for the Troubles?* (Montreal: McGill–Queen's University Press, 2020), preface.

27. Rada Brkić in Zaritsky (dir.), *Romeo and Juliet in Sarajevo*.

28. Nermina Ismić, Zijo Ismić, and Rada Brkić in Zaritsky (dir.), *Romeo and Juliet in Sarajevo*.

29. Nordland, *The Lovers*, 6–22; I am grateful to a colleague in the British Army for information on Afghanistan's ethnic groups.

30. Zaritsky (dir.), *Romeo and Juliet in Sarajevo*; Emma Daly, 'Grave Reunites Lovers Killed by Bosnia's Tribal Passions', *Independent* (10 April 1996), (independent.co.uk/news/world/grave-reunites-lovers-killed-by-bosnia-s-tribal-passions-1304263.html, accessed 31 October 2022); Anon., 'Tearful Goodbye to Tragic Love Girl', *Evening Herald* (4 February 1993), 5.

31. See: Samaritans, 'Media Guidelines for Reporting Suicide', *Samaritans* (2020), (media.samaritans.org/documents/Media_Guidelines_FINAL. pdf, accessed 31 October 2022).

32. Zaritsky (dir.), *Romeo and Juliet in Sarajevo*.

33. Nordland, *The Lovers*, 237, 46.

34. Nordland, *The Lovers*, 103.

35. Ibid, 117.

36. Andrew Gibbs, Nader Said, Julienne Corboz, and Rachel Jewkes, 'Factors Associated with "Honour Killing" in Afghanistan and the Occupied Palestinian Territories: Two Cross-sectional Studies', *PLoS One* 19 (8 August 2019), (ncbi.nlm.nih.gov/pmc/articles/PMC6687286, accessed 31 October 2022).

37. Nordland, *The Lovers*, 238–9.

38. Sontag, *Regarding the Pain of Others*, 93.

39. Ibid.

40. Myriam Gurba, 'Pendeja: You Ain't Steinbeck: My Bronca with Fake-Ass Social Justice Literature', *Tropics of Meta* (12 December 2019), (tropicsofmeta.com/2019/12/12/pendeja-you-aint-steinbeck-my-bronca-with-fake-ass-social-justice-literature/, accessed 31 October 2022).

41. Carol Chillington Rutter, *Clamorous Voices* (London: Women's Press, 1988), 49.

42. UK Government, 'Guidance on Promoting British Values in Schools Published', Gov.uk (27 November 2014), (gov.uk/government/news/guidance-on-promoting-british-values-in-schools-published#:~:text=All%20have%20a%20duty%20to,'Prevent'%20strategy%20in%202011., accessed 31 October 2022).

43. Willingdon School, 'British Values in the Curriculum' (2021), (willingdonschool.org.uk/assets/documents/British-Values-in-the-Curriculum.pdf, accessed 31 October 2022); Saint John Houghton Catholic Voluntary Academy, 'Promoting British Values – Curriculum Audit 2016/2017' (2016) (stjohnhoughtonilkeston.srscmat.co.uk/wp-content/uploads/sites/19/2021/09/british-values-curriculum-audit.pdf, accessed 31 October 2022).

44. Stretton Sugwas Church of England Academy, 'The Terrific Tudors Topic Web: Spring Term' (2020), (strettonsugwas.com/LTP%20 Topic%20Webs%20Y56%20Spring%20Cycle%201-2.pdf, accessed 31 October 2022); The Downs School, 'Promoting British Values in The Downs School' (2021), (thedownsschool.org/372/promoting-british-values, accessed 31 October 2022); St Bernard's School, 'English Language – GCSE' (2021), (st-gregorys.bolton.sch.uk/wp-content/uploads/2021/11/Y6-Key-Texts.docx, accessed 31 October 2022); Triple Crown Centre, 'Promoting British Values: English' (2021), (triple-crown.solihull.sch.uk/wp-content/uploads/2021/09/British-Values-English.pdf, accessed 31 October 2022).

45. Philip Sidney, *A Defence of Poetry* (Oxford: Oxford University Press, 1973), 73–121.

46. British Government, 'Revised Prevent Duty Guidance: For England and Wales', Gov.uk (1 April 2021), (gov.uk/government/publications/prevent-duty-guidance/revised-prevent-duty-guidance-for-england-and-wales, accessed 31 October 2022).

47. For pedagogical texts that explore this in an open-minded way, see: Holly Faith Nelson and Sharon Alker, 'Balancing Relatability and Alterity in Teaching Scottish Restoration Literature: A Case Study', *Studies in Eighteenth-Century Culture* 50 (2021), 217–30; Sara Atwood, 'The Past as Persistent Presence: Teaching Victorian Nonfiction' in Jen Cadwallader, Laurence W Mazzeno (eds), *Teaching Victorian Literature in the Twenty-First Century: A Guide to Pedagogy* (Cham, Switzerland: 2017), 181–96.

48. Rebecca Onion, 'The Awful Emptiness of "Relatable"', *Slate* (11 April 2014), (slate.com/human-interest/2014/04/relatable-the-adjective-is-everywhere-in-high-scchool-and-college-discussions-of-fiction-film-and-other-popular-culture-but-it-doesn-t-mean-anything.html, accessed 31 October 2022).

49. Geoffrey Chaucer, *Troilus and Criseyde*, V.698–9, in Walter W. Skeat (ed.), *The Complete Works of Geoffrey Chaucer*, vol. 2 (Oxford: Oxford University Press, 1900).

50. Alan Bennett, *The History Boys* (London: Faber & Faber, 2004), 56. Enid Tsui, 'Why China's love affair with Shakespeare endures', *Post Magazine* (29 July 2016), (scmp.com/magazines/post-magazine/long-reads/article/1996061/why-chinas-love-affair-shakespeare-endures, accessed 31 October 2022); Ashwin Desai, *Reading Revolution: Shakespeare on Robben Island* (Chicago: Haymarket, 2014); Penelope Wood, '"But Mutes and Audience to this Act" – Globe to Globe Hamlet World Tour and Its Local Reception', *Histories of Emotion* (11 December 2015), (historiesofemotion.com/2015/12/11/but-mutes-and-audience-to-this-act-globe-to-globe-hamlet-world-tour-and-its-local-reception/, accessed 31 October 2022).

51. Mark Turner, *The Literary Mind* (Oxford: Oxford University Press, 1998), 4–5.

52. John Culler, *Literary Theory: A Very Short Introduction* (Oxford: Oxford University Press, 2011), 92.

53. Ibid.

54. David Francis Taylor, *The Politics of Parody: A Literary History of Caricature, 1760–1830* (New Haven, CT: Yale University Press, 2018), 13.

55. Robin Dunbar, Ben Teasdale, Jackie Thompson, Felix Budelmann, Sophie Duncan, Evert van Emde Boas, and Laurie Maguire, 'Emotional Arousal When Watching Drama Increases Pain Threshold and Social Bonding', *Royal Society Open Science* 3 (2016), (royalsocietypublishing. org/doi/pdf/10.1098/rsos.160288, accessed 31 October 2022).

56. Joan Didion, 'The White Album' [1979] in *We Tell Ourselves Stories in Order to Live* (New York: Knopf, 2006), 185.

57. Sue Corbett, 'Triumph and Tears for a Brave Mum', *Sunday Life* (15 May 1994), 5.

58. Anon., 'UVF Victim's Friend Dies', *Evening Herald* (2 February 1993), 7; Kathleen Synnott, letter to the editor, *Evening Herald* (24 February 1993), 15.

59. Patrick McGarry, 'Tragic Victim of a Broken Heart', *Irish Independent* (6 February 1993), 28.

60. Frédéric Tonolli (dir.), 'Belfast, mon amour'.

61. Coleridge, 'On the Slave Trade'.

62. Rod Nordland, 'Two Star-crossed Afghans Cling to Love', *New York Times* (10 March 2014), (nytimes.com/2014/03/10/world/asia/2-star-crossed-afghans-cling-to-love-even-at-risk-of-death.html, accessed 31 October 2022); Nordland, *The Lovers*, xvii–xviii.

63. Ibid.

64. John F. Burns, 'Gangs in Sarajevo Worry Diplomats', *New York Times* (4 October 1993), (nytimes.com/1993/10/04/world/gangs-in-sara-jevo-worry-diplomats.html, accessed 31 October 2022).

65. Paul Harris, *Boško and Admira* (Paul Harris, 2019), 245–6.

66. Zaritsky (dir.), *Romeo and Juliet in Sarajevo*.

67. Nordland, *The Lovers*, 254.

68. Jeanette Lartius, 'Are They Still Taking Help from Various People [. . .]', *Rod Nordland* [Facebook page] (9 September 2017), (facebook.com/profile.php?id=100050322736835, accessed 31 October 2022); Estefhane Ventura, 'Ali is stupid [. . .]', *Rod Nordland* [Facebook page] (22 May 2016, accessed 31 October 2022).

69. Nordland, *The Lovers*, 254.

70. Nordland, *The Lovers*, 233.

71. Hester Lees-Jeffries (ed.), *Romeo and Juliet* (Cambridge: Cambridge University Press, 2023), forthcoming.

72. *A common place book* (c. 1622–5), 359.

73. Jill Levenson (ed.), *The Excellent Conceited Tragedie of Romeo and Juliet* [Q1, 1595] (Oxford: Oxford University Press, 2000), 2.1.95, 2.4.36.

74. *OED*.

75. Nordland, *The Lovers*, 252.
76. Ed Moloney, *A Secret History of the IRA* (London: Penguin, 2007), 322; J. Bowyer Bell, *The IRA, 1968–2000: An Analysis of a Secret Army* (Oxford: Taylor & Francis, 2013), 119; Tim Pat Coogan, *The IRA* (New York: St Martin's Publishing Group, 2002), 404.
77. Tonolli (dir.), 'Belfast, mon amour'. Since December 2020, Baron Maginnis of Drumglass has been suspended from the House of Lords for homophobic bullying and harassment.
78. Dominic Cunningham, '"Distressed" Priest Urges No Reprisals', *Irish Independent* (5 January 1993), 9; Anne McHardy, 'Monsignor Denis Faul', *Guardian* (22 June 2006), (theguardian.com/news/2006/jun/22/guardianobituaries.mainsection1, accessed 31 October 2022); CNI, 'Fr Denis Faul branded as "offensively sectarian" in McAleese's new memoir', *Church News Ireland* (22 September 2020), (churchnewsireland.org/news/irish-uk-news/fr-denis-faul-branded-as-offensively-sectarian-in-mcaleeses-new-memoir/, accessed 31 October 2022).
79. Laurence McKeown, 'Denis Faul saw Church power slipping away', *An Phoblacht* (27 July 2006), (anphoblacht.com/contents/15553, accessed 31 October 2022); McHardy, 'Monsignor Denis Faul'.
80. McGarry, 'Tragic victim of a broken heart', 28.
81. Zaritsky (dir.), *Romeo and Juliet in Sarajevo*.
82. Rod Nordland, *The Lovers*.
83. Andrew Quilty, 'Zakia, 18', *New York Times* (7 June 2014), (nytimes.com/2014/06/08/world/asia/for-afghan-lovers-joy-is-brief-ending-in-arrest.html, accessed 31 October 2022).
84. Rod Nordland, Johan-Frédérik Hel-Guedj (trans.), *Un Amour Interdit* (Paris: Tallandier, 2017).
85. Steve McCurry, 'Afghan Girl', *National Geographic* (June 1985), cover image.
86. Adam Talib, 'Translating for Bigots', American University in Cairo (2013), quoted in Colleen Lutz Clemens, 'Phoenix Rising: The West's Use (and Misuse) of Anglophone Memoirs by Pakistani Women' in Aroosa Kanwal and Saiyma Aslam (eds), *The Routledge Companion to Pakistani Anglophone Writing* (London: Routledge, 2019), 162–71; Marcia Lynx Qualey, Why So Many "Saving Muslim Women" Book Covers?', *Arab Lit* (30 June 2014), (arablit.org/2014/06/30/from-whence-and-whither-so-many-saving-muslim-women-book-covers, accessed 31 October 2022).
87. Nordland, *The Lovers*, 72–6.
88. Rod Nordland, in PBS, 'A chronicle of Afghanistan's modern-day Romeo and Juliet', *PBS NewsHour*, YouTube (8 March 2016) (youtu.be/3xjS2nB3CBg, accessed 31 October 2022).
89. *The Lovers*, 202, 249.
90. *The Lovers*, 262.
91. Rae Lynn Schwartz-DuPre, 'Portraying the Political: National

Geographic's 1985 *Afghan Girl* and a US Alibi for Aid', *Critical Studies in Media Communication* 27.4 (2010), 336–56.

92. Jenny Gross, '"Afghan Girl" from 1985 National Geographic Cover Takes Refuge in Italy', *New York Times* (26 November 2021), (nytimes. com/2021/11/26/world/europe/afghan-girl-national-geographic. html, accessed 31 October 2022).

93. Nordland, *The Lovers*, 2; Marianne Szegedy-Maszak, 'Wherefore Art Thou, Mohammad?', *Mother Jones* (January 2016), (motherjones.com/media/2015/12/rod-nordland-afghanistan-romeo-juliet).

94. 'Tearful Goodbye to Tragic Love Girl', *Evening Herald*, 7.

95. Anon., 'Heartbroken Girl Joins Her Beloved', *Irish Independent* (5 February 1993), 4.

96. McGarry, 'Tragic Victim of a Broken Heart', 28.

97. Corbett, 'Triumph and Tears for a Brave Mum', *Sunday Life* (15 May 1994), 5; McGarry, 'Tragic Victim of a Broken Heart'.

98. Anon. [Julie Statham], tribute to Diarmuid Shields in the *Dungannon Courier* (3 February 1993), 1.

99. Anon., 'Suicide Girl Blames Killers', *Sandwell Evening Mail* (5 March 1993), 2.

100. Sontag, *Regarding the Pain of Others*, 13.

101. Nordland, *The Lovers*, 78.

102. Brigid Shields, interviewed by Laura Haydon, *Wave Trauma Centre* (2016) (wavetraumacentre.org.uk/stories_from_silence/brigid-shield, accessed 31 October 2022).

103. Tonolli (dir.), 'Belfast, mon amour'.

104. Peter Murtagh, 'Grim Tale of Slain Romeo and Juliet', *Irish Times* (25 July 2008), (irishtimes.com/opinion/grim-tale-of-slain-romeo-and-juliet-1.946689, accessed 31 October 2022).

105. Nic Robertson, 'Tragic "Romeo and Juliet" Offers Bosnia Hope', *CNN* (5 April 2012), (edition.cnn.com/WORLD/Bosnia/updates/9604/10/, accessed 31 October 2022).

106. Simon Hattenstone, 'Come on You Capulets!', *Guardian* (8 February 2007), (theguardian.com/football/2007/feb/08/britishidentity.uk, accessed 31 October 2022).

107. Freddy Rokem, 'Postcard from the Peace Process', *Palestine-Israel Journal* 2.1 (1995), (pij.org/articles/685, accessed 31 October 2022).

108. Tonolli (dir.), 'Belfast, mon amour'.

109. Letter from Admira Ismić to Boško Brkić, quoted in Zaritsky (dir.), *Romeo and Juliet in Sarajevo*.

110. *The Lovers*, 229.

111. Ibid.

112. PBS, 'A Chronicle of Afghanistan's Modern-day Romeo and Juliet'.

113. Lisa McGee, *Erin's Diary: An Official Derry Girls Book* (London: Orion, 2020).

114. Ryan North, *Romeo and/or Juliet* (London: Orbit, 2016).

115. Sue Divin, *Guard Your Heart* (London: Macmillan, 2021), 294.

Chapter 8: By the Time She Understands Her

1. John Genest, *Some Account of the English Stage* (Bath: H.E. Carrington, 1832), VIII.419.

2. Bridget Byrne, 'Patrick Stewart Goes Western', *Kentucky New Era* (31 May 2002).

3. Michael Billintgon, 'Olivier, Laurence Kerr, Baron Olivier (1907–1989)', *DNB* (23 September 2004); personal information.

4. Roger Michell (dir.), *Michael Redgrave: My Father* (BBC1: *Omnibus*, 13 July 1997), VHS, BFI no. 487416, London.

5. Herbert Farjeon, 'John Gielgud Essays: The Shakespearean Lear', *Sunday Mirror* (19 April 1931), 10; 'King Lear' *The Era* (15 April 1931), 11.

6. Bernard Braden and Barbara Kelly (prods), 'Kim Braden Part Six' (Adanac Productions: 22 March 1968), BFI 750788, Mediatheque, London.

7. Paramount, 'The Teen-Age Lovers of Verona' (1968) promotional film, 7 mins.

8. Lolita Chakrabarti, *Red Velvet* (London: Bloomsbury, 2012), scene 6.

9. Anon., 'Drury-Lane Theatre', *Times* (7 November 1815), 3.

10. Richard Edmonds, 'Infinite Variety Keeps This Affair Fresh', *Birmingham Post* (7 November 1992).

11. Charles Spencer, 'RSC Resorts to Adolescent Shock Tactics', *Daily Telegraph* (25 June 1999).

12. Billy Wilder (dir.) and Charles Brackett (prod.), *Sunset Boulevard* (Paramount: 1950), 115 mins.

13. Ryan Gilbey, 'The Dresser Review – Matthew Kelly and Julian Clary Face the Final Curtain', *Guardian* (16 September 2021), (theguardian.com/stage/2021/sep/16/the-dresser-review-bath-matthew-kelly-julian-clary, accessed 31 October 2022).

14. Joan Plowright, quoted in Sophie Duncan, 'Judi Dench and Shakespearean Personas in the Twenty-First Century', *Persona Studies* 5.2 (2019), (ojs.deakin.edu.au/index.php/ps/article/view/913, accessed 31 October 2022).

15. Nicky Clark, 'Acting Your Age', *Mrs Nicky Clark* (2018–22), (mrsnicky-clark.com/-acting-your-age--campaign.html, accessed 31 October 2022).

16. Gwen Ffrangcon-Davies, in David Spenser (dir.), *Gwen – A Juliet Remembered* (BBC1: 7 October 1988); Clark, 'Acting Your Age'.

17. Marda Vanne, diary entry dated 15 September 1935, quoted in Martial Rose, *Forever Juliet: The Life and Letters of Gwen Ffrangcon-Davies 1891–1992* (Dereham: Larks Press, 2003), 80–1.

18. Roy Plomley (presenter), *Desert Island Discs* (BBC Home Service: 8 October 1962). An 8-minute fragment can be heard at bbc.co.uk/sounds/play/p009y5vj.

19. Carol Chillington Rutter, 'Shakespeare Performances in England (and Wales), 2008' in Peter Holland (ed.), *Shakespeare Survey 62* (Cambridge: Cambridge University Press, 2009), 349–85; 361–2.

20. Jane Edwardes, 'Have They Got Old News for You', *Sunday Times Culture* (21 March 2010), 20–1.

21. Kate Emery Pogue, *Shakespeare's Family* (New York: Praeger, 2008).

22. Marlowe, *Dido, Queen of Carthage* 4.5.32 in Roma Gill (ed.), *Complete Works of Christopher Marlowe* (Oxford: Oxford University Press, 2012), I.113–74.

23. Thomas Lupton, *All for Money* (London: 1578), D4v.

24. The Nurse was the last Shakespearean film role for Edna May Oliver (1936), Flora Robson (1954), Pat Heywood (1968), and Miriam Margoyles (1996). It was the last Shakespearean stage role for Mary Ann Stirling in 1882–4 and the final professional stage role for Ellen Terry (by then cognitively and visually impaired) in 1916. See: Duncan, 'Judi Dench and Shakespearean Personas in the Twenty-First Century'.

25. Paul Taylor, 'Juliet and Her Romeo, Old Vic, Bristol', *Independent* (18 March 2010), (independent.co.uk/arts-entertainment/theatre-dance/reviews/juliet-and-her-romeo-old-vic-bristol-1922947.html, accessed 31 October 2022).

26. Mary Anderson de Navarro, *A Few More Memories* (London: Hutchinson & Co., 1936), 101–2.

27. Anon., 'Notes by the Chiel', *Evesham Standard* (28 August 1915), 4.

28. Jacques Gheusi, 'Roméo cherche Juliette', *Opéra L'Avant scene* 41 (May–June 1982), 74–7; Anon, 'Melba Sings Farewell', *Westminster Gazette* (9 June 1926), 1; 'Dame Nellie Melba', *Scotsman* (9 June 1926), 8.

29. 'Madmozarteanfelinefantasy', 'ballet is so funny [. . .]', Tumblr (3 June 2022) (madmozarteanfelinefantasy.tumblr.com/post/686094221304872960/ballet-is-so-funny-bc-they-will-be-like-oh-the, accessed 21 October 2022).

30. Sarah L. Kaufman, 'Dancing Juliet', *Washington Post* (8 July 2016), (washingtonpost.com/entertainment/theater_dance/dancing-juliet-the-power-stillness-and-pain-of-one-of-ballets-greatest-heroines/2016/07/08/3fb2bd04-406f-11e6-a66f-aa6c1883b6b1_story.html, accessed 31 October 2022).

31. Ibid.

32. Quoted in Martial Rose, *Forever Juliet*, 37.

33. S. P. B. Mais, *Daily Graphic* (29 May 1924) and letter to Ffrangcon-Davies (29 May 1924), quoted in Martial Rose, *Forever Juliet*, 38–9.

34. Gwen Ffrangcon-Davies, in David Spenser (dir.), *Gwen – A Juliet Remembered* (BBC1: 7 October 1988).

35. BBC News, 'RSC "Appalled" after Romeo and Juliet Cast Called "Garishly Diverse"', BBC (15 June 2020), (bbc.co.uk/news/uk-england-coventry-warwickshire-53049720, accessed 31 October 2022).

36. 'Discrimination: Your Rights', Gov.uk (gov.uk/discrimination-your-rights, accessed 31 October 2022).

37. Equity, 'Manifesto for Casting' (2018), (equity.org.uk/getting-involved/campaigns/manifesto-for-casting/, accessed 31 October 2022); 'CDG Code of Conduct' (2018), (equity.org.uk/media/3286/equity_casting-questions.pdf, accessed 31 October 2022).

38. Roger Michell (dir.), 'Michael Redgrave: My Father'.
39. Gwen Ffrangcon-Davies, *Desert Island Discs* (BBC Radio 4: 19 June 1988) (bbc.co.uk/programmes/p009mgol, accessed 31 October 2022).
40. Martial Rose, *Forever Juliet*, 181.
41. Alessandra Ferri, quoted in Kaufman, 'Dancing Juliet'.

Epilogue

1. James Christensen, 'Shakespearean Fantasy' (1986).

Select Bibliography

All references are given in the endnotes, including online sources, and (many) more anonymous cuttings from the Fondazione Franco Zeffirelli and elsewhere.

Primary

Select Manuscript Sources

Barbacci, Antonio, letter to Direzione Generale delle Antichità e Belle Arti (5 March 1936), Archivio Soprintendenza Beni Architettonici e Paesaggio (ASBAPVr), f. 91/163, Verona

---. letter to Marcello Vaccari (27 October 1938), ASBAPVr, f. 91–3

Bernstein, Leonard, MS annotation to p. 3 of George Kittredge (ed.), *Romeo and Juliet* (Boston: Ginn & Co., 1940), Leonard Bernstein Collection, Box 73, Folder 9, Library of Congress, Washington DC

---. MS notes to typescript 'WEST SIDE STORY | AUDITIONS – Tuesday, May 7, 1957' in *West Side Story [notes re auditions, casting, and orchestra]* (c. May 1957), Leonard Bernstein Collection, Box/Folder 75/5, 1; 29, Library of Congress

---. letter to Felicia Bernstein (23 August 1957), Leonard Bernstein Collection, Box/Folder 5, 1–2, Library of Congress

Crawford, Cheryl, undated letter to Arthur Laurents (early 1957), Cheryl Crawford Papers, Box 83, Folder 4, Billy Rose Theatre Division, New York Public Library

Crow Cushman, Emma, 'Charlotte Cushman: A Memory', Charlotte Cushman Papers 15: 4019–36, Library of Congress

Faucit, Helena, MS annotations to promptbook of *Romeo and Juliet* (c. 1836–45), Folger Library (Rom 8)

Field, Kate, MS letter to Emma Crow (10 July 1860), Charlotte Cushman Papers 11: 3300–01, Library of Congress

Irving, Henry, MS letters to Ellen Terry (c. January 1882), THM/384/6/4, V&A Museum, London

Laurents, Arthur, outline for 'Romeo and Juliet' (1949) and untitled outline (c. 1955), both in Leonard Bernstein Collection Box/Folder 73/10, Library of Congress

MS Sancroft 29, Bodleian Library, Oxford

MS ER82/1/21, Shakespeare Birthplace Trust, Stratford-upon-Avon

'MSS 19 – The "Platt" (or Plot) of The Second Part of the Seven Deadly Sins 1612–1626', Henslowe-Alleyn Papers, Archive of Dulwich College, London

Office of Registry of Colonial Slaves and Slave Compensation Commission: Records, Class T 71, National Archives, UK

Robbins, Jerome, 'Outline "Romeo and Juliet"', undated typescript in attrib. Leonard Bernstein, *West Side Story scene and musical sequence outlines, draft scripts, song lists, lyrics* ([incorrectly dated to] 1955 [whole bundle actually c. 1949–57]), Leonard Bernstein Collection, Box/Folder 73/10, 2, Library of Congress

---. untitled MS notes (c. 1957), Jerome Robbins Dance Division, Box 85, Folder 5, New York Public Library

Secretaries of State: State Papers Domestic, Charles II, *Manuscript SP29/8/1*, National Archives, Kew

Terry, Ellen, MS notes and annotations in 1882 promptbook of *Romeo and Juliet* (London: Chiswick Press, 1882), Harvester Microform 1974 microfilm of TS Promptbook, SH154.348, British Library

Zeffirelli, Franco, MS notes to ring-bound notebook script of *Romeo and Juliet* (c. 1960), 39; 57–8; 73–4, in *Materiali preparatori* for *Romeo and Juliet*, FFZ

Further Primary Sources

'A Modern Romeo and Juliet', *Worcestershire Chronicle* (12 July 1890), 8

'A new Romeo & Juliet', *Look* (1 October 1967), n.p., Box 194.2, FFZ

'A Romeo and Juliet in Cuba', *Hartlepool Free Press* (14 April 1860), 2

Acton, William, *A New Journal of Italy* (London: Richard Baldwin, 1691)

Allam, Roger, 'Mercutio from *Romeo and Juliet*' in Russell Jackson and Robert Smallwood (eds), *Players of Shakespeare* 2 (Cambridge: Cambridge University Press, 1988), 107–19

Allen, Grant, *European Tour* (New York: Dodd, Mead, 1909)

Allott, Robert, *England's Parnassus* (London: N.L., C.B. and T.H, 1600)

Altemus, Jameson Torr, *Helena Modjeska* (New York: J. S. Ogilvie, 1883)

Ancestry, 'Former British Colonial Dependencies, Slave Registers, 1813–1834', *Ancestry* (2020)

Arnold, Matthew, 'The French Play in London', *The Nineteenth Century* 6 (1879), 228–43

Barker, Felix, 'The Very Beautiful Murder of Romeo and Juliet', undated press cuttings, Box C.194, FFZ

Barnes, Clive, 'An Italian Gives Juliet a Beatnik Heart', unattributed cutting, FFZ

Bellamy, George Anne, *An Apology for the Life of George Anne Bellamy*, 5th edn (London: J. Bell, 1786)

Bennett, Alan, *The History Boys* (London: Faber & Faber, 2004)

Bernstein, Leonard, 'Excerpts from a West Side Log', *Playbill* (30 September 1947), 47–8

Bodenham, John, *Bel-vedére* (London: Hugh Alley, 1600)

Braden, Bernard, and Barbara Kelly (prods), 'Kim Braden Part Six' (Adanac Productions: 22 March 1968), BFI 750788, Mediatheque, London

Bradley, John Lewis, and Ian Ousby (eds), *The Correspondence of John Ruskin and Charles Eliot Norton* (Cambridge: Cambridge University Press, 1987)

'Brady, Francis Bridgford', *Principal Probate Registry / Index of Wills and Registrations* (London: Crown Copyright, 1981), H16

Brady, Francis Bridgford, Letter to the Librarian, Christ Church (24 November 1977), F. B. Brady Collection, Christ Church

Breval, John, *Remarks on Several Parts of Europe* (London: Bernard Lintot, 1726)

Burnet, Gilbert, *Some Letters Containing an Account of What Seemed Most Remarkable in Switzerland, Italy, &c* (Amsterdam: Abraham Ascher, 1687)

Burns, John F., 'Gangs in Sarajevo Worry Diplomats', *New York Times* (4 October 1993)

'Callous Murders', *Dungannon Courier* (6 January 1993), 1

Campbell, Jenny, 'Elopement', *Petticoat* (9 March 1968), 22–3

Campbell, Mrs Patrick [Beatrice Stella Tanner], *My Life and Some Letters* (London: Hutchinson & Co., 1928)

Campbell, Robert, *The London Tradesmen* (London: T. Gardner, 1747)

Carlei, Carlo (dir.), Julian Fellowes (screenplay), *Romeo & Juliet* (Echo Lake Entertainment/Swarovski Entertainment, 2013), 118 mins

Cashin, Fergus, 'The Other Face of Juliet', *Daily Sketch* (28 February 1968), n.p., FFZ

'Censor's "A" for Romeo Angers Zeffirelli', *Evening Standard* (5 March 1968), n.p., FFZ

Chakrabarti, Lolita, *Red Velvet* (London: Bloomsbury, 2012)

Charke, Charlotte, *Narrative of the Life of Mrs Charlotte Charke*, ed. Robert M. Rehder (Abingdon: Routledge, 2016)

Chaucer, Geoffrey, and Walter W. Skeat (ed.), *The Complete Works of Geoffrey Chaucer*, vol. 2 (Oxford: Oxford University Press, 1900)

Chavet, Louis, 'Roméo et Juliette', *Figaro* (no date, 1967), n.p., Box C.194, FFZ

Chereau, Jacques (artist), Noël-Nicolas Coypel (engraver), invitation to accompany the funeral procession of John Boyfield on 22 October (1747), E.864-1939, V&A Museum, London

Child, Theodore, *Summer Holidays* (New York: Harper & Bros, 1889)

Christie, Ian, 'Too Young to Be in Love', *Daily Express* (5 March 1968), n.p., FFZ

Cibber, Theophilus, *Four Original Letters* (London: T. Read, 1739)

---. *Romeo and Juliet, A Tragedy, Revis'd, and Alter'd from Shakespeare* [1744] (London: C. Corbett, 1748)

---. *A Serio-Comic Apology for the Life of Mr Theophilus Cibber* (Dublin: A. Long, 1748)

---. *The Girlhood of Shakespeare's Heroines* (London: J.M. Dent & Co., 1907)

'The Coburg Theatre', *The Times* (11 October 1825), 2

Cockin, Katharine (ed.), *Collected Letters of Ellen Terry*, vol. 4 (Abingdon: Routledge, 2016)

Coleman, John, *Fifty Years of an Actor's Life* (New York: James Pott & Co., 1904)

---. 'Little Stars', *New Statesman* (8 March 1968), n.p., FFZ

Coleridge, Samuel Taylor, 'On the Slave Trade', *The Watchman* (25 March 1796), 130–40

---. 'The Monk. A Romance', *Critical Review* (February 1797), 194–200

A common place book (c. 1622–5), MS. Eng. misc. d.28, Bodleian Library, Oxford

Cook, Eliza, 'Poetical Dedication of a Volume', *Hampshire Advertiser* (25 November 1848), 7

Cooke, Richard P., 'The Old Vic in Verona', *Wall Street Journal* (15 February 1962), press cutting, FFZ

Corbett, Sue, 'Triumph and Tears for a Brave Mum', *Sunday Life* (15 May 1994), 5

Coryat, Thomas, *Coryat's Crudities* (Glasgow: J. MacLehose & Sons, 1905)

Cowden Clarke, Mary, 'Shakespeare as the Girl's Friend', *Girl's Own Paper* (4 June 1887), 562–4

Cuffe, Henry, *The Differences of the Ages of Man's Life* (London: Martin Cleare, 1607)

Cunningham, Dominic, '"Distressed" Priest Urges No Reprisals', *Irish Independent* (5 January 1993), 9

---. 'UVF Victim's Bride-to-be Found Dead', *Irish Independent* (3 February 1993), 7

Curry, Julian, *Judi Dench on Juliet* (London: Nick Hern Books, 2010)

Da Porto, Luigi, *Historia novellamente ritrovata di due nobili amanti* (Venice: s.n., 1531)

Dalla Corte, Girolamo, *L'Istoria di Verona* (Verona: Girolamo Discepolo, 1594)

'Dame Nellie Melba', *Scotsman* (9 June 1926), 8

Davies, Thomas, *Memoirs of the Life of David Garrick* (London: s.n., 1780)

Dickens, Charles, *Pictures from Italy* (London: Bradbury & Evans, 1846)

Digges, Leonard, 'To the Memorie of the Deceased Authour Maister W. Shakespeare', *Mr. William Shakespeares Comedies, Histories & Tragedies* [First Folio], Bodleian Arch. G c.7

Divin, Sue, *Guard Your Heart* (London: Macmillan, 2021)

Dominiani, José, 'Romeo y Julieta ante la reina', *Back To Back* (21 April 1968), 37–9

[Dorynne, Jess] *The True Ophelia: And Other Studies of Shakespeare's Women* (London: Sidgwick & Jackson, Ltd, 1913)

Dowden, Edmund, *Shakspere* (London: Henry S. King, 1875)

Downes, John, *Roscius Anglicanus* (London: s.n., 1708)

'Drury-Lane Theatre', *The Times* (7 November 1815), 3

Durling, Robert M., and Robert L. Martinez (eds), *The Divine Comedy of Dante Alighieri: Volume 2: Purgatorio* (Oxford: Oxford University Press, 2003)

Earthenware transfer-printed mug with blue enamel (1800 to 1850), 127 x 86 mm, 3650-1901, V&A Museum, London

Edmonds, Richard, 'Infinite Variety Keeps This Affair Fresh', *Birmingham Post* (7 November 1992), 27

'Enfin Roméo et Juliette ont leur âge', *France-Soir* (24 September 1967), 5D, Box C.194, FFZ

Engraved invitation to the funeral of Mrs Rebecca Hale on 20 April (1776), E.235-1963, V&A Museum, London

'Exeter Theatre', *Western Times* (14 October 1848), 5

Farjeon, Herbert, 'John Gielgud Essays: The Shakespearean Lear', *Sunday Mirror* (19 April 1931), 10

Faucit, Helen, *On Some of Shakespeare's Female Characters* [1885] (London: William Blackwood & Sons, 1905)

Ferrand, Jacques, *Erotomania* (Oxford: Edward Forrest, 1640)

[Fielding, Henry], *An Apology for the Life of Mr T---- C-----, Comedian* (London: J. Mechell, 1740)

'Film Review', *Daily Variety* (11 March 1968), n.p., photocopied cutting, FFZ

Fletcher, George, *Studies of Shakespeare* (London: Longman *et al.*, 1847)

Galiffe, Jacques, *Italy and its Inhabitants* (London: John Murray, 1820)

Garrick, David, *Romeo and Juliet* (London: J. and R. Tonson, 1753)

---. 'Prologue for the Opening of the Bristol Theatre' in *The Poetical Works of David Garrick, Esq.* (London: George Kearsley, 1785), 1.213–4

Genest, John, *Some Account of the English Stage* (Bath: H.E. Carrington, 1832)

Gentleman, Francis, *The Dramatic Censor* (London: J. Bell, 1770)

Giroud, Françoise, 'God Save The Queen', *L'Express* (11 March 1968), n.p., FFZ

Goldsmith, Oliver, *The Vicar of Wakefield* [1766] (London: John Van Voorst, 1842)

Graves, Clotilde, 'O' Both Your Houses', *Gentlewoman* (25 January 1913), 101–2

Hardy, Thomas, *Tess of the D'Urbervilles* (Oxford: Oxford University Press, 1989)

'Heartbroken Girl Joins Her Beloved', *Irish Independent* (5 February 1993), 4

'Here Unentombed van Butchell's Consort Lies' in C. J. S. Thompson, *The Quacks of Old London* (London: Brentano's, 1928), 323–4

Heywood, Thomas, *An Apologie for Actors* (London: Nicholas Okes, 1612)

Hill, John, *The Actor* (London: R. Griffiths, 1750)

'Honour Thy Father and Thy Mother', *Girl's Own Paper* 6, no. 250 (October 11, 1884), 22–23, and no. 257 (November 29, 1884), 139–40

Howitt, Mary, 'The Miss Cushmans', *People's Journal* (18 July 1846), 30

Hurley, Joseph, 'The Old Vic's Master', *New York Herald Tribune* (11 February 1962), newspaper cutting, FFZ

Hussey, Olivia, *The Girl on the Balcony* (New York: Kensington, 2018)

J. R., 'Zeffirelli's "Romeo" – Fresh, Alive, Young', *Los Angeles Advocate* (January 1969), 11

Jackson, Henry, letter to 'G.P.' (September 1610), Corpus Christi Fulman Papers, X. 83r–84v

Jackson, John, *The History of the Scottish Stage* (Edinburgh: Hill and Robinson, 1793)

Jameson, Anna, *Characteristics of Women* (New York: Ottley, 1837)

Jenkins, Richard, *Memoirs of the Bristol Stage* (Bristol: W.H. Somerton, 1826)

Johnston, Karen, 'In a Word!', *Mirabelle* (14 December 1968), 2

Jordan, Thomas, 'I Come, unknown to any of the rest' (1660), reprinted in Fiona Ritchie, *Women and Shakespeare in the Eighteenth Century* (Cambridge: Cambridge University Press, 2014), 4

Kendal, Madge, *Dramatic Opinions* (London: privately printed, 1890)

---. *Dame Madge Kendal by Herself* (1933)

Kerr, Walter, 'First Night Report', *New York Herald Tribune* (14 February 1962), n.p, FFZ

Kielmansegge, Frederick, *Diary of a Journey to England* (London: Longmans, Green & Co., 1902)

'King Lear', *The Era* (15 April 1931), 11

Lane, Trilby, 'Happy News', *Mirabelle* (30 November 1968), 17

Larkin, Philip, 'Annus Mirabilis' (16 June 1967), reprinted in Anthony Twaite (ed.), *Philip Larkin: Collected Poems* (London: Faber & Faber, 2003), 146

Lathrop, Elize, *Sunny Days in Italy* (New York: James Pott & Co., 1907)

Laurents, Arthur, Leonard Bernstein, and Stephen Sondheim, *West Side Story* (New York: Random House, 1958)

Leen, Nina, 'Teen-Age Girls: They Live in a Wonderful World of Their Own', *Time* (11 December 1944), 91–9

Lingard, Joan, *Across the Barricades* (London: Penguin, 2016)

'London', *Daily Post* (26 January 1733), 1

'London. Thursday, Jan. 28th', *Reading Mercury* (1 February 1779), 2

Luhrmann, Baz (dir.), *William Shakespeare's Romeo + Juliet* (Bazmark Productions, 1996), 120 mins

Lyly, John, *Euphues* (London: Gabriel Cawood, 1580)

McClain, John, 'Love That New Love Affair!', *Journal American* (14 February 1962), press cutting, FFZ

Macfarlane, Ursula (dir.), *West Side Stories – The Making of a Classic* (17 January 2017), BBC2, 60 mins

McGarry, Patrick, 'Tragic Victim of a Broken Heart', *Irish Independent* (6 February 1993), 28

McGee, Lisa, *Erin's Diary: An Official Derry Girls Book* (London: Orion, 2020)

McKeown, Laurence, 'Denis Faul Saw Church Power Slipping Away', *An Phoblacht* (27 July 2006, online)

Macready, William, *Macready's Reminiscences* (London: Macmillan & Co., 1875)

Mantel clock, drum-shaped movement inset into bronze rockwork with an ormolu figure of Shakespeare (1840), 395 x 312 x 105 mm, NT 514785, Anglesey Abbey, Cambridgeshire

Marlowe, Christopher, Roma Gill (ed.), *Complete Works of Christopher Marlowe* (Oxford: Oxford University Press: 2012)

'Marriage Bond and Allegation for William Ellis and Jane Cibber, Aldenham, Hertfordshire' (28 February 1761), *London and Surrey Marriage Bonds and Allegations 1597–1921*, DL/A/D/005/MS10091/103

Marston, John, *The Scourge of Villainie* (London: John Buzbie, 1598)

---. *Jacke Drums Entertainment* (London: Richard Olive, 1601)

Marston, Westland, *Our Recent Actors* (Boston: Roberts Brothers, 1888)

'Melba Sings Farewell', *Westminster Gazette* (9 June 1926), 1

Meres, Francis, *Palladis Tamia* (London: Cuthbert Burbie, 1598)

Merrill, Lisa, *When Romeo Was a Woman* (Ann Arbor, MI: University of Michigan Press, 2000)

Michell, Roger (dir.), *Michael Redgrave: My Father* (BBC1: *Omnibus*, 13 July 1997), VHS, BFI no. 487416, London

Modjeska, Helena, *Memories and Impressions of Helena Modjeska* (New York: B. Blom, 1910)

Moore, Thomas (ed.), *Life of Lord Byron* (London: John Murray, 1854)

Moore, Rebecca, 'A Month in Italy', *The Woman's Journal* (23 January 1892), 2

Mulrayne, J. R. (ed.), *The Spanish Tragedy* (London: A&C Black, 2014)

Murphy, Arthur, *The Life of David Garrick, Esq.* (Dublin: Brett Smith, 1801)

Nashe, Thomas, *Pierce Penniless's Supplication to the Devil* [1592] (London: Shakespeare Society, 1842)

Navarro, Mary Anderson de, *A Few Memories* (New York: Harper & Bros, 1896)

---. *A Few More Memories* (London: Hutchinson & Co., 1936)

Nelthorpe, Frances Mary (ed.), *Mrs Mary Carter's Letters* (London: Clayton & Co., 1860)

Nordland, Rod, 'Two star-crossed Afghans cling to love', *New York Times* (10 March 2014)

---. *The Lovers* (London: Hodder & Stoughton, 2016)

---. and Johan-Frédérik Hel-Guedj (trans.), *Un Amour Interdit* (Paris: Tallandier, 2017)

North, Ryan, *Romeo And/Or Juliet* (London: Orion, 2020)

'Notes by the Chiel', *Evesham Standard* (28 August 1915), 4

Noyer, Paul, *Conversations with McCartney* (London: Random House, 2015)

'Nurses make the best wives!', *19 Magazine* (March 1968), 14

The Office of Christian Parents (Cambridge: s.n., 1616)

'Old & New Play in Manhattan', *Time* (20 May 1940), 69

Oppenheim, David (prod.), *Inside Pop: The Rock Revolution* (25 April 1967), CBS

Otway, Thomas, *The History and Fall of Caius Marius* (London: Thomas Flesher, 1680)

'Our Prize Competition', *Girl's Own Paper* (10 March 1888), 380–3

Paramount, 'The Teen-Age Lovers of Verona' (1968) promotional film, 7 mins

Pepys, Samuel, diary entry dated 23 May 1660, *Pepys Diary* (pepysdiary.com/diary/1660/05/23/, accessed 1 October 2020)

---. diary entry dated 1 April 1662, *Pepys Diary* (pepysdiary.com/diary/1662/04/01/, accessed 1 October 2020)

Peters, Jenny, 'Shakespeare's Mister', *More* (26 March 1997), 46–7

Philodramatus, 'A Proposal for the Better Regulation of the Stage', *Weekly Miscellany* (27 January 1738), 1–2

Pinero, Arthur Wing, *The Second Mrs Tanqueray* [1893] in *Pinero: Three Plays* (London: Methuen, 1985)

'Pistol's a Cuckold, or Adultery in Fashion' (London: s.n., 1738)

Plate, Thomas Gordon, 'The Teen-agers of Verona', *Newsweek* (14 October 1968), Box C.194/2, FFZ

Poe, Edgar Allan, 'The Philosophy of Composition', *Graham's Magazine* (April 1846), 163

Porter, Henry, *The pleasant historie of the two angrie women of Abington* (London: Edward Allde, 1599)

The Problemes of Aristotle (Edinburgh: s.n., 1595)

Prujean, Thomas, 'Love's Looking-Glasse', *Aurorata* (London: Hugh Perry, 1644)

Rabinyan, Dorit, trans. Jessica Cohen, *All the Rivers* [2014] (London: Random House, 2017)

Richardson, David (ed.), *Bristol, Africa, and the Eighteenth-century Slave Trade to America, Vol. 3: The Years of Decline 1746–1769*, Bristol Records Society Publications Vol. XLII (1991)

Robinson, David, 'Apollos of Verona', *Financial Times* (8 March 1968), n.p.

'Romeo and Juliet', *Mirabelle* (9 November 1968), 6–8; (16 November 1968), 10–11; (23 November 1968), 6; (14 December 1968), 11

'Romeo and Juliet in Modern Life', *South Wales Daily News* (7 August 1893), 6

'Romeo and Juliet in Real Life', *South Wales Daily News* (24 April 1894), 5

Ruskin, John, 'Of Queen's Gardens' [1864] in Tyas Cook and Wedderburn (eds), *Works of John Ruskin* (Cambridge: 2010), VIII.109–44

Sala, George, *Rome and Venice, with Other Wanderings in Italy* (London: Tinsley, 1869)

Schork, Kurt, 'Kurt Schork's Signature Dispatch from the Siege of Sarajevo', *KS Memorial* (23 May 1993, online)

'Scrutator', 'A Polish Juliet', *Truth* (31 March 1881), 15

Shakespeare, William, *An Excellent Conceited Tragedie of Romeo and Juliet* (London: John Danter, 1597)

---. Bate, Jonathan and Eric Rasmussen (eds), *William Shakespeare: Complete Works* (Basingstoke: Macmillan, 2008)

---. Burrow, Colin (ed.), *The Oxford Shakespeare: The Complete Sonnets and Poems* (Oxford: Oxford University Press, 2002)

---. Kastan, David Scott (ed.), *King Henry IV, Part 1* (London: Bloomsbury, 2002)

---. Levenson, Jill (ed.), *The excellent conceited tragedie of Romeo and Juliet* (Oxford: Oxford University Press, 2000)

---. Lees-Jeffries, Hester (ed.), William Shakespeare, *Romeo and Juliet* (Cambridge: Cambridge University Press, 2022)

---. Loehlin, James N. (ed.), *Romeo and Juliet (Shakespeare in Production)* (Cambridge: Cambridge University Press, 2002)

---. Taylor, Gary, John Jowett, Terri Bourus, and Gabriel Egan (eds), *The New Oxford Shakespeare: Modern Critical Edition* (Oxford: Oxford University Press, 2016)

Shaw, G[eorge] B[ernard], 'Romeo and Juliet', *Saturday Review* (28 September 1895), 409–10

Shelley, Mary, *Rambles in Germany and Italy* (London: Edward Moxon, 1844)

Shulman, Irving, *West Side Story* (London: W.H. Allen & Co., 1987)

Sidney, Philip, *Sir P.S. his Astrophel and Stella* [1580s] (London: John Danter, 1591)

---. *A Defence of Poetry* (Oxford: Oxford University Press, 1973)

Simeone, Nigel (ed.), *The Leonard Bernstein Letters* (hereafter *LB Letters*) (New Haven, CT: Yale University Press, 2013)

Spencer, Charles, 'RSC Resorts to Adolescent Shock Tactics', *Daily Telegraph* (25 June 1999)

Spencer, George, 'Romeo is a Really Horny Guy', *Mizz* (26 March 1997), 8–9

Spenser, David (dir.), *Gwen – A Juliet Remembered* (7 October 1988), BBC1, 60 mins

Sperlinger, Tom, *Romeo and Juliet in Palestine: Teaching Under Occupation* (London: Zero Books, 2015)

[Statham, Julie], tribute to Diarmuid Shields in the *Dungannon Courier* (3 February 1993), 1

Stebbins, Emma, *Charlotte Cushman* (Boston: Houghton, Osgood & Co., 1879)

Stevenson, Robert Louis, 'A Penny Plain and Twopence Coloured' in *Memories and Portraits* (London: T. Nelson, 1924), 203–16

Stokes, John, *In the Nineties* (Hemel Hempstead: Harvest Wheatsheaf, 1989)

Stow, John, *The Annales of England faithfully collected out of the most autenticall authors* (London: Ralfe Newbury, 1600)

Stransom, Nora, 'The Woman in Shakespeare's Plays', *Englishwoman* (April 1914), 198–205

'The Stroller', *Sporting Life* (10 May 1893), 8

'Suicide girl blames killers', *Sandwell Evening Mail* (5 March 1993), 2

Swift, Taylor, 'Love Story', *Fearless*, Big Machine Records, 2014

Swinhoe, Gilbert, *The Tragedy of the Unhappy Fair Irene* (London: J. Place, 1658)

Synnott, Kathleen, letter to the editor, *Evening Herald* (24 February 1993), 15

Terry, Ellen, *The Story of My Life* (London: Hutchinson & Co., 1908)

---. Untitled MS lecture draft on Shakespeare's heroines (c. 1912–16), British Library Loan, MS. 125/31/1

Terry, Ellen, and Christopher St John (ed.), *Four Lectures on Shakespeare* (London: Hopkinson, 1932)

Thomas, James, 'Romeo is My Kind of Boy, Says Juliet . . .', *Daily Express* (26 May 1967), 3

Thrale, Hester Lynch, diary entries dated 17 June 1790 and 9 December 1795, reprinted in Alison Oram and Annmarie Turnbull (eds), *The Lesbian History Sourcebook* (London: Routledge, 2002), 58–9

'Tomorrow Is Today', *Romeo* (6 January 1968), 1–3

Thurlwell, A. R., letter to the editor, *Evening News* (13 March 1968), n.p., FFZ

Truelove, Francis, *The Comforts of Matrimony* (London: s.n., 1739)

The Tryal of a Cause for Criminal Conversation (London: T. Trott, 1739)

'UVF Victim's Friend Dies', *Evening Herald* (2 February 1993), 7

Vasari, Giorgio, *Le vite de' piu eccellenti pittori, scultori, e architettori*, 3 vols (Florence : Appresso i Giunti, 1568)

'Verona', *The Christian Lady's Magazine* (December 1837), 543–6

'Visiting the Tomb of the Capulets', *The Methodists* (28 April 1877), 11

Voller, Jack G. (ed.), *The Graveyard School* (Richmond, VA: Valancourt Books, 2015)

Watts, George Frederick, *Found Drowned* (1849–50), oil on canvas, 213 x 120 cm, Watts Gallery, Compton, Surrey

White, Martin (ed.), *The Roman Actor* (Manchester: Manchester University Press, 2007)

Wigg, David, 'Olivia Likes Rude Romeos', *Evening News* (16 February 1968), n.p., FFZ

Wilkinson, Tate, *Memoirs of His Own Life* (York: Wilson, Spence, and Mawman, 1790)

Williamson, C. H., 'A Lay Sermon', *Wesleyan Methodist Magazine* (October 1898), 764–6

Wise, Robert, and Jerome Robbins (dirs), *West Side Story* (Mirisch Pictures/ Seven Arts Productions, 1961), 152 mins

'Without You', *Mirabelle* (9 November 1968)

Wood, Victoria, 'Bronteburgers', *Up To You, Porky!* (London: Methuen, 1985), 17

Wright, James, *Historia Histrionica* (London: s.n., 1699)

'Yesterday, about one o'clock [. . .]', *General Advertiser* (2 February 1779), 3

Zaritsky, John (dir.), *Romeo and Juliet in Sarajevo*, *Frontline* (PBS/CBC/NFB/ WDR: 10 May 1994), 90 mins

Zeffirelli, Franco, *An Autobiography* (London: Weidenfeld & Nicolson, 1986)

'Zeffirelli with His X Certificate Stars', *Town* (January 1968), n.p., FFZ

Zingarelli, Niccolò Antonio, *Romeo and Giulietta* (New York: E. M. Murden, 1826)

Secondary

Alderton, Zoe, '"Snape Wives" and "Snapeism": A Fiction-Based Religion within the Harry Potter Fandom', *Religions* 5.1 (2014), 219–67

Allen, Richard B., *European Slave Trading in the Indian Ocean, 1500–1850* (Ohio: Ohio University Press, 2015)

Apter, Terri, *What Do You Want from Me?: Learning to Get Along with In-Laws* (New York: W. W. Norton, 2009)

Ariès, Philippe, *Western Attitudes Towards Death: From the Middle Ages to the Present* (Baltimore: Johns Hopkins University Press, 1975)

Badeni, June, 'Meynell [*née* Thompson], Alice Christiana Gertrude (1847– 1922)', *DNB* (7 January 2016)

Bald, R. C., *John Donne* (Oxford: Oxford University Press, 1970)

Bell, J. Bowyer, *The IRA, 1968–2000: An Analysis of a Secret Army* (Oxford: Taylor & Francis, 2013)

Belsey, Catherine, *Romeo and Juliet: Language and Writing* (London: Bloomsbury, 2014)

Benbow, R. Mark, 'Dutton and Goffe Versus Broughton: A Disputed Contract for Plays in the 1570s', *Records of Early English Drama* 6.2 (1981), 3–9

Bennett, Judith, 'Death and the Maiden', *Journal of Medieval and Early Modern Studies* 42.2 (2012), 269–305

Berezin, Mabel, *The Making of the Fascist Self* (New York: Cornell University Press, 2018)

Berson, Misha, *Something's Coming, Something Good: West Side Story and the American Imagination* (Milwaukee, WI: Applause Theatre and Cinema Books, 2011)

Best, Gary, 'Dark Detours: Celebrity Car Crash Deaths and Trajectories of Place' in Leanne White and Elspeth Frew (eds), *Dark Tourism and Place Identity* (Oxford: Routledge, 2016), 202–16

Bigliazzi, Silvia, and Lisanna Calvi, 'Producing a (R&J)space: Discursive and Social Practices in Verona' in Bigliazzi and Calvi (eds), *Shakespeare, Romeo and Juliet, and Civic Life* (Oxford: Routledge, 2015), 238–59

Black, Annetta, 'The Incorruptible St. Zita', *Atlas Obscura* (2021)

Block, Geoffrey, *Enchanted Evenings: The Broadway Musical from Show Boat to Sondheim* (Oxford: Oxford University Press, 2004)

Bolin, Alice, *Dead Girls* (New York: HarperCollins, 2018)

Bosworth, R. J. B., *Mussolini's Italy* (London: Penguin, 2005)

Bourne, Claire, and Jason Scott-Warren, '"Thy unvalued Booke": John Milton's Copy of the Shakespeare First Folio', *Milton Quarterly* 56.1–2 (2023)

Bowling, Benjamin, *Violent Racism: Victimisation, Policing, and Social Context* (Oxford: Oxford University Press, 1999)

Braham, George C., 'The Genesis of David Garrick's *Romeo and Juliet*', *Shakespeare Quarterly* 35.2 (1984), 170–9

Brown, John Russell (ed.), *Shakespeare Handbooks: Macbeth* (Basingstoke: Palgrave Macmillan, 2005)

Burden, Michael, 'Shakespeare and Opera' in Fiona McGill and Peter Sabor (eds), *Shakespeare in the Eighteenth Century* (Cambridge: Cambridge University Press, 2012), 204–24

Burton, Humphrey, *Leonard Bernstein* (London: Faber & Faber, 1994)

Bush-Bailey, Gilli, *Treading the Bawds: Actresses and Playwrights on the Late Stuart Stage* (Manchester: Manchester University Press, 2006)

Clemens, Colleen Lutz, 'Phoenix Rising: The West's Use (and Misuse) of Anglophone Memoirs by Pakistani Women' in Aroosa Kanwal and Saiyma Aslam (eds), *The Routledge Companion to Pakistani Anglophone Writing* (London: Routledge, 2019), 162–71

Coogan, Tim Pat, *The IRA* (New York: St Martin's Publishing Group, 2002)

Coursen, H. R., *Shakespeare in Production: Whose History?* (Athens, OH: Ohio University Press, 1996)

Culler, John, *Literary Theory: A Very Short Introduction* (Oxford: Oxford University Press, 2011)

D'Anniballe Williams, Maria, 'Recreating the Past: The Controversies Surrounding the Refashioning of the Medieval Castle of Castelvecchio in Verona under the Fascist Regime', *Athanor* 28 (2010)

---. *Urban Space in Fascist Verona: Contested Grounds for Mass Spectacle, Tourism, and the Architectural Past*, unpublished doctoral dissertation (University of Pittsburgh, 2011)

Dickerson, James L., *Natalie Portman: Queen of Hearts* (Toronto: ECW Press, 2002)

Dobson, Jessie, 'Some Eighteenth Century Experiments in Embalming', *Journal of the History of Medicine* (October 1953), 431–41

Driscoll, Richard, Keith E. Davis, and Milton E. Lipetz, 'Parental Interference and Romantic Love: The Romeo and Juliet Effect', *Journal of Personality and Social Psychology* 24.1 (1972), 1–10

Dunbar, Robin, Ben Teasdale, Jackie Thompson, Felix Budelmann, Sophie Duncan, Evert van Emde Boas and Laurie Maguire, 'Emotional Arousal When Watching Drama Increases Pain Threshold and Social Bonding', *Royal Society Open Science* 3 (2016, online)

Duncan, Sophie, *Shakespeare's Women and the Fin de Siècle* (Oxford: Oxford University Press, 2016)

---. 'Judi Dench and Shakespearean Personas in the Twenty-First Century', *Persona Studies* 5.2 (2019, online)

Duncan-Jones, Katherine, '"O Happy Dagger": The Autonomy of Shakespeare's Juliet', *Notes and Queries* 45.3 (September 1998)

---. 'Grudge Fudged', *Times Literary Supplement* (20 October 2000), 19

Edmond, Mary, 'Davenant [D'Avenant], Sir William (1606–1668)', *DNB* (8 October 2009), (oxforddnb.com, accessed 1 October 2020)

Edwardes, Jane, 'Have They Got Old News for You', *Sunday Times Culture* (21 March 2010), 20–1

Emelyanova-Griva, Marina, 'La tombe de Victor Noir au cimitière du Père-Lachaise', *Archives de sciences sociales des religions* 149 (2010), 89–108

Equiano, Olaudah, *The Life of Olaudah Equiano* [1789] (Boston: Isaac Knapp, 1837)

Erkens, Richard, 'The Earliest *Romeo and Juliet* Operas: The Happy Lovers of Johann Gottfried Schwanberger (1773) and Georg Anton Benda (1776)' in Maria Ida Biggi and Michele Girardi (eds), *Shakespeare All'Opera: Riscritture e Alletestimenti di 'Romeo e Giulietta'* (Bari: edizioni di pagina, 2018), 15–32

The Fashion Law, 'Why Do Ads and Editorials Depicting Violence Happen In Fashion?', *The Fashion Law* (4 October 2017), (thefashionlaw.com/why-ads-editorials-depicting-violence-keep-happening/, accessed 1 September 2021)

Fernie, Ewan, *Shakespeare for Freedom* (Cambridge: Cambridge University Press, 2017)

Finstad, Suzanne, *Natasha: The biography of Natalie Wood* (London: Arrow, 2002)

Forward, Susan, *Toxic In-Laws: Loving Strategies for Protecting Your Marriage* (New York: Harper Perennial, 2002)

Friedman, Lise, and Ceil Friedman, *Letters to Juliet* (New York: Stewart, Tabori, and Chang, 2006)

Friedman, Terry, *The Eighteenth Century Church in Britain* (New Haven, CT: Yale University Press, 2011)

Gheusi, Jacques, 'Roméo cherche Juliette', *Opéra L'Avant scene* 41 (May–June 1982), 74–7

Gibbs, Andrew, Nader Said, Julienne Corboz, and Rachel Jewkes, 'Factors Associated with "Honour Killing" in Afghanistan and the Occupied Palestinian Territories: Two Cross-sectional Studies', *PLoS One* 19 (8 August 2019)

Gibbs, Kenneth F. (transcrib.), and William Brigg (ed.), *The Parish Registers of Aldenham, Hertfordshire, 1559–1669, with Appendix* (St Alban's, Gibbs and Bamforth, 1902)

Gilbert, James, *A Cycle of Outrage: America's Reaction to the Juvenile Delinquent in the 1950s* (New York: OUP, 1988)

'Godfather of Loyalist Death Squads Given Life Sentences', *Irish Independent* (17 June 1994), 5

Goldby, David J., 'Arne, Thomas Augustine (1710–1778)', *DNB* (23 September 2004)

Gordon, Robert, *The Holocaust in Italian Culture* (Stanford: Stanford University Press, 2012)

Gordon, Stephen, 'Life and Times of King Rat', *Sunday Life* (28 December 1997), 6–7

Gurr, Andrew, 'The Date and Expected Venue of *Romeo and Juliet*' in Stanley Wells (ed.), *Shakespeare Survey 49* (Cambridge: Cambridge University Press, 1996), 15–26

Haywood, Charles, 'William Boyce's: "Solemn Dirge" in Garrick's Romeo and Juliet Production of 1750', *Shakespeare Quarterly* 11.2 (Spring 1960), 173–87

Highfill, Philip H., Kalman A. Burnim, and Edward A. Langhans (eds), *A Biographical Dictionary of Actors* (Carbondale, Il: Southern Illinois University Press, 1978)

Hochschild, Adam, *Bury the Chains: Prophets and Rebels in the Fight to Free an Empire's Slaves* (Boston: Mariner, 2005)

Hodgdon, Barbara, '*William Shakespeare's Romeo + Juliet*: Everything's Nice in America?' in Catherine M. S. Alexander (ed.), *Shakespeare and Politics* (Cambridge: Cambridge University Press, 2004), 247–62

Hohenhaus, Peter, 'Commemorating and Commodifying the Rwandan Genocide: Memorial Sites in a Politically Difficult Context' in White and Frew (eds), *Dark Tourism*, 142–54

Holmgren, Beth, *Starring Madame Modjeska* (Bloomington, IN: Indiana University Press, 2012)

Honigmann, E. A. J., and Susan Brock, *Playhouse Wills, 1558–1642* (Manchester: Manchester University Press, 1993)

Hosmer, Katie, 'Fantasizing About the Perfect Elegant Death', *My Modern Met* (20 May 2013), (mymodernmet.com/izima-kaoru-landscape-with-a-corpse/, accessed 2 September 2018)

Houlbrook, Ceri, *Unlocking the Love-Lock* (Oxford: Berghahn, 2021)

Houlbrooke, Ralph, *Death, Religion, and the Family in England, 1480–1750* (Oxford: Oxford University Press, 2000)

Ian, Janis, *Society's Child* (New York: Penguin, 2009)

Jones, Emma, *The Business of Sculpture in Venice 1525–1625,* unpublished DPhil thesis (Cambridge, 2016)

Kathman, David, 'Reconsidering *The Seven Deadly Sins*', *Early Theatre* 7.1 (2004), 13–44

Keefer, Katrina H. B., 'Marked by Fire: Brands, Slavery, and Identity', *Slavery & Abolition* 40.4 (2019), 659–81

Kelly, John Alexander, *German Visitors to English Theatres* (Princeton: Princeton University Press, 1936)

Knapp, Raymond, *The American Musical and the Formation of National Identity* (Princeton: Princeton University Press, 2006)

Kolchin, Margaret, *American Slavery* (London: Penguin, 1995)

Koon, Helene, *Colley Cibber: A Biography* (Kentucky: Kentucky University Press, 2014)

Kott, Jan, *Shakespeare Our Contemporary* (New York: W. W. Norton, 1974)

Lahr, John, *Prick Up Your Ears: The Biography of Joe Orton* (London: Allen Lane, 1978)

Lake, Howard, 'Jump on In, You're in Safe Hands: Flash-Frames from the Automobile Cargo Bay Experience' in Mikita Brottman (ed.), *Car Crash Culture* (New York: Palgrave, 2001), 45–72

Lathrop, Elize, *Where Shakespeare Set His Stage* (New York: Haskell House, 1906)

Laversuch, Iman Makeba, 'Runaway Slave Names Recaptured: An Investigation of the Personal First Names of Fugitive Slaves Advertised in the Virginia Gazette Between 1736 and 1776', *Names* 54 (2006), 331–62

Lewis, Anna, 'The Woman Who Looks After a Decade-old Shrine to a Fictional Sci-fi Character in Cardiff Bay', *Wales Online* (27 January 2020)

Macaulay, Zachary, *Negro Slavery* (London: Hatchard & Son, 1823)

Maderno, Stefano, *St. Cecilia* (1600), marble, Saint Cecilia in Trastevere, Rome

Mai, R., and J. Rutka, 'The Irony of Being Oscar: The Legendary Life and Death of Oscar Wilde', *Journal of Otolaryngology* 29.4 (August 2000), 239–43

Marini, Paula (ed.), *Medioevo ideale e Medioevo reale nella cultura urbana: Antonio Avena e la Verona del primo Novecento* (Verona: Assessorato alla cultura, 2003)

McGirr, Elaine M., *Partial Histories: A Reappraisal of Colley Cibber* (Basingstoke: Palgrave Macmillan, 2016)

---. '"What's in a Name?": *Romeo and Juliet* and the Cibber Brand', *Shakespeare* 14.4 (2018), 399–412

Minutella, Vincenza, *Reclaiming Romeo and Juliet: Italian Translations for Page, Stage, and Screen* (Amsterdam: Rodopi, 2013)

Moloney, Ed, *A Secret History of the IRA* (London: Penguin, 2007)

Murtagh, Patrick, 'Grim Tale of Slain Romeo and Juliet', *Irish Times* (25 July 2008, online)

Nelson, Holly Faith, and Sharon Alker, 'Balancing Relatability and Alterity in Teaching Scottish Restoration Literature: A Case Study', *Studies in Eighteenth-Century Culture* 50 (2021), 217–30

NHS, 'Early or Delayed Puberty' (nhs.uk/conditions/early-or-delayed-puberty/, accessed 29 October 2022)

Nicholl, Charles, 'Marlowe [Marley], Christopher', *DNB* (23 September 2004)

Orgel, Stephen, *Imagining Shakespeare: A History of Texts and Visions* (London: Palgrave, 2003)

Orlin, Lena Cowen, *The Private Life of William Shakespeare* (Oxford: Oxford University Press, 2020)

Parker, J., rev. K. D. Reynolds, 'Howard, Leslie [Real Name Leslie Howard Steiner] (1893–1943), Actor and Film Director', *DNB* (23 September 2004)

Perry, Maria, *Sisters to the King* (London: André Deutsch, 2002)

Pirohakul, Teerapa, *The English Funeral in the Long Eighteenth Century*, unpublished PhD thesis (London: LSE, 2015)

Pogue, Kate Emery, *Shakespeare's Family* (New York: Praeger, 2008)

Pringle, Heather, *The Mummy Congress* (New York: Hyperion, 2001)

Qualey, Marcia Lynx, 'Why So Many "Saving Muslim Women" Book Covers?', *Arab Lit* (30 June 2014, online)

Ramirez, Juan Antonio, *Architecture for the Screen* (Jefferson, NC: McFarland, 2004)

Ritchie, Leslie, 'Pox on Both Your Houses: The Battle of the Romeos', *Eighteenth-Century Fiction* 27.3–4 (Spring–Summer 2015), 373–93

Rose, Martial, *Forever Juliet: The Life and Letters of Gwen Ffrangcon-Davies 1891–1992* (Dereham: Larks Press, 2003)

Ross, Emily, 'Ripe to Be a Bride? Marriage Age in *Romeo and Juliet*', *JJPC* 19.3 (2011), 145–59

Rutter, Carol Chillington, *Clamorous Voices* (London: Women's Press, 1988)

---. 'Shakespeare Performances in England (and Wales), 2008' in Peter Holland (ed.), *Shakespeare Survey 62* (Cambridge: Cambridge University Press, 2009), 349–85

Sauers, Jenna, 'Vice Published a Fashion Spread of Female Suicides', *Jezebel* (17 June 2013)

Schachar, Hila, 'The "Dead Girl" Aesthetic & Ballet Online', *Notes on Metamodernism* (21 August 2015, online)

Schwartz-DuPre, Rae Lynn, 'Portraying the Political: National Geographic's 1985 *Afghan Girl* and a US Alibi for Aid', *Critical Studies in Media Communication* 27.4 (2010), 336–56

Seaton, A. V., 'Guided by the Dark: From Thanatopsis to Thanatourism', *International Journal of Heritage Studies* 2.4 (1996), 234–44

Shapiro, James (ed.), *Shakespeare in America* (New York: Library of America, 2014)

Shapiro, Michael, 'Patronage and the Companies of Boy Actors' in Paul Westfield White and Suzanne R. Westfall (eds), *Shakespeare and Theatrical Patronage in Early Modern England* (Cambridge: Cambridge University Press, 2002), 272–94

Simone-Charteris, Maria Teresa, Stephen W. Boyd, and Amy Burns, 'The Contribution of Dark Tourism to Place Identity in Northern Ireland', in White and Frew (eds), *Dark Tourism*, 60–78

Sinclair, Colleen H., Kristina B. Hood, and Brittany L. Wright, 'Revisiting the Romeo and Juliet Effect: Reexamining the Links Between Social Network Opinions and Romantic Relationship Outcomes', *Social Psychology* 45.3 (May 2014), 170–8

Smith, Emma, *Shakespeare's First Folio: Four Centuries of an Iconic Book* (Oxford: Oxford University Press, 2016)

Smock, Kirk, *Guyana* (Chalfont St Peter: Bradt, 2008)

Solnit, Rebecca, *Recollections of My Non-Existence* (London: Granta, 2020)

Sontag, Susan, *Regarding the Pain of Others* (New York: Picador, 2003)

Sprague, Arthur Colby, *Shakespeare and the Actors* (Cambridge, MA: Harvard University Press, 2013)

Stirrup, Emma, 'Time Concertinaed at the Altar of Saint Cecilia in Trastevere' in Dorigen Caldwell and Lesley Caldwell (eds), *Rome: Continuing Encounters Between Past and Present* (Oxford: Ashgate, 2011), 57–78

Stokes, John, *In the Nineties* (Hemel Hempstead: Harvest Wheatsheaf, 1989)

Stone, P. R., 'A Dark Tourism Spectrum: Towards a Typology of Death and Macabre Related Tourist Sites, Attractions and Exhibitions', *Tourism: An Interdisciplinary International Journal* 52.2 (2006), 145–60

Tamassia, Giulio, *Dear Juliet: Letters from the Lovestruck and Lovelorn to Shakespeare's Juliet in Verona* (San Francisco: Chronicle Books, 2019)

Taylor, David Francis, *The Politics of Parody: A Literary History of Caricature, 1760–1830* (New Haven, CT: Yale University Press, 2018)

Taylor, Gary, *Reinventing Shakespeare* (New York: Weidenfeld & Nicolson, 1989)

Tebbutt, Melanie, *Making Youth: A History of Youth in Modern Britain* (London: Macmillan, 2016)

Thomas, Julia, *Shakespeare's Shrine* (Philadelphia: University of Pennsylvania Press, 2012)

Thompson, Ron, 'Royal Film Gamble by Zeffirelli Pays Off', *Sheffield Morning Telegraph* (5 March 1968), n.p., FFZ

Thomson, Peter, *The Cambridge Introduction to English Theatre, 1660–1900* (Cambridge: Cambridge University Press, 2006)

Tisdall, Laura, '"What a Difference It Was to Be a Woman and Not a Teenager": Adolescent Girls' Conceptions of Adulthood in 1960s and 1970s Britain', *Gender and History* 34.2 (22 June 2021), 495–513

Turner, Mark, *The Literary Mind* (Oxford: Oxford University Press, 1998)

Vercellotti, Giuseppe, Sam D. Stout, Rosa Boano, and Paul W. Sciulli, 'Intrapopulation Variation in Stature and Body Proportions: Social Status and Sex Differences in an Italian Medieval Population (Trino Vercellese, VC)', *American Journal of Physical Anthropology* 145.2 (June 2011), 203–14

Watson, Nicola, 'At Juliet's Tomb: Anglophone Travel-Writing and Shakespeare's Verona, 1814–1914' in Bigliazzi and Calvi (eds), *Shakespeare, Romeo and Juliet, and Civic Life*, 224–37

Webb, Caroline, *Visitors to Verona* (London: I. B. Tauris, 2017)

Weiss, Nicole M., Giuseppe Vercellotti, Rosa Boano, Marilena Girotti, and Sam D. Stout, 'Body Size and Social Status in Medieval Alba (Cuneo), Italy', *American Journal of Physical Anthropology* 168.3 (March 2019), 595–605

Wells, Elizabeth A., *West Side Story: Cultural Perspectives on an American Musical* (Plymouth: The Scarecrow Press, 2011)

Wiggins, Martin, and Catherine Richardson (eds), *British Drama 1533–1642: A Catalogue, Vol. 3, 1590–1597* (Oxford: Oxford University Press, 2013)

Williamson, Margaret, 'Africa or Old Rome? Jamaican Slave Naming Revisited', *Slavery & Abolition* 38 (2017), 117–34

Winkler, Henry August, *The Age of Catastrophe: A History of the West 1914–1945* (New Haven, CT: Yale University Press, 2015)

Wright, John (ed.), *Letters of Horace Walpole* (Philadelphia: Lea & Blanchard, 1842)

Yoch, James, *Landscaping the American Dream* (New York: H. N. Abrams, 1989)

Index